WITHDRAWN

A gift to

COLORADO COLLEGE
1 8 7 4

from

Constance Sontag
Book Fund

TUTT LIBRARY

CLASSICAL PRESENCES

General Editors
Lorna Hardwick   James I. Porter

Classical Presences

The texts, ideas, images, and material culture of ancient Greece and Rome have always been crucial to attempts to appropriate the past in order to authenticate the present. They underlie the mapping of change and the assertion and challenging of values and identities, old and new. Classical Presences brings the latest scholarship to bear on the contexts, theory, and practice of such use, and abuse, of the classical past.

Romantic Antiquity

Rome in the British Imagination, 1789–1832

JONATHAN SACHS

OXFORD
UNIVERSITY PRESS
2010

OXFORD
UNIVERSITY PRESS

Oxford University Press, Inc., publishes works that further
Oxford University's objective of excellence
in research, scholarship, and education.

Oxford New York
Auckland Cape Town Dar es Salaam Hong Kong Karachi
Kuala Lumpur Madrid Melbourne Mexico City Nairobi
New Delhi Shanghai Taipei Toronto

With offices in
Argentina Austria Brazil Chile Czech Republic France Greece
Guatemala Hungary Italy Japan Poland Portugal Singapore
South Korea Switzerland Thailand Turkey Ukraine Vietnam

Copyright © 2010 by Oxford University Press, Inc.

Published by Oxford University Press, Inc.
198 Madison Avenue, New York, New York 10016
www.oup.com

Oxford is a registered trademark of Oxford University Press.

All rights reserved. No part of this publication may be reproduced,
stored in a retrieval system, or transmitted, in any form or by any means,
electronic, mechanical, photocopying, recording, or otherwise,
without the prior permission of Oxford University Press.

Library of Congress Cataloging-in-Publication Data
Sachs, Jonathan.
Romantic antiquity : Rome in the British imagination, 1789–1832 / Jonathan Sachs.
p.   cm.—(Classical presences)
Includes bibliographical references.
ISBN 978-0-19-537612-8
1. English literature—19th century—History and criticism. 2. English literature—18th century—History and criticism. 3. Rome—In literature. 4. History in literature. 5. Politics and literature—Great Britain—History—19th century. 6. Politics and literature—Great Britain—History—18th century. 7. English literature—Roman influences. 8. Romanticism—Great Britain. I. Title.
PR457.S33 2009
820.9'35823702—dc22   2009003973

1 3 5 7 9 8 6 4 2
Printed in the United States of America
on acid-free paper

*for Cecily
and
in memory
of
Donn MacMinn
(1967–1997)*

---

*Multas per gentes et multa per aequora vectus
    advenio has miseras, frater, ad inferias,
ut te postremo donarem munere mortis
    et mutam nequiquam alloquerer cinerem.
quandoquidem fortuna mihi tete abstulit ipsum,
    heu miser indigne frater adempte mihi,
nunc tamen interea haec, prisco quae more parentum
    tradita sunt tristi munere ad inferias,
accipe fraterno multum manantia fletu,
    atque in perpetuum, frater, ave atque vale.*

                                      —Catullus

[Carried through many lands and across many seas,
    I have come, brother, to these sad funeral rites
So that I may give to you the final offices of the dead
    And speak in vain to your silent ashes.
Since fate has taken yourself
    From me unfairly, wretched brother,
Now, for all that, take these forlorn offerings,
    Made according to our parent's custom
And wet with a brother's tears. This is it
    Forever, my brother, hail and farewell.]

Acknowledgments

This book has been long in the making, and I am grateful at last to have the opportunity to thank the many colleagues, institutions, and friends who have helped to bring it to fruition. Research for this book has been supported by the University of Chicago Division of Humanities, a Mellon Foundation Dissertation Fellowship, the Society of Fellows at the University of Chicago, the Concordia University Faculty of Arts and Sciences, a Connell Fellowship from the Huntington Library, a Special Collections Research Fellowship at the University of Chicago Library, a Carl H. Pforzheimer, Jr. Research Grant from the Keats-Shelley Association of America, the Folger Shakespeare Library, and a Nouveaux professeurs-chercheurs grant from the Fonds québécois de la recherche sur la société et la culture. I thank all of these institutions for their generous support. Earlier versions of chapters 2 and 4 appeared as articles: "From Roman to *roman:* The Jacobin Novel and the Roman Legacy in the 1790s," *Studies in the Novel* 37.3 (2006): 253–272; "'Yet the Capital of the World': Rome, Repetition, and History in Shelley's Later Writings," *Nineteenth-Century Contexts* 28.2 (2006): 105–126. I am grateful to the publishers for their permission to use this material again here.

My early thinking about British Romanticism and classical antiquity, historicism and historicity began at the University of Chicago, and I extend thanks to the many faculty members there who helped to shape my ideas. In the Classics Department, Michael Allen, David Wray, Shadi Bartsch, and Chris Farone were all extravagant with their time and patience during my engagement with classical languages and cultures. In the English department, particular thanks are due to Paul Hunter and Bill Brown, while Steven Pincus in History offered early mentorship and a sustained model of scholarly rigor. In addition to providing an unforgettable model of erudition and intellectual curiosity, Katie Trumpener was an attentive and insightful reader of my work in its early stages and a great source of support at key moments of the process. My greatest intellectual debt, however, is to James Chandler. Not only has Jim taught me most of what I know about Romanticism, but he has been an exemplary mentor. Our ongoing conversation about Romanticism, historicism, and other matters has been invaluable. Since leaving Chicago, Montreal has provided a most welcome environment in which to expand and develop the archive and arguments of this book, and I am grateful to my colleagues in the English department, to my department chairs, Terry Byrnes, Marcie Frank, and Jason Camlot, and, especially, to Mary Esteve and Omri Moses for spirited argument and engagement with my work. I have also benefited from the friendship and support of a widening circle of colleagues, including, in Montreal, Michael Eberle-Sinatra, Tom Mole, and, especially, Andrew Piper; and in Ottawa, Ina Ferris and Mark Phillips. As the project neared completion, its prospectus was bolstered by the comments of Dan White and Andy Stauffer. Thanks also to Noel Jackson, Daniella Garofalo, and Joel Faflack. For research assistance in the later stages, I thank Valerie Medzalabanleth. This book never would have taken the shape it has without the sustained interest and enthusiasm of James Porter, the comments of Kevin Gilmartin and the anonymous readers for Oxford University Press, and the care of my editor, Stefan Vranka.

Ultimately this book would not have been possible at all without the extended community of friends and family who surrounded its composition. Present at the project's conception, Andrew Hebard and Katie Skeen have been encouraging and good humored ever since. For warm and generous hospitality during extended research trips, special thanks are due to Robin Brand and Neda Ulaby in Washington, D.C.; to Danny Richter and Anne Marie Yasin in Los Angeles; and to Susan Olle, Will Pryce, and Colette Camden in London. Will in particular has been the epitome of friendship, and, with three books published during the composition of this one, a model of efficiency. My parents, Sora and Marvin Sachs, have been a constant source of enthusiasm, affection, and unquestioned support. This is, in the end, a book made possible by a smile—and debts and inspirations way to great to name or account—and for all of these, I thank Cecily Hilsdale.

Contents

Introduction   3

PART I. POLITICAL WRITING AND THE NOVEL

1. Rome and the Revolution Controversy   49
    Burke's Use of Rome in the Reflections   52
    Roman Heroes as the Model of Godwin's Selfless Benevolence   65

2. From Roman to *roman*: The Jacobin Novel and the Roman Legacy in the 1790s   77
    Emma Courtney *and the Problem of Roman Reading*   82
    The Moral and Pedagogical Potential of the Novel Form   90
    Godwin and the Case for the Novel as an Agent of Social Change   93
    Holcroft, Inchbald, and the Critical Account of Classical Learning   101

PART II. POETRY

3. A Roman Standard: Byron, Ancient Rome, and Literary Decline   115
    Rome, the Decline of Poetry, and the Letter to John Murray   116
    Childe Harold *and the Ruins of Rome*   131

4. "Yet the Capital of the World": Rome, Repetition, and History in Shelley's Later Writings   146
    Rome in Shelley's Historical Imagination   151

x	Contents

Rome and Greece in Shelley's Philosophical View	154
Thomson, Shelley, and Liberty	156
Rome and Hellas	161
Rome, Athens, and Imitation in Shelley's
  Defence of Poetry	164
The Bureaucratization of the Imaginative	172

PART III. DRAMA

5. Rome-antic Shakespeare: *Coriolanus* on
   Stage and Page, 1789–1820	179
   Shakespeare and the Classics	184
   Shakespeare and Romantic Performance:
     Kemble's *Coriolanus*	189
   Kean's Challenge to Kemble's *Coriolanus*	206
   Hazlitt, *Coriolanus*, and the Aristocratic Imagination	209

6. What Is the People? Rome on the Romantic Stage
   after Kemble	221
   John Howard Payne's *Brutus: Staging Regicide after
     the Revolution*	231
   J. S. Knowles's *Caius Gracchus: Agrarian Revolt and
     the Politics of Corn*	247
   *Catiline: Democracy, Empire, and the Reaction to
     the Roman Revival*	261

Conclusion	272

Bibliography	279
Index	295

ROMANTIC ANTIQUITY

Introduction

I.

This book examines the dispute over the Roman republican legacy in Romantic Britain, a sustained and embattled struggle over the meaning and use of ancient Roman events, precedents, heroes, and texts and their relevance for contemporary Britain. Most broadly, it is concerned with the relationship between classical antiquity and the formation of British national identities, aesthetic values, and political ideologies from 1789 to 1832. I trace how Romantic authors use Rome to contest central aspects of what we now call political modernity, including the expansion of political franchise, the rise of mass democratic movements, and the spread of empire. In turn, such contests also reveal Rome's position in the formation of the Romantic aesthetic and theories of the imagination. Scholars have long noted the fascination with Roman literature and history by many preeminent British cultural figures of the early and middle eighteenth century, which is, indeed, often referred to as the "Augustan" period. Rome remained equally if not more important during the Romantic period, though its increasingly vexed role during this time has been little noted. In part, this is because the Romantic period has traditionally been conceived as constituting a modernity distinguished by its embrace of Greece at the expense of Rome or by its rejection of classical precedents, especially the literary authority of the ancients. I argue, in contrast, that republican Rome becomes increasingly relevant in Romantic Britain because in a period of political unrest and imperial expansion, the appositeness of the Roman example for Britain provokes a conceptual enhancement of what Rome means.

My emphasis on republican Rome revises a narrative about the rise of Hellenism and the increasing importance of Greece in eighteenth- and nineteenth-century Britain. This narrative recognizes the dominant importance of the Roman example for the eighteenth century as Britain, with its mixed constitution and balance of powers between Crown and Parliament, is repeatedly characterized through categories drawn from the Roman republic. Analogies to the Roman republic cease to be useful by the end of the eighteenth century because its associations with the French Revolution made it too radical while, simultaneously, the secular view of politics, to which Rome was central, gave way to a more Christian and nationalist understanding of British politics.[1] In addition to the radicalization of the Roman example, this narrative suggests that the shift away from Rome resulted also from the development of commercial society through the eighteenth century as the stability of landed property was confronted with such alternative forms of value as the equivalence and market price of capital. In the resulting confusion between "virtue" and "commerce," Hellenism came to function as an accommodating force, one that "transcended equivalence and calculability."[2] Through the early nineteenth century, the narrative continues, we see the continued rise of Hellenism and a Victorian fascination with Greece whereby Greece ultimately eclipses Rome as a source of cultural value. Eventually, however, "the high-cultural claims of Victorian Hellenism gave way in the twentieth century to a lower-key disciplinary formation whose center of gravity was Latin rather than Greek."[3] As a result of these claims, the importance of Rome in the Romantic period has been not merely ignored, but actively denied.

In asserting the renewed relevance of Rome for the formation of British Romanticism, I understand Rome to be both transformed and

---

[1] Frank Turner, "British Politics and the Demise of the Roman Republic: 1700–1939," *Historical Journal* 29.3 (September 1986): 587. See also Frank Turner, "Why the Greeks and Not the Romans in Victorian Britain?," in *Rediscovering Hellenism*, ed. G. W. Clarke (Cambridge: Cambridge University Press, 1989), 69; Frank Turner, *The Greek Heritage in Victorian Britain* (New Haven, CT: Yale University Press, 1981); Christopher Stray, *Classics Transformed: Schools, Universities, and Society in England, 1830–1960* (Oxford: Clarendon Press, 1998); and Richard Jenkyns, *The Victorians and Ancient Greece* (Oxford: Basil Blackwell, 1980).
[2] Stray, *Classics Transformed*, 21.   [3] Ibid., 1.

transformative: transformed in the sense that new models of historical understanding produced a changed conceptualization of the Roman past for certain Romantic thinkers and transformative because Rome became the locus of new conceptualizations of historicity itself and a way to understand the changes associated with the spread of empire and the rise of mass political movements. In denying Rome's importance, Frank Turner concentrates mainly on high-impact scholarly production, whereas Christopher Stray focuses on school and university curricula, teaching, textbooks, and the social organization of classical knowledge more generally. I focus rather on close readings of novels, canonical poetry, and drama in combination with materials from political writing, history, and classical studies to show how conflicts over the meaning and use of the Roman republican past shaped Romantic literary and historical writing in ways that have not yet been adequately recognized by scholars. Stephen Bann has argued that Romanticism brings a "remarkable enhancement of the consciousness of history" and that "this historical consciousness is the product of the Romantic period, when the whole range of our contemporary concerns with the past first became accessible to representation."[4] For Bann, in other words, the Romantic sense of history is different from its precursors, and he suggests that "history— far from being a localized and specific practice within the cultural topology—became a flood that overrode all disciplinary barriers and, finally, when the barriers were no longer easy to perceive, became a substratum to almost every type of cultural activity" (6–7). James Chandler also underscores the importance of historicity in this period when he suggests that "Romanticism is the age of the spirit of the age—that is the period when the normative status of the period becomes a central and self-conscious aspect of historical reflection."[5] Accordingly, Chandler demonstrates at length how what we call British Romanticism was constituted as a practice for specifying the dated state of historical cultures and literary texts. Following the claims of Bann and Chandler, I believe that one of the more significant

---

[4] Stephen Bann, *Romanticism and the Rise of History* (New York: Twayne, 1995), 5. Subsequent page references will be provided parenthetically in the text.
[5] James Chandler, *England in 1819: The Politics of Literary Culture and the Case of Romantic Historicism* (Chicago: University of Chicago Press, 1998), 78.

implications of Romanticism was a diffusion of historical sense, one that pervaded Romantic literary, political, and artistic culture.

This diffusion of historical sense, in turn, has implications for how we understand the use of ancient Roman models and precedents in the period. Although Turner argues for the decreased importance of Rome because there were no significant historical studies of the Roman republic between 1799 and 1902,[6] we need to look for engagement with history beyond the production of historical narrative. Early-nineteenth-century literary culture confronted aspects of modernity through recourse to Rome, and because literature has been a prominent locus for the critical discussion of Romantic historicism, it provides a privileged site for thinking about the relationship between cultural production, history, and politics in this period. One could imagine an alternative account of Roman influence focused on more topical discourses such as oratory, journalism, or caricature, or, similarly, one devoted to classical scholarship or visual culture, or even an account devoted to a particular genre like satire, which has a long and sustained tradition in Roman writing. Although my argument does at points engage with all of these topics, I focus predominantly on literary events—including the British response to the French Revolution, the Jacobin novel, Lord Byron's late rejection of Romantic poetics, Shelley's Hellenism, and London theaters, where, I argue, the staging of Rome is directly responsible for essayist William Hazlitt's understanding of poetry as antidemocratic, or "right royal"—to demonstrate that a focus on Rome forces us to rethink our understanding of how British literature and British national identity are constructed in relation to the ancient world. This is why the book defines its historical scope between political events in 1789 (the French Revolution) and 1832 (the First Reform Bill, which produced a modest expansion of the franchise). It is significant that these political events also correlate with changes in the way that Rome is understood in literary texts, from the first staging of *Coriolanus* by John Kemble (1789) to the first installment in *Blackwood's Edinburgh Magazine* of Thomas de Quincey's essays on the Caesars (1832), which provide an account

---

[6] The dates refer to the second edition of Adam Ferguson's *History of the Progress and Termination of the Roman Republic* (1799) and William Heitland's *The Roman Republic* (1902). See Turner, "Why the Greeks," 62.

and justification for the fall of the Roman republic and the emergence of the empire under the dictatorship of the Caesars. In using these dates to frame my book, I mean to call attention to the way that these dates are simultaneously political and literary, which in itself signals the interpellation of politics and literature in the period.

It will help to consider a particular example. Only four years after the publication of *Political Justice* (1793) made him the preeminent British philosopher of his age,[7] William Godwin announced not just a change in method, but a change in attitude. Having become more "tranquil," he emphasized the connection between reform, amiable personal manners, and miscellaneous inquiries; in short, Godwin was "persuaded that the cause of political reform and the cause of intellectual and literary refinement are inseparably connected."[8] This connection is made explicit in the volume's sixth essay, "Of the Study of the Classics," in which Godwin credits the rediscovery of classical knowledge in the fifteenth century with awakening the human mind from slumber. All present wisdom, Godwin claims, comes from antiquity: "From the Greek and Roman authors the moderns learned to think" (38). Though Godwin here equates Greece and Rome, he reserves his strongest praise for the Latin language, which instills in the mind the habit of ordered thinking and whose authors demonstrate the quintessence of decorum and stylistic precision. Not only are such Roman historians as Livy, Sallust, and Tacitus "the best that ever existed" (41), but

> add to this that the best ages of Rome afford the purest models of virtue that are anywhere to be met with. Mankind are too apt to lose sight of all that is heroic, magnanimous and public-spirited. Modern ages have formed themselves a virtue, rather more polished than sublime, that consists in petty courtesies, rather than the tranquil grandeur of an elevated mind. It is by turning to Fabricius and men like Fabricius, that we are brought to recollect what human nature is, left to ourselves we are apt to sink into effeminacy and apathy. (41)

---

[7] Citing Godwin as the foremost philosopher, William Hazlitt later observed that "no work gave such a blow to the philosophical mind of the country as the celebrated *Enquiry Concerning Political Justice*." Hazlitt, *The Complete Works of William Hazlitt*, ed. P. P. Howe (London: J. M. Dent, 1930–1934), 11:17.

[8] Willliam Godwin, *The Enquirer* (London, 1797), vi. Subsequent page references to this edition will be provided parenthetically in the text.

For Godwin, Rome represents masculine virtue, which prevents "effeminacy" and instills an ethos, "that republican spirit" (42).[9] As these comments suggest, the Rome that Godwin values is the Rome of the republic, the Rome of Fabricius,[10] which he interprets as a model of "virtue" and action without calculation of personal gain. Godwin's logic here is what we might call "exemplary." Rome provides "the purest models of virtue," and the heroic individuals of republican Rome provide a series of exemplary figures and historical parallels that can serve as transhistorical models for virtuous behavior.

Some years later, in 1812, Godwin exchanged a series of letters with an adoring, at times recalcitrant, self-proclaimed disciple. The disciple, nineteen-year-old Percy Bysshe Shelley, professed himself to be entirely in accord with the principles of *Political Justice* and sympathetic with the claims of *The Enquirer*, although he notes that "the arguments there in favour of classical learning failed to remove all my doubts on that point."[11] In short, Shelley declares bluntly, "the evils of acquiring Greek and Latin considerably overbalance the benefits" (1:316). In contrast to Godwin, who hoped to establish continuity between the perceived virtues of such Roman heroes as Fabricius and the morality and politics of "modern ages," Shelley asserts a fundamental break with antiquity. "Are not the reasonings on which your system is founded," he asks Godwin, "utterly distinct from & unconnected with the excellence of Greece and Rome?" (1:317). Shelley

---

[9] For a reading of seventeenth- and eighteenth-century civic humanism and dynamics of "virtue" and "corruption" as discourses largely based in an understanding of Roman republicanism and a martial ideal of masculinity, see Linda Dowling, *Hellenism and Homosexuality in Victorian Oxford* (Ithaca, NY: Cornell University Press, 1994). Dowling reads the rise of Victorian Hellenism as producing a new ideal of Greek civilization that ultimately replaced this masculine model and produced the possibility of a powerful model of homosexual identity.

[10] The reference is to Gaius Fabricius Luscinus, the Roman statesman and general celebrated for his probity who most famously rejected a bribe for the release of prisoners in 281 BCE. The likely source of the incident is Plutarch's life of Pyrrhus. See *Plutarch's Lives*, Vol. 9, Loeb Classical Library, trans. Bernadotte Perrin (Cambridge: Harvard University Press, 1920), 406–413. The story is also mentioned in the lost thirteenth book of Livy's *Ab Urbe Condita*. See *Livy*, Vol. 4 (books 8–10), Loeb Classical Library, trans. B. O. Foster (Cambridge: Harvard University Press, 1926), 548–549.

[11] PBS to William Godwin, 29 July 1812, *The Letters of Percy Bysshe Shelley*, ed. Frederick L. Jones (Oxford: Clarendon Press, 1964), 1:316. Subsequent page references to this edition will be provided parenthetically in the text.

further claims that there is nothing to be learned either from the poets of antiquity (with the exception of Lucretius) or from its politics: "Was not the government of republican Rome, & most of those of Greece as oppressive & arbitrary, as liberal of encouragement to monopoly, as that of Great Britain is at present?" (1:317). Shelley excoriates "the thirst of conquest with which even republican Rome desolated the earth" and sees Rome not as a locus of virtue, but rather of self-aggrandizing honor, which makes virtue "nothing but an empty name" (1:317).

The problem for Shelley is as much the example of antiquity, which in his view promotes honor over virtue, as the way that classical languages are taught to young students before they can comprehend the concepts discussed in ancient texts:

> You say that the time of youth could not be better employed than in the acquisition of classical learning. But *words* are the very things that so eminently contribute to the growth & establishment of prejudice: the learning of *words* before the mind is capable of attaching correspondent ideas to them, is like posessing [sic] machinery with the use of which we are so unacquainted as to be in danger of misusing it. But words are merely signs of ideas, how many evils, & how great spring from the annexing inadequate & improper ideas to words. The words honor, virtue, duty, goodness, are examples of this remark. (1:317)

Shelley argues that children forced to study classical languages are taught the words for concepts before they understand the significance of the concepts themselves, and, although he makes an exception for Godwin, Shelley considers the "vindicators of ancient learning...as the vindicators of literary despotism" (1:318). He makes a direct connection between a reverence for ancient learning and support for the "establishment" position, for classicists are "the tracers of a circle which is intended to shut out from real knowledge...all who do not breathe the air of prejudice, & who will not support the established systems of politics, religion & morals" (1:318). Shelley is particularly vehement here in linking the study of classical antiquity with support for establishment positions. To know about classical antiquity, Shelley suggests, is to have learned about the classical past in a manner that prescribes an understanding of links between antiquity and the present that validates the status quo, while proscribing more radical and reformist possibilities. Against Godwin's emphasis on classical learning as the best employment of youth, Shelley proposes that youths should be taught not classical languages, but "natural philosophy, medicine, astronomy, & above all History" (1:318).

The apparently sharp difference between Godwin and Shelley is complicated when set in the context of Shelley's other letters to Godwin. Elsewhere, Shelley acknowledges the "virtues and genius of Greece and Rome," which lead him to doubt the Christian religion as a revelation from divinity: "Shall Socrates and Cicero perish, whilst the meanest hind of modern England inherits eternal life?"[12] He reports a change in his opinion on the *Georgics* and proudly updates the rapid progress of his wife Harriet's Latin learning; at the new year in 1813, Harriet is mastering Horace, and by 7 February, she requests, through Shelley, a copy of Ovid from Thomas Jefferson Hogg, Shelley's friend since Oxford and his eventual biographer. Ironically, Shelley himself closes his longwinded denunciation of the classics with a wonderfully apt quotation of Horace, from Horace's longest letter to Augustus:

> ... in publica commoda peccem,
> si longo sermone morer tua tempora...[13]
> [I would sin against the general good were I to take up your time with long speeches.]

The case of Shelley shows how, with the right education, even the bitterest opponents of antiquity are infected by classical learning.

As Shelley's phrase "literary despotism" would suggest, Godwin and Shelley agree on the close connection between literary taste and political reform. Both articulate this link in conjunction with their understanding of republican Rome, although they disagree on the value of the Roman example. Their exchange is striking for a number of reasons. For a start, the Greco-Roman classics are for Shelley and Godwin an active and vital topic of debate and the two are specifically concerned with the importance of the classics as a potential inspiration for progressive political activity. Godwin emphasizes this link, and

---

[12] PBS to WG, 11 June 1812, *Shelley's Letters*, 1:307.
[13] The reference is to Horace's *Epistles*, book 2, epistle 1, lines 3–4. See Horace, *Satires, Epistles, and Ars Poetica*, Loeb Classical Library, trans. H. Rushton Fairclough (Cambridge: Harvard University Press, 1929), 396–397.

Shelley disputes it. Even in disputing it, however, Shelley uses republican Rome in his effort to comprehend the present state of Britain when he wonders whether republican Rome was "as liberal of encouragement to monopoly, as...Great Britain is at present?" (1:317). Shelley's comment suggests a particular apposition between republican Rome and contemporary Britain, and the exchange shows that both he and Godwin think in terms of historical parallels between antiquity and the present.

Although Godwin and Shelley refer to "the classics" as a coherent entity, there is within this category an inherent sense of distinction between Greece and Rome. Godwin's initial remarks occur in an essay broadly titled "Of the Study of the Classics," but, as his praise for Livy, Sallust, and Tacitus and his reference to Fabricius show, his emphasis is clearly Roman and republican. Shelley makes no distinction between Greece and Rome, though he does single out republican Rome as if it might be an exception, with phrases such as "the thirst of conquest with which even *republican* Rome desolated the earth" (emphasis mine). This kind of distinction, even if it is not explicitly articulated, suggests an awareness (especially in Godwin's case) of what we might call an internally differentiated classicism, by which I mean to invoke the awareness of distinctions between Greece and Rome and the recognition that for certain historical situations Roman precedents might be more appropriate than Greek ones, or vice versa.[14] Frequently, initial reference to "the classics" or "classical antiquity" or the conjoint invocation of Greece and Rome encourages readers to gloss over this distinction. Although Godwin's essay, for example, is titled

---

[14] For a particularly lucid account of these distinctions in the German context, see Glenn W. Most, "On the Use and Abuse of Ancient Greece for Life," *Cultura Tedesca* 20 (2002): 31–53. Most explains that nineteenth-century German classicism and Humboldtian humanism strongly favor Greece. He links this in part to German rivalry with French culture, which had shown how a modern political and artistic identity could be established through the emulation of Rome. By reaching behind Rome to Greece, the Germans "could retain the structure of ancient models but choose to follow a culture which was not only more ancient even than Rome but was also acknowledged by most of the canonical Latin authors to be their own unattainable model and source of inspiration" (42). As Most makes clear, however, this distinction between Greeks and Romans and the strong preference for the Greeks were not without contradictions, especially the emphasis of the German *Abitur* examination on Latin rather than Greek language.

"Of the Study of the Classics," he is clearly invested in advancing an ethos that he identifies more closely with Rome than with Greece. In other situations, a clear preference for Rome or Greece may mask the way such sympathies are worked out comparatively in recognition of internal differentiations. As I argue in chapter 4, Shelley's Hellenism is a case in point. Shelley's clear preference for Greek precedents and values should not blind us to the frequency with which Shelley establishes this preference by comparing Greece and Rome or to certain situations and problems in which he recognizes the greater value and relevance of Roman examples. For Shelley, the understanding of contemporary Britain as it actually exists is commonly understood through Rome, whereas his fantasy of desired outcomes and his invocation of ideal future possibilities are more commonly elaborated through Greek examples.[15]

The possibilities for making such distinctions were significantly enhanced during the Romantic period. This is in part because of the rise of Hellenism itself, which produced greater awareness of Greek, art, literature, and culture.[16] The growth of Hellenism, in Timothy Webb's account, has its roots in the concrete empirical experiences of English and French travelers in Greece in the late seventeenth and early eighteenth centuries "who provided a new impetus towards an understanding of the Greek achievement in terms not of an idealized and abstract set of landscapes but of topographical and social specificity."[17] As a result, the rediscovery of Greece is grounded not so much in the appreciation and transmission of texts, but rather in a set

---

[15] In this particular exchange with Godwin, Shelley's lack of distinction between Greece and Rome is especially surprising given our understanding of Shelley as one of the most prominent mouthpieces for Romantic Hellenism. Timothy Webb has even called this lack of distinction the most significant feature of Shelley's letter to Godwin: "What is perhaps most significant about this letter is that Shelley, the future philhellene, as yet makes little distinction between Latin and Greek." Although there are hints of it here, the internally differentiated classicism that I am characterizing here would come later for Shelley. See Webb, *The Violet in the Crucible: Shelley in Translation* (Oxford: Clarendon Press, 1976), 53.

[16] For a discussion of these developments and their significance, see Bruce Graver, "Romanticism," in *A Companion to the Classical Tradition*, ed. Craig Kallendorf (Oxford: Blackwell, 2007), 72–85; and Timothy Webb, "Romantic Hellenism," in *The Cambridge Companion to British Romanticism*, ed. Stuart Curran (Cambridge: Cambridge University Press, 1993), 148–176.

[17] Webb, "Romantic Hellenism," 157.

of objects and experiences which are seen to stand for an entire way of life.[18] The experience of travelers combined with a newfound appreciation for Greek art, architecture, and sculpture, much of which took its impetus from the German art historian J. J. Winckelmann. For Winckelmann, the perceived elemental simplicity of Greek art came to stand for a proximity to nature and an unmediated relationship to the world. The profound appreciation for Greek sculpture articulated by Winckelmann was based on an environmental theory of production that underscored the connection between the climate of Athens and its democratic institutions. If the renewed interest in Greece was not predominantly textual, it did, nonetheless, have textual ramifications, most significantly the reevaluation of Homer and the Homeric poems, which formed the basis for the precise historical criticism of ancient texts, and the related revival of Greek studies at British universities, which resulted in meticulous new editions of Greek authors. In addition, archaeological excavations at Pompeii and Herculaneum provided new information about the details of ancient Roman life while the importation of Greek and Roman antiquities into Britain for both private enjoyment and display in public museums further enhanced the possibilities for the appreciation of ancient art and the understanding of Greek and Roman culture through material as well as textual sources. The removal from the Parthenon of the Parthenon (or Elgin) marbles sparked debate not only about neoclassical ideals, but also over the distinctions between Greek and Roman society, as Richard Payne Knight argued that the stones were Roman copies of Greek originals.[19] All of these developments enabled increasingly refined distinctions between Greece and Rome.

That changes in the way that antiquity was understood enable more refined distinctions between Greece and Rome suggests a further issue in the exchange between Godwin and Shelley: the historical mediation of the classical world. Godwin calls our attention to this issue explicitly when he locates the rise of classical learning in the fifteenth century.

---

[18] On the contrast between the text-based understanding of Roman antiquity and Hellenism's emphasis on artifacts and material culture, see Marilyn Gaull, "Romans and Romanticism," *Wordsworth Circle* 36.1 (2005): 15–20.

[19] On the controversies over the Marbles, see William St. Clair, *Lord Elgin and the Marbles* (Oxford: Oxford University Press, 1967); and Christopher Hitchens, *The Elgin Marbles: Should They Be Returned to Greece?* (London: Chatto and Windus, 1987).

What we would today call the Renaissance was notable in Godwin's interpretation both for the preservation of the material remains of antiquity and for the recovery of ancient manuscripts, which then became the subject of extensive commentary. Such attention, for Godwin, allows Greek and Roman writers to be "understood and relished in a degree scarcely inferior to their contemporaries" (37). Despite Godwin's optimism about the resulting transparency of ancient texts, we of course recognize that the process of commentary also produces further layers of interpretation, and just as Renaissance commentaries on classical texts mediate the ancient world for their readers, the classical world was further mediated for Romantic period culture by the Renaissance, the Enlightenment, and neoclassicism. Furthermore, classical historians of the ancient world including Livy and Plutarch themselves produced texts mediated by a profound distance from the events, institutions, and heroes that they described. Harold Parker underscores these nestled historical frames with regard to the French tradition when he describes Manon Phlipon's (Mme. Roland's) longing for antiquity, which, she imagined, would have allowed her to have the career and happiness denied her under the French ancien régime. "She knew that this was true," Parker observes, "because two *philosophes*, Montesquieu and Rousseau, had told her that it was so."[20] The British understanding of Rome could be shaped by the same Enlightenment thinkers and also, as I discuss in the pages that follow, by native sources including Shakespeare, whose *Coriolanus* was performed throughout the Romantic period, and by the classical republican or civic humanist tradition, which relied heavily on Roman examples.

In addition, as Parker's example suggests, the process by which the classical world would have been mediated for Godwin, Shelley, and other Romantic thinkers is further complicated by the visual and textual appropriation of classical, especially Roman, examples by the artists, writers, and propagandists of the French Revolution.[21] The

---

[20] Harold T. Parker, *The Cult of Antiquity and the French Revolutionaries* (Chicago: University of Chicago Press, 1937), 62.

[21] On the French appropriation of Rome, see Parker, ibid.; Robert L. Herbert, *David, Voltaire, Brutus, and the French Revolution: An Essay in Art and Politics* (New York: Viking, 1972); Mona Ozouf, *Festivals and the French Revolution* (Cambridge: Harvard University Press, 1988), 271–278; Norman Vance, *The Victorians and Ancient Rome* (Oxford: Blackwell, 1997), 24–26.

Constituent Assembly of August 1789 to June 1791 included a broad range of opinion as to whether the French should admire, imitate, or condemn the example of republican antiquity, with more conservative members seeking to condemn antiquity and radicals desiring to imitate it.[22] Such positions could change with circumstance, and with the initial high promise of the Revolution, many felt that France would achieve a constitution superior to any in antiquity and need no longer admire the republican past.[23] With the further progress of the revolution, however, what Parker calls the "cult of antiquity" advanced. Towns began to name themselves after the great figures or cities of the classical past—Montfort-l'Amaury became Montfort-le-Brutus— revolutionaries took classical names such as Scaevola and Gracchus, and republicans Brutus, Cato, and Publicola were featured on the assignat.[24] The new meeting place of the National Convention in 1793 was decorated with enormous statues of Demosthenes, Lycurgus, Solon, and Plato, opposite which stood Camillus, Publicola, Brutus, and Cincinnatus. The painted image of Brutus stood facing speakers, and his sculpted bust was placed in front of the rostrum. Busts of Brutus protected Jacobin meeting places throughout France, and "Je jure sur la tête de Brutus" became an oratorical cliché. As Robert Herbert indicates, "It would be hard to exaggerate the prevalence of Brutus in 1793 and 1794."[25] The widespread presence of Brutus as a revolutionary symbol lends special significance to the revival of Brutus on the London stage in 1818 after the revolutionary wars had ended, as I discuss in chapter 6. Although the prevalence of models from the Greek republican tradition in the National Convention and elsewhere underscore that the cult of antiquity encompassed Greece and Rome, the particular place of Brutus in the symbolic economy of the French Revolution suggests that Rome came to occupy a dominant position. Karl Marx, for example, emphasizes this Roman influence in the *Eighteenth Brumaire,* and Walter Benjamin observes how "to Robespierre ancient Rome was a past charged with the time of the now which he blasted out of the continuum of history. The French

[22] Parker, *Cult of Antiquity*, 83–84.
[23] Ibid., 96.
[24] Parker, *Cult of Antiquity*, 139, 142, 143.
[25] Herbert, *David, Voltaire,* Brutus, 105.

Revolution viewed itself as Rome reincarnate."[26] The identification of the new Republic with Rome was not lost on her enemies, especially the British. In Commons debate after Commons debate British speakers noted how the French Republic attempted to align itself with Rome, thus leaving England to play the losing role of Carthage.[27] The French association with Rome exacerbated the polarization and politicization of the Roman legacy. However, as I discuss in the chapters that follow, more conservative interpretations of Rome, such as that of John Kemble's staging of *Coriolanus*, could push back against the French, and many British radicals actively sought to align themselves with the Roman example in spite of (or perhaps on account of) its French associations. The whole matter became more complicated with the fall of Napoleon and subsequent attempts to reappropriate Rome after 1815.

While the French use of Rome provides perhaps the most important new factor for the historical mediation of the classical world, one further context of mediation, vernacular histories of Rome, remains to be considered. Even if there were no significant new histories of the Roman republic written in English between 1799 and 1902, Romantic readers had abundant access to histories of Rome written in vernacular languages. The most famous of these was Gibbon's history of the Roman Empire (1776–1788), but Adam Ferguson's immensely sophisticated and detailed *History of the Progress and Termination of the Roman Republic* was first published in 1783 and revised and reissued in 1799. For younger readers, Goldsmith's *Roman History* (1769) was

---

[26] Benjamin, "Theses on the Philosophy of History," in *Illuminations*, ed. Hannah Arendt (New York: Schocken Books, 1969), 261.

[27] See, for example, debates about the Protest of Earl Fitzwilliam against the Rejection of his Amendment to the Address (1796): "They resort to that well-known and constant allusion of theirs to ancient history, by which representing 'France as a modern Rome, and England as modern Carthage,' they accuse us of a national perfidy, and hold England up 'as an object to be blotted out from the face of the earth,'" in *Cobbett's Parliamentary History of England* (London: R. Bagshaw, 1806–1820), 32:1189; Debate on the Papers Respecting the Negotiation for Peace with France (1797): "Our enemies continually affect to put themselves in the place of ancient Rome, and us in that of its rival, Carthage; and an hon. baronet asked, the other night, if we were prepared to submit, like Carthage, to stipulate the reduction of our fleet" (33:1020); Debate in Commons on the Assessed Taxes Bill (1798): "Our enemies were constantly holding up the examples of Rome and Carthage" (33:1180).

repeatedly reprinted and revised during the period and served as a leading school text. Richard Johnson's *New Roman History, from the Foundation of Rome to the End of the Commonwealth* (1770; sometimes reprinted as part of *Cooper's Histories of Greece and Rome*) also was used in schools, and it was reprinted even more frequently than Goldsmith's work. In addition, William Godwin published a *History of Rome* (1809) for young readers under the pseudonym Edward Baldwin, and Henry Bankes's *The Civil and Constitutional History of Rome, from its Foundation to the Age of Augustus* appeared in 1818. Toward the end of the period, Barthold Georg Niebuhr's *Römische Geschichte* (1811–1812), with its extensive reconsideration of the sources of early Roman history, helped to transform the study of Rome into a more critical endeavor. Julius Hare and Connop Thirlwall published their translation of the second edition of Niebuhr's Roman history (1827–1832) starting in 1828. Finally, Jules Michelet's *Histoire romaine* was published in 1831. Collectively, these histories reveal a heterogeneity of possible interpretations of the Roman past that ranges from a continued reliance on exemplary heroes and tidy moral lessons (Goldsmith, Johnson, Godwin) to more sophisticated attempts to apply new standards of critical accuracy, including the careful scrutiny of source material (Niebuhr).

The increasing importance of an internally differentiated classicism and the many layers through which the classical world was mediated suggests that Godwin and Shelley's dispute makes sense when seen not simply as part of Shelley's path to Hellenism, but rather as symptomatic of a more far-reaching and widespread dispute over the Roman republican legacy in Romantic Britain. The Roman republican past could be construed positively as a training ground for republican virtue and the reform cause, as it was for Godwin, or negatively, as a seedbed of reaction, Toryism, and imperialist aggression, as it was for Shelley.[28] Of course, it was possible to embrace the connection between classical texts and Establishment conservatism, as did Prime

---

[28] Similarly, William Blake declared, "The Classics, it is the classics! & not Goths nor Monks, that desolate Europe with Wars." See Blake, "On Homer's Poetry," *The Complete Poetry and Prose of William Blake*, ed. David Erdman (Berkeley: University of California Press, 1982), 270. Blake's comment echoes those of earlier novelists, Richardson especially, who reject what they see as the warmongering ethos of the classical epic.

Minister and 1st Earl of Chatham William Pitt (Pitt the Elder) when he recommended Homer and Virgil to his son as containing "the finest lessons of the age to imbibe."[29] These positions suggest some of the possible meanings attached to the Roman example in late eighteenth- and early nineteenth-century Britain: Rome could represent a powerful model of European culture, of literary authority, of liberty and civic participation, of *imperium sine fine* (empire without end)— but also of decline and ruin. In all of these instances, and in a series of others that I examine in the pages that follow, references to republican Rome work to negotiate with the past in a strategic effort to influence competing visions of the present and future. That Rome should function in this manner is, of course, not surprising, and from the Renaissance forward the events from classical history and the narratives of classical authors frequently served as the standards by which later generations measured themselves. Throughout the Romantic period and beyond, we would not be at all surprised to hear of the repeated invocation of Roman precedent in Parliamentary debates (a suspicion borne out by even a cursory glance at Hansard), but there is a widespread assumption among literary scholars and historians that the importance of Rome as a model, and the importance of classical antiquity more broadly, diminishes during the Romantic period— especially as a source of inspiration for the period's literary production. But this does not mean that Rome ceased to be a topic of debate. The recognition of republican Rome's place in Romantic period writing changes our understanding of the cultural dynamics of the period and reveals the shaping presence of a differentiated classical world in the period's culture wars.

The importance of Rome has been widely overlooked because the Romantic aesthetic has commonly been understood as a departure from classical models,[30] and, when the relevance of antiquity is recognized, scholars have tended to emphasize the importance of Greece

---

[29] As quoted by Timothy Webb, *English Romantic Hellenism, 1700–1824* (Manchester: Manchester University Press, 1982), 31.

[30] The constitution of a Romantic modernity through the rejection of classical precedents can be seen as early as the 1790s among German theorists who articulated a notion of the Romantic in contrast to the classical, a distinction that Coleridge introduced to Britain in 1811 and that gained momentum shortly thereafter with Mme de Stael's English stay and the translation of A. W. Schlegel's lectures. Among

and not Rome in the constitution of Romantic modernity.³¹ In addition, the neglect of Rome may reflect an assumption of its diminished importance as the standards and references associated with aristocratic classical education (seen, for example, in Shelley's above remarks) declined with the spread of print culture and the changing demographics of literature.³² There have, nonetheless, been a number of useful shorter studies that address the relevance of Rome for the Romantic period. Jerome McGann offers a sustained meditation on

contemporary scholars, our understanding of the Romantic reaction against the classical has been consolidated by the canonical work of M. H. Abrams, with its distinction between the mimetic critical standards of neoclassicism to the expressive emphasis of Romanticism. See Abrams, *The Mirror and the Lamp: Romantic Theory and the Critical Tradition* (New York: Oxford University Press, 1953). See also Walter Jackson Bate, *From Classic to Romantic* (Cambridge: Harvard University Press, 1946). For a survey of the reception of classical standards in the period with a useful distinction between classicism and neoclassicism, see Paul H. Fry, "Classical Standards in the Period," in *The Cambridge History of Literary Criticism*, Vol. 5: *Romanticism*, ed. Marshall Brown (Cambridge: Cambridge University Press, 2000), 7–28.

[31] On the importance of Greece, see Turner, *Greek Heritage*, "British Politics," and "Why the Greeks," and Stray, *Classics Transformed*; see also Jenkyns, *Victorians and Ancient Greece*. In literary studies, the most thorough exponent of British Romantic Hellenism has been Timothy Webb. See his *English Romantic Hellenism, 1700–1824* and, more recently, his "Romantic Hellenism." See also Marilyn Butler, "The Cult of the South," chap. 5 of *Romantics, Rebels, and Reactionaries* (Oxford: Oxford University Press, 1981); Jennifer Wallace, *Shelley and Greece: Rethinking Romantic Hellenism* (New York: St. Martin's Press, 1997); Karl Kroeber, "History, Hellenism, and Eternal Evanescence," chap. 7 of *British Romantic Art* (Berkeley: University of California Press, 1986); Simon Goldhill, *Who Needs Greek: Contests in the Cultural History of Hellenism* (Cambridge: Cambridge University Press, 2002), esp. 1–12, 178–195; Gaull, "Romans and Romantics."

[32] See Fry, "Classical Standards," 14, for this explanation. On the changing demographics of Romantic reading audiences, see William St. Clair, *The Reading Nation in the Romantic Period* (Cambridge: Cambridge University Press, 2004). Much recent work has been done on print culture and the rapid expansion of the periodical press—and especially on the link between the press and radical political culture. In this connection, see Iain McCalman, *Radical Underworld: Prophets, Revolutionaries, and Pornographers in London, 1795–1840* (Cambridge: Cambridge University Press, 1988); James Epstein, *Radical Expression: Political Language, Ritual, and Symbol in England, 1790–1850* (New York: Oxford University Press, 1994); David Worrall, *Radical Culture: Discourse, Resistance, and Surveillance, 1790–1820* (Detroit, MI: Wayne State University Press, 1992); Marcus Wood, *Radical Satire and Print Culture, 1790–1822* (Oxford: Clarendon Press, 1994); Kevin Gilmartin, *Print Politics: The Press and Radical Opposition in Early Nineteenth-Century England* (Cambridge: Cambridge University Press, 1996); Paul Keen, *The Crisis of Literature in the 1790s: Print Culture and the Public Sphere* (Cambridge: Cambridge University Press, 1999).

the fascination with Roman ruins for Byron, Goethe, and Stendahl, whereas Peter Manning's account of Wordsworth's response to German historicism, most specifically Niebuhr's, concentrates on Wordsworth's handling of Roman history and Latin literature in his late poetry of the 1830s and 1840s. Most recently, through readings of Coleridge, Hazlitt, and Byron, Stephen Cheeke has suggested that the Roman past gains renewed importance in the Romantic period as the response to the French Revolution and the rise of Napoleon produced accentuated attempts to understand contemporary events through their parallel with ancient Roman history.[33] My work builds on these studies, and, taking my cue from Cheeke's explanation of the importance of the Roman parallel after the French Revolution, I show how contests over the meaning of the ancient Roman past structure Romantic poetics and theories of the imagination, and how this aesthetic work in turn affects such aspects of political modernity as mass democracy and the spread of empire.

The Roman past was a "usable past."[34] It was not a static tradition, but an available set of examples that could be deployed to make authorized statements about the present. More than other kinds of historical example, Rome and Greece are exceptionally usable: "For much of European history, classical antiquity has provided a symbolic repertoire of great power and flexibility; its power stemming from its exemplary achievements and its endurance through a long history of reception, its flexibility from its incorporation of the dual poles of Greece and Rome."[35] Christopher Stray characterizes the use of this

---

[33] Jerome McGann, "Rome and Its Romantic Significance," *The Beauty of Inflections: Literary Investigations in Historical Method and Theory* (New York: Oxford University Press, 1985), 313–333; Peter Manning, "Cleansing the Images: Wordsworth, Rome, and the Rise of Historicism," *Texas Studies in Literature and Language* 33 (1991): 271–326; and Stephen Cheeke, "The Sword 'Which eats into itself': Romanticism, Napoleon, and the Roman Parallel," *Romanticism* 10.2 (2004): 209–227. See also Stephen Cheeke, "'What So Many Have Told, Who Would Tell Again': Romanticism and the Commonplaces of Rome," *European Romantic Review* 17 (2006): 521–541.

[34] I borrow the term "usable past" from Lawrence Lipking, who also uses it to distinguish from a tradition, in this case arguing for the way that literary, music, and art historians in the eighteenth century resorted to the past as a kind of mythmaking in their effort to discover their forebears and produce the initial histories of their respective arts. See Lipking, *The Ordering of the Arts in Eighteenth-Century England* (Princeton, NJ: Princeton University Press, 1970), especially 10–12.

[35] Stray, *Classics Transformed*, 10.

symbolic repertoire for present purposes as "classicizing," which he defines as "a mode of action in which present interests act on the symbolic resources of antiquity to produce 'classics.'"[36] The term calls attention to the way that antiquity can be used to make authoritative sense of the present and serves as an apt characterization of the moves made by both Godwin and Shelley in their dispute over the meaning and relevance of antiquity. Godwin and Shelley can also be understood as akin to the classicists described by James Porter who adapt "poses and strategic identities, so as to manipulate and negotiate with, rather than to serve the past—always with an eye to solving a problem in specific historical and cultural circumstances."[37] The sustained and intense struggle over the Roman legacy in the Romantic period suggests a culture war over the meaning of republican Rome as politicians, novelists, poets, dramatists, pundits, and others struggled, as did Shelley and Godwin, to use the Roman past to shape their understanding of the present and anticipate the direction of the future. As Jeffrey Cox makes clear, the classical ideal was a source of contest in the nineteenth century, and much of "the struggle was clearly over exactly how one was to define classical culture and the nineteenth century's relationship to it."[38] Cox dates what he describes as these "culture wars" from the defeat of Napoleon, but we can locate them even earlier in the celebrations surrounding the centennial of the Glorious Revolution and in the British response to the French Revolution—both key events in shaping Romantic period political culture generally and more specific questions about the nature of and future for Britain's political system.

Consistent with my suggestion that we can locate a struggle over the definition of classical culture—one that turns around distinctions between Rome and Greece—long before Waterloo, we can look not only to Godwin for the range of meanings associated with the Roman republican past, but also to two other prominent participants in the

---

[36] Ibid. As Stray points out, "classicizing" is "thus analogous to 'orientalizing,' producing exemplars of Self rather than Other" (10 n. 8).

[37] James I. Porter, "What Is 'Classical' about Classical Antiquity? Eight Propositions," *Arion* 13.1 (2005): 127.

[38] Cox, *Poetry and Politics in the Cockney School: Keats, Shelley, Hunt, and Their Circle* (Cambridge: Cambridge University Press, 1998), 185.

revolution controversy of the 1790s, Edmund Burke and John Thelwall. As I discuss in more detail in chapter 1, Burke's *Reflections* draw continuously on the example of Cicero to support and substantiate his opposition to events in France. In part, this is common rhetorical practice for Burke and other classically educated parliamentarians of the eighteenth century. But Burke's use of Cicero is more deliberate, for it allows him to align himself with the protector of the Roman republic in a time of conspiracy and threat and, further, to suggest that this threat comes not as previously feared in the shape of an aristocratic conspiracy from within, but rather from those British supporters of reform sympathetic with the rights declared by the French. Furthermore, through Cicero, Burke attempts to claim republican Rome for the establishment—he attempts to use his citation of Cicero to align Rome with the aristocratic resistance to French ideals and the rejection of those arguing for an expansion of the franchise and the "rights of man." Thelwall, in contrast, would have it differently. Thelwall was a prominent radical orator, agitator, and supporter of the French Revolution. When limited by the Two Acts of late 1795[39] from speaking about contemporary politics, Thelwall responded with a series of lectures on Roman history. The first of these was to concern "The importance of the study of History in general; and of the Roman history in particular," which would be followed by a general review of "the rise, progress, and decline of Roman grandeur," and a more specific investigation of, among other topics, the Roman mixed government, the abuses of kingly power, the "arrogance, rapacity, and usurpations of the Roman aristocracy," and the advent, limitations, and decline of tribunician power.[40] Thelwall claimed that "there is hardly an individual topic important for the cause of Liberty, which might not be embraced in such a course of lectures," and his subject would even be "more instructive" than the French Revolution.[41] Thelwall's attack on the aristocracy and his

---

[39] The first of the Two Acts made it a treasonable offense to incite the populace to hatred or contempt of king, constitution, or government by speech or writing, and the second banned meetings of more than fifty people without prior permission from a magistrate. Defiance of the magistrate's orders was punishable by death. The acts were introduced by William Pitt on 10 November 1795 and received royal assent on 18 December 1795.

[40] John Thelwall, *Prospectus of a Course of Lectures...in Strict Conformity with the Restrictions of Mr Pitt's Convention Act* (London, 1796), 29.

[41] Ibid., 20, 19.

emphasis on the tribunes make clear that his lectures would mine Roman history as a source for the popular democratic politics advocated by many radicals in the 1790s.[42]

These simultaneous attempts by Burke and Thelwall to enlist the Roman legacy for the disparate causes of the establishment and of reform offer an introduction to what was at stake in the struggle over ancient Rome in the Romantic period. Those attempting strategically to manipulate Rome for contemporary causes, might, however, also find themselves manipulated by their use of Roman models and precedents.[43] As I show in chapter 1, William Godwin is traditionally considered a radical thinker, but his use of Rome in *Political Justice* and later in *The Enquirer* (as we see in his comments on Fabricius) remains tied to an eighteenth-century model of classical exemplarity that is fundamentally backward looking, and may, as Shelley speculates, inhibit the more progressive application of his ideas for those who refuse to recognize the relevance of historical parallels between classical antiquity and contemporary Europe. A similar problem occurs in the Jacobin novels of Godwin, Holcroft, Hays, and others which, as I explain in chapter 2, rewrite this model of classical exemplarity to create their own exemplary figures and incidents for a public-minded republican audience not trained in classical literature. Most of these

---

[42] Thelwall even proposed that the lessons of the most radical British thinkers could be extrapolated from the classics: "Locke, Sydney and Harrington are put to silence; and Barlowe, Paine, and Callandar it may be almost High Treason to consult: but Socrates and Plato, Tully and Demosthenes, may be eloquent in the same cause" (*Prospectus*, 18–19). Thelwall made a similar claim in another pamphlet: "Every man who will take the trouble to make himself acquainted with ancient or foreign history, may discuss, with the utmost freedom, every political principle, and every question connected with the good government and permanent happiness of the human race. He must not apply his arguments, it is true, to this particular country, nor illustrate them by the trying reports and occurrences of the day; but ancient history will abundantly furnish him with illustrations, much more interesting to the strong and noble feelings of the heart; and if the Orator is at all adroit in the management of his subject, he will find reason to exult in the many and grand advantages for the display of genuine and impassioned eloquence, which historical discussion possesses over the local topics to which our public speakers have hitherto confined their attention." See *An Appeal to Popular Opinion against Kidnapping and Murder* (London, 1796), 10.

[43] Again, I follow Porter, who notes that "one should also allow for the possibility that the exponents of classicism could be as much manipulated by their assumed positions as they could manipulate them." See "What Is Classical," 127.

novels, however, are not considered to be aesthetic successes, and a focus on their use of Rome reveals the tension between a backward-looking model of exemplarity and the attempt to seize the progressive potential of the emerging novel genre. At points like this, the recognition that these episodes are part of a broader struggle over the meaning of republican Rome reveals how certain problems need to be understood not only in connection with generic changes in the novel form, but more specifically in the intersection of these problems with the struggle over the meaning of the antique past. To some extent, the contours of this struggle are already familiar to us through our understanding of Romantic Hellenism. But, as will become clear in my reading in chapter 4 of Shelley's later works, we cannot properly understand the meaning and importance of Romantic Hellenism unless we set it in the context of the struggle over the Roman legacy in this period.

II.

In seeking to explain republican Rome as an imaginative space that helps to organize Romantic period political, historical, and aesthetic practices, this book develops from a series of new research trajectories in British Romantic literature and culture. For a start, it follows new historicist scholarship in thinking through the complex ways that literary writing in the Romantic period responds to extraliterary social and cultural pressures.[44] More recent work by James Chandler shows

---

[44] Among Romanticists, influential new historicist methodologies can be found in Marilyn Butler, *Romantics, Rebels, and Reactionaries* (Oxford: Oxford University Press, 1981); Jerome McGann, *The Romantic Ideology: A Critical Investigation* (Chicago: University of Chicago Press, 1983), and *The Beauty of Inflections: Literary Investigations in Historical Method and Theory* (New York: Oxford University Press, 1985); Marjorie Levinson, *Wordsworth's Great Period Poems* (Cambridge: Cambridge University Press, 1986); Alan Liu, *Wordsworth: The Sense of History* (Stanford, CA: Stanford University Press, 1989); David Simpson, *Wordsworth's Historical Imagination: The Poetry of Displacement* (New York: Methuen, 1987). These critics follow in the wake of an earlier group of historically-minded British scholars, most prominently Raymond Williams, *Culture and Society* (London: Chatto and Windus, 1958), and *The Long Revolution* (London: Chatto and Windus, 1961); E. P. Thompson, *The Making of the English Working Class* (New York: Pantheon, 1963); and David Erdman, *Blake: Prophet against Empire* (Princeton, NJ: Princeton University Press, 1954).

further how the very fact that new historicist scholars are concerned with historicity can itself be seen as a Romantic phenomenon.[45] Chandler's argument is that the "Romantic ideology" is not, as Jerome McGann argues, a systematic retreat from history, but rather a turn toward it, and his work forces us to think more carefully about the uses of historical thinking in Romantic period writing. Chandler's work focuses predominantly on Romantic poetry and historical fiction (especially the historical novels of Walter Scott); my attention to the importance of republican Rome across a variety of genres includes poetry, but it also offers an opportunity to extend the conversation sparked by Chandler's claims about Romantic historicity to encompass writing in a variety of other genres, including histories of ancient Rome written during the period and the dramatization and staging of episodes from Roman republican history.

Textually, the events and heroes of ancient Rome frequently provided models for imagining alternative ideals of political prudence and public-minded virtues (alternatives that became important as the political future of the nation became increasingly uncertain and more deeply contested), though we should not forget that scenes from Roman antiquity were also a physical reality in Romantic Britain. Plays on Roman themes were staged repeatedly, often by the period's most popular actors, as we see with John Kemble and Sarah Siddons, who performed *Coriolanus* more than forty times from 1789 to 1811 (when Siddons retired) to packed houses, and in subsequent post-Waterloo portrayals of Roman figures by Edmund Kean and Charles Macready. Sometimes the Theatres Royal even produced competing plays featuring the same heroes and events from Roman republican lore, as was the case in May of 1820, when Macready played Virginius in James Sheridan Knowles's play of that title at Drury Lane, while Kean enacted the same role in similar drama by an unknown author at Covent Garden. Through its attention to the representation of Rome on the Romantic stage, my focus on the use and meaning of

---

[45] James Chandler, *England in 1819: The Politics of Literary Culture and the Case of Romantic Historicism* (Chicago: University of Chicago Press, 1998). On genres of historical writing in this period, see the excellent work of Mark Salber Phillips, *Society and Sentiment: Genres of Historical Writing in Britain, 1740–1820* (Princeton, NJ: Princeton University Press, 2000).

republican Rome engages the recent recovery and reassessment of Romantic period drama.[46] My thinking about the staging of Roman historical themes builds specifically on attention to the cultural and political significance of the stage and on critical accounts of the relationship between theatrical production and the Romantic imagination, but my particular focus on the Roman republic allows me to integrate work in theater studies with other literary and discursive fields. If, for example, we want to consider the relationship of the theater to the concept of imagination, Rome is a crucial starting place because when Hazlitt explicitly politicizes the faculty of imagination by calling it "right royal," he does so in a review of John Kemble's staging of a Roman play: Shakespeare's *Coriolanus*. Critics often overlook the context in which these remarks were made, but Hazlitt's general concession of the imagination as aristocratic derives from the specificity of Kemble's performance and its portrayal of a particular aristocratic ideal of Rome. Similarly, if we want to think about the theater as a public sphere and as political space—as perhaps more representative of the nation than even Parliament in the years before the 1832 Reform Bill expanded the franchise and recast the districts of representation—then Rome provides a vehicle for staging displaced political concerns. Because of state censorship and licensing acts that governed theatrical production through the Romantic period, explicit engagement with politics was rare on stage. But, as Hazlitt claimed in an 1816 review, anyone who sees *Coriolanus* "may save himself the trouble of reading Burke's *Reflections*, or Paine's *Rights of Man*, or the

---

[46] David Worrall, *Theatric Revolution: Drama, Censorship, and Romantic Period Subcultures, 1773–1832* (Oxford: Oxford University Press, 2006); Jane Moody, *Illegitimate Theatre in London, 1770–1840* (Cambridge: Cambridge University Press, 2000); Julie Carlson, *In the Theatre of Romanticism: Coleridge, Nationalism, Women* (Cambridge: Cambridge University Press, 1994); Jeffrey Cox, "Ideology and Genre in the British Antirevolutionary Drama of the 1790s," *ELH* 58.3 (1991): 579–610; Judith Pascoe, *Romantic Theatricality: Gender, Poetry, and Spectatorship* (Ithaca, NY: Cornell University Press, 1997); Daniel O'Quinn, *Staging Governance: Theatrical Imperialism in London, 1770–1800* (Baltimore: Johns Hopkins University Press, 2005). As a further index of this renewed interest in the stage, Broadview recently published *The Broadview Anthology of Romantic Period Drama*, ed. Jeffrey N. Cox and Michael Gamer (Peterborough, ON: Broadview, 2003). See also Betsy Bolton, *Women, Nationalism, and the Romantic Stage: Theatre and Politics in Britain, 1780–1800* (Cambridge: Cambridge University Press, 2001).

Debates in both Houses of Parliament since the French Revolution or our own."[47] Simply put, the meaning of the ancient Roman legacy was a crucial site of contestation between radicals and conservatives in post-1789 British political and literary culture, and the theater provides us with a clear locus to examine the contours of that struggle.

What makes this book of central importance for such innovations in the field is its emphasis on the significance of Rome's republican history for Romantic aesthetic practices and for our understanding of the complex interaction between the development of these practices and such aspects of an emergent political modernity as mass democracy and the spread of empire. Much work has been done regarding the general influence of Italian culture on British Romanticism and on the Italian experiences of writers including Byron, Shelley, and John Keats.[48] Considerable attention has also been paid to the influence of classical Roman writers Virgil, Juvenal, and Catullus.[49] Finally, following Marilyn Butler, recent work by Jeffrey Cox and Jane Stabler has examined how Mediterranean culture provided liberal writers,

---

[47] *The Complete Works of William Hazlitt*, ed. P. P. Howe (London: J. M. Dent and Sons, 1931), 5:347.

[48] See, for example, Roderick Cavaliero, *Italia Romantica: English Romantics and Italian Freedom* (London: Palgrave, 2005); C. P. Brand, *Italy and the English Romantics: The Italianate Fashion in Early Nineteenth-Century England* (Cambridge: Cambridge University Press, 1957); Kenneth Churchill, *Italy and English Literature, 1764–1930* (Totowa, NJ: Barnes and Noble Books, 1980); on the use of Italian writers by British Romantics, see especially Karl Kroeber, *The Artifice of Reality: Poetic Style in Wordsworth, Foscolo, Keats, and Leopardi* (Madison: University of Wisconsin Press, 1964).

[49] For reasons which I will explain, the purpose of this book is not to trace the reception of Roman authors in the Romantic period, a topic on which some excellent work has appeared recently. See, especially, the special issue on "Romans and Romantics" edited by Kurt Heinzelman in Texas Studies in Literature and Language 33 (Summer 1991): 125–326; Kevis Goodman on Virgil in *Georgic Modernity and British Romaniticism: Poetry and the Mediation of History* (Cambridge: Cambridge University Press, 2004); Andrew Stauffer on Seneca, Juvenal, and Longinus in *Anger, Revolution, and Romanticism* (Cambridge: Cambridge University Press, 2005); on Juvenal, see also Gary Dyer, *British Satire and the Politics of Style, 1789–1832* (Cambridge: Cambridge University Press, 1997), 39–56; on Catullus, see Cox, *Poetry and Politics*, 146–186. Finally, Arnd Bohm has shown the importance of Ovid for Keats's "Ode on a Grecian Urn." See "Just Beauty: Ovid and the Argument of Keats's 'Ode on a Grecian Urn,'" *Modern Language Quarterly* 68.1 (March 2007): 1–26. On the uses of Roman stoicism in Romantic poetry, see Bruce Graver, "Romanticism," in *A Companion to the Classical Tradition*, ed. Craig Kallendorf (Oxford: Blackwell, 2007), 80–86.

and especially women, with powerful models of alternative social and political ideals.[50] The important bearing of Roman republicanism on British Romantic thought about politics, history, and literature, however, has not been adequately examined. One reason for this is certainly the overwhelming attention that has been paid to classical Greek culture among both Romantic writers themselves and recent scholarship in the field. Another explanation, though, is that scholars have only recently begun to attend to the importance of historiographical thought among the period's writers. There is a vast, important field of Romantic writing on Roman history and politics that remains largely untouched.

One way of understanding Rome's importance for the Romantic period relates to the British republican, or civic humanist, tradition. At its most basic, republicanism would connote any political philosophy advocating a government without a monarch, one in which the supreme authority resides with the people. This is complicated in England, however, by a post-Restoration political tradition in which a government anchored in the balance between Crown, nobles, and commons was seen to constitute an ideal republic. The stability of such a republic, its ability to keep corruption at bay, was maintained by the virtue of its citizenry. Within this logic, a republic ruled by laws was contrasted not with a monarchy, but with despotism.[51] The logic of the British republican tradition might be described as "exemplary": certain key figures— Cicero, Brutus, Fabricius, Cincinnatus, and, especially, Cato—are continually called upon to license contemporary notions of citizenship and patriotism on the assumption that these figures have a transparent relevance to current affairs. Because the ideal of a virtuous citizenry is so crucial to the stability of the republican state, such Roman models of virtue play a central role in republican ideology.

As a mode of relating present to past, the republican tradition's exemplary logic is sometimes thought to be supplanted by the rise of

---

[50] See Butler, "Cult of the South"; and Cox, *Poetry and Politics*, and *Unfolding the South: Nineteenth-Century British Women Writers and Artists in Italy*, ed. Allison Chapman and Jane Stabler (Manchester: Manchester University Press, 2003).

[51] See J. G. A. Pocock, *The Machiavellian Moment* (Princeton, NJ: Princeton University Press, 1975), and *Virtue, Commerce, and History* (Cambridge: Cambridge University Press, 1985).

historicism, which denies the basis of exemplarity and offers a vision of social change distinct from the republican emphasis on the dynamic of virtue and corruption. Understood as a tendency to explain events and human characteristics with reference to particular times and places, historicism was a direct challenge to the universal human nature implied by exemplarity.[52] Arguably, this idea is not new in the Romantic period. We can sense such an attitude as early as Bacon's essays, and by the late seventeenth century, historicist conceptions began to underwrite a new understanding of political prudence, as we see in the charter of the Bank of England's rejection of the Machiavellian, republican notion of wealth through land in favor of the possibility of wealth through trade.[53] This is precisely the change emphasized by Hume when, in his essay "Of Civil Liberty," he rejects the political wisdom of Machiavelli because it was based too narrowly on the "tyrannical governments of ancient times," and could not accommodate trade, which "was never esteemed an affair of state till the last century."[54]

What seems distinctive about the conjunction of Romanticism and historicism, however, is the way that an awareness of historical difference became the dominant idea of the age. As John Stuart Mill suggested in 1831, "The idea of comparing one's own age with former ages, or with our notion of those which are yet to come, had occurred to philosophers; but it never before was itself the dominant idea of any age."[55] Given the historicist challenge to the exemplary logic of republicanism, its denial that history could reach across ages and teach by example, one way of conceptualizing the Romantic period would be as a transition from the reverence for antiquity, with its emphasis on exemplarity and history's teaching by example, to the more critical and

---

[52] My understanding of historicism as described here is indebted to James Chandler. See his *England in 1819*, and also his essay "History," in *The Oxford Companion to the Romantic Age: British Culture 1776–1832*, ed. Iain McCalman (Oxford: Oxford University Press, 1999), 354–361.

[53] See Steven C. A. Pincus, "Whigs, Political Economy, and the Revolution of 1688–89," in *Cultures of Whiggism: New Essays on English Literature and Culture in the Long Eighteenth Century*, ed. David Womersley (Newark: University of Delaware Press, 2005), 62–85.

[54] David Hume, "Of Civil Liberty," *Essays: Moral, Political, and Literary*, ed. Eugene F. Miller (Indianapolis, IN: Liberty Classics, 1987), 88.

[55] [John Stuart Mill], "The Spirit of the Age," *The Examiner*, 9 January 1831, 20.

analytical approach of historicism, which distinguishes past ages based on contextual particularity. Rome provides an especially apt locus from which to elaborate and complicate this transition because of its central position in republican ideology and because of the dominant hold that classical models, Roman in particular, are commonly thought to have on the British political, historical, and aesthetic imagination in the eighteenth century. Indeed, the long shadow cast by Rome across the British eighteenth century has meant that despite the potential usefulness of Rome for thinking about changes in the understanding of the past during the Romantic period, it remains a somewhat counterintuitive focus because of the degree to which discussions of the concept and the period have been characterized by the description of Romanticism as a rupture with the faith in ancient learning and texts characteristic of the "neoclassical" or "Augustan" eighteenth century.[56] But for this reason, the relevance of the classical, and especially the Roman, persists in a Romantic period that was fully engaged with the Romantic past. We must recognize, in other words, that the paradoxical classicism of Romanticism and the careful scrutiny of the range of meanings assigned to Rome and of the process by which Rome is compared to contemporary Britain is fundamental to an interpretation of Romantic modernity.

---

[56] As a term for characterizing the reception of antiquity in eighteenth-century Britain, "neoclassical" has consistently been contested. See, for example, J. W. Johnson, *The Formation of English Neo-Classical Thought* (Princeton, NJ: Princeton University Press, 1967). Among art historians, the role of antiquity in generating a discourse of aesthetic reinvigoration, whereby the embrace of artistic modernity comes through the embrace of classical values and aesthetic standards, is widely recognized. The literature is vast and ongoing. For an introduction, see Robert Rosenblum, *Transformations in Late Eighteenth-Century Art* (Princeton, NJ: Princeton University Press, 1967); more recently, see Martin Myrone, *Bodybuilding: Reforming Masculinities in British Art, 1750–1810* (New Haven, CT: Yale University Press, 2005). Among art historians, neoclassicism as a "stylistic label has latterly been superceded by the rubric of taste and the antique," according to Viccy Coltman ("Representation, Replication and Collecting in Charles Townley's Late Eighteenth-Century Library," *Art History* 29 [2006]: 304).

See Francis Haskell and Nicholas Penny, *Taste and the Antique: The Lure of Classical Sculpture, 1500–1900* (New Haven, CT: Yale University Press, 1981). A revival of the term neoclassical, and a useful discussion of the relationship between the use of antiquity and the forging of modernity, can be found in Viccy Coltman, *Fabricating the Antique: Neoclassicism in Britain, 1760–1800* (Chicago: University of Chicago Press, 2006) and in Coltman's *Art History* article, cited above.

III.

Literary historians often refer to the British eighteenth century as an Augustan era. This reference to the emperor Augustus Caesar is meant to suggest both the political stability that followed the rise of Augustus (and by implication the revolution settlement in England) and the aesthetic triumphs of Horace and Virgil and their British admirers Dryden, Pope, Swift, and others.[57] Though widely used as a descriptor of British culture in the eighteenth century, "Augustan" has always been a subject of contestation, and the dispute over the relevance of the term concerns an extended reflection on the interconnections between literature, literary criticism, and politics. The furor surrounding the term has abided considerably since its peak from the late 1960s to the early 1980s, and it now seems safe to suggest that three distinct positions have emerged: those defending the relevance of the term "Augustan"; those who prefer a broader term (usually, "classical" or "neoclassical"); and, finally, those who reject all such terms and argue that the eighteenth-century reliance on the classics has been overstated.[58] The most polemical antagonists in this debate have been Howard Erskine-Hill and Howard Weinbrot.[59]

---

[57] In the hands of literary scholars, "Augustan" has been broadly applied to the literary forms, styles, and themes associated with Dryden and his followers, especially Pope. But the term can also be used to suggest more overtly political connotations, most commonly in discussions of Dryden's *Astrea Redux* or Pope's *Epistle to Augustus*. In addition, the term is used to describe a specific temporal period, the "Augustan Age," either associated with a specific ruler, Charles II, Queen Anne, or the early Georges, or a specific literary figure, most commonly Dryden and Pope, Addison, or Johnson, in a span whose specific contours start as early as 1660 and end as late as 1800. See Ian Watt, *The Augustan Age* (Greenwich, CT: Fawcett, 1968).

[58] On the neoclassical, see Johnson, *English Neo-Classical Thought*; for the defense of the term "Augustan," see Watt, *Augustan Age* and, especially, Howard Erskine-Hill, *The Augustan Idea in English Literature* (London: Edward Arnold, 1983); for the rejection of "Augustan," see Howard D. Weinbrot, *Augustus Caesar in Augustan England: The Decline of a Classical Norm* (Princeton, NJ: Princeton University Press, 1978), and Weinbrot's extended review of Erskine-Hill, "The Emperor's Old Toga: Augustanism and the Scholarship of Nostalgia," *Modern Philology* 83 (1986): 286–297.

[59] For a full account of the dispute, see Weinbrot, *Augustus Caesar in Augustan England*, 3–7; Erskine-Hill, *Augustan Idea*, 235 n. 4, which includes a detailed reply to the arguments in Weinbrot's book; and Weinbrot, "The Emperor's Old Toga." For a more recent commentary, see Thomas Kaminski, "Rehabilitating 'Augustanism': On the Roots of 'Polite Letters' in England," *Eighteenth-Century Life* 20.3 (1996): 49–65.

Weinbrot associates Augustanism with royal absolutism and denies its relevance to a period shaped by the landmarks of 1688 and 1776, both of which did so much to restrict the royal prerogative in England. Erskine-Hill, in contrast, claims that throughout the eighteenth century, "Augustan" was a shaping concept for defining an age of political stability and literary refinement fostered by the monarchy, and he claims that the eighteenth century saw no change in opinion about Augustan Rome and that the adjective "Augustan" was uniformly used in a positive sense. It is not my purpose here to mediate or resolve the dispute between Weinbrot and Erskine-Hill; rather I want to suggest how both of their positions underscore the importance of Rome as a model and source of reference for Britain in the Restoration and eighteenth century. Weinbrot's argument, which associates Augustanism with absolutism and suggests that such a concept is discordant with what he sees as the sustained limitations on monarchial power through the eighteenth century, accords with a view of English history that emphasizes 1688 as the crucial date for establishing the political context for what it then describes as a liberal and progressive eighteenth century. But even if, as Weinbrot argues, the reverence for classical antiquity was replaced by a strong national identity, then we must recognize the degree to which even the negative references to Rome that Weinbrot reproduces so copiously were instrumental in forging this identity. Erskine-Hill's emphasis on the authority of the monarch for establishing a favorable climate for the arts is a position coherent with a view of English history, most commonly associated with J. C. D. Clark, that downplays the political significance of 1688 and claims instead that the structures of the "old regime" were firmly in place until the First Reform Bill of 1832.[60] But regardless of which position one takes, it is clear that the Roman past, imperial and republican, was crucial in eighteenth-century Britain for articulating a coherent yet flexible set of models with which one could both attack or defend various models of political power and competing understandings of an emergent national identity.[61]

---

[60] See J. C. D. Clark, *English Society, 1688–1832: Ideology, Social Structure, and Political Practice during the Ancien Regime* (Cambridge: Cambridge University Press, 1985).

[61] Weinbrot, however, would likely disagree with this assessment. *Brittania's Issue: The Rise of British Literature from Dryden to Ossian* (Cambridge: Cambridge University Press, 1993) resumes his earlier arguments about the unsuitability of Augustus as a model for eighteenth-century Britain, and it documents what he sees as "the

Rome, in other words, was a site of conflict in the eighteenth century, and the struggle over its meaning and relevance was not limited to the defense of or attack on Augustus. Republican Rome was also an important model. Explaining the increased use of Roman analogies after 1688, Philip Ayres suggests that eighteenth-century gentry and aristocrats reimagined themselves as Romans, assuming the role of defining and safekeeping the principles of political liberty and civic virtue in an effort to dignify and legitimize a new political order. Ayres claims that:

Republican Rome, its civic virtues and vices, its politics and class structure, the dangers it faced not just from Julius Caesar and autocracy but, it was implicitly understood, from the democratic element since the days of Marius and (for many) the Gracchi, all this became a compound metaphor for the state of England in the decades following 1688, exploitable by Whigs and Tories alike. Louis XIV might identify with Augustus but he thereby denied to the French state, insofar as it existed outside of himself, any connection with the free Roman Republic and its old institutions. It is the English ruling class's deep sense of affinity with this Rome and its oligarchic, not its popular, traditions, which gives English classicism an entire dimension of meaning absent from any of the contemporary continental classicisms until the French

---

frequent and growing disapproval of or indifference to the classics" (21). Weinbrot asserts that when Rome is cited, it is increasingly as a negative example. In this reading, to become a nation Britain needed to recognize the limits of the great classical achievements so important to her educated classes, and this reverence for classical antiquity is gradually replaced by the development of a strong national identity that sees life in eighteenth-century Britain as better than classical times. Weinbrot's Britain is one that integrates a diverse range of cultural traditions into what he terms the "synthetic compromise that characterizes the complex eighteenth-century British identity" (74); but he also notes the "mistrust, suspicion, and outright hostility as well as competition or emulation of the best sort" (74). Weinbrot acknowledges this conflict only to ignore it in favor of his attempt to characterize the amiable synthesis and harmony of the period. In a particularly astute review, Alok Yadav calls attention to the way that Weinbrot's emphasis on synthesis has the unfortunate effect of muting the cultural conflicts that were so much a part of an expanding and quasi-homogenizing British identity. Although Yadav is especially concerned with cultural imperialism and the way that Weinbrot reproduces and endorses what Yadav describes as the ideology of imperialism, we could just as easily apply the same scrutiny to Weinbrot's treatment of Rome and the classical heritage, in which conflict and struggle are muted in the effort to describe a coherent national identity that uniformly sees Britain as better than Rome. See *Criticism* 36 (Fall 1994): 611–616.

Revolution and the assimilation of Roman-republican iconography under the Republic.[62]

Ayres's claims underscore the deeply political meanings of Rome in the eighteenth century, and they suggest further how diverse the meanings assigned to Rome could be. Although Rome's history could be adapted for the monarchical ideal of an "Augustan" eighteenth century, Ayres's argument contests the importance of Augustus in favor of Roman republican history as a means of structuring oligarchic power plays; its suggestion that such a strategy was meant to combat the dangers of Rome's democratic element also hints at the possibility of republican Rome as the source for the rhetoric of popular revolution. For Ayres, the importance of republican Rome in the English tradition provides a rationale for distinguishing English classicism from its Continental contemporaries, and he thus offers an additional reason for attending to changes in the meaning of republican Rome beyond the period of his study.

What happens to the use of republican Rome in England when, with the onset of the French Revolution, the French also begin to make use of the Roman republican tradition? Furthermore, how does the understanding of republican history change with the reception of the French Revolution in Britain and the persistent and widespread fear of an insurrection from below that it produced? These questions are further complicated during the second half of the century when, as Britain's power increased abroad, analogies to the classical world became less and less deferential—a decline in deference that placed Britain in the same relation to Rome as Rome was with Greece. Just as Rome was seen to borrow, extend, and ultimately surpass Greek ideals in the production of a dominant empire, so eighteenth-century British thinkers began to conceive of their emergent empire as the apotheosis and extension of Roman ideals. The logic of this analogy implies another possible explanation for Romantic anxieties about imitation, and it also suggests how an emphasis on the originality of the Greeks as being unsurpassed by the Romans could be a potentially political gesture in that it rejects a particular logic of progress through

---

[62] Philip Ayres, *Classical Culture and the Idea of Rome in Eighteenth-Century England* (Cambridge: Cambridge University Press, 1997), 12–13.

history by which Greece then Rome then Britain become the standard-bearer for political organization, artistic expression, and imperial dominance. In the context both of the particular relevance of republican Rome in eighteenth-century Britain and the increasingly prevalent understanding of Britain as the apotheosis of Roman ideals, the interpretation of the Roman past assumes prominent political implications for the British present.

Marilyn Butler has similarly highlighted the political implications of the increased attention to classical cultures in the second decade of the nineteenth century. She argues that Byron, Shelley, and Keats, along with Thomas Love Peacock, Leigh Hunt, and Hazlitt, recognize themselves as part of a distinct group that emerges from a specific place, Marlow in the Thames valley in spring 1817. Although the emergence of this group was not so much induced as crystallized by what she terms a "post-war right-wing cult of the Germanic," in its deliberate rejection of the literature of the North and its defense of the classical and Mediterranean South, the Marlow group believed that they were fighting for their political principles. Moreover, their work is deliberately pagan, and the shared taste for Greece, especially in the case of Peacock and Shelley, "stands for a whole ideal of harmony, a challenge to arbitrary divisions between mind and body, man and his environment, man and God; and a challenge also to an institutionalized Christianity that was part of the apparatus of State."[63] Such claims coincide with the political implications of an insistence that the originality of the Greeks was unsurpassed by the Romans. In both interpretations, Hellenism is public and deeply political, a covert discourse in a game of opposition politics. We should be careful, however, before we accept Butler's claim that the fidelity to Enlightenment tastes and values of such periodicals as the *Edinburgh Review* and the *Quarterly Review* when combined with the classical interests of the Marlow circle represents "the distinctive and remarkable late flowering of Neoclassicism in England in the second decade of the century."[64] These examples clearly indicate the continued attention to classical cultures, especially among the later Romantics, but this does not necessarily mean that such attention is neoclassical in focus or import.

---

[63] Butler, "Cult of the South," 121, 136.
[64] Ibid, 117.

Although the neoclassical is a notoriously difficult term to specify, its invocation is most commonly associated with eighteenth-century standards of taste and, as Paul Fry suggests, "Many Romantic texts could be cited in which the decline of the Classical to the neoclassical is seen precisely as the transformation of the normative from internal necessity to external constraint."[65] This does not mean, however, that Romanticism rejected a classical standard entirely. This book seeks to address certain fundamental changes in the way that classical antiquity was understood in the Romantic period and thus to distinguish Romantic classicism from the neoclassicism of the eighteenth century and, further, to suggest how an understanding of Romantic attention to antiquity as something distinct from eighteenth-century neoclassicism can refine our understanding of Romanticism itself.

This book is a study, then, of the way one historical period uses another historical period and of the meaning of that use. For this reason, the problem of Romantic historicism and the widening hermeneutic circle of the relationship of present to past are of overriding concern. This book reflects upon the process it examines; just as the Romans looked to the Greeks and the Romantics looked to Rome, so this book looks back to the Romantics. The pattern is further complicated by the rhetorical structure of the classical historians themselves. No histories of republican Rome written during the republic survive, and the historians that we do have (most important, Livy, Sallust, and Tacitus) present the bright background of the republic contrasted with a morally diminished present.[66] Within this circle, certain issues of periodization are immediately apparent: though the issue is contested, many scholars argue—including Godwin in his *Enquirer* essay on the classics—that the modernity of the Renaissance comes from its use of the classics.[67] How, then, does the modernity of the Romantics

---

[65] Fry, "Classical Standards," 9.

[66] To get a strikingly clear, condensed sense of this contrast, we need only look as far as the first ten chapters of book 1 of Tacitus's *Annali*, noting the speed and stinging irony with which Tacitus moves through the republic (chap. 1) and the reign of Augustus (chaps. 2–10).

[67] See, for example, Hans Baron, *The Crisis of the Early Italian Renaissance* (Princeton, NJ: Princeton University Press, 1966) and a work which draws heavily, if subtly, on Baron's categories and concerns, J. G. A. Pocock, *The Machiavellian Moment* (Princeton, NJ: Princeton University Press, 1975).

differ? In other words, it is simply not enough to say that the Romantics know the classics or even to point to the places where they refer to them; the more important question is, What is the meaning of that use?

One possibility is suggested by Mona Ozouf, who argues that the rhetorical structure of the ancient historians lends itself to a view of ancient history that is dehistoricized and utopianized, a sort of sacred past, infinitely usable as a kind of beginning.[68] This position dovetails nicely with that of Marx, who, in the opening of *The Eighteenth Brumaire of Louis Bonaparte* (1852), argues that the French revolutionaries use Roman examples as a means of cloaking the initiation of a new, bourgeois order in the forms of established and venerated precedent:

> Unheroic as bourgeois society is, it nevertheless took heroism, sacrifice, terror, civil war and battles of peoples to bring it into being. And in the classically austere traditions of the Roman republic its gladiators found the ideals and the art forms, the self-deceptions that they needed in order to conceal from themselves the bourgeois limitations of the content of their struggles and to keep their enthusiasm on the high plane of the great historical tragedy.[69]

Marx emphasizes the way that modernity can be initiated through the borrowed clothing of the Roman past. His focus is squarely on the co-optation of republican ideals and art forms by the French, but his comments could also be applied to Britain. Indeed, Marx's comments suggest that the use of Roman examples by some British Romantics may have been a reaction to French efforts to colonize and deploy the same examples, the result being a kind of pamphlet war for cultural capital, transpiring alongside a Continental war for material capital. Stephen Cheeke, for example, describes Coleridge's use of the historical parallel between France and Rome to anticipate a process of accelerated decline and to predict the triumph of England over France. Cheeke also notes the increasing doubts that surround the construction of such parallels, whereby contemporary events in France clarify

---

[68] Ozouf, *Festivals*, 271–278.
[69] Karl Marx, *The Eighteenth Brumaire of Louis Bonaparte* (New York: International Publishers, 1963), 16–17.

the terror and violence of Roman history and lead to a questioning of the value of Roman ideals and the classical legacy more broadly. For Cheeke, this is part of a shift in the relation of the present to the ancient past, central to which "is a reconfiguration of the historical parallel, a darkening of the notion of the double, in which instead of the idea of the repeated 'type,' the notion of the double becomes essentially a moral bifurcation within the subject, a schizophrenia or an 'angel-demon' duality of the kind De Quincey identified in Roman history, which is easily translated into Freudian, Nietzschean or Foucauldian paradigms."[70] Pressure on the historical parallel here results in Romanticism's inward turn, a splitting "within the subject." I argue, in contrast, that this inward turn is only part of the story and that the more critical understanding of the ancient past is an index of its sheer difference from the present. The recognition of this difference results in a fundamental shift in the perception of history during the Romantic period, a shift clarified by this book's attention to the meaning and use of republican Rome.

Reinhart Koselleck emphasizes the significance of this changed understanding of history, which he evaluates as part of a much broader shift in intellectual history.[71] For Koselleck, the late eighteenth century produces a transition from a backward-looking concept of history which uses exempla from the past to offer lessons for the present to a forward-looking concept in which history has a determined logic of progress. "History as a totality places the person who has learned to understand it in a state of learning which was to work directly on the future" (38). History becomes not a plural collection of exempla, but capital-H History, a systematic unity and the sole path to true knowledge of one's condition. Koselleck's argument is, of course, but one narrative of the birth of historicism and the philosophy of history, but given the way that this book treats the use of classical exempla in the Romantic period, it is a particularly relevant narrative. Walter Jackson Bate makes a similar, though less sophisticated, claim in his biography

---

[70] Cheeke, "The Sword 'Which eats into itself'," 221.

[71] Reinhart Koselleck, "Historia Magistra Vitae: The Dissolution of the Topos into the Perspective of a Modernized Historical Process," in *Futures Past: On the Semantics of Historical Time*, trans. Keith Tribe (Cambridge: MIT Press, 1985), 21–38. Subsequent references to this essay are provided parenthetically in the text.

of Keats. "Keats began to think of history," states Bate, "as a process in which the changes that take place are fundamental."[72] And it is this recognition of the pastness of the past, this historicism, that Bate claims underwrites Keats's turn to "the inner life." The point in juxtaposing the two examples is to suggest that the evaluation of Romanticism and ancient Rome itself provides a crucial series of exempla with which to think about the meaning and significance of Romantic historicism and the further possibility that such historicism may underwrite the individualism, expressionism, and imagination long perceived as the essence of the period.[73]

IV.

In considering the importance of republican Rome for Romantic period Britain, then, my thinking is framed by what I see as a fundamental shift in historical understanding in this period: the transition from "exemplarity," where historical examples are removed from specific contexts and made to teach lessons for all times, to "historicism," here considered as a tendency to explain events and human characteristics with reference to particular times and places and thus as a direct challenge to the universal human nature implied by exemplarity. Republican Rome functions as a heuristic device through which to observe more particularly the implications and tensions within this shift, though it also has a more specific importance. The French Revolution, with its deliberate borrowing of the symbols and heroes of republican Rome—"the ideals and the art forms" as Marx would have it—emphasized the significance of Roman parallels and invited sustained comparison between the history of Rome and more contemporary European events. Such borrowings, in turn, make the history of republican Rome important not only for understanding events in

---

[72] Walter Jackson Bate, *John Keats* (Cambridge: Harvard University Press, 1963), 322.
[73] I do not claim this insight as my own, and it may indeed have by now become a commonplace. For a convincing explanation, see McGann, *Romantic Ideology*, and "Keats and the Historical Method in Literary Criticism," *Beauty of Inflections*, 15–65.

France, but also for understanding the response to those events in Britain, where an extant republican political tradition had assigned its own values and interpretations to the virtuous heroes of Rome—values that often stood in opposition to a more complacent and confident set of Augustan parallels prominent in the eighteenth century, especially its earlier decades. As radicals such as John Thelwall began to encourage a different set of conclusions from Roman history, the result was a prolonged struggle—a culture war, even—over the proper significance and applicability of republican Rome, and this struggle marks the interrelation of political, historical, and aesthetic practices in Romantic Britain. A focus on the meaning and significance of republican Rome can therefore clarify the specific contours of this struggle, while also recognizing and conceptualizing a significant shift in historical thinking in this period, one that questions the efficacy of exemplarity and historical parallels in favor of explanations rooted in historical particularity. This book elucidates this transition by considering how the understanding of specific Roman figures and events changes and how these changes are constructed differently in different genres.

Section 1 consists of two chapters, focusing respectively on political writing and the novel. Chapter 1, "Rome and the Revolution Controversy," argues that an understanding of the discourse of republicanism[74] is crucial for thinking about the meaning and use of ancient Rome at the start of the Romantic period through a look at the bitter polemics over the British response to the French Revolution in which Edmund Burke, John Thelwall, William Godwin, and many lesser known writers deploy Roman texts and the exemplary mention of exalted Roman heroes for opposing sides in the conflict (what Carl Woodring refers to as "Latinate moral statesmanship"). More specifically, I show how a focus on Roman references recasts an important debate on political philosophy as something more complicated than a simple opposition

---

[74] In the past three decades of eighteenth-century scholarship, "republicanism" as a dominant political concept has assumed increased—and hotly contested—explanatory importance. The contested nature of republicanism is not new; none other than John Adams claimed that "there is not a more unintelligible word in the English language than republicanism." David Wooton concurs and observes that "one of the problems with much modern scholarship on republicanism is that it has taken this unintelligible word too much for granted" (both quotations can be found in Wooton, "The Republican Tradition: From Commonwealth to Common Sense," *Republicanism*,

between "radical" and "conservative" positions. Burke, for example, relies on the citation of Roman texts, but he also, to an extent, undermines the relevance of these examples because his emphasis on prescription (the application of past precedent to concrete circumstances) and on the organic accumulated wisdom of the English national past suggests that the analogous mode of directly relating ancient history to contemporary events (the mode that Koselleck calls *historia magistra vitae* and that I have described as exemplarity) is no longer so obviously relevant. Godwin, in contrast, relies on exactly this exemplary mode when he praises Roman heroes, and, although he is traditionally considered a "radical" thinker, Godwin's use of Rome in *Political Justice* and later in *The Enquirer*, I show, reproduces a more traditional eighteenth-century model of classical exemplarity.

The second chapter, "From Roman to *roman:* The Jacobin Novel and the Roman Legacy in the 1790s," considers changes in the eighteenth-century reading public to elaborate the contours of what I call "republican poetics" in the Jacobin novels of Godwin, Thomas Holcroft, Mary Hays, and Elizabeth Inchbald. Key radicals like Godwin and Thomas Paine modeled the progressive's ideal republic upon the republic of letters.[75] Godwin, as we saw above, claimed boldly that "the cause of political reform, and the cause of intellectual refinement are inseparably connected,"[76] whereas, more famously, Shelley saw in poetry the seeds of "social renovation." Marilyn Butler has argued that the "revolutionary factor" responsible for the literary situation of the late eighteenth

---

Liberty, and Commercial Society [Stanford, CA: Stanford University Press, 1995], 1). This is certainly the case for scholars of the Romantic period, in whose works the word, though often referred to, remains ill defined, and as a result the concept remains undertheorized. Part of the problem may lie in the polysemic connotations of the word "republic," with each specific definition constituting a definite political choice. The problem may also relate to the way "republican" was used through the eighteenth century as a straightforward term of abuse, despite the simultaneous existence of an extensive public literature that appealed to republican principles and values while claiming them to be perfectly compatible with constitutional monarchy. Finally, much of the confusion may be a question of how a notion of civic participation largely anchored in a land-based theory of property responds to changes in the very notion of property that arise with commercial modernity.

[75] John Klancher, "Godwin and the Republican Romance: Genre, Politics, and Contingency in Cultural History," *MLQ* 56 (1995): 145–165.

[76] Godwin, *The Enquirer*, vi. Quoted above on page 1 and by Klancher, ibid., 154.

century "was the new audience for imaginative literature."⁷⁷ Taking this new audience as its starting point, this chapter considers the use of Roman figures and classical historical models in the Jacobin novel as a way of revealing how the radical novel trades upon the model of exemplarity so prominent in republican discourse as it strives to create its own set of exempla as models for imitation or avoidance.

Section 2 focuses on poetry. It explores how later Romantic poets struggled over the meaning of the Roman legacy as they attempted to enlist it for their competing systems of poetics and politics. Chapter 3, "A Roman Standard: Byron, Ancient Rome, and Literary Decline," evaluates how Roman literary history structures Byron's concept of literary decline and enables him to reject Romantic modes and his immediate poetic precursors. Looking backward in a famous letter to Murray, Byron writes:

> With regard to poetry in general I am convinced the more I think of it—that he and *all* of us—Scott—Southey—Wordsworth—Moore—Campbell—I—are all in the wrong…that we are upon a wrong revolutionary poetical system—or systems…and that the present & next generations will finally be of this opinion.—I am the more confirmed in this—by having lately gone over some of our Classics—particularly *Pope*—whom I tried in this way—I took Moore's poems & my own & some others—& went over them side by side with Pope's—and I was really astonished (I ought not to have been so) and mortified—at the ineffable distance in point of sense—harmony—effect—and even *Imagination Passion*—& *Invention*—between the little Queen Anne's Man—& us of the lower Empire—depend upon it [it] is all Horace then, and Claudian now among us—and if I had to begin again—I would model myself accordingly—⁷⁸

Setting these and other comments by Byron in the context of the controversy over the reputation of Pope, this chapter argues that because the historicization of taste is such an important point of contention

---

⁷⁷ Marilyn Butler, "Romanticism in England," *Romanticism in National Context*, ed. Roy Porter and Mikulas Teich (Cambridge: Cambridge University Press, 1988), 38–39. Butler further claims that this audience was "literate but not perhaps well-educated: there is more emphasis on feeling and on life-experience (or hunger for it) than on prior knowledge gained from reading." She explains that because this new audience was excluded from direct political power, late-eighteenth-century poetry and fiction "had a political content" that "tended to oppose the central British state and its institutions" (39). On the Romantic reading public, see also St. Clair, *Reading Nation in the Romantic Period*.

⁷⁸ Byron to John Murray, 15 September 1817, *Byron's Letters and Journals*, 5:265.

in the Pope controversy, we would do well to consider how Roman texts and the concept of Roman literary history work in the constitution of Byron's claims. If, as Robert Griffin asserts, Romanticism defines itself by reconfiguring its literary past, then Byron's contribution to the Pope controversy shows him grounding his attempted manipulation of a malleable English canon on the more solid stuff of Roman literary history, on the canon of Latin poets. In Byron's case, he uses a specific concept of classical poetics to locate the greatness of English literary history in Milton, Dryden, and Pope, and he suggests that the present age, though distinguishable from its predecessors, represents not a progressive development but a frightening decline. With this in mind, I turn to Byron's poetry and show how an understanding of Byron's sense of Roman poetics and literary history allows us to read beyond his self-mythologizing and see that when Byron speaks of ancient Roman ruins in *Childe Harold*, he is both using the ruins to amplify his expression of self but also developing a particular expression of his post-Waterloo historical consciousness. Focusing on the way Rome thus figures in Byron's prose, letters, and poetry, I argue, lends not only a fresh perspective to the Pope controversy, but also to a consideration of uneven and dissonant qualities within the category "Romantic" itself.

One explanation for the lack of focus on Rome is the widespread conception of a turn to Greece as early as the mid-eighteenth century—a turn which, with the importation and display of the Parthenon Marbles, developed into a philhellenic furor by the end of the 1810s. Shelley's work has been a consistent focal point for the critical understanding of this Romantic Hellenism, and chapter 4 takes up his later writing, which, despite (and perhaps because of) its obvious fascination with Greece, represents the period's most complicated engagement with Rome. "We are all Greeks," Shelley famously claimed in his 1821 preface to *Hellas*. But immediately after his statement, he continues, "But for Greece, Rome, the instructor, the conqueror, the metropolis of our ancestors would have spread no illumination with her arms."[79] Greece is immediately linked to Rome. It is a pattern that persists throughout Shelley's work, although scholars have focused on

---

[79] *Shelley's Poetry and Prose*, ed. Donald H. Reiman and Sharon B. Powers (New York: W. W. Norton, 1977), 409.

Shelley's Hellenism and have had little to say about his use of Rome. This critical oversight, I argue, has left us with an incomplete understanding of the meaning and importance of Shelley's Hellenism, one that cannot be remedied without a sharper sense of his appreciation of antiquity more broadly and of the relationship between Greece and Rome in particular. To watch the changing fortunes of Athens and Rome in such later works as the *Philosophical View*, the "Ode to Liberty," the *Defence of Poetry*, and *Hellas* exposes the critical role that Rome plays in Shelley's historiographical inclinations and his strategies for understanding the past, which, in turn, exposes the relationship of these techniques to the deeply political functions of Shelley's classicism and his historiography.

Section 3 considers the importance of drama on Roman republican themes for the political and cultural struggles of the Romantic period. It considers the possibility, stated explicitly by John Thelwall (and later echoed by Hazlitt), that ancient Rome provided a means to engage British politics in forms acceptable to censors and licensers who were wary, especially after the publication of Paine's *Rights of Man* (1792), of the volatile popular response to explicit political commentary. But if Rome and matters Roman were often thought to be the province of educated elites trained in classical languages, then the representation of Rome in the theater demonstrates how people who did not have classical educations could nonetheless gain awareness of Rome and Roman figures. Put simply, the theater made Rome available to masses and elites alike. Chapter 5 focuses on *Coriolanus*, which was performed repeatedly by the most popular actors to packed houses. With its representation of grain shortages, conflicts between the populace and the patricians, and the dependence of political leaders on the approval of the people, *Coriolanus* was a very topical play for Romantic period audiences. The play was associated with John Philip Kemble, the most dominant actor of the Romantic period, who used the role to portray the rightness of patrician rule in a time of popular unrest. He added, for example, a large processional scene with two hundred actors to show Coriolanus's ability to control the populace, and his stage sets relied (anachronistically) on the columns and might of imperial Rome. This chapter examines these and other aspects of Kemble's production of the play from 1789 to 1817, including the omissions and additions to the text, set designs, and the commentaries of contemporaries who saw the performance. It then compares Kemble's staging with Edmund Kean's brief tenure in the role in an 1820 production that returned the scene to the mud huts of early Rome and diminished the haughty dominance of the central character. The chapter concludes with a discussion of Hazlitt's distinction between imagination and understanding—made initially in a review of *Coriolanus*—where imagination is seen as an "aristocratical faculty," and poetry as "right royal." To what extent does this judgment relate less to Shakespeare's play and more to Kemble's interpretation of it? In response to this question, I show how the performance history of *Coriolanus* provides the crucial subtext for understanding this key Romantic period theorization of the imagination and can help us better to understand Romantic anxieties about Shakespearean performance generally.

It is not an accident that many new plays on Roman themes appear after 1817, the year Kemble retired from the stage, and this forms a crucial aspect of the story that I tell in this book. Because Kemble's *Coriolanus* was Rome for so much of the period, only after he retired did other imaginings become possible. Accordingly, chapter 6 ("What Is the People? Rome on the Romantic Stage after Kemble") considers the competition over the Roman legacy through readings of an entirely new archive of plays on which minimal scholarly work has been done, with particular focus on John Howard Payne's *Brutus* (1818), James Sheridan Knowles's *Caius Gracchus: A Tragedy* (1823), and George Croly's *Catiline: A Tragedy* (1822). The chapter is framed around questions of expanded popular participation in the political process and the related problem of public opinion. Roman plays, I argue, show how the theater functions as a public space for debate on these issues along with related problems—all similarly topical—such as the relation between foreign wars and domestic policy; scarcity; conspiracy; revolt; and the use of violence to achieve political ends. *Brutus* and *Caius Gracchus* clearly align themselves with Reform politics, whereas *Catiline* uses an episode from Roman republican history to criticize popular democracy by linking it to both domestic misrule and corrupt imperial governance. Regardless of their apparently different political sympathies, all three plays are uniformly critical of the Roman populace, which is most often depicted as a mob incapable of acting as a people. With the clamor for voting reform that resumed after Waterloo and culminated in the First Reform Bill of 1832, this depiction of the populace as confused and incapable of articulating a coherent representation of its interests can be read as skepticism about the expansion of the franchise and demonstrates further the continued relevance of republican Rome for shaping British responses to even the most contemporary of events.

Rome has been made to stand for literary authority, republican heroism, imperial power and decline, the Catholic Church, and the pleasure of ruins. This book extends these concerns—so central to the eighteenth-century reception of Rome—to the realm of British Romanticism, where the often overlooked presence of Rome helps to reveal how a distinctive field of historical reference and mode of historical understanding structure the period's more obvious fascination with imagination, nature, and the self. The book thus constitutes a work about republicanism that does not occlude the republic of letters, a work about historicism that affirms its importance without obfuscating the diversity and tensions of Romantic thought, and a work of intellectual history that does not overlook the particularly literary quality of British Romanticism and the complicated relationship between political and aesthetic positions that it presents.

Part I

Political Writing and the Novel

Chapter One

Rome and the Revolution Controversy

On 10 February 1796, at the Beaufort Buildings in London, John Thelwall began a series of some twenty lectures that would last seven weeks. Thelwall was an active participant in the London Corresponding Society and the Society for Constitutional Information who became notorious when he was tried alongside Horne Tooke and Thomas Hardy in the infamous 1794 Treason Trials. The previous year, he had lectured on contemporary British politics to crowds that exceeded the building's capacity, but after the draconian prohibitions of the Two Acts, Thelwall needed a different topic. The subject he chose was Roman history. Though the lectures were not published, Thelwall's *Prospectus* suggests that his reading of Roman history would be a radical interpretation, emphasizing the merits of popular sovereignty through an analysis of the abuses of Rome's early kings, the corruption of the Roman aristocracy, and the conditions surrounding the establishment and decline of the tribunes.[1] For these lessons, Thelwall thought Rome would be more instructive even than the French Revolution or the pantheon of radical English thinkers from John Locke, Algernon Sydney, and James Harrington through Thomas Paine. Although the London lectures were unsuccessful, when Thelwall made a tour of the provinces, his audiences sometimes numbered as many as five thousand. The lectures were so controversial. that Thelwall was set upon by a gang of sailors at Yarmouth who threatened impressments to the antipodes. Thelwall escaped with his life, but most of his books were destroyed.[2]

---

[1] John Thelwall, *Prospectus of a Course of Lectures...in Strict Conformity with the Restrictions of Mr Pitt's Convention Act* (London, 1796).
[2] For details of this incident, see John Thelwall, *An Appeal to Popular Opinion against Kidnapping and Murder* (London, 1796).

It is somewhat remarkable that a series of lectures on Roman history should draw so much attention both from those attending and from those clamoring to interrupt. That this was the case speaks both to Thelwall's notoriety as a public figure and to the politically charged circumstances of the 1790s. Such attention, however, also suggests that the interpretation of Roman republican history was a sharply contested aspect of 1790s political disputes. The English use of Rome after the Glorious Revolution is, according to Philip Ayres, distinguished from any on the Continent because the English ruling class identified its traditions not with Augustus, but with the civic virtue and oligarchic traditions of republican Rome.[3] Ayres's emphasis on the use of oligarchic and aristocratic traditions helps to explain the challenge of Thelwall's intended lectures, which, with their emphasis on tribunician power and the abuses of the aristocracy, clearly invoked an alternative republican tradition. Thelwall's Roman lectures are part of the so called Revolution Controversy, a prolonged print dispute over the significance of events in France and their relevance for Britain. This conflict is often referred to as the "Burke-Paine controversy," although recent scholarship has complicated the significance of Edmund Burke and Thomas Paine, respectively, as the epitomes of conservative and radical positions and, indeed, further complicated the parameters of the broad opposition between radical and conservative.[4] James Epstein, for example, suggests that the dispute turns

---

[3] See Ayres, *Classical Culture and the Idea of Rome in Eighteenth-Century England* (Cambridge: Cambridge University Press, 1997), 12–13.

[4] Gregory Claeys, for example, concludes that "for most of its participants, neither Burke nor Paine defined the British response to the French Revolution." See Claeys, "Republicanism versus Commercial Society: Paine, Burke, and the French Revolution Debate," *History of European Ideas* 11 (1989): 313. For an argument on how British radical language relies on a constitutionalist idiom and thus departs from the natural rights language favored by Paine, see James Epstein, *Radical Expression: Political Language, Ritual, and Symbol in England, 1790–1850* (New York: Oxford University Press, 1994), especially pages 4–28. For a corresponding expansion of conservative rhetoric beyond the terms set by Burke, see Kevin Gilmartin, *Writing against Revolution: Literary Conservatism in Britain, 1790–1832* (Cambridge: Cambridge University Press, 2007). For further arguments that leading conservative writers owe less to Burke than often imagined, see H. T. Dickinson, "Popular Conservatism and Militant Loyalism, 1789–1815," in *Britain and the French Revolution, 1789–1815,* ed. H. T. Dickinson (Basingstoke, UK: Macmillan, 1989), 103–125; and J. G. A. Pocock, introduction to *Reflections on the Revolution in France* (Indianapolis, IN: Hackett, 1987), vii–xlviii, esp. xl.

less on an opposition between a conservative appeal to past precedent associated with Burke and the radical rejection of history in favor of arguments from natural right associated with Paine, and more on the struggle over what he describes as a shared constitutionalist idiom, which "was distinguished not so much for being the ideological property of any one class or political tendency, but as defining the contested terrain between different social and political groups."[5] Epstein's emphasis on the constitutionalist idiom characterizes the dispute over Britain's political future as a contest over the interpretation of significant events in the British past. But, as Thelwall's lectures on Roman history would suggest, the appeal of historical precedent was not limited to British examples. Thelwall even goes so far as to suggest that his engagement with Roman history presents an inviting alternative to a specifically native tradition of radical thought.

This chapter argues that a focus on contests over the Roman republican legacy in the Revolution Controversy exposes tensions among key protagonists that make the dispute's traditionally understood alignments of radical versus conservative look different. Paine's legacy does not enter into the discussion because he largely excludes references to Rome, and though he occasionally appeals to the ancient constitution, his injunction, as Epstein says, is quite clear: "Radicals must eschew arguments seeking to derive political rights from historical precedent and drink solely from the purely rationalist fountain of natural rights theory. *The Rights of Man* is an essentially antihistorical work; democratic rights thrive in an imminent present freed from reference to the past."[6] In contrast, two other major protagonists in the dispute, Edmund Burke and William Godwin, make extensive use of Rome. Burke uses references to Latin satirists to accentuate the authority of his position, and the force of his rhetoric aligns him with Cicero as the clearsighted savior of his country. Although Burke's argument is bolstered by his use of Roman texts, the appeal to Roman precedent implied by his references rests uneasily with his emphasis on the organicism of the British nation and the importance of specifically national precedent. Godwin's use of Rome is less textual, but no less important. For him, certain Roman heroes function as key

[5] Epstein, *Radical Expression*, 27.
[6] Ibid., 5.

proof for the possibility of benevolent sacrifice for the good of the community—the very kind of rational selflessness upon which Godwin establishes the basis of his philosophical anarchism. Godwin's use of Roman heroes, however, invokes past precedent in a manner that can be understood to work against his progressivism.[7] Both Godwin and Burke seek to align aspects of the Roman republican legacy with their position in the dispute. My focus on their use of Rome reveals unexpected similarities alongside more widely recognized differences in their positions, and, further, it exposes how in each case the manner in which Roman precedent is invoked often undermines the ends to which those precedents are applied.

BURKE'S USE OF ROME IN THE *REFLECTIONS*

For scholars of the 1790s, the importance of Burke's *Reflections* hardly requires a defense. Burke's argument is critical both for its fundamental statement of a principled British conservatism[8] that staunchly dismisses the abstract rights of citizenship in favor of local and specific qualities of British national life and for its provocation of a radical response. As such it is a key text—if not the key text—for thinking about 1790s political discourse[9] and is a promising starting place for a close reading of the usage and implication of Roman references. Written ostensibly in response to Richard Price's speech to the Revolution

---

[7] Recall Shelley's objection to Godwin in his letter of 29 July 1812: "Are not the reasonings on which your system is founded utterly distinct from & unconnected with the excellence of Greece and Rome?" See *The Letters of Percy Bysshe Shelley*, ed. Frederick L. Jones (Oxford: Clarendon Press, 1964), 1:317.

[8] On the cadences of this often misleading word, see J. G. A. Pocock's introduction to Burke's *Reflections*, vii; and Robert Hole, *From Jacobite to Conservative: Reaction and Orthodoxy in Britain, c. 1760–1832* (Cambridge: Cambridge University Press, 1993), 1–7. Kevin Gilmartin prefers the term "counterrevolutionary." See *Writing against Revolution*, 2–3.

[9] And, I would add, Burke's influence is of course not limited to the 1790s. For a clear account of Burke's legacy to liberal and conservative thought in the nineteenth and twentieth centuries, see John Whale's introduction to *Edmund Burke's* Reflections on the Revolution in France: *New Interdisciplinary Essays*, ed. John Whale (Manchester: Manchester University Press, 2000), 3–5.

Society on 4 November 1789, Burke's *Reflections* is simultaneously an attempt to clarify his vision of government through an explication of the 1688–1689 Revolution Settlement and to use these principles to criticize the recent revolution in France. In this sense, though it announces itself as a response to events in France, Burke's argument is really more about his understanding of the English nation and the political wisdom of its institutions and customs as proven over time.

In his speech to the Revolution Society, Price had argued for a radical interpretation of the Revolution Settlement that would provide British subjects with "the right to chuse [sic] our own governors, to cashier them for misconduct, and to frame a government for ourselves."[10] In his critique of Price, Burke associates each of these ostensible rights not with the bloodless changes of 1689, but with the feared logic of 1649; he accuses Price of trying to create an abstract rule out of an exceptional circumstance. For Burke, there can be no right to choose governors because the Revolution Settlement clearly establishes by law the principles of succession. There can be no right to rebel because the Settlement was not a nursery for future changes but rather an exception that establishes only the settlement of an extraordinary question of state by asserting the right of Parliament as a corporate body to check the power of the sovereign. Finally, there can be no right of subjects to frame the government for themselves because the English government is based on a series of inherited and not abstract rights—conflicts settled not by abstraction but by an appeal to precedent.[11] In each case, Burke checks Price's move to establish an abstract right with the assertion of a concrete circumstance. Burke's emphasis on his particular interpretation of the Revolution Settlement of 1689 and his attempt to align opponents like Price with the bloody civil war of the mid-seventeenth century may explain why so many of Burke's contemporary critics, including Catharine Macaulay, George Rous, Thomas Christie, and James Mackintosh, included in their response a competing explanation of

---

[10] Richard Price, *A Discourse on the Love of Our Country*, in *Political Writings*, ed. D. O. Thomas (Cambridge: Cambridge University Press, 1991), 190.
[11] Edmund Burke, *Reflections on the Revolution in France*, ed. Pocock (Indianapolis, IN: Hackett, 1987), 10–30. Subsequent references to this edition are provided parenthetically in the text.

the Revolution Settlement and often an accusation that Burke himself had violated its principles in his defense of monarchy.[12]

The English government, in Burke's conception, is a mixed government in which each of the three orders—Crown (sovereign), lords (landowners), and commons (people)—has certain claims over and against one another. Conflicts between these orders create a balance of power. Such conflicts are further mitigated by manners and what Burke calls "public affections." "To be attached to the subdivision, to love the little platoon we belong to in society, is the first principle (the germ as it were) of public affections," he writes. "It is the first link in the series by which we proceed toward a love to our country and to mankind" (41). This vision of an organic society bound together by a shared set of customs, manners, and affections helps to explain why Burke depicts the French Revolution through its violent infringement upon the order established by such public affections and why he represents events in France (most famously in his description of Marie Antoinette) in terms of a romance gone wrong. Literary critics have been quick to seize on the gendered terms of this incident with their translation of revolutionary violence into sexual energy, which can then be read alongside Burke's earlier distinction between the sublime and the beautiful.[13] Within Burke's vision of social hierarchy softened and maintained through public affection, history stands as a counterforce of uncontrolled passions that works to destabilize the local and specific bonds created by affection; it consists of all "the miseries brought upon the world by pride, ambition, avarice, revenge, lust, sedition, hypocrisy, ungoverned zeal, and all the train of disorderly appetites which shake the public with the same" (124). Accordingly, the state (for Burke) is a balance of institutions that enables a hierarchy of public affection in an effort to protect individuals from the vices and exigencies of such history. Price's state, in contrast, is a composite of individuals organized to ensure best the collective assertion of individual will.

---

[12] For an effective summary of major initial responses to Burke, see Gregory Claeys, "The *Reflections* Refracted: The Critical Reception of Burke's *Reflections on the Revolution in France* during the Early 1790s," in Whale, *New Interdisciplinary Essays*, 44–50.

[13] See Ronald Paulson, *Representations of Revolution (1789–1820)* (New Haven, CT: Yale University Press, 1983), 59–73; and Tom Furniss, *Edmund Burke's Aesthetic Ideology: Language, Gender, and Political Economy in Revolution* (Cambridge: Cambridge University Press, 1993), 138–163.

Burke's conception of government as a set of practices and conventions accruing over time and inherited by succeeding generations lies at the heart of his argument. It clearly establishes the basis of government as national and not comparative or abstract. National precedent, not abstract principle, becomes the key determinant for Burke's defense of the status quo. Thus, unlike his opponents who argue for abstract natural rights that can be deduced from an originary entry into a social compact, Burke need provide no account of the origins of society. For him, "Government is a contrivance of human wisdom to provide for human *wants*.... Among these wants is to be reckoned the want, out of civil society, of a significant restraint upon their passions" (52). This, however, is a far from straightforward matter because "the real effects of moral causes are not always immediate" (53)—which is precisely why good government must draw upon sustained experience. If the causes and effects of governmental matters are not always apparent, then effective government requires "even more experience than any person can gain in his whole life" (53). The argument carries echoes of Bernard Mandeville's and Adam Smith's defenses of luxury and its indirect benefits to an entire economy, but it also becomes something much more specific in Burke's hands. No longer simply a justification of inequality, it now becomes a vital bolster to any theory of government that rests on the sanctity of past precedent. And, by implication, it provides a theoretical justification and a political imperative for the continued relevance of arguments based on the national past—as opposed to abstract reason—as the best teacher of the present. We see this logic not in the direct expression of carefully expostulated principles, but rather in Burke's continued emphasis on prescription— the application of past precedent to concrete circumstances—which B. T. Wilkins suggests is integral to Burke's understanding of political, social, and economic rights and obligations.[14] Hence, the importance of first principles—so central to Mary Wollstonecraft's and Paine's claims—is exactly what Burke argues against. For him, the past constrains present possibilities, and although certain 1790s radicals see this as a limitation to

---

[14] Wilkins, *The Problem of Burke's Political Philosophy* (Oxford: Clarendon Press, 1967), 61. On Burke's logic, see also James T. Boulton, *The Language of Politics in the Age of Wilkes and Burke* (London: Routledge and Kegan Paul, 1963), and Pocock, "The Political Economy of Burke's analysis of the French Revolution," *Virtue, Commerce, and History*, 193–212.

be transcended, Burke views the same limitations as ensuring a prudent caution.

To bolster his arguments, Burke uses evidence ranging from transcripts of contemporary French proceedings to European history, English history, and English poetry. Although Burke's interpretation of the English past has received much scholarly attention, the most consistently deployed examples are from classical literature and history, especially Roman. From the beginning to the end of the *Reflections*, Burke cites examples from Roman history and quotes Latin poetry.

At the most basic level, Burke's references to Latin texts identify him as man of a certain learning and education—he quotes widely from classical sources ranging from Terence and Cicero through Horace and Virgil to Juvenal. His quotations are most often untranslated and most frequently unattributed, suggesting that his readers could not only comprehend the Latin but would also recognize the source of his quotations. Although they were certainly not the only people able to do this (witness the self-educated John Thelwall), those most likely to be in this position were members of a privileged class, likely educated at England's more prestigious public schools prior to finishing at Cambridge or Oxford. Burke is clearly directing his remarks at this landholding and governing class, and his emphasis on the importance of rank, precedent, and the preservation of tradition is meant to be heard by this class. Part of the issue here, however, is that this class was by no means united in its opposition to the French Revolution. Nor for that matter was the Whig Party, and Burke's strong opposition to events in France helped to further a split among the Whigs that led to an irreconcilable division between Burke and his former Whig allies Charles James Fox and Richard Brinsley Sheridan. Given Burke's strong support for the American colonies, Burke's opposition to events in France could not have been predicted. For more than thirty years now, the apparent tension between Burke's defense of the American Revolution and his attack on the French Revolution—foremost among other tensions and ambivalences in Burke's thought—has been discussed in the context of the "Burke problem."[15] Hazlitt famously saw the Burke who

---

[15] On the "Burke problem," see Isaac Kramnick, *The Rage of Edmund Burke: Portrait of an Ambivalent Conservative* (New York: Basic Books, 1977), 3–11; C. B. Macpherson, *Burke* (Oxford: Oxford University Press, 1980), 1–7.

supported the colonists and the Burke who opposed the revolution as two different people, and a sense of division within Burke himself is precisely what Isaac Kramnick characterizes as central to the problem. As one lacking "magnificent ancestry," Burke had always occupied an ambivalent position in relation to the governing class that he defended so strenuously in the *Reflections*, and with his further alienation from his party over his opposition to the French Revolution, he found himself in an increasingly isolated position.[16] Burke was a political man of letters writing against other political men of letters, and his extensive use of Latin citation can be read as an attempt to position himself as part of this lettered elite while simultaneously opening up a second front (the first being his particular understanding of 1688–1689 and the Revolution Settlement) in his fight against the French Revolution by enlisting a powerful network of Roman associations and precedents for his position in the controversy.

Consider, for example, a moment later in the *Reflections*, when Burke reports M. de la Tour du Pin's speech to the French National Assembly regarding the state of the war department and the army. Quoting du Pin's reference to the "the authority of the king himself," Burke inserts the parenthetical remark *risum teneatis* (186; "can you keep from laughing"). The reference comes from the opening sentence of Horace's *Ars Poetica*, in which Horace asks his readers to imagine a horse's neck joined to a human head and other sorts of monstrous, grotesque juxtapositions. In the context of the *Ars Poetica*, the image serves as a warning against the kind of wild, meaningless imagery that Horace sees as prevalent in the poetry of his time.[17]

---

[16] Burke was an Irish Protestant who was not from a titled family and made his living as a man of letters before winning a seat in the House of Commons. For biographical information on Burke, see Conor Cruise O'Brien, *The Great Melody* (Chicago: University of Chicago Press, 1992). As William Godwin writes in his public letter to Burke, "I know, Sir, that it has been affirmed, that your want of a magnificent ancestry and a splendid patrimony, has formed one principal cause of the clamour with which you have been decried, and will prove an everlasting bar to your complete success." See *Political and Philosophical Writings of William Godwin*, ed. Mark Philp (London: William Pickering, 1993), 1:267.

[17] The full sentence reads:

Humano capiti cervicem pictor equinam
iungere si velit, et varias inducere plumas
undique collatis membris, ut turpiter atrum

Burke omits the *amici* with which the sentence concludes, but the effect is the same. The phrase creates a common perspective among his readers, and the sardonic, clubby tone and the use of the Latin second person plural align Burke with presumably upper-class Latin initiates. Placing the citation back within its original Horatian context has the further effect of linking the beautiful woman (*mulier formosa*) who ends up horribly as a fish (*piscem*) with the movement of the French Revolution. Focusing on Burke's use of Horace here allows us to recognize not only the rhetorical strategy in Burke's use of Latin citation, but also how the moral force of his claims is amplified through their echo of Horace's treatise of poetry.[18]

In another example, Burke looks at what he interprets as the French effort to form a state based on philosophical principles:

These paradoxes become with them serious grounds of action upon which they proceed in regulating the most important concerns of the state. Cicero ludicrously describes Cato as endeavoring to act, in the commonwealth, upon the school paradoxes which exercised the wits of the junior students in the Stoic philosophy. If this was true of Cato, these gentlemen copy after him in the manner of some persons who lived about this time—*pede nudo Catonem*. (150)

The reference is to Cato's habit as a philosopher of walking barefoot and the habit of fools to pretend to be like him by doing the same. The explicit source is the letter to Maecenas in Horace's *Epistles* (book 1, letter 19), in which the line mocks those who think that drinking wine

> desinat in piscem mulier formosa superne,
> spectatum admissi risum teneatis, amici?

["If a painter chose to join a human head to the neck of a horse, and to spread feathers of many a hue over limbs picked up now here now there, so that what at the top is a lovely woman ends below in a black and ugly fish, could you, my friends, if favoured with a private view, refrain from laughing?"]

See Horace, *Satires, Epistles, and Ars Poetica*, Loeb Classical Library, trans. H. Rushton Fairclough (Cambridge: Harvard University Press, 1929), 450–451.

[18] The phrase is also used by John Thelwall as the frontispiece epigraph to his 1795 verse pamphlet, "John Gilpin's Ghost." In the context of the poem, which was written as an occasion to mock the interception of some of Thelwall's papers by the squirearchy of Oakham, the epigraph shows Thelwall, having been recently acquitted from a treason charge, trying to cast satirical scorn upon the government's rabid suspicion of certain radical figures, himself included. See John Thelwall, *John Gilpin's Ghost* (London: T. Smith, 1795).

will make them a poet. "What," Horace asks Maecenas, "if a man were to ape Cato with grim and savage look, with bare feet and the cut of a scanty gown, would he thus set before us Cato's virtue and morals?"[19] To be a philosopher, Horace implies, one must do more than simply dress as one. As with the earlier reference to Horace's *Ars Poetica*, the reference aligns Burke with the cultural force of Latin reference, but here again, the context of the original redoubles the force of the citation. Part of what Burke attacks here and throughout the *Reflections* is the use of philosophical first principles to regulate political decisions. A reference to Horace's similar scorn for *faux* philosophers brings the weight of classical precedent to support Burke's position.

Burke's use of Latin thus shows more than his targeting of and alignment with a certain social group, for Burke frequently refers, as in the instances above, to the work of Roman satirists like Juvenal and Horace. In so doing, he aligns himself with a particular sensibility and point of view, one set above the scene, with acerbic and pointed wit, casting scorn upon the contemporary degradation of morals. Consider his first reference in Latin: "But I may say of our preacher [Price] '*utinam nugis tota illa dedisset tempora saevitiae.*'—All things in this his fulminating bull are not of so innoxious a tendency" (12).[20] Here,

---

[19] The original reads:
>...si quis voltu torvo ferus et pede nudo
>exiguaeque togae simulet textore Catonem,
>virtutemne repraesentet Moresque Catonis?

See *Horace: Satires, Epistles, and Ars Poetica*, Loeb Classical Library, ed. and trans. H. Rushton Fairclough (Cambridge: Harvard University Press, 1970), 380–381.

[20] The reference is to the closing of Juvenal's Satire IV:
>Atque utinam his potius nugis tota illa dedisset
>tempora saevitiae, claras quibus abstulit urbi
>inlustresque animas impune et vindice nullo.
>sed periit postquam cerdonibus esse timendus
>coeperat; hoc nocuit Lamiarum caede madenti.

["And yet would that he had rather given to follies such as these all those days of cruelty when he robbed the city of its noblest and choicest souls, with none to punish or avenge! He could steep himself in the blood of the Lamiae; but when once he became a terror to the common herd he met his doom."] See *Juvenal and Persius*, Loeb Classical Library, ed. and trans. G. G. Ramsay (Cambridge: Harvard University Press, 1940), 68–69. The specific quotation translates as "Would that he had rather given to follies such as these all those days of cruelty."

Burke scathingly declares that Price's speech, far from being harmless rhetoric, has an explicit tendency to violence. By making this declaration through Juvenal, he situates himself and his perspective with the Juvenalian point of view and situates Price with the object of Juvenal's satire and the moral degradation of Rome. Rome and its decline were clearly a powerful force in the British empirical/imperial imagination, and as many commentators on the eighteenth century have shown, interpretations of Rome's fall could constitute an explicitly contemporary political statement.

The logic of Burke's writing, then, extends beyond his continued emphasis on prescription and specifically national precedents as, through the careful use of classical texts and examples, Burke deploys Roman satire to consolidate a consensus among the governing elite and to position himself within it. Gary Dyer has called our attention to the explicitly political connotations of satirical writing in this period. Although his most striking claim is for the emergence of "Radical satire" that combines the Juvenalian and Horatian traditions, the main significance of his work for this context is that it suggests that, far from disappearing, satirical writing gains new importance in this period—especially as strategy to avoid persecution. Dyer's account pays scarce attention to Burke (whose writing can hardly be characterized as satirical), but Burke's deployment of Roman satire provides a further context in which to place Dyer's claims.[21]

An elevated satirical outlook, however, is not the only perspective that Burke attempts to cultivate. Just prior to his "Society is indeed a contract" statement, as he is about to celebrate the virtues of prejudice and established institutions, Burke makes the first of a series of references to Cicero, the Roman rhetorician, statesman, and philosopher. "We know, and what is better, we feel inwardly," Burke claims, "that religion is the basis of civil society and the source of all good and of all comfort."[22] In forging this connection between religion and civil society, a footnote directs the reader to Cicero's *De Legibus*, where Cicero suggests that "the gods are the lords and rulers of all things" (*dominos*

---

[21] See Gary Dyer, *British Satire and the Politics of Style, 1789–1832* (Cambridge: Cambridge University Press, 1997). On Romantic satire, see also Steven E. Jones, *Satire and Romanticism* (New York: St. Martin's, 2000); and Marcus Wood, *Radical Satire and Print Culture, 1790–1822* (Oxford: Oxford University Press, 1994).

[22] See Burke, *Reflections*, 79.

esse omnium rerum ac moderators, deos).[23] There are, of course, many sources for the pious appeal to a power higher than the human. Burke's choice of Cicero here provides a clue for the extent to which he wants to align himself with the Roman orator. Indeed, further references to Cicero dominate the second half of the *Reflections*. Burke hardly cites Cicero at all in his earlier work, referring to him only once in *A Philosophical Inquiry into... the Sublime and Beautiful* (1759) and once in his speech on Fox's East India Bill (1783). And yet in the *Reflections* Burke refers to Cicero thirteen times.[24] He cites Cicero's *Pro Sestio* to defend the value of the nobility as part of the civil order (122);[25] later, when Burke refers to the sanctity of private property as a means of

---

[23] In his footnote, Burke gives two full sentences, with a reference to "Cic. *de Legibus*, 1.2": "Sit igitur hoc ab initio [for "hoc iam a principio"] persuasum civibus, dominos esse omnium rerum ac moderators, deos; eaque, quae gerantur, eorum geri vi, ditione, [for "iudicio"] ac numine; eosdemque optime de genere hominum mereri; et qualis quisque sit, quid agat, quid in se admittat, qua mente, qua pietate colat religiones intueri; piorumque [for "piorem"] et impiorum habere rationem. His enim rebus imbutae [for "inbutae"] mentes haud sane abhorrebunt ab utili et [for "aut"] a vera sententia." I quote the passage as Burke does, noting minor variants from the Loeb edition. For the full passage in context, which comes not from 1.2, but rather from 2.vi–vii, see Cicero, *De Re Publica De Legibus*, Loeb Classical Library, trans. Clinton Walker Keyes (Cambridge: Harvard University Press, 1943), 388–389. The passage translates, "So in the very beginning we must persuade our citizens that the gods are the lords and rulers of all things, and that what is done, is done by their will and authority; that they are likewise great benefactors of man, observing the character of every individual, what he does, of what wrong he is guilty, and with what intentions and with what piety he fulfills his religious duties; and that they take note of the pious and the impious. For surely minds which are imbued with such ideas will not fail to form true and useful opinions."

[24] For this count, see Frans DeBruyn, "William Shakespeare and Edmund Burke: Literary Allusion in Eighteenth Century British Political Rhetoric," in *Shakespeare and the Eighteenth Century*, ed. Peter Sabor and Paul Yachnin (Aldershot, UK: Ashgate, 2008), 85–102.

[25] In context, the citation reads as follows: "Nobility is a graceful ornament to the civil order. It is the Corinthian capital of polished society. *Omnes boni nobilitati semper favemus*, was the saying of a wise and good man" (122). The reference is to Cicero's *Pro Sestio*, 9.21, where the full sentence reads, "Omnes boni semper nobilitati favemus, et quia utile est rei publicae nobiles homines esse dignos maioribus suis, et quia valet apud nos clarorum hominum et bene de re publica meritorum memoria etiam mortuorum." ["All we who are good citizens always favor noble birth, both because it is good for the State that there should be noblemen, worthy of their ancestors, and because the memory of distinguished men and of those who have deserved well of the State lives in our hearts even after they are dead."] See Cicero, *The Speeches: Pro Sestio and In Vatinium*, Loeb Classical Library, trans. R. Gardner (Cambridge: Harvard University Press, 1958), 60–61.

protecting church lands or any property from confiscation by the state, he again refers to Cicero, this time in citing the *De Officiis* in a long footnote (136).[26] Further examples abound throughout the text. In each case, the precedent and authority of Cicero's writing lend authority and the force of time to Burke's claims.

Cicero was famous for, among other actions, saving Rome from the internal conspiracy of Catiline. Burke is clearly trying to identify himself with this great hero and warning siren of the Roman republic. Early in the *Reflections*, as he approaches his description of Marie Antoinette and his lamentation for the loss of chivalry, Burke refers explicitly to Catiline. The remark is part of his description of the illegitimacy and consequent impotence of the French National Assembly. Burke states:

It is notorious that all their measures are decided before they are debated. It is beyond doubt, that under the terror of the bayonet and the lamp post, and the torch to their houses, they are obligated to adopt all the crude and desperate measures suggested by clubs composed of a monstrous medley of all conditions, tongues, and nations. Among these are found persons, in comparison of whom Catiline would be thought scrupulous. (59–60)

Burke describes all of the early events of the French Revolution as a conspiracy of the monied interest against the legitimacy of the aristocracy and the church, and his reference to Catiline here serves further to connect events in France with republican Rome. On a general level, Burke suggests that the French National Assembly is being directed by an unscrupulous mob, and he thus links the motor force

[26] In context, the reference is as follows: "It is not the confiscation of our church property from this example in France that I dread, though, I think this would be no trifling evil. The great source of my solicitude is, lest it should ever be considered in England as the policy of a state to seek a resource in confiscations of any kind, or that any one description of citizens should be brought to regard any of the others as their proper prey." Here, Burke includes a footnote with a lengthy citation from Cicero's *De Officiis*. Cicero's comments in the cited passage concern land reform. Cicero is specifically denouncing those politicians that propose agrarian laws in order to appear as friends of the people. In the second part of the passage, he praises Aratus of Sicyon ("ille Graecus") for his handling of land redistribution after the overthrow of tyrants. The passage runs from "si plures sunt ii quibus improbe datum est...profectae manarunt latius" (2.79–80) and then concludes with two more sentences, "Sic par est agree cum civibus...omnis aequitate eadem continere." See Cicero, *De Officiis*, Loeb Classical Library, trans. Walter Miller (Cambridge: Harvard University Press, 1913), 254–259.

behind the assembly's actions and decisions with one of the most notorious conspirators of ancient history. Here, however, the force of Catiline is not concentrated in a single individual but, rather, is spread across an entire segment of the population. Burke moves the threat from an aristocratic conspiracy from above to a popular conspiracy from below; he multiplies the insidious qualities of Catiline and magnifies his threat. In addition, his "monstrous medly" echoes the later reference to the opening of Horace's *Ars Poetica*. On a more specific level, the association in the *Reflections* between Catiline, the French National Assembly, and their English supporters attacks aristocratic politicians on both sides of the channel who enlist themselves in radical causes to promote their pursuit of elected office. Such English nobles as Fox and the Duke of Bedford, who identify themselves with contemporary revolutionary principles, become traitors to their class, as loathsome as Catiline was to Cicero, while Burke plays the role of Rome's savior.[27] This identification with Cicero, seen throughout the second half of the *Reflections*, puts Burke in the place of the one sober and rational voice that can save the British state both from the subtle menace of French philosophy and its treacherous appeal even to members of the governing class and from the unscrupulous mob.

Far from being peripheral to or mere decoration for his argument in the *Reflections*, Burke's use of Latin literature and Roman history is absolutely crucial. A focus on Burke's use of Roman examples demonstrates how Burke's logic of prescription and his emphasis on the particularity of the national past is framed by his use of Roman references to garner cultural authority and consolidate his position. This centrality of Rome to Burke's rhetoric was clearly recognized in the first important printed response to Burke, Wollstonecraft's *Vindication of the Rights of Men* (1790). At one point, Wollstonecraft plays upon the British (and indeed, European) fascination with Roman ruins and the habit of seeing the British Empire as heir to the Roman. She notes, with a tone evocative of Gibbon's *Decline and Fall* (and anticipatory of Volney's *Les Ruines*, which would be published the following year), that

the time may come when the traveler may ask where proud London stood? when its *temples*, its laws, and its trade, may be buried in one common ruin,

[27] On this point, see Pocock's introduction to *Reflections*, xxii–xxv.

and only serve as a byword to point a moral, or furnish senators, who wage a wordy war, on the other side of the Atlantic, with tropes to swell their thundering bursts of eloquence.[28]

The temporality of Wollstonecraft's statement is complex. She posits three distinct empires—Rome, Britain, and America ("the other side of the Atlantic")—in three distinct times (past, present, and future), each of which draws upon the examples of its immediate precursor. The passage identifies most closely with the projected American empire and imagines a time when its senators will use the ruins of London as a trope with which to inflate superfluous rhetoric. Reading her analogy back one step, it implies that British senators (parliamentarians) were using the ruins of Rome to authorize and "swell" their own zealous rhetoric. Because Wollstonecraft responds expressly and explicitly to one member of Parliament, the author of the *Reflections*, this is a clear reference to Burke that her contemporary readers would have immediately recognized. As such, Wollstonecraft's need to dismiss such rhetoric as a "wordy war" implies that his contemporaries clearly recognized how important Burke's use of Roman references was to his argument.

But if Burke's use of Rome, dependent as it is on Latin quotation and classical moral statesmanship, is recognizable as an eighteenth century mode, the implications of Burke's organicism and his vehement defense of an established Christian church undermine, to some extent, the relevance of these very examples. For a start, the *Reflections* itself can be read as turning political debate away from a reliance on Roman precedent. As Frank Turner explains, because of Burke's emphasis on the importance of religion in public life and his traditional view of the ancient constitution, "British history and traditions rather than Roman became the appropriate source of knowledge about the political structures of the nation. The intense religiosity of Burke's polemic similarly crushed for a time the concept of politics as a realm of secular human activity that could be profitably illustrated through the model of the pagan republic."[29] Roman precedents, such as the

---

[28] Mary Wollstonecraft, *A Vindication of the Rights of Men*, in *A Vindication of the Rights of Men and A Vindication of the Rights of Woman*, ed. Sylvana Tomaselli (Cambridge: Cambridge University Press, 1995), 37.

[29] Turner, "British Politics and the Demise of the Roman Republic: 1700–1939," *The Historical Journal* 29.3 (September 1986): 587.

parallel between Cicero and Burke as the saviors of their respective nations, and Roman texts such as the satires of Horace and Juvenal can be used to accentuate and structure an argument; the creation of direct parallel between an event from the ancient past and one from the modern present as a model of political prudence, however, loses its efficacy because the structure through which a particular historical situation needs to be understood is one of national particularity and not transnational comparison. Burke's emphasis on prescription and on the organic accumulated wisdom of the English national past suggests that the analogous mode of directly relating ancient history to contemporary events, the mode that Reinhardt Koselleck calls *historia magistra vitae*,[30] is no longer so obviously relevant. Ancient history can no longer be the teacher of life, because in Burke's vision of the organic nation, the only precedents that matter are national ones.

ROMAN HEROES AS THE MODEL OF GODWIN'S SELFLESS BENEVOLENCE

If Burke's use of Rome is citational, his Roman examples are not, as Mary Wollstonecraft implies, mere decoration. Rather, they function as an integral component of Burke's argument, helping him to make a direct appeal to members of a particular class of men, to position his opponents with the legendary and longstanding opprobrium heaped upon Catiline, and to assume for himself the laurels of Cicero. In contrast, William Godwin, who began his career as an ardent admirer of Burke, rarely quotes Latin text in the original.[31] Godwin's writings—from his earliest published works in 1783 to his 1831 volume, *Thoughts on Man*—are, however, littered with references to Rome and Latin

---

[30] Reinhart Koselleck, "Historia Magistra Vitae: The Dissolution of the Topos into the Perspective of a Modernized Historical Process," in *Futures Past: On the Semantics of Historical Time*, trans. Keith Tribe (Cambridge: MIT Press, 1985), 21–38. See my discussion of Koselleck's argument in the introduction.

[31] In book 2, appendix 1, of *Political Justice*, for example, Godwin states, "There is a proverb which affirms, 'that the blood of the martyrs is the seed of the church.'" He does not cite Tertullian in the original, which would read, "Plures efficimus quoties metimur a vobis, semen est sanguis Christianorum." See *The Political and Philosophical Writings of William Godwin*, ed. Mark Philp (London: Pickering, 1993), 3:56.

literature. And yet Godwin is a curious figure because he demonstrates what Koselleck would call "a typical eighteenth century mixture of rational prediction and salvational expectation."[32] Through this combination, he expresses in *Political Justice* a classical Enlightenment belief in historical and social progress, and yet he continuously places great emphasis on the ancients. My discussion of Burke was focused on the significance of specific references to classical texts and a general rhetorical structure that Burke used to align himself with the wisdom and virtue of Cicero. My discussion of Godwin looks less at particular citations and more at what Godwin's references to Roman heroes and episodes can tell us about his attitude toward the past in his theorization of an ideal future in *Political Justice*. Godwin's belief in the selfless virtue of certain Roman heroes provides him with the model for the selfless benevolence that will be able to act in a manner that maximizes human good and enables Godwin's idealization of a future without government or institutions. But this comes at a certain cost, for Godwin's utopic vision of the future is constrained by the intensity with which he looks backward and idealizes the Roman past.

Because I will argue that republican Rome provides key evidence for the continuity of Godwin's political, philosophic, and literary positions, I begin by evaluating Godwin's use of republican Rome in some of his earlier writings. Godwin's political writings prior to *Political Justice* suggest that he sees the past as a guide to the present through the mode of exemplary experience. He makes protracted use of Roman examples—in arguments that read unmistakably like those that Koselleck describes as *historia magistra vitae*—to make sense of contemporary events. Between August 1785 and December 1786, Godwin published a series of six letters in *The Political Herald and Review*, which he signed as Mucius. As Mark Philp explains in his brief introduction to these writings, the paper was part of a campaign for public opinion organized by the Whig Party of Charles James Fox and the Duke of Portland after the failure of the Fox-North coalition.[33] Godwin's letters are addressed to leading figures of the government including William Pitt and Henry Dundas; they contain protracted praise of Burke,

---

[32] Koselleck, "Modernity and the Planes of Historicity," *Futures Past*, 17.
[33] *The Political and Philosophical Writings of William Godwin*, ed. Mark Philp (London: William Pickering, 1993), Vol. 1. Subsequent references to this edition will be provided parenthetically in the text.

the addressee of the second letter, and are both an attack on prominent Whigs and an exhortation to reform their ideals. The choice of Mucius as a pseudonym is significant. In the second book of *Ab Urbe Condita*, Livy presents the story of Gaius Mucius Scaevola in which Mucius, after a failed attempt to assassinate the king of Clusium, showed his immunity to pain by holding his right hand over a sacrificial fire, and the astonished king let him go free.[34] As the king had threatened to restore the tyrannical rule of Tarquinius Superbus, Mucius's actions can be seen as a quintessential example of the virtuous patriotism that Godwin was anxious to uphold—a point further borne out by the reputation of the family of Roman jurists (Quintus Mucius Scaevola [Scaevola the Pontifex] and his cousin Quintus Mucius Scaevola [Scaevola the Augur]) whose name the legend dignified.

Not surprisingly, the Mucius letters are written in an elevated diction, full of long, Ciceronian clauses, and contain consistent references to Rome. The fifth letter in particular, addressed to Henry Dundas, treasurer of the navy, is a protracted analogy between the prosecution of Warren Hastings, spearheaded by Burke, and Cicero's prosecution of Verres. Here we find Godwin using untranslated Latin, which, as was the case with Burke, suggests a narrow and highly educated audience. Godwin declares explicitly that

the utility of history is to enable us to discover from former examples, the clue that may guide us through the intricacies of those which are present. It may happen that causes, not very dissimilar to those which defeated the earlier prosecutions in Rome, have contributed to the escape of criminals in our own day. (1:284)

Within the terms of this analogy, General Burgoyne becomes Caesar, one of the *juvenes nobilissimi* who fail in their prosecution because of hasty and ill-advised measures; the venal and corrupt Whigs are paralleled to the rapacious *quadruplatores*;[35] and, not surprisingly, Burke

---

[34] The episode can be found in Livy, book 2, chap. 12. See *Livy*, Vol. 1 (books 1 and 2), Loeb Classical Library, trans. B. O. Foster (Cambridge: Harvard University Press, 1925), 254–261.

[35] The term *quadruplatores* refers to public informers or accusers so called because in the event of a successful prosecution they were given one quarter of the condemned's property or because those violating laws governing gambling and usury were required to pay a fourfold fine. In Cicero's usage, it is a derogatory term that refers to false or mercenary accusers.

emerges as Cicero, the redeemer of England: "I have told you, Sir, that I would not insult you with the eulogium of Mr Burke, and I will endeavor to keep my engagement. Let us not talk then of Britain, but of Rome. Let us forget the redeemer of England, and talk of the avenger of Sicily" (1:286).

In the length and explicitness of Godwin's analogy, we have a hint of what Thelwall's Roman lectures must have been like—although Godwin, under no prohibitions from the Two Acts, can make his analogy explicit. He concludes somewhat histrionically that "it is perhaps from the sentence against Verres that we are to account for the protracted duration of the Roman empire" (1:287), and we are thus invited to read the same significance into the prosecution of Hastings, which now wears the exalted robes of historical precedent. This brief piece shows Godwin thinking through historical parallel in a manner that skillfully eliminates the difference between past and present. It enacts a process by which a considerable similarity is perceived between past situation and present situation, allowing an abridgment of deliberation and producing present action conformable with and constrained by past precedent. The situation in Rome then is a direct equivalent to the situation in England now, Godwin implies, and if we accept his logic and the *historia magistra vitae* paradigm, we are left with a severely curtailed set of present possibilities.

But Godwin is of particular interest because his other writings show him pushing away from this highly political model of a backward looking, imitative exemplarity and toward an imitative model with a different "temporal structure," as Koselleck would put it. Considered in the context of this shift, Godwin's writings on education, though published before the Mucius letters, help to explain how his position changes between the Mucius letters and *Political Justice*. Written as a prospectus for his planned school at Epsom, "An Account of the Seminary" (1783) argues that for established societies, education is more important than government for general happiness and morality. In contradistinction to Burke, then, it is not government and political forms that produce a stable society, but a mode of education.

In the "Account," Godwin proposes a system of education with language learning at its core. Although he suggests that students should begin with a modern language, Godwin scorns the "refined geniuses of the present age"[36] who dismiss the value of the ancients, and he stresses that the importance of ancient writers cannot be overlooked. Because the ancients were "not encumbered and hedged in with the multitude of their predecessors" (5:6), they wrote directly from experience, and their prose is a model of untranslatable decorum. Asserting the indispensability of language learning for effective grammar and style, Godwin cites the Roman Cornelia, mother of the Gracchi, "who never suffered a provincial accent, or a grammatical barbarism in the hearing of her children, [and] has always been cited with commendation; and the subsequent rhetorical excellence of the Gracchi has been in a great degree ascribed to it" (5:10). Grammar, however, is not the end of language learning, but Godwin cautions against introducing beginning students "to the sublime flights of Virgil, the philosophical investigations of a Cicero, or the refined elegance and gay satire of Horace" (5:17). Instead, students should begin with history, where Plutarch and Vertot, the French historian of Rome, lead the way; these figures "treat of that simplicity and rectitude of manners of the first Greeks and Romans, that furnish the happiest subject that can be devised for the initiating youth in the study of history" (5:18). Admittedly, the proposal of a school is the explicit purpose of this tract, and it is thus unsurprising that Godwin emphasizes the importance of education even over and against politics—just as we would expect him to stress the importance of politics in a piece for the *Political Herald*. Nonetheless, the piece is striking for the way that its logic differs from the Mucius letters and anticipates the claims of *Political Justice*. The aim of the educational system in the "Account" is to use classical texts and examples, supplemented by the moderns, to allow the early commencement of benevolent affections—a usage based on the same guiding principle as *Political Justice:* that "self love is not the source of all our passions, but that disinterested benevolence has its seat in the human heart" (5:20).

This pedagogical emphasis on education as a means for general improvement—and the place of republican Rome within it—provides an important frame with which to think about *Political Justice*. Many contexts for the interpretation of *Political Justice* have been proposed by

---

[36] *The Political and Philosophical Writings of William Godwin*, ed. Mark Philp (London: William Pickering, 1993), 5:7. Subsequent references to this edition will be provided parenthetically in the text.

scholars. These range from utilitarianism to republicanism to eighteenth century religious dissent.[37] It is my claim here that Godwin's tracts on education form a crucial backdrop for a reading of *Political Justice*, that Roman exempla shift their implications from a political to a pedagogical application, and that Godwin's classical exempla here constitute a use of Roman references imbued with a temporality distinct from the Mucius letters. References to the history of the Roman republic in *Political Justice* are consistent and continuous, though not profuse. Godwin cites Cato's desire to suppress Greek philosophy as a negative model in an effort to suggest that untrammeled opinion is always a positive good (book 6, chap. 3); and he uses Livy's suggestion that Romulus settled Rome with vagabonds, criminals, and runaway slaves to illustrate the point that banishment is good punishment because it forces men to learn subsistence (7, 6). Godwin's tone in *Political Justice* is more familiar, and his sentences are clearer than in the "Letters of Mucius." He does not quote from the original Latin, and, despite the high cost of the volume, he clearly has a broader audience than the readers of the *Political Herald and Review* in mind. Whereas the "Letters of Mucius" showed a drive to specificity, *Political Justice* reaches for abstraction and universalization. In this context, certain Roman references seem extraneous. They are used to illustrate or fill out a point for which any number of examples could serve equally well.

Other references to Rome, however, are more central—and much less flattering. In the second chapter, Godwin considers the tendency of political society to promote war, of which the Romans are the foremost example: "Indeed the Romans, by the long duration of their wars, and their inflexible adherence to their purpose, are to be ranked among the foremost destroyers of the human species"(1, 2: 84–85).[38]

---

[37] On Godwin and utilitarianism, see Peter Marshall, *William Godwin* (New Haven, CT: Yale University Press, 1984); on Godwin and republicanism, see Klancher, "Godwin and the Republican Romance"; on Godwin and dissent, see Mark Philp, *Godwin's Political Justice* (Ithaca, NY: Cornell University Press, 1986), and, most recently, Daniel E. White, *Early Romanticism and Religious Dissent* (Cambridge: Cambridge University Press, 2006).

[38] When pages numbers are cited explicitly following the indication of book and section number, the reference is to William Godwin, *Enquiry Concerning Political Justice*, ed. Isaac Kramnick (Harmondsworth: Penguin, 1976). Kramnick bases his copy text on Godwin's third edition of *Political Justice* from 1798.

Similarly, Godwin sharply condemns the Roman aristocracy. Aristocracy is inimical to humankind because it constitutes institutionalized privilege and prevents the recognition of merit, which is the essence of justice. Aristocracy is unjust in all of its manifestations, whether in the calls of India, the villainage of the feudal system, or "the despotism of ancient Rome, where the debtors were dragged into personal servitude, to expiate, by stripes and slavery, the usurious loans they could not repay" (5, 11: 475). Nevertheless, Godwin also uses Rome to indicate the degree of excellence to which aristocracy can be raised, and this consideration reveals the aspiration of Godwin's utopic vision. The Roman aristocracy is based on merit, but the talents recognized by merit are confined to aristocrats, because only a liberal education can inculcate such talents. Accordingly, Godwin praises the Roman aristocracy for their "public spirit and an unbounded enthusiasm of virtue" (5, 13: 482). Despite these merits, the aristocracy is still opposed to the essential interests of mankind because of their exclusivity, which Godwin calls "the iniquity of aristocratical usurpation" (5, 13: 483). This exclusivity, in turn, is what girds Roman bellicosity, that "indelible blemish of their history, the love of conquest" (5, 13: 483). The Roman patricians wage war to divert the classes below them "from attending to the sentiments of political truth" (5, 13: 483). Politics and war here become a distraction from the pedagogical possibilities inherent in the spread of political truth. Based on the suggestions of his *Prospectus*, Thelwall likely would have agreed with Godwin's distaste for the aristocracy.

Such opinions seem difficult to reconcile with the untrammeled admiration for Rome that we saw so clearly in Godwin's writings on education. Nonetheless, thinking about such distinct examples together helps us to clarify the important place that Rome holds in Godwin's thought. Some have suggested that Godwin's idealization of Rome presents a problem for his belief in progressive perfectionism. We can see clearly, however, that for Godwin, Rome is not an idealized past age to which a return is desired, but rather a necessary locus for the introduction of certain principles and figures, the examples of which promote a better future. Godwin, after all, claims that he learned to see the corruption inherent in monarchy from "Latin historians."[39] The Roman aristocracy is despotic and bellicose, but they also illustrate how the ethos of a group can develop not around self-love, but around public spirit and manifest virtue—the precise ethos that Godwin would like to generalize to all humankind. The problem with Rome is that, on an individual level, these principles are confined to one group.[40] In contrast to the Roman past, however, Godwin believes that in his late eighteenth-century present, the benefits of knowledge and a liberal education can be extended to all, thanks to the spread of print technology.

Within this context, we can see how central republican Rome is to Godwin's theory of society and social improvement. Individual Roman heroes provide, for Godwin, historical proof of the possibility of general benevolence. Certain figures even become continuously illustrative and assume a talismanic quality. The suicide of Cato and the willingness of Brutus to punish his sons with death both generate energy and virtue for the public good, holding out "the sacred flame" to all lovers of virtue (1793; book 2, chap. 2, appendix 1). Similarly, Mucius Scaevola's refusal to betray emotion provides an example of pain "defied by the energies of intellectual resolution" for an end higher than self. Godwin claims that "all history affords us examples where pain has been contemned and defied by the energies of intellectual resolution. Do we not read of Mutius [sic] Scaevola who suffered his hand to be destroyed by fire without betraying any symptom of emotion"(1, 5: 135). In this sense, Mucius becomes an emblem for the whole work, a mark of consistent admiration carried over from Godwin's days as a party hack. As an exemplum, Mucius is not simply carried over, but transformed by the shift. If, previously, Mucius reflected the backward looking tendency of *historia magistra vitae*, he now assumes a similarly atemporal function—he is the kind of example that "all history affords us"—but his example here becomes proleptic of future possibilities and not a constraining reminder of past precedent.

---

[39] The claim is made in the preface to the first edition of *Political Justice* (1793). It can be found in Kramnick's edition on page 69.

[40] Godwin credits the plebeians "in their corporate capacity" with "the virtues of sincerity, intrepidity, love of justice and of the public," but he claims that only in the Gracchi do these qualities manifest themselves in an individual character (5, 13: 481).

As this instance suggests, the temporal logic of *Political Justice* is fundamentally distinct from that of the Mucius letters. Consider Godwin's description of how enlarged experience may curtail voluntary action:

> In proportion as our experience enlarges, the subjects of voluntary action become more numerous. In this state of the human being, he soon comes to perceive a considerable similarity between situation and situation. In consequence he feels inclined to abridge the process of deliberation, and to act today conformably to the determination of yesterday. Thus the understanding fixes for itself resting places, is no longer a novice, and is not at the trouble continually to go back and revise the original reasons which determined it to a course of action. Thus the man acquires habits from which it is very difficult to wean him, and which he obeys without being able to assign either to himself or others any explicit reason for his proceeding. This is the history of prepossession and prejudice. (125–126)

What Godwin here calls the "history of prepossession" is also the logic of *historia magistra vitae*, here recast implicitly as Burkean prejudice. Instead of deploying the example of ancient precedent as a means to abbreviate current decisions and to curtail present possibilities as he did in the Mucius letters, Godwin uses Roman figures in *Political Justice* to enlarge possibilities and to make a future that is more progressive, more perfect, and more reasonable than classical Rome. Godwin recasts his exempla into a more forward looking distillation, one that draws upon key figures from the past to discern the logic of history—seen here as selfless reason—and the potential of the future, seen in all of its infinite perfectibility.

Godwin is opposed to government, which like Paine he distinguishes from society, because while designed to suppress injustice, it inevitably promotes it. He places his faith for human improvement not in laws or institutions that enforce morality, but in reason, and he believes that because reason is based on knowledge, as knowledge spreads, reason will necessarily advance and thus improve perpetually the lot of humankind. Institutions have no place in this process because truth and virtue "are competent to fight their own battles" (6, 1: 562). For Godwin, social improvement comes through education and the spread of knowledge, a process in which classical examples continue to point the way not to an idealized re-creation of the past, but to a more perfect future. Rome is thus central to the development of Godwin's pedagogical purpose in *Political Justice*, and Roman figures such as Mucius Scaevola and Fabricius are integral to his claims that human endeavors are marked not by self-love, but by generous benevolence, and that the preservation of an individual's right to private judgment is crucial for the improvement of society.

In the sustained debate over the British response to the French Revolution, the so called Revolution Controversy, the Roman republic plays a shaping role in the thought of Burke and Godwin. Burke's thundering denunciation of the French Revolution, which appeared first and established the terms of the debate to follow, is traditionally thought of as the cornerstone of modern conservatism for its normative emphasis on tradition and the particularity of the national past. Burke's continuous references to Roman satirists like Horace and Juvenal and the shaping model of Cicero show how Roman precedents frame Burke's response, lending it rhetorical power and moral force. The implications of Burke's insistence on the importance of national precedent, however, undermine the exemplary logic of antiquity, for it disputes the possibility of a direct parallel of circumstances across time and nation. The appeal to precedent, by virtue of Burke's emphasis on national particularity, must be made within the historical record of a particular nation. Classical antiquity may be relevant to the nation—witness the importance of Roman law in the British common law tradition—but it can no longer act as an incontrovertible model. In this sense, Burke's *Reflections* might be read as an index of a new national confidence in Britain, one which suggests that the British have their own legacies and examples of more relevance to their case than ancient Rome.

Burke utilizes a very traditional Roman mode of Latin quotation and classical moral statesmanship, but his emphasis on organicism and national particularity implicitly undermines the exemplary uses of antiquity, and his emphasis on prescription constitutes a significantly constrained and backward looking vision of present and future possibilities. Godwin, in contrast, is traditionally considered a radical thinker, but his use of Rome remains tied to an eighteenth-century model of classical exemplarity. Godwin especially highlights the self denying intellectual resolution of Roman republican heroes like Mucius and Fabricius, who become for him transhistorical models of virtue. These examples serve to underscore the possibility of selfless benevolence, and they are therefore of fundamental importance for Godwin in establishing the viability of his system of philosophical anarchism, in which abstract reason will enable all to act in a manner commensurate with the selflessness and fortitude of these exemplars of Roman virtue. The importance of these Roman examples for Godwin's system is often overlooked, however, because unlike Burke, Godwin uses the backward-looking model of exemplarity in a manner that attempts to open up future possibilities. This is a quality that Godwin shares with other Jacobin novelists, and might even help to explain Godwin's turn to fiction after completing *Political Justice*. The following chapter will consider Godwin's turn to fiction and the Jacobin novels of the 1790s more generally in connection with what has been described as a diffusion of historical sense in the Romantic period.

Stephen Bann insists that as a result of the historical mindedness that followed the French Revolution, the sense of history in the Romantic period was qualitatively and quantitatively distinct from its predecessors. "An irreversible shift had occurred," Bann explains, "and history—from being a localized and specific practice within the cultural typology—became a flood that overrode all disciplinary barriers and, finally, when the barriers were no longer easy to perceive, became a substratum to almost every type of cultural activity."[41] Given Bann's suggestion that historical-mindedness overrode all disciplinary barriers in this period, we might wonder whether, as Bann poetically suggests, Clio may have dressed some of the other muses in her own apparel such that "her own subject matter can be disseminated through poetry, theatre, and the visual arts, as well as through her chosen medium of the narrative history."[42] Godwin suggests as much in his 1797 manuscript "Of History and Romance," in which he considers the histories of "the progress and varieties of civilization"[43] produced by Hume and Robertson, only to reject them

---

[41] Bann, *Romanticism and the Rise of History* (New York: Twayne, 1995), 5–7.
[42] Ibid., 15.
[43] William Godwin, "Essay of History and Romance," *The Political and Philosophical Writings of William Godwin*, ed. Mark Philp (London: William Pickering, 1993), 5:291. Subsequent references to this edition will be provided parenthetically in the text. The essay was intended for a possible follow up to The Enquirer, but not published until it appeared as an appendix in Maurice Hindle's edition of *Caleb Williams* (Harmondsworth: Penguin, 1987).

in favor of a history that focuses on individual men. This, Godwin argues, has a "higher use" (292) because it "is the contemplation of illustrious men, such as we find scattered through the long succession of ages, that kindles into a flame the hidden fire within us" (293). In this way, "the energy of our minds should lead us to aspire to something more animated and noble than dull repetition" (293). Again, classical historians, especially Plutarch, are central. But, having noted that some see ancient history as a tissue of fables, Godwin affirms that "all history bears too near a resemblance to fable"(297), and this move allows him to suggest that the novel may constitute a more refined type of history.

In the next chapter, Godwin's thoughts about history and romance provide a starting point for my suggestion that it is through the novel that 1790s radicals update classical historical models and produce a progressive vision of commercial society. The discussion will draw significantly upon the concepts introduced in this chapter. As Marilyn Butler has shown, Burke provides a key context for the Jacobin novel,[44] and Godwin himself proposes that "if then history be little better than romance under a graver name, it may not be foreign to the subject here treated, to enquire into the credit due to that species of literature, which bears the express stamp of invention, and calls itself romance or novel" (298). With this in mind, I now turn to the Jacobin novel.

---

[44] Marilyn Butler, *Jane Austen and the War of Ideas* (Oxford: Clarendon Press, 1975), 37–42.

Chapter Two

From Roman to *roman*

The Jacobin Novel and the Roman Legacy in the 1790s

In his 1778 essay "On Novel Reading," Reverend Vicesimus Knox blames novels for their contribution to what he perceives as the corruption and degeneracy of the present age. The sentimentality of these compositions, Knox argues, weakens the mind and prevents it from properly following its duty. Knox further castigates novels for their very success—because they utilize common situations in their effort to depict human nature exactly, they "afford so lively a pleasure" that a reader raised on a diet of novels "cannot submit to the painful task of serious study." In contrast to novels, Knox favors the heroic romances of past times, which, he claims, presented patterns of perfection that inspired emulation and were thus "favourable to virtue."[1]

Knox's comments form one contribution to a longstanding eighteenth-century debate about the intellectual responsibility of the novel. This debate spans the attempt to establish critical standards for the new form—through Aristotelian categories or a comparison with heroic romance—to a discussion of its moral effects, direct or indirect. Knox's argument is certainly not original, and although his nostalgia for the heroic romance reflected widespread concern over the quality and effects of contemporary fiction, it had become, as Ioan Williams (among others) points out, "a platitude of late eighteenth-century

---

[1] Vicesimus Knox, "On Novel Reading," no. 14, *Essays Moral and Literary* (1778); reprinted in Ioan M. Williams, ed., *Novel and Romance, 1700–1800: A Documentary History* (New York: Barnes and Noble, 1970), 304.

conservative criticism."[2] Knox does, however, make one striking comment, revealing what must have been a widespread, if infrequently stated, fear. "The boy who can procure a variety of books like *Gil Blas*, and *Devil Upon Two Sticks*," he declares, "will no longer think his Livy, his Sallust, his Homer, or his Virgil pleasing."[3] In this opposition, the novel becomes not just a new and modern form whose etymological connection with newness and novelty creates an opposition with "the classics," but also, as a specifically pedagogical form here conceived negatively, a potential replacement for the pedagogical function of classical texts, as if the *roman* had displaced the Roman in the republic of letters. Indeed, many of its most eminent critics similarly conceptualize the emergence of the novel in parodic relation to classical genres and critical traditions.[4] Lukács, for example, describes the historical novel as the heir of its epic precursors, whereas Ian Watt describes the entire enterprise of the novel as contingent upon a break with classical learning and classical critical standards.[5] Of course, theories of the rise or origin of the novel do not suggest that the novel organically replaces the classics, and neither Lukács nor Watt conceives the transition as such.

This chapter considers the relationship between the novel and the classics, with particular focus on the use of classical texts and Roman historical models in the Jacobin novels of the 1790s. Emerging at a time when the moral efficacy of the novel was still in debate, in a context of political upheaval, these novels represent an attempt to use the emergent form to educate a diverse audience about specific political

---

[2] Williams, *Novel and Romance*, 14.

[3] Knox, "On Novel Reading," 306.

[4] See Georg Lukács, *The Theory of the Novel*, trans. Anna Bostock (Cambridge: Harvard University Press, 1971); José Ortega y Gassat, *Meditations on Quixote*, trans. Evelyn Rugg and Diego Marín (New York: Norton, 1961); Mikhail M. Bakhtin, *The Dialogic Imagination: Four Essays*, trans. Caryl Emerson and Michael Holquist (Austin: University of Texas Press, 1981). For a discussion of this point, see Michael McKeon, "Prose Fiction: Great Britain," in *The Cambridge History of Literary Criticism: The Eighteenth Century*, ed. H. B. Nisbet and Claude Rawson (Cambridge: Cambridge University Press, 1997), 240.

[5] Lukács, *The Historical Novel*, trans. Hannah Mitchell and Stanley Mitchell (Lincoln: University of Nebraska Press, 1983), 45–47; Watt, *The Rise of the Novel: Studies in Defoe, Richardson, Fielding* (Berkeley: University of California Press, 1957), 35–59; 239–259.

principles. Although seminal critics and historians of the novel including Watt and Michael McKeon often give the novels of this decade (and indeed, prior to Austen, of Romantic period fiction *tout court*) short shrift, Gary Kelly, Marilyn Butler, and others affirm the importance of Jacobin fiction for understanding not only the period in which these novels were published, but also the history of the novel more generally. Kelly, for example, emphasizes the relevance of the Jacobin novelists' belief in the doctrine of necessity—that character originates in external circumstance—for the problem of how to relate character formation and episodic events (or plot) in novelistic form. Necessitarianism, he suggests, produced an integration of character and plot, a unity of design, and thus seemed to the Jacobin novelists "to solve all moral and philosophical paradoxes and to reconcile all aesthetic and moral antinomies. It also seemed to solve the perennial problem of form in the novel, by uniting plot and character."[6] Butler, in contrast, explains the importance of Jacobin novels less for their formal solutions (which, with the exception of Godwin's *Caleb Williams* and Bage's *Hermsprong*, she sees more as formal failures) and more for their deliberate engagement with contemporary social and political issues through their reworking of the sentimental heritage.[7] Regardless of emphasis, for both Kelly and Butler it is impossible to understand the history of the novel without an awareness of the formal qualities and the political and philosophical ideas that inform Jacobin fiction.

The work of both Butler and Kelly has now been in print for more than thirty years. Although no comprehensive revisions of their approaches to the Jacobin novel have been published, a number of recent studies have drawn upon the initial claims of Butler and Kelly to show further the importance of the Jacobin novel's engagement with contemporary changes in political, cultural, and ideological structures and to emphasize the relevance of the Jacobin novel for understanding the relationship between such changes and generic innovation in the novel form. Much of this work has focused on the

---

[6] Kelly, *The English Jacobin Novel 1780–1805* (Oxford: Clarendon Press, 1976), 263.
[7] Butler, *Jane Austen and the War of Ideas* (Oxford: Clarendon Press, 1975).

fiction of William Godwin, especially as it relates to the program outlined in the *Enquiry Concerning Political Justice*.[8] Others have followed Butler to show more broadly how the sentimental heritage shapes generic changes in the Romantic period novel. Nicola Watson, for example, argues that the seduction plot, with its attack on chastity, can be read as a political allegory and that the formal innovations of the novel from 1790 to 1825, especially the decline of the epistolary novel, represent the fictional accommodation of anxiety crystallized by the French Revolution.[9] Collectively, the work of these critics suggests that the political concerns and pedagogical program of the novel can be linked to widespread contemporary changes in the political, economic, and intellectual landscape.

My focus on the invocation of classical texts and Roman historical models in Jacobin fiction reveals how the pedagogical program of the Jacobin novel reworks the residual forms of classical history, with its emphasis on the patriotic virtue to be derived from studying the heroic deeds of exemplary individuals, through a deliberate attempt to produce a new, contemporary set of examples to be imitated or avoided. The Jacobin novel, in other words, attempts to replace the pedagogical lessons to be drawn from the exemplary heroes of classical

---

[8] The most comprehensive work here has been done by Pamela Clemit, who, following Butler, suggests that because most of the Jacobin novels fail to create a new form with which to work out their concerns, Godwin's work must be seen as distinct and distinctly original compared to other Jacobin novels. Clemit argues for a significant continuity between Godwin's fiction and his philosophy, and she claims that with the formal innovations of *Caleb Williams* and *St Leon*, Godwin precedes Scott in using fiction to establish a link between character and historical circumstance. See Pamela Clemit, *The Godwinian Novel: The Rational Fictions of Godwin, Brockden Brown, Mary Shelley* (Oxford: Clarendon Press, 1993). See also recent essays by Jon Klancher and Gary Handwerk: Klancher's "Godwin and the Republican Romance: Genre, Politics and Contingency in Cultural History," MLQ 56.2 (June 1995), 145–165; and its later revision as "Godwin and the Genre Reformers: On Necessity and Contingency in Romantic Narrative Theory," in *Romanticism, History and the Possibilities of Genre: Re-forming Literature, 1789–1837*, ed. Tilottama Rajan and Julia M. Wright (Cambridge: Cambridge University Press, 1998), 21–38; and Handwerk's "History, Trauma, and the Limits of the Liberal Imagination: William Godwin's Historical Fiction," in *Romanticism, History and the Possibilities of Genre: Re-forming Literature, 1789–1837*, ed. Tilottama Rajan and Julia M. Wright (Cambridge: Cambridge University Press, 1998), 64–85.

[9] Watson, *Revolution and the Form of the British Novel, 1790–1825* (Oxford: Clarendon Press, 1994). Other work of note on the novels of the 1790s includes the essays collected in *Women, Revolution, and the Novels of the 1790s*, ed. Linda Lang-Peralta

From Roman *to* roman 81

history while reproducing a mode of exemplarity that we might call "Plutarchian," a mode which suggests that novels, in a manner similar to a traditional understanding of classical history, enable a better understanding of society through knowledge of the individual and that, contrary to Knox's fears, novels can supplement or replace classical history as a means of promoting virtue. One of the ways Jacobin novels underscore this potential of the novel form is through their self-reflexive representation of discursive processes like writing, revision, and, especially, reading, which then becomes an index of how these novels imagine their effects upon a reader.

The process by which fictional characters and novelistic representation are imagined in relation to lived experience is complex and is itself historically determined. My interpretation of Jacobin fiction draws on Catherine Gallagher's discussion of this process in *Nobody's Story*. Gallagher shows how, in the face of criticism that the novel turned its readers into emotional addicts, Maria Edgeworth attempted to redeem fiction by incorporating into her work a depiction of sentimental reading as pathological ("the wrong sort" of reading) to contrast it with other responses to reading that enabled the operation of rational faculties and self-control ("the right sort" of reading). Gallagher clarifies that "the right sort of reading is epitomized by philosophy, the wrong sort by the novel."[10] My reading of Jacobin fiction

---

(Lansing: Michigan State University Press, 1999), Nancy E. Johnson, *The English Jacobin Novel on Rights, Property and the Law: Critiquing the Contract* (Basingstoke, UK: Palgrave Macmillan, 2004), and Eleanor Ty, *Unsexed Revolutionaries: Five Women Novelists of the 1790s* (Toronto: University of Toronto Press, 1993). Ty argues for the separate consideration of 1790s female novelists. She recontextualizes the revolution controversy by suggesting that Burke's most dominant intellectual principle was the patriarchal family and therefore, when women writers respond to his ideas, they rail against patriarchy. She further distinguishes feminine responses to Burke by claiming that because of cultural conditioning, men and women use language differently. The problem with Ty's account is that she must reduce Burke to a simple advocate for patriarchy—a position that is hardly new or remarkable—as a means through which to separate revolutionary principles from gender issues and thus bracket female from male novelists as more concerned with gender issues. In so doing, Ty fails to recognize the significant connection between revolutionary principles and gender issues as articulated by Watson, who reads seduction plots as political allegory.

[10] See Catherine Gallagher, *Nobody's Story: The Vanishing Acts of Women Writers in the Marketplace, 1670–1820* (Berkeley: University of California Press, 1994), 275–288; quotation from 276.

follows Gallagher, but my focus is on how Jacobin novels epitomize the right sort of reading not only through philosophy but also through their use of classical history, although in so doing they attempt to reencode the lessons of the antique past in a manner that promotes certain republican values such as public-mindedness and civic virtue while purging such qualities as the perceived tendency toward war, imperial spread, and corruption. The re-encoding of certain classical values through a Plutarchian exemplarity as a means of moving readers away from the pathologies of sentimental reading, in turn, suggests that references to classical history in the Jacobin novel can be read as an internal critique of sensibility at a time when sensibility was a charge against the Jacobin consciousness. This will become clearer through attention both to Roman references in Jacobin fiction and to the ways that Jacobin novels represent the experience of reading, especially the reading of classical texts.

EMMA COURTNEY AND THE PROBLEM OF ROMAN READING

Mary Hays's *Memoirs of Emma Courtney* (1796) provides a clear example of how Jacobin fiction represents the relationship between sentimental fiction and classical history and how it uses this relationship to promote a type of reading that it sees as more effectively developing virtue. Presented as an extended series of letters from Emma Courtney to her adopted son, Augustus Harley, the novel tells the story of Emma's life and her uncontrolled passion for Augustus's father, also named Augustus Harley. Unfortunately, Augustus senior is the recipient of a large annuity expressly contingent upon his remaining unmarried, and when Mr. Montague, a longstanding admirer of Emma's, proposes marriage, she is faced with a difficult dilemma: indulge her passion or accept security. Emma refuses Mr. Montague—"my reason was but an auxiliary to my passion"[11]—and much of the novel is an extended attempt to rationalize this choice.

---

[11] Mary Hays, *Memoirs of Emma Courtney*, ed. Eleanor Ty (Oxford: Oxford University Press, 1996), 61. Unless otherwise indicated, subsequent page references to this edition will be provided parenthetically in the text.

Eventually, when Emma discovers that Augustus is already married, she agrees to wed Montague but fails to abandon her passion for Augustus. By the end of the novel, Augustus Harley senior is dead; Montague, after Emma's passion for Augustus pushed him to an affair with his servant, Rachael, has killed their illegitimate child and then himself; and Emma is left alone with Augustus junior. She then concludes her story with a plea:

Ere I sink into the grave, let me behold *the son of my affections*, the living image of him, whose destiny involved mine, who gave an early, but a mortal blow, to all my worldly expectations—let me behold my Augustus, escaped from the tyranny of the passions, restored to reason, to the vigor of his mind, to self-control, to the dignity of active, intrepid, virtue! (196)

Emma Courtney is a cautionary tale. It uses Emma's story to show the negative effects of sentimental reading, but then concludes by presenting itself as a series of letters for the benefit of Augustus junior. The novel implies that, when applied to the text of Emma's own story, a different and more reasonable form of reading can serve as a corrective to Emma's addiction to emotion and the passions, and it holds out the possibility that in reading his mother's story, Augustus junior will reflect philosophically on his own literary habits. Ostensibly, then, the novel serves as a case study and a plea for the triumph of reason over "the tyranny of the passions." Throughout, it raises profound questions about what constitutes virtue, and it seems to resolve that true virtue consists in the self-control achieved through reason. *Emma Courtney* runs "the sentimental machinery backward, converting feeling into principle and impression into idea."[12] The act of reading features centrally in this process and *Emma Courtney* is distinguished from other sentimental novels by the way that the struggle between reason and passion is woven together with frequent references to Rousseau, Godwin, Helvetius and other key texts of contemporary intellectual discussion. There are also consistently repeated references to Roman texts and culture. These references begin when Emma describes her upbringing and education, and their use suggests a relationship between the novel's pedagogical program and its handling of the widely acknowledged virtues of a classical education as emphasized by Knox and others.

---

[12] This is the phrase used by Gallagher to describe the work of Maria Edgeworth. See *Nobody's Story*, 282.

In contrast to the case of Miss Milner, the heroine of another novel that calls deliberate attention to the importance of education for character formation—Mrs. Inchbald's *A Simple Story* (1791)—the formative texts of Emma's upbringing are carefully documented. While raised by her aunt and uncle, Emma is exposed to "the Arabian Nights, Turkish Tales, and other works of like marvelous import" (14). Once she learns to read, these pleasures are supplemented by Pope's Homer and Thomson's *Seasons*. But when her uncle dies, to counteract her "deep gloom," Emma subscribes to a circulating library "and frequently read, or rather devoured—little careful in the selection—from ten to fourteen novels in a week" (18). Emma does not read, she devours. A lack of control characterizes this reference to the circulating library.[13] Reading here becomes a process in which one is enveloped by uncontrollable passions, understood in both instances as pure and literal appetite, but with threatening implications of eros and the indulgence of sexual appetite. In this sense, the circulating library has exactly the effect feared by Vicesimus Knox, when he complains that novels "tend to give the mind a degree of weakness, which renders it unable to resist the slightest impulse of libidinous passion." Knox also makes metaphorical use of appetite when he asks rhetorically what may be given to leisured youth in lieu of novels: "To this it may be answered that when the sweetened poison is removed, plain and wholesome food will always be relished. The growing mind will crave nourishment, and will gladly seek it in true histories, written in a pleasing and easy style, on purpose for its use."[14] Here Knox refers pointedly to Plutarch's *Lives*, and as his comments suggest, there is an operative contrast running through the later eighteenth century between

---

[13] Coleridge uses similar imagery to describe his early experience with the circulating library: "I read through the catalogue, folios and all, whether I understood them or did not understand them.... My whole being was, with eyes closed to every object of present sense, to crumple myself up in a sunny corner, and read, read, read; fancy myself on Robinson Crusoe's island, finding a mountain of plumb-cake, and eating a room for myself, and then eating it into the shapes of tables and chairs—hunger and fancy!" See Richard Holmes, *Coleridge: Early Visions* (New York: Viking, 1990), 28. Godwin too lamented in 1832 that *Caleb Williams* had become a book "to amuse boys and girls in their vacant hours, [and was] a story to be hastily gobbled up by them, swallowed in a pusillanimous and unanimated mood, without chewing and digestion." As quoted by Garret A. Sullivan Jr., "'A Story to Be Hastily Gobbled Up': *Caleb Williams* and Print Culture," *Studies in Romanticism*, 32 (Fall 1993): 336–337.

[14] Knox, "On Novel Reading," 306–307.

the controlled, structured rigor of classical learning and the perceived libidinous, appetitive lack of control associated with the young novel.

Emma Courtney presents this contrast most starkly. Emma's early education can be characterized as a mixture of "elevated" poetry, fantastic tales, and a voracious reading of the sort of fiction reviled by Knox and later dismissed by Godwin as the "scum and surcharge of the press."[15] Indeed, when her father asks after Emma's reading, he discovers that her "imagination had been left to wander unrestricted in the fairy fields of fiction" (21). Accordingly, he initiates a more formalized and rigorous schedule of reading, one that produces a fictionalized enactment of the program recommended by Knox. Forced to read only Plutarch, Emma initially resents the restriction, but soon she is gripped, and when summoned to dinner, she comments that "my mind [was] pervaded with republican ardour, my sentiments elevated by a high-toned philosophy, and my bosom glowing with the virtues of patriotism" (22).[16] Emma continues to identify strongly with her reading, but through this "wholesome food," she takes away more practical and socially useful results. Both the program of Emma's father and her response to it are similar to—and likely drawn from—Rousseau's description of discovering Plutarch in the *Confessions* (1782). There, Rousseau describes the pleasure he took in repeated readings of Plutarch's *Lives*, which

> cured me a little of my taste for romance, and I soon preferred Agesilaus, Brutus, and Aristides to Orondates, Artamenes, and Juba. This interesting reading, and the conversations between my father and myself to which it gave rise, formed in me the free and republican spirit.[17]

Similarly, the virtues imbibed by Emma are explicitly classical and also explicitly (and sometimes exclusively) masculine. When one of

---

[15] William Godwin, "Of History and Romance," appendix 3 of Godwin, *Caleb Williams*, ed. Maurice Hindle (Harmondsworth: Penguin, 1988), 369.

[16] The episode might be compared to the beginning of Mary Wollstonecraft's *Mary*, where, having been taught to read by a servant, the heroine, ranging through the library and "left to the operations of her own mind...considered everything that came under her inspection, and learned to think." Wollstonecraft, *Mary* and *The Wrongs of Women*, ed. Gary Kelly (Oxford: Oxford University Press, 1976), 4.

[17] Jean-Jacques Rousseau, *Confessions*, ed. P. N. Furbank (New York: Everyman, 1992), 5.

Mr. Courtney's dinner guests hears about Emma's reading, he protests, "'Heavens, Mr Courtney! you will spoil all her feminine graces; knowledge and learning, are insufferably masculine in a woman'" (22–23).

But Emma's classical reading persists as her father directs her through a course of historical study for which she ultimately fails to acquire a taste. "Accounts of the early periods of states and empires, of the Grecian and Roman republics," she recalls, "I pursued with pleasure and enthusiasm: but when they became more complicated, grew corrupt, luxurious, licentious, perfidious, mercenary, I turned from them fatigued, and disgusted, and sought to recreate my spirits in the fairer regions of poetry and fiction" (25). If before, Emma's education showed the infection of dilatory reading cured by a hearty dose of Plutarch and history, now that very reading becomes a worse kind of infection, one which necessitates a different cure. Rome and Greece become models not of virtue, but of decay. The two cultures are collapsed together as undifferentiated models of corruption, and Emma turns to fiction to find a "cure" for history.

The fiction that Emma finds most engaging—much to the consternation of her father, who snatches the volumes from her—is Rousseau's *La Nouvelle Héloïse* (1761). She notes that "the impression made on my mind was never to be effaced—it was even productive of a long chain of consequences, that will continue to operate till the day of my death" (25). In this context, then, her father's disciplined program of reading is directly contrasted with the example of Rousseau. And because Rousseau is aligned with her passion for Augustus, the ostensible moral of the novel—its suggestion that passions must be combated—underlines the classics as a locus of disciplined reason. But because Emma turns to Rousseau as an escape from the greed, rapacity, and violence of ancient history, such coding is at best ambivalent.

Indeed, the way that the conflicts between reason and passion, prudence and emotion are echoed and aligned in Emma's reading—her juxtaposition of classical history and Rousseau's *La Nouvelle Héloïse*—presents another compelling reason for thinking about Rome and the Jacobin novel. In a letter to Emma, Mr. Francis, whom she meets at her father's house and who is meant to represent William Godwin,[18]

---

[18] In her notes to the text, Ty establishes the connection based on the age of Mr. Francis. Godwin was forty, the same age as Francis, when the novel was published in 1796.

cautions her about her "excessive sensibility" (48), suggesting that it prevents her from contributing fully to "the general reformation" (51). With Godwinian faith in reason and the power of man, however, he also implies that her reason must inevitably triumph over her passion, for the "hordes of barbarians, which overwhelmed ancient Rome, adopted at length the religion, the laws, and the improvements of the vanquished, as Rome had before done those of Greece" (50). Rome here is not a seedbed of corruption, but a society of enduring and contagious values—the legitimate heir to Greece in the same way that Europe is the heir to Rome. Once again, Roman virtues are aligned with reason and rationality, which are in turn linked to the house of her father, where Emma first met Mr. Francis. It is at her father's house, confronted with knowledge locked in cabinets, that Emma encounters Plutarch and Roman history, discipline and reason. Rome thus functions as the anchor of a value system based on methodical reason and disciplined virtue that *Emma Courtney* ostensibly validates. And yet even while Emma's struggle explicitly underlines the importance of reason, the context in which it is presented is more ambivalent—for it is also at her father's house that Emma discovers Rousseau's *Héloïse*.

We can see this ambivalence clearly when, "after some years" Emma meets Mr. Pemberton, a gallant whom she remembers as the antagonist of Mr. Francis at her father's. He recognizes her and notes that she was one who "'I remember was, when a very young lady, a great admirer of Roman virtues'" (110). Here, Emma Courtney is closely linked to Roman virtues, and the reference suggests that although Emma mentions Rome and Greece conjointly and reads Plutarch's *Parallel Lives*, the significant intertext is an internally differentiated classicism, with Rome conceived not simply as the follower but as the subsumer of Greece, the apotheosis and completion of Greek values in an empire powerful enough to spread its virtues. Based on Emma's previous acknowledgment that she greatly admired the Greek and Roman republics, readers of *Emma Courtney* might expect her to concur. Instead, she responds, "'Not of *Roman virtues*, I believe, Sir; they had in them too much of the destructive spirit which Mrs Melmouth thinks so admirable'" (110). The response implies that Emma admires something about Rome apart from Roman virtues, but that something is never named. Once again, Emma's initial thrill at reading Plutarch is qualified, and as we will see is also the case with Holcroft's *Hugh Trevor*, Roman virtues are understood to be deeply ambivalent. For both Emma Courtney and Hugh Trevor, Rome inspires elevated, lofty thinking, which is, however, checked by the recognition of the potentially violent and jingoistic underside of Roman virtue.

It seems, then, that the evaluation of Roman references in *Emma Courtney* produces an interpretive quandary. The consistency with which such references appear prohibits their dismissal, but their meaning is far from clear. Rome is in some sense a locus of virtue and, via Plutarch, a cure for a particular kind of reading, that which Mr. Courtney dismisses as the "fairy fields of fiction." Yet the violence of Roman history becomes a problem in itself for Emma, one which, in turn, necessitates a cure of its own—here, her reading of Rousseau. And by Emma's account that reading of Rousseau produces the entire chain of events that she recounts. Despite this ambivalence, the use of Rome as a corrective to the perceived frivolous business of reading novels reveals *Emma Courtney*'s critique of contemporary novelistic fare; but unlike the corrective described by Rousseau in the *Confessions*—one that "cures" its readers of their taste for romance in the manner proposed by Vicesimus Knox and imposed by Emma's father—Hays suggests that classical reading can have its own adverse effects, and that the cure sometimes acts as a poison.

In this context, it is possible to speculate on the significance of Augustus as the name of Emma's beloved: is this too a veiled and continuous reference to Roman history? When Emma first begins to read history, it is the "early period of states and empires"—the "Grecian and Roman republics"—that provide "pleasure and enthusiasm." But when these republics mature into empires, Emma resents their complications and corruption, and she describes these empires as "luxurious, licentious, perfidious, mercenary." All of these qualities might be considered uncontrolled passions—which is precisely the way Emma ashamedly presents her own passion for Augustus. Emma's later reference, in a letter to Mr. Francis, to the "pernicious ambition of an Augustus Caesar" (147) sustains this reading. Further, if the Roman corruption that Emma shuns is indeed Augustan, then her turn to Rousseau gives license to her passions and produces another, equally problematic Augustus—her beloved Augustus

Harley—and this might be a way of suggesting that *both* versions of Augustus show great but squandered potential—much as Emma presents herself.[19]

These questions about the relationship of the two Augustuses are provisional, but they raise a larger question. Rome, Rousseau, and Augustus all function to one degree or another as textual entities: Emma's reading of Roman figures and Roman history is presented in considerable emotional detail, she ascribes great weight to her reading of Rousseau, and she presents the story of Augustus Harley in writing for the later reading and edification of her adopted son, Augustus. Based upon the detail with which these and other experiences of reading are presented, Hays would appear to be well aware of the ongoing debate, glimpsed at the start of this chapter, over the history of the novel as it relates to classical education and the reading of classical texts, especially classical history. Such awareness suggests that attention to Roman references exposes how the Jacobin novel operates in what we can describe as a Plutarchian mode. These novels are simultaneously critical of the novel's potential frivolity but hopeful about the possibility of using the form to educate readers about republican virtue in the manner that Rousseau and Knox describe the Plutarchian ideal. Hays and other Jacobin novelists were aware of the perceived threat to classical learning posed by the novel, and they attempted to use the form to preserve and recast certain classical, republican values (public-mindedness and civic virtue in particular) and jettison others (bellicosity, imperial expansion, and corruption) within the form of their fiction. Thinking about these issues helps to unpack the apparent ambiguities of *Emma Courtney*, but it also underscores how the pedagogical program of the Jacobin novel draws upon and recasts the residual forms of classical history, with its emphasis on the study of particular individuals. To understand better how this might work, however, we need a clearer sense of the late-eighteenth-century case for thinking that literature could change social attitudes in particular

---

[19] Given these potential resonances, it is curious that Eleanor Ty glosses Emma's reference to Augustus as a reference as to Gaius Julius Caesar and not to his adopted relative and avenger, Octavius Caesar, the first Roman emperor, who adopted the cognomen "Augustus." The mistake is at a certain level trivial, but given that both Emma's love object and her adopted son are named Augustus, Ty's confusion forecloses a potentially important echo.

ways and that particular kinds of literature could do this especially well. How exactly was literature thought to do this? What did the novel as a genre offer to the philosophical radicals?

THE MORAL AND PEDAGOGICAL POTENTIAL OF THE NOVEL FORM

The ongoing eighteenth-century debate over the formal qualities and latent moral potential of the emergent novel form offers an initial response to these questions. Within this debate, the persistent discussion of the critical rules and moral implications of the novel suggests a lack of critical consensus about the form, and comments like Vicesimus Knox's underline the gravity with which these discussions were conducted. In the preface to *Joseph Andrews*, for example, Fielding applies classical critical rules to his writing in an effort to define his work as a "comic-epic poem in prose" and thus to distinguish it from what he perceives as the common rabble of romance.[20] Fielding's argument suggests both the ungrounded status of the novel form and the desire to establish critical and qualitative standards for it. Richard Hurd, however, rejects Fielding's claims. In "On the Idea of Universal Poetry," he distinguishes poetry from other forms of writing because it takes pleasure for its end, on account of which it must have well-chosen words (decorum) and figurative expression, a particular imaginative quality that outstrips nature, and not only rhythm but numbers. From this it follows that a work of prose fiction conducted according to the rules of epic poetry cannot be called a poem because it is not in verse, and Hurd denounces novels and romances as hasty, imperfect, and abortive poems. He further harangues them as ephemeral works that appeal to the sickly imagination and not to "true taste," which requires only chaste, severe, and simple pleasures.[21] With Hurd,

---

[20] Henry Fielding, *Joseph Andrews*, ed. Martin C. Battestin (London: Methuen, 1961), 7–12.

[21] Richard Hurd, *Dissertation I: On the Idea of Universal Poetry* (London, 1766); reprinted in *Literary Criticism in England, 1660–1800*, ed. Gerard Wester Chapman (New York: Alfred A. Knopf, 1966), 388–396.

who first attracted public attention with his editions of Horace (in 1749 and 1751, respectively), we see how close critical positions are to moral ones; his argument is geared toward keeping the tastes of erudite readers conservative.

Johnson, in the famous *Rambler #4* (31 March 1750), presents another more optimistic possibility for the moral efficacy of the novel. Although the piece is renowned for its denunciation of the so-called "mixed character," Johnson also emphasizes the pedagogical possibilities of the novel form. Since, like its reader, the hero of the novel is an ordinary figure, Johnson argues that the author of the novel has an advantage over real life: the novelist can select only those parts of nature worthy of representation. The realism of the form makes it approachable, and provided that the best examples are selected, the novel becomes the ideal means with which to inculcate morality to impressionable youth.[22] This would become a crucial calculation for the Jacobin novel.

While some, including George Canning, saw the novel and the romance as essentially identical with only certain names and situations changed, others, among them John Moore in *The Progress of Romance*, located a progression within the romance genre from ancient to modern. Moore, like Johnson, defended the instructive potential of the form, for "modern romances" presented an accurate representation of life and manners within a particular setting. Indeed, Moore continues to lament the lack of such representations in antiquity: "Had works of this nature existed in the flourishing ages of the Greek and Roman republics, and had some of the best of them been preserved, how infinitely would they be relished at present! as they would give a much more minute and satisfactory picture of private and domestic life than is found in history, which dwells chiefly on war and affairs of state."[23] Moore's comment is significant for two reasons: it further confirms the tendency to think about the modernity of the novel form by comparing it with ancient precedents, and he, like so many of his contemporaries, distinguishes the form not by its

---

[22] Johnson's essay is reprinted in Chapman, *Literary Criticism*, 405–409.
[23] Moore, *A View of the Commencement and Progress of Romance* (London, 1797), reprinted in *Eighteenth-Century British Novelists on the Novel*, ed. George L. Barnett (New York: Appleton-Century-Crofts, 1968), 172.

adherence to critical rules but by the nature of its content: novels are about private and domestic life. As Clara Reeve states in her volume, also titled *The Progress of Romance*, "The Romance is an heroic fable, which treats of fabulous persons and things. The Novel is a picture of real life and manners and of the times in which it is written."[24] This is precisely the position from which the reviewer for the *Analytical Review* objected to Godwin's *Caleb Williams*. By focusing on such topics as "the admiration of chivalry, love of reputation, fatal effects of indiscreet curiosity," Godwin, the reviewer claims, restricts the power and affect of his composition: "He has no tale of rational love, no marked insistence of personal attachment, no fondly anxious parent, or child devoted to filial duty, in the development of his story."[25] Comments like these show—as the work of Watt and McKeon would lead us to believe—that by the late eighteenth century enough of a consensus had emerged about the form for its readers to expect that the novel would deploy consistent themes and plots.

The point, then, is that if there was no contemporary critical agreement at the time of the formal consolidation of the novel as described by Watt and McKeon, then by the end of the eighteenth century those writing about the novel show a much clearer consensus about the form. Even those who see novels as merely a contemporary version of the romance form are willing to concede that there is a qualitative difference between the modern novel and previous fictional forms. The novel, most contemporary commentators agree, is a form that addresses personal and domestic life through its representation of scenes that could possibly and probably occur in "real" daily life, and it gains its potential moral force by the accessibility of these examples. If novel reading was initially seen as a scandalous moral threat—especially to such readers as women and boys without a proper, classical education—an increasingly positive construal of its realism and accessibility began to impart substantial moral and pedagogical potential to the emergent form. Sometimes, as the comments of John Moore show, novels were even construed positively as an invaluable supplement to the kinds of knowledge imparted by the classics.

---

[24] Barnett, *Eighteenth-Century Novelists*, 135.
[25] The review is reprinted in Williams, *Novels and Romance*; quoted material is from 397.

Surveying the same critical territory, McKeon has argued that the eighteenth century produces a shift in the location of the theorization of the emergent novel form. During the first half of the period, he claims, "the theory of the novel appears in a variety of discourses in which the epistemology of fiction is being treated, and often in the interstices of narrative itself." By the end of the period, however, novel theory is not "so commonly embedded in practice itself because it is being separated out and institutionalized within the discourse of the periodical review."[26] But as Kelly, Butler, and others argue, a close look at the fictions of the 1790s suggests that their authors were keenly aware of the history and critical debates surrounding the form and—I would add further—of the ways that the novel usurps the pedagogical functions of classical knowledge. A focus on Roman references reveals how these works pick up on significant strains from that debate—Hurd's emphasis on the moral duties of poetry, Johnson's optimism about the pedagogical possibilities of the novel, Moore's favorable comparison of novels with classical texts. These positions are then recast into a narrative that fits critical consensus about the content and internal coherence of the form, while also reinscribing many of the moral and pedagogical functions of classical texts. This theory suggests a possible context of significance for the above-noted classical references in Mary Hays. That such references recur, sporadically but consistently, throughout other Jacobin novels further suggests that Jacobin novelists were attempting to use their awareness of the history of the novel form to transform the moral significance of the novel into an increased political efficacy in the service of progressive causes.

GODWIN AND THE CASE FOR THE NOVEL AS AN AGENT OF SOCIAL CHANGE

William Godwin most sharply articulates this case for the particular effectiveness of fiction for changing social attitudes. His claims begin

---

[26] McKeon, "Prose Fiction: Great Britain," 238.

in the *Enquiry Concerning Political Justice* (1793) with his belief in the leveling effects of print technology:

> By the easy multiplication of copies, and the cheapness of books, everyone has access to them. The extreme inequality of information among different members of the same community, which existed in ancient times is diminished. A class of men is become numerous which was then comparatively unknown, and we see vast multitudes who, though condemned to labor for the perpetual acquisition of the means of subsistence, have yet a superficial knowledge of most of the discoveries and topics which are investigated by the learned. The consequence is that the possessors of knowledge being more, its influence is more certain.[27]

If, as Godwin develops more fully in *Political Justice*, individuals are the products of their environment, then the diffusion of knowledge through printing becomes a force that undermines repressive social control. But the passage, and *Political Justice* more generally, makes no special case for fiction. Furthermore, as Garrett Sullivan has shown, Godwin is being somewhat disingenuous here, for not all printing—especially *Political Justice*—was particularly cheap. Sullivan uses this point to suggest that with the explosion of new texts and audiences in the 1790s, Godwin's critique of the habits of popular reading through handbills in *Caleb Williams* underscores his attempt to use fiction to popularize his philosophy.[28] Godwin himself says this explicitly in the preface to *Caleb Williams* when he explains that the novel can convey

---

[27] Godwin, *Enquiry Concerning Political Justice*, ed. Isaac Kramnick (Harmondsworth: Penguin, 1976), 280 (book 4, chap. 2).

[28] Garrett Sullivan, "Story to Be Hastily Gobbled Up." The suggestion that Godwin's fiction is intended to bring his philosophy to broader audiences is widespread. What distinguishes Sullivan's account, however, is the way that he reads Caleb's experience with popular handbills, which he codes as lower-class textual consumption, to show how Godwin models both the production and the consumption of these sort of texts, and thus how Caleb can be read as a kind of "solution" to the potential of certain kinds of printed material to distort informed opinion. But of course with the spread of print and the diversification of audience, it becomes even more difficult to control the reception of a text, and Sullivan concludes that Godwin wound up writing for a print culture quite alien from the gentlemanly world imagined in *Political Justice*. As he later lamented, his book had mostly served "to amuse boys and girls in their vacant hours...a story to be hastily gobbled up by them, swallowed in a pusillanimous and unanimated mood, without chewing and digestion" (as quoted by Sullivan, 336–337).

the truth of philosophers to "persons whom books of philosophy and science are never likely to reach."[29]

Godwin more fully articulates his belief in the powers of fiction and imaginative production elsewhere. In *The Enquirer*, for example, he explicitly rejects the systematic mind-set of Latin moralists in favor of writers "whose composition is fraught with irresistible enchantment." Godwin explains, "I can guess very nearly what I should have been if Epictetus had not bequeathed to us his Morals, or Seneca his Consolations. But I cannot tell what I should have been, if Shakespear[e] or Milton had not written. The poorest peasant in the remotest corner of England, is probably a different man from what he would have been but for these authors."[30] Comments like these acknowledge Godwin's belief in the ineffable qualities of imaginative composition, his belief that, "the unity of spirit and interest in a tale truly considered, gives it a powerful hold on the reader, which can scarcely be generated with equal success in any other way."[31] For Godwin, imaginative writing is to be valued because more than any kind of explicitly philosophical or scientific discourse it reaches the broadest possible audience and holds the attention of its readers.

But Godwin's belief in the efficacy of the novel and fictional production as an agent of social change is based on more than its accessibility and concerns also its selectivity. In an unpublished 1797 essay "Of History and Romance"—originally intended for *The Enquirer*—Godwin argues that romance (a term that he uses interchangeably with the novel) is the more accurate version of history. Godwin bases his distinctive claims about the importance of romance on his belief that the purpose of history is to enable a better understanding of society and that this can best be done through "knowledge of the individual."[32] The argument is twofold. First, Godwin considers the

---

[29] Original preface, reprinted in *Caleb Williams*, ed. Maurice Hindle (Harmondsworth: Penguin, 1988), 3.

[30] William Godwin, *The Enquirer: Reflections on Education, Manners, and Literature* (London: G. G. and J. Robinson, 1797), 139–140.

[31] From Godwin's 1832 preface to his collected novels, as quoted by Kelly, *Jacobin Novel*, 15.

[32] William Godwin, "Of History and Romance," appendix 3 of Godwin, *Caleb Williams*, ed. Maurice Hindle (Harmondsworth: Penguin, 1988), 363; subsequent page references to this edition will be provided parenthetically in the text.

"broken fragments and the scattered ruins of evidence" (367) to emphasize the constructed nature of historical narrative, the contradictions inherent in the assembly of disparate facts. Next, Godwin turns to the "romance or novel."[33] He notes the "obloquy and censure" (368) to which this genre has been exposed and claims that such denigration results from an unreasonable failure to distinguish the finest examples from the "whole scum and surcharge of the press" (369). Further, the imaginative component of the romance—its supposed distance from factual reality in the eyes of most critics—is "not wholly inapplicable to...the graver and more authentic name of history" (370). Combining his critique of the factual basis of history with his elevation of the intellectual value of the best romances allows Godwin to declare:

> Romance, then, strictly considered, may be pronounced to be one of the species of history. The difference between romance and what ordinarily bears the denomination of history, is this. The historian is confined to individual incident and individual man, and must hang upon that his invention or conjecture as he can. The writer collects his materials from all sources, experience, report, and the records of human affairs; then generalises them; and finally selects, from their elements and the various combinations they afford, those instances which he is best qualified to portray, and which he judges most calculated to impress the heart and improve the faculties of his reader. In this point of view we should be apt to pronounce that romance was a bolder species of composition than history. (370)

Inherent in Godwin's elevation of romance, as we might expect from his predecessors who defended the intellectual responsibility and moral agency of the novel, is its improving quality, its singular potential to direct "the machine of society...to its best purposes" (363) by impressing the heart and improving the faculties of its readers.

In addition to the rather surprising elevation of the romance genre by the author of one of the most abstract and analytical philosophical treatises of the eighteenth century, Godwin's essay is striking for at least two more reasons: first, its emphasis on the greatness of the ancients; and, second, its almost programmatic explication of the

---

[33] References like this make clear that although Godwin uses the term "romance," he sees the form as interchangeable with the novel.

moral aims and philosophic rationale of the Jacobin novel. The two points, as should be clear from my argument, are closely related. Godwin pronounces the greatness of ancient history in rapturous, emphatic tones, in contrast to which the history of post-Revolution Britain "assumes its most insipid and insufferable form" (367). Unlike those souls blighted by modern governments and institutions, the ancients "are men of free and undaunted spirit" (365); and Godwin cites Plutarch to back his declaration that "something in the nature of the Greek and Roman republics... expanded and fired the soul" (364). Godwin even announces that he "would rather be acquainted with a few trivial particulars of the actions and dispositions of Virgil and Horace, than with the lives of many men and the history of many nations" (364). Godwin's reverence for the ancients, then, works in a Plutarchian mode, in which the exemplary nature of ancient individuals gives meaning and greatness to ancient history. History is understood biographically, and biography acts as a kind of moral fable.

This Plutarchian mode relates directly to Godwin's program for the Jacobin novel. "True history," Godwin affirms in defense of the romance form, "consists in a delineation of consistent, human character, in a display of the manner in which such a character acts under successive circumstances, in showing how character increases and assimilates new substances to its own, and how it decays, together with the catastrophe into which by its own gravity it naturally declines" (372). The "true history" that Godwin defines here could be a description of Plutarch's *Lives*, and, indeed, Godwin and his Jacobin contemporaries bring the pedagogical functions and moral seriousness of ancient history into the novel form. The *roman* subsumes the Roman, and although the historical process is presented only allegorically, the way that these novels use the allegorical presentation of history to explain how character is determined by circumstance suggests that they precede the acknowledged initiation of this process in the historical novel as defined by Lukács.[34]

---

[34] For Lukács, what distinguishes the novels of Scott from their predecessors is their "derivation of the individuality of characters from the historical peculiarity of their age" (*Historical Novel*, 19).

If the social improvement envisioned by Godwin can best be conveyed through fiction, it follows that the novel has a primary role in social, political, and moral improvement. When read in the context of Godwin's earlier novel, *Caleb Williams* (1794), "Of History and Romance" enables us to see just how the Jacobin novel inherits the Plutarchian mode of history and how changes in reading practices and reading publics can produce a movement from Roman history to romance conceived positively and progressively. *Caleb Williams* represents the "true history," later outlined in "Of History and Romance." In his suppressed original preface to *Caleb Williams*, which appeared first with the 1796 edition, Godwin explicitly offers his novel as an allegory in which a single story will stand for "a general review of the modes of domestic and unrecorded despotism by which man becomes the destroyer of man."[35] Godwin's reference here to those "whom books of philosophy and science are never likely to reach" implies that he locates the efficacy of the novel form in its potential for reaching a public without a formal classical education.

Kelly and Butler have both speculated on the way that certain names in *Caleb Williams*, especially Falkland, constitute a purposeful allusion to historical characters—specifically Lucius Cary and Edmund Burke—thus giving the novel's critique of contemporary society historical range and depth;[36] more recently, Pamela Clemit has argued convincingly that through the use of first-person narrative Godwin "seizes on the narrative potential of Burke's emotive defence of hierarchical society and turns it into a complex fable," one that moves beyond a simple parable of Burke "to present psychological self-division as a product of Burkean society."[37] In addition to its critique of contemporary political values, *Caleb Williams*, much like *Emma Courtney*, also offers, albeit subtly, a related evaluation of shifts in contemporary reading practices.

Immediately after beginning his narrative, Caleb acquaints his readers with his restless curiosity, a trait that manifests itself not only in an attachment to mechanics and natural philosophy, but also in "an

---

[35] Hindle reprints this preface at the start of his edition of *Caleb Williams*, ed. Maurice Hindle (Harmondsworth: Penguin, 1988); the quotation comes from page 3.
[36] See Kelly, *English Jacobin Novel*, 198–207; Butler, *Jane Austen*, 69–73.
[37] Clemit, *Godwinian Novel*, 69, 54.

invincible attachment to books of narrative and romance."[38] He continues, in a vein similar to Emma Courtney and Coleridge, "I read, I devoured compositions of this sort" (6). As before, the reading of romance is here associated with a lack of control and with an unhealthy loss of reason. For both Emma Courtney and Caleb Williams, the effects of fictional reading cannot be controlled, and both of these novels depict readers who lack the ability to detach themselves from the stories that they read. Caleb notes that the effects of his obsession with such books "were frequently discernible in my external appearance and my health" (6). Similarly, the first sentence of the first chapter devoted to Falkland notes his reading preferences: "Among the favourite authors of his early years were the heroic poets of Italy. From them he imbibed the love of chivalry and romance" (12). During this early narrative of Falkland's stay in Italy, the only specific locale mentioned is Rome. But given Falkland's preference for romance, it is as if Rome itself has shifted in its association from the classical texts of ancient Rome to the current fad for romance, a shift that directly mimics an awareness among Jacobin novelists that the *roman* had displaced the Roman in the republic of letters. Caleb's unquenchable curiosity fuels his feverish reading, while Falkland imbibes his love of romance from Italian heroic poets. The association of each individual's reading of romance with his downfall highlights *Caleb Williams* as a different kind of novel, one that draws upon the plot-driven elements of romance to produce a more progressive code of social and moral values. This claim assumes further credence when considered in the context of Godwin's qualitative distinctions between fictional productions in "Of History and Romance," but the implications of such a shift are not fully manifest until we consider the novel's references to ancient Rome.

Given the largely accepted connection of the novel form with the minute representation of the everyday, its status as a kind of counterknowledge to the more aristocratic classical education, the novel seems an unlikely place to seek classical references. But as "Of History and Romance" suggests, ancient models may be important to the

---

[38] William Godwin, *Caleb Williams*, ed. Maurice Hindle (Harmondsworth: Penguin, 1988), 6; subsequent page references to this edition will be provided parenthetically in the text.

Jacobin novel in ways other than through direct, overt reference. At different points in the novel, Falkland is associated with Alexander (115–118) and with the tyrannous Roman emperors Nero and Caligula (324). Butler notes this link and further speculates that, "Rather more shadowily, Caleb perhaps suggests some of the simplicity and virtue of the plain citizen of the Roman Republic, in primitive days before the sophisticated and tyrannous emperors destroyed the fibre of that people. Elsewhere in his work Godwin consistently admired two periods, the Roman Republic and the English Commonwealth, as times when the egalitarian spirit had flourished."[39] Though Butler introduces this point with considerable caution, it is substantially confirmed when Caleb is among the band of thieves. Here, "fatigued with continual contemplation" he pulls out "a pocket Horace," where he reads "with avidity the epistle in which he so beautifully describes to Fuscus, the grammarian, the pleasures of rural tranquility and independence" (239). Previously, in his initial description of his curiosity in relation to his reading habits, Caleb presented the absorbing qualities of narrative as something over which he had no control. This moment, in contrast, presents a competing model for the impact of a book on its reader. Horace enables a type of absorption that helps Caleb overcome fatigue, and the poetry transports him into a fantasy of independence and tranquility that better enables a reengagement with the world in contrast to the sickly effects produced by narrative fiction. Furthermore, the emphasis on the "rural tranquility and independence" of the epistle in what is the only explicit citation of any text that Caleb reads lends textual support to Butler's theory. We have seen Godwin's reverence for the classics,[40] and these views, taken in the context of the above discussion, allow us both to reconfirm and to recontextualize Butler's observations. They suggest *why* such potential symbolism is not only likely but also significant.

Godwin clearly has a great stake in the moral efficacy of classical texts, and *Caleb Williams* borrows the focus of certain classical historians on exemplary figures to exploit the potential of the "romance" as "true

---

[39] Butler, *Jane Austen*, 72.
[40] Present not only in "History and Romance," but also in "Of the Study of the Classics," in the opening section of *The Enquirer* (1797)—the volume for which "History and Romance" was intended.

history" to produce an enriched understanding of society through individual example. The story of Caleb and Falkland not only borrows the Plutarchian mode of history as moral fable, but it is possible to link it rhetorically to the histories of Sallust. In the *Bellum Catilinae*, for example, Sallust juxtaposes the corruption of Rome with the corrupt character of Catiline, such that the latter becomes the quintessential example of the former: "In a city so great and so corrupt Catiline found it a very easy matter to surround himself, as by a bodyguard, with troops of criminals and reprobates of every kind."[41] The way in which corrupt social contexts mark all individuals recurs throughout Sallust, and, as Butler notes, "Among historians, the biographical Sallust is [Godwin's] favourite."[42] In light of the exemplary status of ancient individuals and the centrality of the novel form to Godwin's vision of social and moral improvement, we can begin to read the Plutarchian project of the Jacobin novel as providing a new and more progressive set of exemplars—as an alternative locus of exemplarity, one that builds from the examples of the ancients, and the received mode of interpreting exemplarity, but one that directs this mode to a distinct moral and social vision.

HOLCROFT, INCHBALD, AND THE CRITICAL ACCOUNT OF CLASSICAL LEARNING

In comparison to the work of other Jacobin novelists, Thomas Holcroft and Elizabeth Inchbald offer a more critical account of classical learning. Both Inchbald and Holcroft, however, continue to draw upon the rhetorical model of classical biography as moral fable. Considering these novelists collectively reveals a pattern by which the Jacobin novel—whether it offers a critique of the function and substance of classical learning (Inchbald, Holcroft), or a more positive assessment (Godwin, Hays)—reinscribes certain classical virtues into a more accessible set of

---

[41] In tanta tamque corrupta civitate Catilina, id quod factu facillumum erat, omnium flagitorum atque facinorum circum se tamquam stipatorum catervas habebat" (14, 1). The text and translation are from the Loeb edition, *Sallust*, trans. J. C. Rolfe (Cambridge: Harvard University Press, 1921), 24–25.
[42] Butler, *Jane Austen*, 63.

examples for readers often unversed in classical texts. The dominant virtues of Jacobinism (a belief in the individual's power to use reason, civic participation, plain speaking, etc.), in other words, can be described as classical Roman virtues, and it is thus fair to say that the Jacobin novel democratizes the often elitist doctrines of classical republicanism.

Although the 1790s novels of Holcroft are quite distinct in tone—critics often compare the heavy-handed didacticism and epistolary form of *Anna St. Ives* (1792) to Richardson and suggest that Smollett was a key influence on the more picaresque *bildungsroman Hugh Trevor* (1794–1797)—both novels underline the importance of experience as a kind of education, whereby the lofty ideals of their respective protagonists cannot help but triumph. In *Anna St. Ives*, this process comes about largely through the superior and exemplary moral virtue of Frank Henley. Although Anna does not initially consider Frank as a potential mate because he is of a different social class, the force of his example is so strong that he not only wins her affection—he reshapes her worldview and wins the approval of her family. Similarly, in *Hugh Trevor*, continued engagement with the mores and structures of British society produces only disenchantment, setbacks, and the exposure of deep corruption, thus teaching the initially misguided Hugh Trevor the virtues of plain speaking, sympathy, and altruistic personal morality as a source of social improvement.

Roman references are critical to the central themes and pedagogical thrust of each of Holcroft's novels. Cato, the great Roman statesman and quintessential symbol of republican virtue, appears twice in *Anna St. Ives*. First, he is used by Coke Clifton to characterize Frank Henley. Coke suggests to his correspondent and fellow cavalier, Guy Fairfax, that Frank is a leveler who lacks all sense of social inferiority and he then compares his altruism to Cato:

You may think that I do not fail to humble the youth whenever opportunity offers. But no! Humble him, indeed! Shew him boiling ice! Stew a whale in an oyster-shell! Make mount Caucasus into a bag pudding! But do not imagine he may be moved! The legitimate son of Cato's eldest bastard, he! A petrified Possidonius, in high preservation.[43]

---

[43] Thomas Holcroft, *Anna St. Ives*, ed. Peter Faulkner (London: Oxford University Press, 1970), 96. Subsequent page references to this edition will be provided parenthetically in the text.

The reference is meant to be arch and disparaging, but for the reader of the novel, who has the advantage of superior perspective achieved by comparing all of the letters, it comes off differently. Having seen numerous examples of Frank's actions, we recognize his reasonable objectivity, his virtue, and his selfless willingness to help others—even at risk to himself—as the value system of the novel. As the symbol of Roman virtue, republican and abstemious, Cato exemplifies all of these qualities. Coke's jest thus aligns Frank explicitly with Cato while simultaneously suggesting that his own value system is warped enough to poke fun at a Roman republican hero. Coke makes a similar reference in a subsequent letter to Fairfax, this time as part of an extended series of references contrasting high-minded moral philosophy with his own epicurean hedonism:

Let speculative blockheads brew metaphysical nectar, make a hash of axioms, problems, corollaries and demonstrations, and feed on ideas and fatten. Be theirs the feast of reason and the flow of soul. But let me banquet with old Homer's jolly gods and heroes, revel with the Mahometan houris, or gain admission into the savoury sanctorum of the gormandizing priesthood, snuff the fumes from their altars, and gorge on the fat of lambs. Let cynic Catos truss up each in his slovenly toga, rail at Heliogabalus, and fast; but let me receive his card with—"Sir, your company is requested to dine and sup." (144)

In Coke's dichotomy, Homer is aligned with the greed and gorging of a victor sacking a conquered city, and an internally differentiated classicism allows Holcroft to criticize certain aspects of classical education, while still pointing to the potential worth and civic virtue of other republican and Roman classical figures. Cato is particularly relevant because, as a charged example of civic abstemiousness, he adds intellectual depth to the contrast between the hero and villain of *Anna St. Ives*. This is clearly not a simple difference between men, but a sharp distinction of value systems: Coke disparages the self-denying patriotism of Cato because his values are coded as purely aristocratic—driven by pride and not patriotism, passion and not reason, self-indulgence and not altruistic virtue. His classical education becomes mere decadence, a set of references with which to carry off a fine phrase and a turn of wit. And in the way that exposure to Cato produces only mocking references, Coke represents the corruption of the republic into the empire—the dressing of republican forms for imperial power. Frank, in contrast, is thus explicitly aligned with the hero of the Roman republic, a kind of recoding of the importance of classical history and the attempt to align the "new man" with a reinterpreted and differently emphasized set of classical references, one safe from the corruption and imperious spread of empire.

A later Roman reference in *Anna St. Ives* further elaborates this line of thought. As Coke gets worked up over his elaborate plot to take Anna by force, he begins to construe Seneca as a means to calm down and gather himself. "I have been throwing up my sashes," he writes to Fairfax, "striding across my room, and construing ten lines of Seneca, and my pulse again begins to beat more temperately" (286). In this way, while the novel symbolically links the actions of Frank with the figure and stature of Cato, Coke is clearly identified as one who has received training in classical languages and learned how to read Latin texts. But such learning fails to influence his moral system and instead, Coke values Latin for its forms, devoid of content and meaning. Because of the manner in which Coke reads—or rather construes instead of reads—his reading is shown to have no effect on his thinking. He does not turn to the substance of Senecan stoicism, but merely to its style; he figures out the cases and forms of the words and is left with the structure of meaning devoid of the substance of meaning itself.

This is precisely how Rome and Roman culture figure into Holcroft's next novel, *Hugh Trevor*. After a period of economic hardship that forces him to apprentice himself to an abusive farmer, the eponymous hero is taken in by his grandfather and sent to a provincial grammar school. Here, full of zeal, his "progress both in Latin and Greek was rapid."[44] The lessons of such ancient texts, however, can only be described as ambivalent. Hugh implies that he has acquired strong "moral propensities" as a result of his classical studies and, moreover, that such propensities are not unusual but the norm for anyone not corrupted by "habit and example":

I speak from experience, and well know how much the accounts I had read of Aristedes, Epaminondas, Regulus, Cato and innumerable other great

---

[44] Thomas Holcroft, *Hugh Trevor*, ed. Seamus Deane (London: Oxford University Press, 1973), 53. Subsequent page references to this edition will be provided parenthetically in the text.

characters among the ancients inflamed my imagination, and gave me a rooted love of virtue; so that even the vulgarly supposed dry precepts of Seneca and Epictetus were perused by me with delight; and with an emulous determination to put them in practice. (63)

Classical texts here inspire not just a "love of virtue," but an "emulous determination" to act upon that love. Like the narratives that Emma and Caleb find so absorbing, classical texts inspire imitative behavior in their readers, only here that emulation is explicitly directed toward virtue and action in the world. So far, so good, but Hugh also concedes that despite moral propensities, his morality remains "far from pure." He notes, "From the glow of poetry I learnt many noble precepts; but from the same source I derived the pernicious supposition that to conquer countries and exterminate men are the acts of heroes" (63). For Hugh, then, classical texts teach an uneasy blend of civic and martial virtues, and his virtue remains misdirected. This is the commonly expressed critique of the classics—so prominent in Richardson—that they contain noble precepts that are all too often directed toward bellicosity and imperial expansion.

Soon, however, Hugh discovers another outlet for his classical knowledge. In a chapter that includes the episodic subheading, "The honey changed to gall, or rules for fine writers" (117), Hugh accepts an invitation to write a letter on reform for Lord Idford. Though Idford denounces government corruption, it is clear that his ambitions are personal, that his positions are chosen for expediency and not principle, and that Hugh himself is a mere hack. Nonetheless, he throws himself into the task. As a "model of style" and "masculine ardor," Hugh has already praised Junius, whom he sets out to rival. His beginning is auspicious: "So copious was my elocution that in less than four hours I had filled eight pages of paper; two of which at least were Greek and Latin quotations, from Aristotle, Demosthenes, and Cicero. I meant to astonish mankind with my erudition" (119). The tone of this passage, written retrospectively, suggests that such references are of no efficacy but are merely a demonstration of vanity. We also sense, however, that allusions to the classics serve as a sort of entrance fee to public discourse, that without the vain demonstration of such erudition, no one will listen.

This seems to be precisely the position that Holcroft is attacking, for after a favorable reception from Enoch, a sycophantic aspirant to the company of the good and great, Hugh takes his piece to Turl, the novel's Jacobin conscience. Far from praise, Turl finds the piece execrable, and he attempts to show Hugh the rules of rational composition, "We certainly write to be understood, and should therefore never write in a language that is unknown to a majority of our readers. The rule will apply as well to the living languages as to the dead, and its infringement is but in general a display of the author's vanity" (122). Coming as baldly and directly as it does, Turl's critique initially offends Hugh, but he soon recognizes its "infinite service," concedes his mistakes, and rewrites the piece. "I now arranged my thoughts, omitted my quotations, discarded many of my metaphors, shortened my periods, simplified my style, reduced the letter to one forth of its former length, and finished the whole by one o'clock" (123). There is a direct, matter-of-fact tone to these lines, suggesting a lesson well and clearly learned. The episode works on a number of levels. Most basically, it is one of a series of incidents in which Hugh errs, is corrected, and initially resents his comeuppance before ultimately recognizing, comprehending, and amending his mistakes. Indeed, the novel itself can be seen as one long chain of such incidents; the efficiency with which Hugh learns his lessons after initial resistance allows space for Holcroft to demonstrate the persuasive power of reason and truth clearly perceived, and the favorable outcome of each of these episodes performs the inevitable triumph of reason over things as they are.

Next, the act of revision can be understood in light of my discussion of how these novels imagine an effect upon their readers. In contrast to the novels and romances that were shown to have such an electric and absorbing effect on Emma Courtney and Caleb Williams, we can assume that the problem with Hugh Trevor's letter is that its breadth of reference makes it turgid and prevents it from having its desired effect on its reader. Only through clear writing and plain speaking, Holcroft implies, can a text hope to engage and sustain the interest of its reader. More specifically, however, the scene can be read as a critique and emendation of a particular kind of public discourse. Hugh signs his letter "Themistocles," and refers favorably to the letters of Junius. Godwin himself wrote a series of letters from "Mucius." All of these letters participate in a kind of high-minded, allusive discourse in which their authors attempt to harness unsullied and irreproachable classical virtues for present purposes. Through the drafting, criticism, and revision of Hugh's letter, Holcroft offers a pointed attack on this kind of discourse in which classical learning is seen as mere indusium for present ends, and the whole frame of debate is seen as unnecessarily complicated and exclusive of common sense and plain speech. By moving Hugh away from classical references, Holcroft suggests that they are inherently exclusive and prejudiced, for they say things that can easily be said other ways and thus appeal only to those with a certain education. Furthermore, especially when we recall Hugh's description of his own classical training, this view becomes an implicit critique of a whole system of education, one which, Holcroft implies, produces not thoughtful patriots and principled thinkers, but jingoistic hacks who work as spin doctors for the wealthy and powerful. What remains unclear is whether Holcroft thinks that it can be otherwise: Frank Henley is identified with Cato and Hugh Trevor's classical reading inflames his imagination to virtue, but we see little explicit praise for or redeployment of classical authors and heroes. With his eponymous heroes and his undisguised moralism, however, Holcroft reinscribes the same Plutarchian mode that we saw in Godwin; and given Hugh Trevor's ambivalence about the lessons of classical poetry, it is as if Holcroft writes his novels to clarify that ambivalence by, in effect, writing in the civic virtue and the decorum (here as plain speaking), while separating out the bellicosity and the drive to expand.

In this, Holcroft's position is similar to that of Mrs. Inchbald in *Nature and Art* (1796). As its title would suggest, the novel unfolds the contrasts between a series of dualisms: nature and art, body and soul, adversity and prosperity, literacy and illiteracy, self and other, and so on. Initially, the operative characters for these qualities are the brothers Henry and William, although the focus of the novel soon shifts to their respective sons. Education forms perhaps the most prominent distinction between the two brothers. Henry, who received no formal education, begins to prosper as a fiddler and returns home one day to find William "poring over the orations of Cicero."[45] William goes on to Oxford, with Henry's fiddle playing supporting his studies.

---

[45] Elizabeth Inchbald, *Nature and Art*, ed. Shawn L. Maurer (London: Pickering and Chatto, 1997), 6. Subsequent page references to this edition will be provided parenthetically in the text.

William's learning, however, serves only to lay the groundwork for a sycophantic and hypocritical life. He marries into a titled family and receives a bishopric, but, in contrast to Henry, dies unhappy and unloved. Inchbald not only questions the results of William's classical education, she also calls attention to frequent poor teaching: "Poor Hannah had learned to write as some youths learn Latin: so short a time had been allowed for the acquirement, and so little expert had been her master, that it took her generally a week to write a letter of ten lines, and a month to read one of twenty" (55). The reference is a casual one and seems initially to be mere decoration. It serves, however, to offer a pedagogical critique of classical education from a different direction. Holcroft condemns the successes of classical education through Coke Clifton, who uses his classical learning for style and affect, and Hugh Trevor, who uses his to dress up his hack work and engage in public discourse. Inchbald's comment, in contrast, points to the failures of classical education and suggests that if classical learning is meant to be a standard of erudition and an entry to the public sphere, then too many students are denied these benefits by poor instruction.[46]

Classical references in Holcroft and Inchbald suggest a sharply critical attitude to classical learning. Though Holcroft recognizes certain virtues in classical texts, the classics are coded as exclusive and impractical, contributing in no way to the general good and preventative of plain, direct speech. Nonetheless, Holcroft and Inchbald both deploy clearly and carefully developed characters who are meant to represent abstract virtues and failings. In this way, they continue to draw upon the kind of exemplarity, the Plutarchian mode, that Godwin cites as the chief virtue of classical authors and figures. This is not to suggest that Holcroft and Inchbald fail to ground their critiques and fall into the same system that they criticize. Rather, the reading of the novels themselves becomes an alternative kind of education, one that enacts the process they describe as their readers are forced to use their own reason and experience to assess the characters and actions depicted.

---

[46] Such a critique accords with historians of classical education such as M. L. Clarke who note the poor state of classical studies at Oxford and Cambridge in the later eighteenth century. See Clarke, *Classical Education in Britain, 1500–1900* (Cambridge: Cambridge University Press, 1959).

Emma Courtney, Caleb Williams, and other so-called "Jacobin" novels manifest a core set of values and beliefs. They can be characterized by their indignant sensibilities, their opposition to distinctions not founded in moral quality or virtue, their detestation of tyranny and oppression, and their hope for an improved future enabled by the triumph of reason over superstition and the status quo. Moreover, as Gary Kelly has suggested, the most distinctive feature of the Jacobin novel is its production of a form in which a belief in the doctrine of necessity—that character originates in external circumstance—produces a carefully thought integration of character and plot.[47] All of these novels focus on a small number of individuals, and we watch the process by which the central figures of each novel change as a result of the circumstances thrust upon them.

If the references to Rome, Roman history, and Roman texts in *Emma Courtney* initially seemed disjunctive, it is now possible to clarify their significance. Considered in the context of the eighteenth-century debate about the intellectual responsibility of the novel, *Emma Courtney* can be read as a novel about reading. As such, those features of Emma's reading—romances, classical texts, and Rousseau—to which the novel calls deliberate attention indicate both Hays's awareness of the debate surrounding the novel form and her response to it, and Emma's specific experience can be read, like that of Caleb Williams, with a more generalizable significance. Two features of Emma's early reading stand out: first, the voracious lack of control with which she reads contemporary romances, and second, her father's attempt to correct these reading habits with a solid dose of Plutarch and Roman history. In this way, the novel shows both Knox's great fear that frivolous romances will usurp the minds of young readers and his prescribed cure, a healthy dose of classical writing, in this case Plutarch. But Hays does not stop there. Emma's (illicit) reading of Rousseau completes her program and adds a third kind of reading—a novel written based upon a specific intellectual program. It is this third category with which the novel grapples most profoundly, for Rousseau becomes at once the most powerful influence on Emma and—because of the way that she suggests reading Rousseau gives free reign to her passion—her own explanation for her undoing.

---

[47] Kelly, *English Jacobin Novel*, 14.

But Emma Courtney is not silently undone by her passions, and the novel uses its thematization of reading to present its own text as a novel that deliberately considers eighteenth-century shifts in reading practices away from classical texts and toward domestic fiction. Hays, like her fellow Jacobin novelists, marks the shift in an effort to direct it. Her novel subsumes all three categories of Emma's literary experiences—romance, classics, and Rousseau—into a programmatic narrative that shows how the novel form can guide its readers to the critical and rational evaluation of texts, in other words, to a kind of interpretive virtue. Just as Gallagher characterizes Edgeworth as encoding the "right sort" of reading into her fiction, *Emma Courtney* thus performs its own solution to the failure of these other narratives to lead Emma to virtue, and like other Jacobin novels it attempts to bridge the contrast between the Roman and the *roman* by producing a novel of civic and secular virtue, one that uses a mode of exemplarity borrowed from ancient history to take advantage of a more accessible form in which to present a new and updated set of exemplars. To suggest that *Emma Courtney* thematizes reading is perfectly consistent with its location in an intellectual program built on ideas and a priori systems, a program that puts great emphasis on the possibility of achieving moral, social, and political change simply by changing the way people think.

The depiction of reading practices in the Jacobin novel engages strains of the eighteenth-century debate over the moral functions of the novel to perform a transformative critique of that debate in a fictional form. These novels not only criticize the negative results of classical learning but also refashion their more productive qualities in an effort to carve the process of novel reading as a new locus of virtue for their readers. Such a redeployment of classical virtues also suggests the importance of ancient histories, with their emphasis on civic virtue and individual exemplarity, for shaping the form and moral concerns of the novels of the 1790s. McKeon has argued that questions of truth—a central category of his analysis—become drastically reformulated when the ascendancy of Romanticism produces a separation of "history" and "literature."[48] My discussion of the Jacobin

---

[48] Michael McKeon, *The Origins of the English Novel 1600–1740* (Baltimore: Johns Hopkins University Press, 1987), 419.

novel, however, when read in the context Godwin's claims for the selectivity of fiction in "History and Romance," suggests that for one prolonged cultural moment that coincides with the initial stirrings of Romanticism, history and literature were far from separate. These novels all usurp the moral and pedagogical functions of a Plutarchian historical mode to redeploy its exemplarity for progressive causes. They all present an allegory of the historical process that precedes its more explicit and extended presentation by Walter Scott. Indeed, the way that these novels work with the civic lessons and moral fables of classical history make it somewhat unsurprising that Godwin, the great scion of the Jacobin novel, would later be mistaken for the anonymous author of *Waverley*.

Part II

Poetry

Chapter Three

A Roman Standard

Byron, Ancient Rome, and Literary Decline

This chapter evaluates the use of Roman precedent in Byron's understanding of the decline of literature and literary standards, the decline of ancient civilization, and the decline of the self. The first part considers Byron's unforgiving assessment of "Romanticism" and his defense of Pope and what we might call "Augustan poetics" in letters to Thomas Moore, John Murray, and others from 1817 to 1821. It focuses most closely on Byron's published contribution to the so-called Pope controversy, the 1821 *Letter to **** ******* [John Murray], the longest of a small number of prose pieces published by Byron in his lifetime. What is particularly germane to the purposes of this book about the *Letter to John Murray* is how Byron uses the transition from republic to empire to construct a model of literary decline, one which he then applies to contemporary poetic practice as part of an argument that the poets we call "Romantic" have taken a wrong turn. Byron's use of Roman precedents to revalue negatively the work of his contemporaries and the Romantic movement generally, I argue, shows Byron reaching back behind his dissatisfaction with Romantic poetics to invoke what is ultimately a Roman standard. The same emphasis on decline seen in Byron's advocacy of Pope also forms a dominant theme in *Childe Harold*, canto IV (1818), which was written during the years that Byron defended Pope. In canto IV, Byron uses the ruins of Rome to present a more intense expression of self and to imagine his own decline. A focus on Byron's engagement with classical Roman authors and the decline of the Roman republic, however, shows how Byron's sense of decline is more than mere self-mythologizing and represents rather the development of a particular post-Waterloo historical consciousness. Together, both sections of this chapter affirm the centrality of ancient Rome for Byron's sense of self, for his understanding of literary history and his place within it, and, finally, for what Kenneth Burke would call his attitude toward history.

ROME, THE DECLINE OF POETRY, AND THE *LETTER TO JOHN MURRAY*

The most prominent feature of Byron's conception of British poetry in both his private letters and his published remarks is the idea of decline. In a characteristic remark that typifies a position held throughout Byron's post-1816 letters, he wrote to Murray, "There never was such a *Set* as your ragamuffins—(I mean *not* yours only but everybody's) what with the Cockneys and the Lakers—and the *followers* of Scott and Moore and Byron—you are in the very uttermost decline and degradation of literature.—I can't think of it without all the remorse of a murderer."[1] With its emphasis on "decline and degradation," Byron's thinking about the state of British literature draws upon a prominent debate in eighteenth-century historiography as to whether cultural production moves through time in a process of progression or decline, a problem present in the work of classic historiographers from Hume and Gibbon to Rousseau, Condorcet, Volney, Kant, Schiller, and Hegel. In his discussion of the controlling narrative structures in the work of these figures, Greg Kucich points out that the key factor "for literary historians of both the eighteenth and the nineteenth centuries was the tendency in these narrative models to conflate lines of progress and decline as essential components of a single pattern of contrary motion."[2] Byron favors strongly the

---

[1] *Byron's Letters and Journals*, ed. Leslie Marchand (Cambridge, MA: Belknap, 1973–1982), 7:175. Hereafter abbreviated as *BLJ*.

[2] Greg Kucich, "Eternity and the Ruins of Time: Shelley and the Construction of Cultural History," in *Shelley: Poet and Legislator of the World*, ed. Betty T. Bennett and Stuart Curran (Baltimore: Johns Hopkins University Press, 1996), 19.

narrative structure of decline, and his position is shaped by the way that thoughts about antiquity and the vanished civilizations of Greece and Rome enforce interpretations of the present state of European society. Consider Byron's first extended comments on Pope in a letter to Murray of 15 September 1817 in which Byron suggests that

> with regard to poetry in general I am convinced the more I think of it—that he [Moore] and *all* of us—Scott—Southey—Wordsworth—Moore—Campbell—I—are all in the wrong—one as much as another—that we are upon a wrong revolutionary poetical system—or systems—not worth a damn in itself—& from which none but Rogers and Crabbe are free—and that the present & next generations will finally be of this opinion.—I am the more confirmed in this—by having lately gone over some of our Classics—particularly *Pope*—whom I tried in this way—I took Moore's poems and my own & some others—& went over them side by side with Pope's—and I was really astonished (I ought not to have been so) and mortified—at the ineffable distance in point of sense—harmony—effect—and even *Imagination* Passion—& *Invention*—between the little Queen Anne's Man—& us of the lower Empire—depend upon it [it] is all Horace then, and Claudian now amongst us—and if I had to begin again—I would model myself accordingly. (*BLJ*, 5:265)

This passage is striking for a number of reasons, not the least of which is Byron's wholesale dismissal of his contemporaries with the exception of Crabbe and Rogers. Furthermore, it shows what sounds, for Byron, like a rather systematic and meticulous process of comparison through which Pope gains concrete favor. Finally, and of the most relevance for my argument here, Byron's reference to a "wrong revolutionary poetical system" raises a number of questions, the more prominent of which concern the problem of historical situation: What is the state or "system" of contemporary poetry? To what extent can analogies carry between the fields of politics, history, and poetry? Can revolutions occur in the field of poetry comparable to the way they occur in politics, and do such revolutions represent progress or decline, or do they perhaps just repeat the past? What, for Byron, is the relationship between poetry and politics? Similarly, the reference to "our Classics" serves to narrow the field of poetry in general to British poetry specifically, a narrowing that becomes somewhat oxymoronic when we consider that often a key aspect of classicism is its transnational, cosmopolitan quality; to trade *the* classics for *our* classics is to encourage a distinctly national identity as opposed to a European one. Byron's reference to how he would "model" himself also raises more general questions about models and modeling, especially as these relate to the performance of identity and the understanding of historical change. Byron's acknowledgment that he would "model" himself differently alludes to the constructed quality of Byron's identity and poetic persona. Recent accounts of such modeling, most prominently those of Peter Manning and Jerome Christensen, have stressed the relationship between this performed, constructed quality of Byron's identity—its modeling—in relation to the emergence of a market economy and commercial society. Manning, for example, emphasizes that in Byron, "the self acquires its image—not its essence—by telling tales that negotiate or, to use a more Byronic term, navigate impersonal structures," by which he refers to changing structures of publication and the professionalization of authorship.[3] Like Manning and Christensen, I see questions of personal identity and historical situation as related, but one response to commercial modernity was a hearkening back to antiquity, and thus questions of identity may be performed in relation to changing conditions of commerce, but through a response to the remnants of vanished civilizations. The second part of this chapter engages further with this argument in connection with the relationship between commerce, identity, and Roman ruins in *Childe Harold* canto IV. For now, however, I will evaluate how Byron's comments here about modeling relate to historical change: what historical models does one use to make historically informed judgments of the present?

The reference to "the lower Empire" and the transition from Horace to Claudian suggests a tentative response to these questions. It places Byron's perceived change of poetical systems in explicitly Roman terms, and shows how Rome serves as the model for his understanding of literary decline. More specifically, the reference links Pope with Horace, and by extension, the epitome of

---

[3] See Peter Manning, "The Nameless Broken Dandy and the Structure of Authorship," in *Reading Romantics: Texts and Contexts* (New York: Oxford University Press, 1994), 145–162, quoted passage from 148.

the Latin poetic tradition and the height of imperial power, whereas Byron and his contemporaries are aligned with Claudian, often called the last poet of Rome. Labeled by Gibbon as "a poet worthy to celebrate the actions of heroes,"[4] Claudian was best known for his panegyrics of the Roman general Stilicho and of Honorius, the weak son of Theodosius I, the last sole emperor of Rome. In this way, Byron's characterization of a literary transition conveys a political claim as well: if it is "all Claudian now amongst us," then the implication is that his contemporaries may be accomplished poets, but they are not nearly as good as their precursors, and, worse, they are doomed to be linked to a corrupt imperial regime in its dying days. Indeed, as this comment implies and as Jane Stabler has recently argued, Byron converted the cause of literary taste into the cause of political reform; he sees his defense of Pope in explicitly political terms, envisioning his crusade to shape popular taste as being as worthy as Hobhouse's devotion to the cause of political reform.[5]

The reference to "us of the lower Empire" resonates with a similar phrase in *Don Juan*. This occurs in canto XI, after Juan arrives in England, where, "admitted as an aspirant to all the coteries," he sees "the eighty 'greatest living poets'" (11.54). The scare quotes deride such classifications; indeed, Byron is just as scornful when he compares the contest and rivalry among poets to that between boxers (champions "in the fisty ring") and also to political monarchs, with each poet king for a time of "foolscap subjects." The stanzas that follow then stretch this comparison of literary and political sway as Byron famously describes himself as "the grand Napoleon of the realms of rhyme," and mentions Southey, Scott, Moore, Campbell, and Coleridge as contenders, while casting mocking dismay on such lesser writers—"pretenders"—as George Croly, Barry Cornwall (Bryan Waller Procter), Walter Savage Landor, and Keats. It is a virtuoso performance, and the passage slides lithely across references to

---

[4] Edward Gibbon, *The History of the Decline and Fall of the Roman Empire*, ed. David Womersley (London: Allen Lane, 1994), 2:106.
[5] Jane Stabler, *Byron, Poetics, and History* (Cambridge, Cambridge University Press, 2002), 84–105.

the Napoleonic Wars, *Henry IV Part II*, and the second satire of the second book of Horace as it plays with references to episodes described in the work of these pretenders before finally dismissing all analogies to boxing, monarchic rule, and contemporary post-Napoleonic imperial politics as inappropriate, for unquestioned rule in the realm of verse has become impossible.

Ultimately, a Roman analogy clarifies Byron's description of the situation. His broad survey concludes with the claim that the chances of these men to rule alone is low, for the number of contenders for literary sway are

> ... too numerous, like the thirty
>   Mock tyrants when Rome's annals waxed but dirty.
>
> This is the literary lower empire,
>   Where the Praetorian bands take up the matter,
>
> A "dreadful trade" like his who "gathers samphire,"
>   The insolent soldiery to soothe and flatter
>
> With the same feelings as you'd coax a vampire.
>   Now were I once at home and in good satire,
>
> I'd try conclusions with those Janizaires
>   And show them what an intellectual war is. (11. 61–62)

After the grand buildup of rulers and pretenders to the poetical throne, the reference to the thirty tyrants and the "literary lower empire" serves to deflate all claimants, and the throne itself comes to be seen as tarnished, a tawdry thing for sale in a corrupt polis.[6] The passage obviously dovetails nicely with Byron's earlier comments to Murray about the passage from Horace to Claudian. It also, of course, demands to be read in connection with *Don Juan*'s sustained engagement with contemporary literary politics, and its persistent efforts to link the apostasies of the Lake poets, especially Southey, with the

---

[6] The "thirty tyrants" is a reference to the "Tyranni Triginta," a group of pretenders to the throne under the legitimate emperor Gallienus (co-ruler with his father, Valerian, from 253 to 260 CE and sole ruler from 260 to 268 CE), as described in the *Historia Augusta*. See *Scriptores Historiae Augustae*, Vol. 3, Loeb Classical Library, trans. David Magie (Cambridge: Harvard University Press, 1932), 64–151.

corrupt government epitomized by Castlereagh. This begins in the (suppressed) dedication and continues through such well-known moments as the poetical commandments in canto I and the "sad trimmer" poet in canto III. What distinguishes this passage, however, is its concern with the entire field of literary production, here conceived deliberately and self-consciously as a field, as the *Macbeth*-like passage of ten-thousand living authors of which perhaps eighty vie for supremacy. Byron returns to Wordsworth, Coleridge, and Southey in stanza 59, but he does not target them, and their mention here serves only to place them in the broader field that also includes such now-forgotten figures as George Croly and Barry Cornwall. Byron does not use the word "decline," but Chandler notes the work's preoccupation with "decline and decay"[7] in his discussion of *Don Juan*, and these stanzas provide a perfect example. They show once again, and with distinct clarity, how the attempt to think comparatively through the field of contemporary poetry characterizes it as in a late stage of decline, and how this emphasis on decline inevitably also elicits the need to understand the literary field through references to Rome, here Roman imperial history even more than Roman literary history. For Byron, the contemporary literary field can be characterized only through the idea of decline, and when he seeks to characterize or understand this decline, the analogy is inevitably Roman.

Still, there is a sense in which this was not always the case, and Byron's contenders for the literary throne of British poets recall an earlier effort to map the field of contemporary poetry, the "triangular 'Gradus ad Parnassum!'"[8] that Byron drew in his diary in 1813. There, on the 24th of November, after noting Scott's unfortunate monetary circumstances, he again uses the field of politics to characterize the field of poetry when he calls Scott "undoubtedly the Monarch of Parnassus" and then continues to sketch the rest of the field in the following diagram:

---

[7] Chandler, *England in 1819*, 381.
[8] This phrase means literally "steps to Parnassus," with Parnassus referring to the mountain that was, in Greek mythology, the home to the Muses.

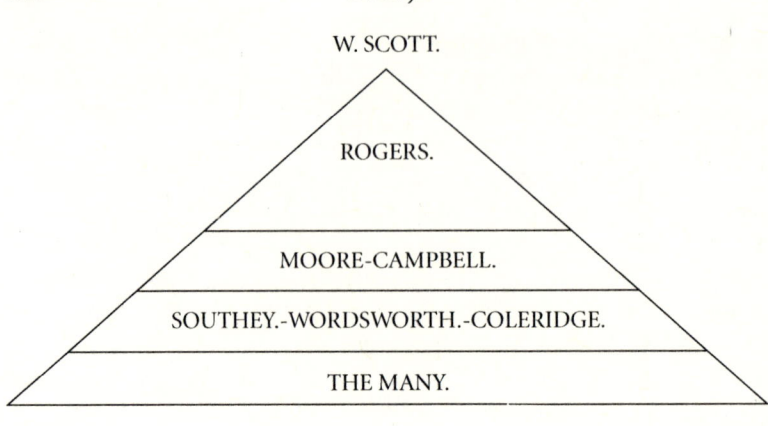

(*BLJ*, 3:220)

Now, there is nothing unusual in Byron's describing his contemporaries with reference to Parnassus, and it might even be considered a cliché. A comparison of his comments here to his later characterization of the same field, however, reveals that his critical and less dismissive description builds upon a Greek concept of the poetic field (and Byron here even refers to "the many" in his prose as the οι πολλοι [hoi polloi, or "the people"]), and makes no mention of Rome. The use of Rome comes later. A comparison of this earlier, Greek-inflected model of Parnassus with Byron's later use of Rome suggests what I have called a differentiated classicism. Byron clearly relies for his modeling on what we would understand as classical antiquity or the classical tradition, but within these larger formations there is clearly a sense of differentiation between Rome and Greece, and we might further infer that certain aspects of Greece and Rome vary in their relevance to the contemporary situation. For example, as Byron's enthusiasm for contemporary poetry fades—as he comes to see it as "the very uttermost decline and degradation" in his comments to Murray—Rome becomes a more prominent point of reference and the precedent and model for how Byron understands decline, both literary and imperial.

This is clear in Byron's 15 September 1817 letter to Murray and in the letters that Byron wrote defending Pope starting in 1817, but it is clearest in Byron's more formal assessment of Pope in his published 1821 *Letter to* **** ****** [John Murray]. Byron's comments here are part of a mounting argument over the place of Pope in contemporary poetry, a controversy that resulted in more than a dozen publications between 1819 and 1826. The controversy centers on Bowles's *The Works of Alexander Pope, Esq. in Verse and Prose* (1806, 10 vols.), of which the first volume savaged Pope's moral character while the "Concluding Observations" asserted what Bowles saw as the invariable principles of poetry. "I presume it will be readily granted," Bowles wrote,

that "all images drawn from what is beautiful or sublime in the works of NATURE, are more beautiful and sublime than any images drawn from ART;" and that they are therefore, *per se*, more poetical.

In like manner, those *Passions* of the human heart, which belong to Nature in general, are, *per se*, more adapted to the *higher species* of Poetry, than those which are derived from *incidental* and *transient* MANNERS.[9]

By this reasoning, Pope was seen to be the first poet among "the polished literature of a polished aera," but not one of the first poets overall. When years later Thomas Campbell disagreed vehemently with these claims in his introductory essay to his *Specimens of the British Poets* (1819), Bowles responded by elaborating the claims made in his "Concluding Observations" in a separately published volume, *The Invariable Principles of Poetry* (1819). This set off a flurry of responses from Isaac D'Israeli, Oliver Gilchrist, Byron, and others.[10] The dispute is notable for the intensity and vehemence of its contributors and for the way that disagreements over Pope's work quickly degenerate into literary mudslinging over Pope's moral character and that of his detractors and defenders. Despite this, it is also a serious and sustained dispute over the shaping of a national canon.

James Chandler suggests that this dispute over Pope "is arguably the canonical canon controversy in English literary history, the one associated with that nation's major revolution in poetry and taste."[11] Chandler argues that the controversy can be traced back to the views

---

[9] Quoted by Andrew Nicholson, in Lord Byron, *The Complete Miscellaneous Prose* (Oxford: Clarendon Press, 1991), 400–401. Hereafter abbreviated *CMP*.

[10] For an excellent, concise overview of the controversy, see *CMP*, 399–408; for a chronological list of publications, see 408–410.

[11] James Chandler, "The Pope Controversy: Romantic Poetics and the English Canon," *Critical Inquiry* 10 (1984): 482.

on Pope expressed by Joseph and Thomas Warton's *An Essay on the Genius and Writings of Pope* (1756), and that even in its hottest moments from 1819 to 1826, it is already replaying earlier arguments. Based on this analysis, Chandler can claim that Pope is not rejected because of the sudden domination of a new "Romantic" aesthetic, but that this Romantic aesthetic itself is constituted by the critical rejection of Pope: that the two developments are mutually generative.[12] Expanding this argument along similar lines, Robert Griffin maintains that the opposition to Pope is "constitutive of Romantic identity," but that the quarrel with Pope begins in the mid-eighteenth century, well before the traditional start of the Romantic period.[13] Given the nature of his argument, Griffin attends only occasionally to the Pope controversy because he is more concerned to show that its battle lines are drawn long before 1819. While Chandler's argument concludes with a reading of Byron's *Letter to Murray*, Griffin hardly mentions Byron's essay, though he does make frequent reference to Byron's comments on Pope. It thus seems fair to say, with Andrew Nicholson, that Byron's contribution to the Pope controversy "has received scanter critical attention than it deserves."[14]

Byron first contemplated an answer to Bowles in a letter to Murray of 4 November 1820,[15] but not until February 1821, while writing *Sardanapalus*, did the impulse revive. In his Ravenna journal, Byron

---

[12] In a further component of his argument, Chandler uses the dispute to show how his own historicist approach to the question of canon is not an objective, twentieth-century development, but is itself a product of the historicist attitude played out and developed in the Pope controversy. See Chandler, "The Pope Controversy," 481–509.

[13] Robert J. Griffin, *Wordsworth's Pope: A Study in Literary Historiography* (Cambridge: Cambridge University Press, 1995), 3.

[14] *CMP*, 408. One notable recent exception is Andrew Franta, who argues that "Byron's stake in the debate has to do with the difference between the form of literary authority that Pope represents and that which is epitomized for Byron in the poetic judgments being rendered by representatives of the new schools." The problem for Byron, as Franta represents it, is that because public opinion is expressed as a group, or more accurately a school, the schools "have developed a strategy that makes it possible for Wordsworth's influence to extend far beyond his readership." By association with the Lake School, Wordsworth gains for his views "a public standing unwarranted by his poetic success (or, more precisely, the lack thereof)." See Franta, *Romanticism and the Rise of the Mass Public* (Cambridge: Cambridge University Press, 2007), 35–45; quoted passages from 40, 42, and 43.

[15] "Mr. Bowles shall be answered," LB to JM, 4 November 1820, *BLJ*, 7:217.

records reading some of the essays in the dispute, and he then adds, "Perceive that my name has been lugged into the controversy, but have not time to state what I know of the subject. On some 'piping day of peace' it is probable that I may resume it" (*BLJ*, 8:43). Despite Byron's involvement with the Carbonari and their efforts to free Italy from the Austrian yoke, that day would come sooner rather than later. Byron began writing the letter on 7 February, completed it on 10 February, and sent it to Murray on 12 February. Byron's contribution to the Pope controversy establishes a comparison of ancient and contemporary literary history to locate the greatness of British poetry in Milton, Dryden, and Pope; he suggests that the present age represents not a progressive development but a frightening decline. Specifically, Byron denigrates the emphasis on imagination and invention, promotes a relativistic conception of poetic merit, and suggests that by diminishing the greatness of Pope, his contemporaries are simply trying to rescue their own reputations because "they are also fighting for Life—for if he maintains his station—they will reach their own—by falling" (*CMP*, 148).[16]

Although the argument is by no means straightforward, it is widely seen to have turned attention away from scurrilous quibbles over Pope's personal life and returned the focus of the debate to Pope's poetry. It is also considered an explicit statement of Byron's faithful adherence to the "classical tradition." Nicholson asserts "the singular status the letter holds in Romantic literature. For however tenuous its argument may have appeared to the contemporary reader, and however eccentric or unorthodox its convictions, it documents a long-held and firm belief in the sovereignty of the classical tradition of literature."[17] Chandler notes the link between the construction of literary history and the national character. He suggests that Pope is associated with France and French tastes in a manner that helps to

---

[16] Ironically, this echoes Moore's comments on Byron's rankings in which he makes a similar accusation of Byron. As Manning notes, "Moore shrewdly saw this deprecation as a tactic to confirm his own eminence: 'being quite sure of his own hold upon fame he contrives to loosen that of all his contemporaries, in order that they may fall away entirely from his side, and leave him unencumbered, even by their floundering'"(Manning, "Nameless Broken Dandy," 147, quoting Moore's journal).

[17] *CMP*, 408.

consolidate a national literature and that only the cosmopolitan Byron was "sufficiently alienated from contemporary English life to recognize the nationalistic premises of its literary arguments."[18] Byron responded by urging "a classical canon that cuts across national boundaries and rises above national interests,"[19] Chandler writes—the important difference from Bowles here being that Byron's canon cannot be based on "invariable principles."

I agree with Nicholson and Chandler that Byron's contribution to the Pope controversy is grounded in the classical tradition and an international perspective on the classical canon. What this emphasis on "the classics" as a category overlooks, however, is the distinctly Roman dimension of Byron's classicism, and, more broadly, Byron's differentiated classicism, his understanding of Greece and Rome as distinct traditions within these larger formations. This is not to suggest that Greece is absent, but rather that the literary and political examples that structure Byron's thinking about the state of contemporary British poetry are firmly Roman. Specifically, Byron consistently uses the field of politics to characterize the field of poetry. It is, in other words, a model of Roman literary history as related to the political fortunes of the Roman republic's transition to the Roman empire that furnishes Byron with his most powerful example of literary decline, and the idea of decline, in turn, is crucial to understanding both his contribution to the Pope controversy and his assessment of the contemporary state of English poetry. For this reason, and because the historicization of taste is such an important point of contention within the dispute, we should consider how Roman texts and the concept of Roman literary history work in the constitution of Byron's argument.

Although Byron does not rely exclusively on Roman examples, they recur throughout his essay and serve as a reminder not only of the classical texts and references that are at stake in the conflict, but also of an entire set of standards, values, and judgments about poetry that conceives of British poetry in reference to Greek and Roman precursors. Such classical examples also offer a telling insight into Byron's

---

[18] Chandler, "The Pope Controversy," 502.
[19] Ibid., 503.

position in the conflict, for an interpretation of classical literary history underlies Byron's reaction to contemporary aesthetic trends, and he continually uses Rome both as an example of decline and as a frame for his own assessment of contemporary standards and possibilities—as indicated by his initial comments to Murray about Pope in the September 1817 letter.

Byron objects most vehemently to Bowles's claim that poetry has invariable principles, and his response is a profound assertion of historical and cultural relativism and of the inevitable changes in literary taste:

> Mr. Bowles's title of "*invariable* principles of poetry," is, perhaps, the most arrogant ever prefixed to a volume. So far are the principles of poetry from being "*invariable*," that they never were nor will be settled. These "principles" mean nothing more than the predilections of a particular age; and every age has its own, and a different from its predecessor. It is now Homer, and now Virgil; once Dryden, and since Walter Scott; now Corneille, and now Racine; now Crebillon, now Voltaire. The Homerists and Virgilians in France disputed for half a century. Not fifty years ago the Italians neglected Dante— Bettinelli reproved Monte for reading "that barbarian;" at present they adore him. Shakespeare and Milton have had their rise, and they will have their decline. Already they have more than once fluctuated, as must be the case with all the dramatists and poets of a living language. This does not depend upon their merits, but upon the ordinary vicissitudes of human opinions. Schlegel and Madame de Stael have endeavored also to reduce poetry to *two* systems, classical and romantic. The effect is only beginning. (*CMP*, 142n)

The passage shows Byron's absolute rejection of the possibility of objective literary judgment. The principles of poetry can never be settled because they can never be anything more than "the predilections of a particular age." Byron's specific vision is one that recognizes culturally contingent judgments of value and merit, but also one that, unlike the conjectural history of the Scottish Enlightenment, imposes no developmental scheme. It is a vision neither of progress nor decline, but simply of mutability based on the logic of a particular age: "now Homer, and now Virgil." Value judgments change because of the "ordinary vicissitudes of human opinions"(*CMP*, 142), and such alternation "does not depend upon their merits." What the "ordinary vicissitudes of human opinion" leaves unexplained, of course, is why the changes occur: why do they begin when they do, how do we mark the transition from one age to the next? Is the literary canon a litmus test for broader cultural and political shifts?

There is a tension inherent in Byron's rhetoric, for the suggestion that shifts of taste are unrelated to merit—as opposed to a move that would question the possibility of determining merit because of its contextual basis—implies a concept of objective merit sitting behind Byron's pronouncements. It is unsurprising, then, when Byron rejects Bowles's conception of specific orders of poetry (genres) in favor of what he terms more generally "Ethical poetry." This he further describes as "Didactic poetry...whose object is to make men better" (*CMP*, 143). Didactic poetry is, of course, a classical tradition, running from Hesiod to Lucretius and Virgil and beyond. And, as support for his assertion of the superiority of didactic over epic, Byron cites Virgil: "The Georgics are indisputably—and I believe *undisputedly* even—a finer poem than the Aeneid.—Virgil knew this—he did not order *them* to be burnt" (*CMP*, 143). Regardless of the accuracy of this judgment, the point is that even as Byron denies a hierarchy of poetical orders, he is defending classical categories of poetry with classical examples. Moreover, he explicitly denigrates Romantic categories as ephemeral fads: "It is the fashion of the day to lay great stress upon what they call 'Imagination' and 'Invention' the two commonest of qualities—an Irish peasant with a little whiskey in his head will imagine and invent more than would furnish forth a modern poem" (*CMP*, 143–144). In contrast to this, Byron cites Lucretius, whose poem was unfortunately ruined by his ethics, and Pope, whose poetry was not. Though never explicitly stated, the concept of imitation serves as a backdrop for Byron's claims—much as it did with Bowles. When Byron scorns imagination and invention as the qualities of a drunk Irish peasant, he devalues originality as a "common" quality, and thus implies that imitation is not in any way a demerit.[20] Often chided for his vanity, Byron here holds the mirror to Bowles's lamp.

---

[20] Elsewhere, in one of the addenda to the letter that was not published with the original, Byron declares "when a man talks of his *System*—it is like a woman's talking of her *Virtue*—I let them talk on" (*CMP*, 156). Taken together with his remarks about the drunken Irish peasant, these comments suggest anxieties about both effeminization and professionalization and they thus work similarly to the Botherby stanzas of *Beppo* (74–76). In connection with these stanzas, Peter Manning argues that Byron's

Such use of classical authors in conjunction with Pope offers a hint as to what underwrites Byron's own concepts of poetic merit. For Byron, fluctuations of taste "must be the case with all the dramatists and poets of a living language" (*CMP*, 142n). This implies the alternative of a dead language, and classical literature provides Byron with a system of value and with a concept of poetic permanence. Consider the penultimate paragraph of the letter (the one prior to the postscriptum and addenda—Byron was clearly no less inclined to augment his prose as his poetry). Here, Byron asks, what if Britain were to disappear, leaving only the English language behind to be studied on foreign shores:

> If your literature should become the learning of Mankind, divested of party cabals—temporary fashions—and national pride and prejudice—an Englishman anxious that the Posterity of Strangers should know that there had been such thing as a British Epic and Tragedy—might wish for the preservation of Shakespeare and Milton—but the surviving World would snatch Pope from the Wreck—and let the rest sink with the People.—He is the moral poet of all Civilization—and as such let us hope that he will one day be the National poet of Mankind. (*CMP*, 150–151)

As this statement suggests, a dead language, ironically, becomes permanent, a thing to be studied by future generations. In its very deadness, such a language becomes a transnational standard: "the learning of Mankind divested of party cabals—temporary fashions—and national pride and prejudice." Such a fantasy of decline is striking, for it shows Byron thinking of England as Greece and Rome and asking what should remain; poetic fame, he suggests, is easy to come by, but whether that fame is in any way connected to value, merit, or permanence is another question entirely. Faced with the prospect of decline, Byron reaches for value in a canon of ancients. The point, then, is that the fantasy of decline provokes the need for a standard by which an author can be measured against his contemporaries, and for Byron, that standard is always classical.

---

attacks on Botherby and the bluestockings affirm Byron's "membership in the world from which he had parted; at the same time, dismissing Botherby and the bluestockings, Byron proclaims his masculine independence and denies his implication in the motives that drive professional authors." See Manning, "Nameless Broken Dandy," 151–153; quoted lines come from 153.

It should now be clear how thinking about the classics shapes both Bowles's position and Byron's response to it. Bowles relies for his claims on an Aristotelian concept of poetic orders and rules of composition to set up an *a priori* system of judgment that, in a curious twist, touts a new series of poetic and aesthetic values explicitly geared against Pope's neoclassicism. Byron, however, makes an argument against a hierarchy of poetic genres and, in his emphasis on execution, against any *a priori* rules of judgment. But he does embrace the ancient tradition of didactic poetry—or his version thereof—in making an argument for ethical poetry. But again, while this tradition begins in Greece and continues in Rome, Byron refers most commonly to Roman authors, and it is mainly Roman authors that shape Byron's concept of poetic value. What we saw initially in Byron's reference to the "literary lower empire" in *Don Juan* canto IX we see also in the *Letter to Murray*, where the shadow of Rome underwrites Byron's move away from the question of who the best contemporary poets are, and who best represents what period of British poetry, to a much more long-term concern with those poets who would best represent British poetry when Britain has ceased to be and the English language has died with it. In this way, Byron's input into a contest over the formation of a British canon is always already anticipated by the existence of a Roman canon. The example of Roman decline, and his interpretation of how the best classical texts represent classical values directs him to an evaluation of what matters in British poetry.

But to say that Byron grounds his position on the British canon in an understanding of how Roman texts reflect ancient values is not to say that Byron's position is obvious or uncomplicated. When Byron argues for didactic, ethical poetry, he is claiming a public role for poetry, asserting its potential to educate and inform its audience, and his conception of that public role comes from his interpretation of both ancient poetry—especially the Roman poets Virgil and Lucretius—and his interpretation of the way that Pope, through satire, adapted classical values for a renewed public role. Once again, imitation is crucial here, for satire, perhaps the most public of genres, relies upon imitation—both of generic precedent but also of content and form—for its success. Satire is a genre of topicality and historicity, but one that is constantly updated to fit new social circumstances. As such, Byronic satire, and satire in the mode conceived by Byron, requires an acute understanding of both ancient history and the context of ancient satire which can then be amended and adapted to fit contemporary concerns. In contrast, Bowles and his Romantic contemporaries place a premium not on the poetic intellect remolding ancient examples for contemporary use, but on individual experience, on the direct and unmediated expression of feeling. And so this public role for poetry, this potential for the poet to educate a population in a particular way that is so crucial to the premise of satire, is what Byron sees Bowles and the Romantics as threatening.

It is a threat from which he does not excuse himself or his own earlier poetry. Byron's *Letter to Murray* represents a significant statement of his critical principles and of the value that he places on an internally differentiated classicism in 1821. It echoes and confirms the kind of pronouncements that occur regularly, though not in any developed fashion, in his letters from 1817 forward. Poetry can decline. And Byron's understanding of this, the way he presents it as a fact, as a challenge to public taste, can only be understood when we recognize the degree to which his position relies on his sense of the classical tradition and of the Roman example within it.

CHILDE HAROLD AND THE RUINS OF ROME

Even the most cursory glance at Byron's first poetic success, "English Bards and Scotch Reviewers" (1809), suggests that the concerns Byron expresses so vehemently in reference to the Pope controversy were not new in his later years. Begun in October 1807, completed in September 1808, but continually revised up to 1812, the poem produces a sharp critique of contemporary letters and morals in an angry Juvenalian tone and trades upon ancient themes of a "degenerate" (103) and "diseased" present. Although, as Jerome McGann explains in his textual commentary, the poem began in the aloof and unimpassioned tone of Horatian satire, it became, after Henry Brougham's attack on

Hours of Idleness, increasingly rancorous until it was by its second edition a loose imitation of Juvenal's first satire.[21]

In the poem, Byron surveys a contemporary cultural scene in which he sees Vice and Folly, Knaves and Fools dominant over all. Although he declares that his purpose is to encourage reform, he modestly suggests that he does not own "the arrows of satiric song" (38) but acts merely until one with "A keener weapon, and a mightier hand" (40) comes forward. Byron establishes a connection between the current lapse of poetry and social decline generally, and he believes that poetry, a "genuine Bard," can drive away this pestilence and cure the degradation that he describes. In this sense, poetry for Byron must be public poetry—it must address and attempt to remedy national ills, and it must work to benefit the "public weal." It aspires to efficacy. For this cause, the examples of Milton, Dryden, and Pope, to whom Byron refers in line 187, are his allies, whereas the current crop of poets, aside from a few, represent an example to be avoided. The rhetorical structure of the poem—as with so much ancient verse in this genre—depicts a better age of poetry degraded by the lesser efforts of the present. Byron hopes that by concentrated effort, and the stirring of a genuine bard, past greatness can be restored: "Restore the Muse's violated laws" (892). Such emphasis on restoration is even more particular for Byron because he places upon it a specific and nationally focused emphasis by underlining the connection between political freedom and poetic power. As Britain is "first in freedom," so must she be "dearest to the Muse" (996). We see here in an earlier form the same conflation of literary taste and political reform that critics note in Byron's later efforts to revive Pope's reputation. Byron's claim that Britain is "dearest to the Muse," however, smacks of the kind of nationalism that James Chandler aligns with Pope's enemies in the Pope controversy.[22] Britain is a great name of which a bard must be worthy, and Byron insists upon this with reference to classical empires past:

---

[21] "Most satirists," argue Connery and Combe, "*claim* one purpose for satire, that of high minded and usually socially oriented moral and intellectual reform; however they *engage* in something quite different, namely, mercilessly savage attack on some person or thing that, frequently for private reasons, displeases them" (*Theorizing Satire: Essays in Literary Criticism*, ed. Brian Connery and Kirk Combe, [New York: St. Martin's Press, 1995], 5). Byron would thus appear to be a classic case in point.

[22] See Chandler, "The Pope Controversy."

> What Athens was in science, Rome in power
> What Tyre appeared in her meridian hour,
>   'Tis thine at once, fair Albion!

Greece is here revered for her achievements in knowledge, Rome for her politics, and Carthage for her naval might. In contemporary Europe, Britain combines the virtues of all three, but she must be careful nonetheless, for

> Rome decayed, and Athens strewed the plain,
> And Tyre's proud piers lie shattered in the main;
> Like thee thy strength may sink in ruin hurled,
> And Britain fall, the bulwark of the World. (1003–1006)

With these lines, antiquity assumes a more complex role as Byron enlists the example of ancient fallen empires as rhetorical muscle for poetic reform. Rome works structurally as a formal poetic model through its tradition of satirical literature, and historically, as one of three examples of decline. On close inspection, there is a felt tension between the roles, for the initial grounds of the analogy would seem to be that Greece is to knowledge what Rome is to politics. But if we associate knowledge and poetry in any way, then the heavy reliance on Roman satirical models suggests that Rome's contribution to knowledge was not inconsiderable, and the focus on Roman politics unfairly excludes her contribution to the arts. One way to rationalize this would be to suggest that knowledge originates with Greece, and, though it spreads to Rome, the fascination that wisdom and learning had for the Romans was grounded in Greek precedents: Virgil was the imitator of Homer. This is the sort of logic that, as we will see in the next chapter, marks Shelley's comparison of Rome and Greece in the *Defence*. But in Byron's case this seems only a partial retort for, as will become clear, the analogy further changes shape when Byron returns to Rome in *Childe Harold* canto iv.

If the ruined empires of Athens, Carthage, and Rome are meant to function opportunistically as exemplary warnings in "English Bards," by the time Byron returns to more prolonged thinking about Rome and its fate, in *Childe Harold* canto iv, he is much less optimistic about the possibility of learning from fallen empires past. The poem itself is an extended meditation on ruin, decay, and decline as Byron returns to Italy, the land described in canto iii as "the throne and grave of empires" (canto III, stanza 110). *Childe Harold* is a poem defined by its observing consciousness, a self set in contrast to the world outside it, consolidating itself by reflecting on what the eye confronts in a somewhat meandering, sometimes determined, and sometimes associative way. In this sense, one might call this a quintessentially Romantic poem, whose mood alternates between despair and a small whisper of hope. The Byronic persona takes refuge from the opposition between self and world in the moment of solitude in nature:

> There is a pleasure in the pathless woods,
> There is a rapture on the lonely shore,
> There is a society, where none intrudes,
> By the deep Sea, and music in its roar:
> I love not Man the less, but Nature more,
> From these our interviews, in which I steal
> From all I may be, or have been before,
> To mingle with the Universe, and feel
> What I can ne'er express, yet can not all conceal. (stanza 178)

In this most Wordsworthian of passages, Nature restores, providing pleasure, rapture, music, and, ultimately, a kind of sublime transcendence, a wholeness and a "mingl[ing] with the universe," a feeling unconcealable but beyond language. This situation contains all the qualities—imagination, nature, the self—that have traditionally been defined as Romantic, but alongside these qualities, the poem is also steeped in historical referentiality and filled with the struggle to take meaning from the events and locales of the past. In this sense, if the poem is quintessentially Romantic, it is also quintessentially "Rome-antic," and the relationship is far from accidental. Byron earlier described Italy as the land where

> The fount at which the panting mind assuages
> Her thirst for knowledge, quaffing there her fill,
> Flows from the eternal source of Roman's imperial hill.
> (*Childe Harold*, canto III, stanza 110)

Byron's connection in "English Bards" of Greece with knowledge and Rome with politics has slipped, and Rome now assumes the mantle of knowledge. But if Italy is the land of thought, it is also the land filled with the detritus and flotsam of lost and decayed civilizations. This contrast between Italy as a land of ruin and a land of thought echoes the contrasts of a poem engrossed in historical referentiality and an effort to make meaning for the self not through self-reference, but through historical example. In other words, *Childe Harold*, canto IV is a poem that generates its drama from the juxtaposition of such obsessively Romantic themes as reflection, the powers of mind, the nature and function of the imagination, the experience of personal suffering, and the weight of existence with other "Rome-antic" themes like the relics and ruins of classical civilization and the inevitability of decay. Such juxtaposition produces a burdensome series of questions about the meaning of individual human life, the significance of the past, permanence and impermanence, variability and invariability, and the way that value is determined within a context of perishability.[23]

As it meanders from Venice to Rome and from Rome to Florence before returning to Rome, the poem's tentative response to these anxieties is to place faith in the word and writing more generally—chimerically, perhaps—as that which can serve as a standard of value

---

[23] To suggest that *Childe Harold* canto IV generates its drama from the juxtaposition of what I am calling Romantic and Rome-antic themes as Byron's narrator attempts to carve a place for the self might be read as a way of calling attention to the performed and improvised qualities of Byron's persona, a feature that a number of recent studies have sought to explain in relation to commercial markets. My analysis of the relationship between Byron's self-dramatization and his backward-looking encounter with Roman civilization and ruins, with its emphasis on a self made insecure by the confrontation with the perishability signified by the ruins of antique civilization, might seem here like a counterpoint to these accounts. I want, however, to suggest the possibility of their compatibility and thus to emphasize how a focus on antiquity can contribute to an understanding of the very modernity to which it is often seen as antithetical. Central here are questions of value, exchange, and credit. If conditions of the marketplace—whether the professionalization and structure of production addressed by Manning or the engagement with what Christensen describes more broadly as commercial society and political economy—shape Byron's poetic endeavors, then these endeavors must be understood in relationship to the complacency of literature in an economy dominated by getting and spending, one in which commodities such as literary production have value based on what they can be exchanged for. In Christensen's account, what he calls "Byronism" takes advantage of this system, culminating in *Childe Harold* canto IV, whereas *Don Juan* resists the system through "a strong, ethical challenge to the murmurous complacencies of commercial society" (Christensen, *Lord Byron's Strength: Romantic Writing and Commercial Society* [Baltimore: Johns Hopkins University Press, 1993], xx). But the dangers of commercial society and the marketplace, the traumas of credit with its correspondent questions of credibility (*Crede Byron*), the possibilities of contingency and cataclysm are all issues raised by the symbolic power of Rome's ruins in *Childe Harold* canto IV.

in contexts of perishability and contingency and thus preserve, however imperfectly, the ultimately unpreservable past. Initially, the poem establishes the longevity of writing through its contrast with the ephemerality of historical figures like politicians, statesmen, and generals, culminating with Napoleon. The poem thus turns its emphasis from the actors in historical dramas to the observers and recorders of that action. The appearance and significance of Lake Thrasimene, where Hannibal defeated the Roman legions in the Punic Wars, has changed: "Far other scene is Thrasimene now" (stanza 65)—but if the scene still has meaning, it is because the memory of the battle has been preserved by Livy. Similarly, the glories of the falls of Terni and Soracte are preserved by Horatian lyrics. Looking at Rome, Byron longs for the great authors of Roman antiquity:

> Alas, for Tully's voice, and Virgil's lay,
> And Livy's pictur'd page!—but these shall be
> Her resurrection; all beside—decay. (stanza 82)

In all of these instances, Rome's loss is lamented, but the civilization remains preserved on the page, and through the knowledge produced and information imparted by the page, Rome is resurrected—in comparison to which everything else can only be seen as decay.

But the page itself often acts as the preserver of decay, and there is a sharply self-conscious moment in *Childe Harold* where Byron recalls in his youth tracing the path through Greece of Servius Sulpicius, praetor, legate of Gaul, and friend of Cicero. As Sulpicius saw ruins, so too did Byron, for classical Greece was never rebuilt, and yet Byron observes with a dreadful sense of inevitability:

> That page is now before me, and on mine
> *His* country's ruin added to the mass
> Of perish'd states he mourn'd in their decline,
> And I in desolation: all that *was*
> Of then destruction *is*; and now, alas!
> Rome—Rome imperial, bows to the storm,
> In the same dust and blackness, and we pass
> The skeleton of her Titanic form,
> Wrecks of another world, whose ashes still are warm. (stanza 46)

Byron, in desolation, contemplates the ruin of Rome, and finds in it an unconquerable tendency for all states to decline as the storm moves with dust and blackness and increases the mass in its wake. And, as Byron thinks about Sulpicius considering the ruins of Greece with Rome intact and himself considering Sulpicius with both Greece and Rome lapsed and fallen, there is an unavoidable sense that Britain too will soon have her day. The immanence of destruction, however, is undercut by the very situation it describes, for the letter of Sulpicius survives—or at least the text of it does—and Byron uses it to produce writing of his own, writing which the imaginative structure of the poem suggests might survive the decay of Britain.

In this sense, the potential permanence of the writer—Cicero, recall, is "Rome's least mortal mind"—contrasts with the ephemerality of the politician. There is, of course, a tension in this distinction because Cicero was after all both an author and a politician. He thus functions within the rhetorical pattern of the poem as a symbol of both impermanence and permanence, much like Rome itself. When he turns to Florence, Byron reports with indignation that Dante, Boccaccio, and Petrarch are not buried there, while all the city's most glorious monuments "encrust the bones/ Of merchant-dukes" (60). And yet he reasons, by way of analogy to the omission of Brutus's bust from the pageant of Caesar in Rome, that the absence of the figures only makes their presence more felt in Florence, and that for those whose names are embossed in "mausoleums of the Muse,"

> their tombs
> Are gently prest with far more reverent tread
> Than ever paced the slab which paves the princely head. (stanza 60)

Statesmen receive honors, but the work of the writer endures; it achieves its permanence and receives its due reverence over time. The rhetorical pattern is a familiar one, in which Byron remarks on a cause for grief and indignation but then tries to reverse such despondency with a glimmer of hope—the hope here being the suggestion that time cannot suppress the quality of the writer and that eventually art receives its due. The reference to Brutus resonates with the earlier reference to Sulpicius and anticipates the later allusion to Cicero, Livy, and Virgil. Rome is central to the rhetorical pattern as the epitome of both ruin and transcendence.

This contrast between poet and statesman continues and marks a recurring theme in the poem. It also marks the development of

Byron's earlier analogy in "English Bards." The distinction between knowledge and politics, previously a way of relating the singularity of Greece and Rome, has now become localized within the Roman context. And in this incarnation, one element, knowledge, is valued over the other, politics. When, in stanza 82 (quoted above), Byron declares that the works of Tully, Livy, and Virgil will be Rome's resurrection, he continues on a more despairing note, "Alas for Earth, for never shall we see/ That brightness in her eye she bore when Rome was free" (82). The connection between great writing and freedom recalls the link in "English Bards" in which Britain, "first in freedom," must be "dearest to the Muse" (996). And this lament leads directly to his apostrophe of Sulla and a series of stanzas on statesmen and generals concluding with Napoleon. "I have always looked upon Sylla [sic]," Byron would write in 1821, "as the greatest Character in History—for laying down his power at the moment when it was 'too great to keep or to resign' and thus despising them all" (*BLJ*, 8:106). In the stanzas that follow here, Sulla (though certainly no angel) is praised for exactly that resignation, and he serves as a point of contrast to more zealous leaders such as Cromwell and Napoleon. There is, then, a tension in Byron's value system, for although he is willing to take solace in the literature of a ruined Rome and to eulogize the permanence of art over the fleetingness of politics, he retains a stake in politics and continues to reserve praise for statesmen and leaders. The problem for Byron is that after the fall of Rome, many have imitated her example but they have done so "At apish distance" (89) and never approached a comparable supremacy. There will never be another Virgil, Horace, or Juvenal, but Latin literature serves as a valued standard of imitation, a model to strive for and to bolster the literature of contemporary Europe. Roman politics, or Roman imperial politics, however, work in reverse, for to imitate their standard in the conqueror Caesar and his adapted nephew Caesar Augustus provokes only bathetic and tyrannical attempts at conquest and vanishing greatness.

The one exception to this is Napoleon, who very nearly achieved Roman supremacy. Byron sees Napoleon as "a kind of bastard Caesar," following behind his antique precursor "with steps unequal" (90), a man spoiled by vanity with a more "terrestrial" mind than Caesar, a man lacking the "judgment cold" of the great Roman. Just as Caesar has been bastardized by Napoleon, Rome has been bastardized by

Europe. With the apish distance of imitation, men like Napoleon have produced the bleak worldview represented in stanzas 93–97 ("What from this barren being do we reap?..."), in which "Life is short and truth a gem which loves the deep" (93), and all are slaves; men "plod in sluggish misery" while tyrants struggle with other tyrants. In these stanzas, Roman examples form the basis of Byron's assessment of European politics and the state of contemporary Europe. Caesar provides the means to understand Napoleon and Europe because Napoleon and other European tyrants are motivated by the example of Caesar. It is impossible to avoid linking this with an ongoing discussion of exemplarity, for it shows that even if Byron sometimes does and sometimes does not use Rome as a lesson for contemporary Europe, others do—much of European history, Byron implies, has been shaped by a kind of exemplarity, by the attempt to imitate the example of Caesar. Exemplarity works, then, in the manner of ideology: it is so much a given for the matter at hand that Byron's choice of Roman examples cannot necessarily be read as a conscious subscription to what Koselleck describes as a "*historia magistra vitae*" mode of thought.[24] The point is that Byron's subjects, the tyrants of Europe after Caesar up to Napoleon, are all motivated by the relevance of the Caesarian example, and it would be impossible to discuss their motivation without reference to Rome. But the way that such links resound with other examples, uses, and modes of Roman reference testifies to the distinct but related ways that Rome works throughout Byron's poem, from examples of political wisdom (Sulla) to examples of political tyranny (Caesar), from art as that which survives decay to decline as the lesson of Roman history. It is a bleak vision, but again, in what has by now become a familiar pattern in this poem, it is one with at least a glimpse of hope:

> Yet, Freedom! yet thy banner, torn, but flying,
> Streams like the thunder-storm *against* the wind; (stanza 98)

---

[24] Reinhart Koselleck, "Historia Magistra Vitae: The Dissolution of the Topos into the Perspective of a Modernized Historical Process," in *Futures Past: On the Semantics of Historical Time*, trans. Keith Tribe (Cambridge: MIT Press, 1985), 21–38. See my discussion of Koselleck's argument in the introduction, p. 38ff.

As Byron laments the ephemerality of civilization, he recalls the survival of Roman examples through writing; as he bemoans the spread of tyranny, he delivers the hope of freedom.

Such alternation between abject despair—at decline in life, in history—and glimpses of hope is complicated in *Childe Harold*, canto IV, by the images of Roman ruins echoing through the poem. The ruins seem to function on a different temporal level, subjecting contemporary concerns—political, social, personal—to another level of value, to a more austere and often more hopeless questioning of what human endeavor can be worth if cracked stone is all that remains. Examining the Palatine hill and the destruction of the Imperial Mount, Byron concludes

> There is the moral of all human tales;
> 'Tis but the same rehearsal of the past,
> First Freedom, and then Glory—when that fails,
> Wealth, vice corruption,—barbarism at last. (stanza 108)

The lines read like a redaction of Gibbon's magisterial history of Roman decline. Rome here underwrites a cyclical vision of history, one in which freedom continuously decays to barbarism, thus undercutting even the longing of freedom's banner flying against the wind. At the temporal level of the ruins, even the freedom that Byron so cherishes and hopes to help promulgate will melt to barbarism via an inevitable cycle of wealth, vice, and corruption. The past becomes not a fount of wisdom, but an endless repetition of decline, a "rehearsal." Despair at this decline forms a continuous motif in *Childe Harold* canto IV; as the Byronic persona regards the Palatine, Trajan's arch, the Tarpeian rock, and the Egerian stream, we see the emptiness of decay and the view of nature creeping through to reclaim all monuments of civilization—monuments which then become a marker for the futility of all human endeavor.

The ruins and the sense of futility they inspire are, of course, a metaphor for Byron's personal despair, and it is somewhat unsurprising when the Egerian fount leads to thoughts on love and the failure of love in Byron's life. In what might thus seem a typically Romantic move, the ruins, the symbols and markers of history, provide material for the expression and explication of the self. They enable a profound solipsism and provide an aid with which the self can see the self. But the specificity of the ruins, their historical referentiality—the way that they mark certain figures or battles or sights and places made memorable by the survival of ancient texts—and the persistent return of the ruins suggests that for Byron they are more than a convenient metaphor for Romantic self-pity. And this is another sense in which we cannot understand the Romantic without thinking more carefully about the place of Rome within it.

We have seen how for Robert Griffin, Romanticism defines itself by reconfiguring its literary past and, in Byron's comments on the Pope controversy, we have traced the relevance of Roman literary history for moves of this kind. Byron's use of Roman ruins, and the pattern by which they function as both metaphor for personal despair *and* as a lesson of history shows the close proximity of politics and historical sensibility to Byron's most exalted and despairing sense of himself. Jerome McGann has linked Byron's expression and extension of himself to historical circumstance, and he concludes that "the mode of both his Romanticism and his Romanism is tragic and desperate rather than comic and hopeful because—unlike Goethe's—the history he has inherited includes the crucial years of 1789–1817, when western civilization suffered what he brilliantly called 'man's worst, his second fall.'"[25] McGann also claims that "like everything else in Byron's poem Rome is an expression and extension of himself, a model which Byron receives from de Stael only to appropriate in a gesture of Romantic, even Napoleonic, imperialism."[26] There is a tension between these two claims. One suggests that Byron's Romanticism and his Romanism are part of a tragic relationship to concrete historical circumstances, whereas the other simply declares that Byron's Romanticism colonizes Rome for the self. But there is a more complex relationship in which the Roman ruins stand in *Childe Harold* as that which can be manipulated for the self but never fully appropriated, and Byron is acutely aware of this.[27] If Childe Harold,

---

[25] McGann, "Rome and Its Romantic Significance," in *The Beauty of Inflections: Literary Investigations in Historical Method and Theory* (New York: Oxford University Press, 1985), 325.
[26] Ibid., 324.
[27] Here again, we might speculate about how questions about decline and fall and of perishability and impermanency generated by the ruins and Byron's responses to

the Byronic persona, is the hero of the poem, then it is an ambivalent heroism—and not just because the poem uses the relics and shards of history to question the possibility of heroism in post-Waterloo Europe, but also because the Byronic persona gives to the ruins, perhaps despairingly, a centrality and a permanence that he knows he can aspire to but never securely occupy. The poem then stages and elaborates a dialectic between self and history that ultimately expresses what McGann calls the "tragic and desperate" mode of *both* his Romanticism and his Romanism. And in the relationship between the two, in the way that the Romanism enables us to see the complexity of the Romanticism, its unceasing dialectic between self and history, we begin to see a critical aspect of ancient Rome's importance for Romanticism.

Byron discovers

> a power
> And magic in the ruined battlement,
> For which the palace of the present hour
> Must yield its pomp, and wait till ages are its dower. (stanza 129)

To this sense of power and magic is added a certain clarity, what Byron calls a "sense so deep and clear"—a clarity that, in turn, enables the self to "become a part of what has been" and to "grow unto the spot, all-seeing but unseen" (138). The ruins here enable the kind of

---

these questions can be linked with the traumas of credit and the instability of the self in a commercial economy. The ruins serve as a stark reminder of the decline and fall of antique civilizations and as such they point up questions about the parallel between the ancient world and the modern world. As Michael Sonensher explains, "Chronologically the modern world was its [the ancient world's] heir. What came to matter in the eighteenth century was whether it might also have its fate...[whether] eighteenth century Europe might have to face the prospect of a replay of the ancient cycle of decline and fall under modern conditions of war and debt. Here, the threat to established power and prosperity was not so much the inequality and luxury that, according to a long-standing tradition of political and historical analysis, had been responsible for earlier cycles of decline and fall, but the new financial instruments and fiscal resources that had accompanied the transformation of warfare during the seventeenth and eighteenth centuries" (*Before the Deluge* [Princeton, NJ: Princeton University Press, 2007], 6). What this suggests is a close link between ancient ruins and traumas and anxieties associated with public credit and debt in emergent commercial societies as Byron uses the ruins to imagine his contemporary modernity as the site of a future antiquity.

transcendence, the "mingl[ing] with the universe" that Byron also receives from the "pathless woods" and the "lonely shore" later in the poem (stanza 178, quoted above). And, if that scene was described as an "interview," the ruins have an eloquence of their own:

> Tully was not so eloquent as thou,
> Thou nameless column with the buried base! (stanza 110)

With this comment, we see three distinct transmissions from antiquity. First, at the most basic level, the line trades upon Cicero the orator and rhetorician as the epitome of eloquence. Next, it also echoes earlier comments from stanza 82 in which the writings of Cicero, Livy, and Virgil will be Rome's resurrection, that which survives decay. And yet here, finally, the ruins too survive—as ruins—and offer an eloquence of their own.[28] As I suggested earlier, there is a tension in the message of the text and the message of the ruins, for if the survival of the text is what allows the poet to trump the statesman, if the transmission of ancient literature enables a "bark of hope" (105) amid the wreckage of history, the ruin suggests something different. It is a message of futility and despair. Yet it too offers the possibility of transcendence and clarity, and in this way, Byron returns from the futility of the wreck. Amid the despair of Egeria, Byron calls himself back:

> Yet let us ponder boldly—'tis a base
> Abandonment of reason to resign
> Our right of thought—our last and only place
> Of refuge; (stanza 127)

In this way, the ruin itself provokes thought and the transmission of thought through text. The thought produced in the making of the poem confirms the power and magic in the ruined battlement. While the ruins also underline the worthlessness of human endeavor, it is an ambivalent worthlessness because it inspires the struggle to find meaning, to take something more productive from history than the lesson of inevitable decline, and, perhaps strangest of all, to leave

---

[28] On the complicated relationship between ruins and Romantic historicity, see Sophie Thomas, "Assembling History: Fragments and Ruins," *European Romantic Review* 14 (2003): 177–186.

something behind in history.[29] We see this most clearly when the experience of the ruins produces the declaration that

> there is that within me which shall tire
> Torture and Time, and breathe when I expire; (stanza 137)

Somewhat paradoxically, the ruin produces the desire for permanence, the desire to leave something behind that will transcend the life of the individual, while simultaneously acknowledging the impossibility of any production that can escape destruction.

The fallen empires of antiquity function in "English Bards" as a warning to contemporary Britain that she must live up to her greatness. Despite the angry Juvenalian tone of that poem, its very existence suggests the premise that poetry can effect change—within its own category, but also in events and circumstances beyond the immediate realm of letters. This, I have suggested, is the premise of efficacy inherent in satirical writing. In *Childe Harold* canto IV, however, remnants of antiquity—in the form of transmitted texts and ancient ruins—play both a larger and a more ambivalent role. The decay of ancient civilizations still acts as a warning, and Byron suggests to his country "in the fall/ Of Venice think of thine, despite thy watery wall" (17). But *Childe Harold* is a more Romantic poem than "English Bards," Romantic both in its usual sense and in the terms and categories that I have opened up for its reconception. The poem draws much more attention to the Byronic persona and narrates, in a way that "English Bards" does not, the efforts of its observing consciousness—it begins, after all, with the self ("*I stood in Venice*") and proceeds in a tone of self-consciousness with an associative logic particular to the observing self through the cities and countryside of Italy. In this sense it fits—as it has always been seen to fit—a treatment of Romanticism that focuses on imagination, nature, and the self. Within this context, Roman ruins serve as a metaphor for the experience of the self: they both magnify and confirm personal futility and might thus be seen to express the groundlessness of a self formed and manipulated by the

---

[29] The tension inherent in this ambivalent worthlessness is similar to what McGann refers to when he notes "A promise given twice and lost twice means for Byron a history in which the promise will never fail to be given and will never succeed in being realized." See McGann, "Rome," 325.

marketplace. The way that they do so, however, suggests more than simply a unilateral appropriation, an adaptation of historical event and symbol to amplify the expression of self. The ruins too have their eloquence, and the way that they are compared to and complemented by the texts of Roman antiquity places the observing self within history and expresses what Kenneth Burke would call an attitude toward history—although that attitude is certainly not the comedy that Burke calls "our attitude of attitudes."[30] Indeed, it delivers something more like a tragic attitude in which the poem marks the development of a post-Waterloo historical consciousness that everywhere sees reaction on the rise and civilization as a temporary stay against inevitable decline and destruction and yet still declares the will for energetic and continuous struggle—a variety of faith without hope.

---

[30] Kenneth Burke, *Attitudes Toward History*, 3rd ed. (1937; Berkeley: University of California Press, 1984), introduction, n.p.

Chapter Four

"Yet the Capital of the World"

Rome, Repetition, and History in Shelley's Later Writings

> At Albano we arrived again in sight of Rome—arches after arches in unending lines stretching across the uninhabited wilderness, the blue defined outline of the mountains seen between them; masses of nameless ruins standing like rocks out of the plain; and the plain itself with its billowy & unequal surface announced the neighborhood of Rome. And what shall I say to you of Rome?
>
> —Percy Bysshe Shelley to Thomas Love Peacock, 23 March 1819

Shelley had much to say about Rome, and his letter of 23 March 1819 to his friend and fellow classicist Thomas Love Peacock is a rapturous description of the ruins of the ancient and the splendors of the modern city; Shelley glories in the palaces and temples, the baths and fountains, the trees and flowers, but he takes especial pleasure in Rome's ruins. "Rome is yet the Capital of the World," Shelley affirms. "It is a city of palaces & temples more glorious than those which any other city contains, & of ruins more glorious than they."[1] If the tone of Shelley's letter suggests a wonder and a fascination with the ancient city, one that defies his prodigious verbal capacities ("Come to Rome," Shelley urges Peacock. "It is a scene by which expression is overpowered:

---

[1] Percy Bysshe Shelley to Thomas Love Peacock, 23 March 1819, in *Letters of Percy Bysshe Shelley*, ed. Frederick L. Jones (Oxford: Clarendon Press, 1964), 2:87.

which words cannot convey."), then it is a mood that has, perhaps, the zeal of a convert, for Shelley's earlier comments about ancient civilizations give no hint of one who would eventually speak in such tones.

Seven years prior to this letter from what has been called his annus mirabilis,[2] during the time surrounding his seven-week pamphleteering visit to Dublin early in 1812, the young Shelley—not yet twenty—wrote a series of letters to William Godwin. In the longest of these, dated 29 July 1812, Shelley responds to Godwin's suggestion in his 1797 essay "Of the Study of the Classics" that application to classical learning was the best employment of youth. The young reformer presents himself as a vituperative opponent of Greek and Roman culture because, as he explains, their systems of government and their literature promote a value system anchored in honor and glory at the expense of virtue. Shelley then concludes that "the evils of acquiring Greek & Latin considerably overbalance the benefits."[3] "What is perhaps most significant about this letter," as Timothy Webb notes, "is that Shelley, the future philhellene, as yet makes little distinction between Latin and Greek."[4] Shelley would, of course, soon make that distinction to the point that by 1821 in the preface to *Hellas*, he could claim, "We are all Greeks—our laws, our literature, our religion, our arts have their root in Greece."[5]

But what does it mean to be "Greek," and to what extent are we all Greeks? The question cannot be answered without a clearer sense of how Greece relates to Rome in Shelley's work. After all, immediately following the declaration that we are all Greeks, Shelley continues, "But for Greece, Rome, the instructor, the conqueror, or the metropolis of our ancestors would have spread no illumination with her arms, and we might still have been savages, and idolaters; or, what is worse,

---

[2] Stuart Curran, *Shelley's Annus Mirabilis: The Maturing of an Epic Vision* (San Marino, CA: Huntington Library, 1975).
[3] PBS to WG, *Letters*, 1:316.
[4] Timothy Webb, *The Violet in the Crucible: Shelley in Translation* (Oxford: Clarendon Press, 1976), 53.
[5] *Shelley's Poetry and Prose*, ed. Donald H. Reiman and Sharon B. Powers (New York: W. W. Norton, 1977), 409. All citations from Shelley's poetry are from this edition. Hereafter abbreviated *SPP* and cited parenthetically in the text.

might have arrived at such a miserable state of social institution as China and Japan possess" (*SPP*, 409). Greece is immediately linked to Rome. It is a pattern that persists throughout the Shelleyan oeuvre, although scholars, who have devoted considerable attention to Shelley's Hellenism, have little to say about the use of Rome in Shelley's work. This critical oversight has left us with an incomplete understanding of the meaning and importance of Shelley's Hellenism, one which cannot be remedied without a sharper sense of Shelley's appreciation of antiquity more broadly and of the relationship between Greece and Rome in particular.

This chapter examines Shelley's many scattered references to Rome in an effort to understand the relationship between Greece and Rome in Shelley's work. Shelley's thinking about classical antiquity should be considered as part of an internally differentiated classicism, one that recognizes distinctions between Greece, the Roman republic, and the Roman Empire and that each of these specific moments in antiquity bears a different—and changing—relevance for Shelley's contemporary moment. Shelley's references to antiquity reflect a prolonged rethinking of the past provoked by events to which Shelley refers again and again in his correspondence, such as the Spanish liberal revolution; the beginnings of Greek insurgency against the Turks in 1821; and the Peterloo massacre of August 1819, in which thousands of peaceful demonstrators protesting for the reform of Parliament were charged by the cavalry of the Manchester yeomanry. From 1819 forward in such works as *The Philosophical View of Reform*, the "Ode to Liberty," *The Defence of Poetry*, and *Hellas*, Shelley—who was living in Italy and, as his letters to Peacock and his prefaces to *Adonais* and *Prometheus* show, was continually exposed to ancient ruins and remnants—repeatedly tells a story of the rise and spread of liberty from Athens to Rome to the Italian republics to the more recent American and French revolutions. Within this narrative, Rome occupies a consistent but ambiguous position: always distinguished from Athens, sometimes blamed for crushing Greek liberties, sometimes singled out for particular praise, sometimes marginalized. Viewing these pieces in chronological order, it would be difficult to argue for a telos or even to suggest that in its many successive retellings the story and the position of Rome within it develop in any ordered, definitive way.

Rather, the telling and retelling of the history of liberty reveals Shelley's historiographical strategies for understanding the contemporary moment, his persistent use of the past in an effort to comprehend the present and anticipate the future. Greece is consistently the hero of Shelley's story—in *Hellas*, for example, he suggests that the spirits of Greece "Rule the present from the past" (1. 701)—but Shelley's faith in the Greek ideals that he hopes will come to dominate thought and action ranges from ardent to wavering as he explores what Carl Woodring describes as "the relationship of political idealism to the empirical validity of hope."[6] To watch the changing fortunes of Athens and Rome in Shelley's later prose and poetry is to confirm the importance of Shelley's undeniable Hellenism but also to expose the critical role that Rome plays in Shelley's historiographical inclinations and his strategies for understanding the past, which, in turn, allows us to see the relationship of these techniques to the deeply political functions of both Shelley's classicism and his historiography.

A focus on Shelley's Hellenism can show us the intensity of Shelley's political commitments[7]—especially his attempt to suggest the conditions by which his democratic ideals might be recognized and fulfilled—but it is only by situating this preference for Greece in the broader context of Shelley's internally differentiated classicism, where

---

[6] Carl M. Woodring, *Politics in English Romantic Poetry* (Cambridge: Harvard University Press, 1970), 310.

[7] Although most critical work on Shelley's classicism has been focused on Greece, there remains little consensus about the significance of Shelley's Hellenism. Timothy Webb sees Shelley's interest in Greek literature and culture as a kind of escapism devoted to an ideal of beauty comfortably allied to a spirit of good cheer. See Webb, *Violet in the Crucible*, 51–89, esp. 51–63. Marilyn Butler, however, argues for the deeply political significance of this very remoteness. She sees a distinct flowering of neoclassicism in England in the second decade of the nineteenth century, clustered around the Marlow circle in the spring of 1817. In this way, Shelley's Hellenism is both public and deeply political, a covert discourse in a game of opposition politics. See Marilyn Butler, "The Cult of the South," chapter 5 of *Romantics, Rebels, and Reactionaries* (Oxford: Oxford University Press, 1981), 113–137; Butler explains that in its deliberate rejection of the literature of the North and its defense of the classical and Mediterranean South, the Marlow group's taste for Greece, "stands for a whole ideal of harmony, a challenge to arbitrary divisions between mind and body, man and his environment, man and God; and a challenge also to an institutionalized Christianity that was part of the apparatus of State" (136). In contrast, Karl Kroeber and, more recently, Jennifer

we can see it in relation to Shelley's use of Rome, that we can understand how Shelley uses the antique past to comprehend the possibilities and limitations of the rapidly changing contemporary moment. James Chandler has suggested that Shelley's later work defines a new notion of the historical situation, one that is at once situated in a sociohistorical movement but also acutely self-conscious about the implications of setting the conditions for the production of such a movement. In this way, Chandler shows the deeply political significance of the historiographical procedures present in Shelley's later work, as Shelley "provokes historical awareness of the condition of being historically aware."[8]

Extending Shelley's thinking about the historical situation and our understanding of Shelley's Hellenism to a discussion of the meaning of Rome in Shelley's historiographical strategies can show us—in a way that a too narrow focus on Shelley's Hellenism cannot—how Shelley modifies his understanding of classical antiquity (and the place of republican Rome within it) in the shaping of a historical outlook specifically designed to address the reactionary

---

Wallace caution against interpreting Shelley's Hellenism in any clearly polemical way. The interrogation of the Aeschylean source in Shelley's *Hellas*, Kroeber claims, is the animating impulse behind all Romantic classicism: "Romantic hellenism is of lasting interest because it evokes skeptical scrutiny of the idealizing it articulates, nowhere more anguishingly than in the final chorus of *Hellas*" (*British Romantic Art* [Berkeley: University of California Press, 1986], 165). Wallace is more inclined to read Shelley's Hellenism politically, but she argues that the Marlow circle was less coherent than Butler represents. She emphasizes the problems inherent in the efforts of the Marlow writers "to imply political relevance by alleging irrelevance and lack of concern" (88), and she suggests that Shelley was especially attracted to Greece because of its complex and ambiguous heritage. Any monolithic explanation of Greek influence, Wallace concludes, is consequently untenable. See Jennifer Wallace, *Shelley and Greece: Rethinking Romantic Hellenism* (New York: St. Martin's Press, 1997). For all of these studies, Greece is the dominant factor in Shelley's classicism. Though the significance of Shelley's Hellenism is disputed, the work of all these critics makes clear that it was at once deeply political and deeply ambivalent—qualities which might be said to characterize Shelley's historical understanding more generally. For additional treatments of Shelley's engagement with Greek writing, see Paul Carter, "Shelley & the Greek Spirit," *Art and Artists* 11 (1977): 511–519; and John Buxton, *The Grecian Taste: Literature in the Age of Neo-Classicism, 1740–1820* (New York: Barnes and Noble, 1978).

[8] James Chandler, *England in 1819: The Politics of Literary Culture and the Case of Romantic Historicism* (Chicago: University of Chicago Press, 1998), 490.

situation of post-Waterloo England. The matter of Rome, in turn, affords us more than simply an exposure of how a field of historical reference shapes Shelley's understanding of the past. To think about the development of Shelley's understanding of the relationship between Greece and Rome reveals how—despite Shelley's ardent idealization of Greece and his desire that England and Europe generally imitate the Greek example of democratic liberty—Rome proves to be the ancient example more apposite to the case of England. Shelley comes to recognize that when conceived as a locus of imperialism, cultural spread, and institution building, Rome becomes the more dependable analogy by which to understand the development and repetition of the same process in England. Just as Rome came to seem for Shelley an imitation of Greece, so England, especially the England of the Augustan period, came to seem an imitation of Rome. This use of Rome's relation to Greece to conceptualize historical process as a movement of repetition with difference anticipates Marx's later use of Rome in the *Eighteenth Brumaire* (1852).

ROME IN SHELLEY'S HISTORICAL IMAGINATION

Shelley's correspondence with Godwin shows that in 1812 Shelley saw Greece and Rome conjointly as the promoters of a false system of value that was conducive to violence and imperial expansion. Around the same time that Shelley was writing to Godwin, he was also composing *Queen Mab* (1813), his first major poem detailing his theory of historical evolution. Here, Shelley again associates Athens and Rome in the general process of imperial decay when the Fairy explains to the Spirit "'Where Athens, Rome, and Sparta stood,/ There is a moral desart now'" (*SPP*, 25). Shelley does, however, single imperial Rome out for particular vilification when the poem later denounces Nero as a representative despot:

>   When Nero,
> High over flaming Rome, with savage joy
> Lowered like a fiend, drank with enraptured ear
> The shrieks of agonizing death, beheld

> The frightful desolation spread, and felt
> A new-created sense within his soul
> Thrill to the sight, and vibrate to the sound;
> Thinkest thou his grandeur had not overcome
> The force of human kindness? (*SPP*, 32)

As Shelley's work progresses, Greece emerges as a more central and preoccupying feature of his writing. Rome, however, does not disappear. Nor is Rome always associated, as Kenneth Cameron implies, with the forces of despotism in Shelley's conception of history as a struggle between despotism and liberty (*SPP*, 512). Rather, Shelley's sense of Rome shifts from an earlier negative outlook to a more complex awareness of the strengths and limitations of Rome. In the preface to *Prometheus Unbound* (1819, published 1820), for example, Shelley writes:

This Poem was chiefly written upon the mountainous ruins of the Baths of Caracalla, among the flowery glades, and thickets of odoriferous blossoming trees which are extended in ever winding labyrinths upon its immense platforms and dizzy arches suspended in the air. The bright blue sky of Rome, and the effect of the vigorous awakening of spring in that divinest climate, and the new life with which it drenches the spirits even to intoxication, were the inspiration of this drama. (*SPP*, 133)

And in the preface to *Adonais* (1821), Shelley notes that:

John Keats died at Rome of a consumption, in his twenty-fourth year, on the———of———1821; and was buried in the romantic and lonely cemetery of the protestants in that city, under the pyramid which is the tomb of Cestius, and the massy walls and towers, now mouldering and desolate, which formed the circuit of antient Rome. The cemetery is an open space among the ruins covered in winter with violets and daisies. It might make one in love with death, to think that one should be buried in so sweet a place. (*SPP*, 390)

The prefaces to both of these poems, which take as their inspiration Greek subjects and Greek forms, allude to Rome. Each conjures a specific image of Rome as a modern city while manifesting a more acute fascination with the ruins of ancient Rome. Shelley's experience of modern Rome is clearly marked by the presence of ancient ruins, and the ruins themselves are experienced as part of the modern city. The ruins sneak into the poetry as well, taking three stanzas near the end of *Adonais* (48–50), or, more subtly, in the "Ode to the West Wind" (1819, publ. 1820) when Shelley apostrophizes the wind as:

> Thou who didst waken from his summer dreams
> The blue Mediterranean, where he lay,
> Lulled by the coil of his chrystalline streams,
> Beside a pumice isle in Baiæ's bay. [lines 29–32]

Baiæ's bay, as Shelley observes in a letter to Peacock, contained the ruins of imperial Roman villas that impressed Shelley on a December 1818 tour. It is also an area that he associates with Virgil and the sixth book of the *Aeneid*.[9] Elsewhere, Shelley makes passing reference to Rome and Latin authors, and his letters from Italy contain many passages praising Roman history and culture.

In a letter of 17–18 December 1818, for example, Shelley writes to Peacock, "Behold the wrecks of what a great nation once dedicated to the abstractions of the mind. Rome is a city as it were of the dead, or rather of those who cannot die, & who survive the puny generations which inhabit & pass over the spot which they have made sacred to eternity."[10] We note here the conjunction of Rome with eternity ("those who cannot die"). This sense of the eternal value of classical culture combined with Shelley's deep mistrust of Rome and his association of Rome with despotism suggests, initially at least, a divided and ambivalent attitude toward Rome. In part, such ambivalence can be explained by Greg Kucich's suggestion that Shelley's historical practice constructs what he describes as a progressive model of historical "contrariety," a sustained pattern of historical progress and decline arranged around competing strategies of linear and cyclical narrative.[11] Read this way, we might say that Shelley views Rome's cultural achievement—as he views other high points in Western

---

[9] "We passed Posilipo & came first to the eastern point of the bay of Puzzoli which is within the great bay of Naples & which again incloses that of Baiæ.... Here we were conducted to see the Mare Morto & the Elysian fields, the spot on which Virgil places the scenery of the 6th Æneid.... We then coasted to the bay of Baiæ to the left of which we saw many picturesque and interesting ruins;...The colours of the water & the air breathe over all things here the radiance of their own beauty. After passing the Bay of Baiæ & observing the ruins of its antique grandeur standing like rocks in the transparent sea under our boat, we landed to visit Lake Avernus." PBS to TLP, 17 or 18 December 1818, *Letters*, 2:61.

[10] *Letters*, 2:59.

[11] Greg Kucich, "Eternity and the Ruins of Time: Shelley and the Construction of Cultural History," in *Shelley: Poet and Legislator of the World*, ed. Betty T. Bennett and Stuart Curran (Baltimore: Johns Hopkins University Press, 1996), 19.

culture—as a mixture of the eternal with the flawed or time-bound. But a close look at Shelley's more sustained engagement with the Roman legacy suggests a different picture, one that does not fit with this model of progressive contrariety and its optimistic picture of divided achievement fueling eventual innovation in the endless poem written by time. Shelley clearly sees a deterioration from Greece to Rome, and this sense of decline constitutes an important qualification to Shelley's optimistic historiography, one that might be read as a careful shaping of Rome's retrenchment to fit the politics of the contemporary, post-Waterloo moment. Read this way, we can see that Shelley's understanding of Rome shapes his understanding of the present, but we can also begin to recognize how Shelley's understanding of his contemporary moment alters his understanding of Rome in a dynamic version of historical consciousness.

ROME AND GREECE IN SHELLEY'S *PHILOSOPHICAL VIEW*

Shelley's 1820 pamphlet *A Philosophical View of Reform* (not published until 1920) provides a clear and sustained example of Shelley's inchoate use of Rome for the evaluation of European history and his attempt to comprehend the post-Waterloo present. The comprehensive world history of the first chapter opens with a sentence remarkable for both its exaggerated simplicity and its biting irony: "From the dissolution of the Roman Empire, that vast and successful scheme for the enslaving [of] the most civilized portion of mankind, to the epoch of the present year have succeeded a series of schemes on a smaller scale, operating to the same effect."[12] Shelley's qualifier for the Roman Empire—"that vast and successful scheme for the enslaving [of] the most civilized portion of mankind"—is worthy of Gibbon, but it is Gibbon turned on his head: although Gibbon cast a scornful and distant gaze on the worst excess of empire, he preserved

---

[12] *Shelley's Prose, or the Trumpet of a Prophecy*, ed. David Lee Clark (Albuquerque: University of New Mexico Press, 1954), 230. Subsequent page references to this edition, abbreviated as *SP*, will be provided parenthetically in the text.

a near reverent admiration for the republic and the empire under the Antonines. Shelley here offers no redemptive features of Roman rule. The Roman Empire is simply a scheme, a trick to enslave the majority, but it is nonetheless an important scheme because it provides the model for other "schemes on a smaller scale" and hence begins a series of repetitions that explain the origin of the Church and the European dynasties.

For the remainder of the chapter, Shelley uses Renaissance Florence and Elizabethan England to show how religious and political rethinking produce a resurgence and renewed vitality of intellect, and thus periods of change and disruption toward an increase in freedom are associated with a heightened quality in the arts. The ramifications of this argument are multiple. For a start, Shelley expresses a complex historical vision closely akin to philosophy of history. Shelley sees the past as a series of distinct ages, which shape and are in turn shaped by the individuals that inhabit them. As Shelley looks back through these ages he is able to acknowledge their unique "spirits," but he also notes a correlation between periods of increased freedom and liberty and periods of prolific and memorable artistic production, a correlation that for him has a predictive value. Shelley locates the origin of this link in Greece. When the literary and artistic production of Florence and republican Italy, starting with Dante and continuing with Raphael and Michelangelo, achieves its distinct "union of energy and beauty," it draws "conjointly" from the republican spirit of its government and "the creations of Athens, its predecessor and its image" (*SP*, 231). Shelley's theory of the Italian Renaissance is one that both links it to a distinct political context and describes it as the recovery and retransmission of ancient texts, thoughts, and forms. The ancient texts, thoughts, and forms in question, however, are exclusively Athenian. Although some of his contemporaries, Godwin in particular, describe the thought of fifteenth-century Italy as a recovery of and fascination with classical texts and forms, Greek and Roman, and others, Gibbon especially, see Greece as a developmental stage preceding the peak of Latin civilization, Shelley writes Rome out of the Renaissance. Greece, with her democratic republics, provides the appropriate and chosen model for imitation, whereas Rome becomes merely a vast scheme of enslavement. The juxtaposition is explicit when Shelley sums up his thoughts at the close of the chapter:

Such is a slight sketch of the general condition of the human race to which they have been conducted after the obliteration of the Greek republics by the successful external tyranny of Rome—its internal liberty having been first abolished—and by those miseries and superstitions consequent upon this event which compelled the human race to begin anew its difficult and obscure career of producing, according to the forms of society, the great portion of good. (*SP*, 239)[13]

Here, the empire of Rome chokes Greek liberty. In the *Philosophical View*, Greece is always a paragon of liberty and artistic production, the model of an ideal democratic state that inspires intellectual power. Rome, in contrast, is depicted as the model of an expansionist state, one that quells Greek liberties as it increases in breadth and might. But these same negative qualities—as we shall soon see—may better enable an understanding of European expansion, institution building, and revolution.

THOMSON, SHELLEY, AND LIBERTY

By most accounts, Shelley was still at work on the *Philosophical View* in early 1820, around the time of the Spanish liberal revolution in the spring of that year. The event inspired a verse ode, the "Ode to Liberty," in which Shelley again tells of the emergence and progress of liberty. As in the *Philosophical View*, Shelley's handling of his subject in the "Ode to Liberty" is thoroughly historical. Both of these works conduct an analysis of the past designed to bear upon the present and emphasize the need for change while constructing the hope and logic by which such change is bound to occur. Judith Chernaik has called our attention to the shared theme of Shelley's poem and Thomson's *Liberty* of 1729. For her, the critical distinction between the two poems lies in the position they assign to the poet: for Thomson, the

---

[13] The sentence echoes an earlier lament, made by Shelley in a letter to Peacock early in 1819: "O, but for that series of wretched wars which terminated in the Roman conquest of the world, but for the Christian religion which put a finishing stroke to the antient system; but for those changes which conducted Athens to its ruin, to what an eminence might humanity have arrived" (*Letters*, 2:75).

poet is "simply a specially gifted representative of society," whereas for Shelley—and in what Chernaik calls the "Romantic sublime" more generally—the function of the poem is social, but "the poet is outside society."[14] What Chernaik overlooks, however, is the way that the two poems provide markedly different accounts of ancient history.

In part II of *Liberty*, Thomson's idealization of Greek culture as a whole, in addition to the more customary nod to Greek political wisdom, represents an early example of the Grecian taste that would become more prevalent later in the century.[15] But it is clear that for Thomson, Rome constitutes the pinnacle of ancient liberty and political wisdom. Thomson opens his poem with a contrast between modern and ancient Italy that emphasizes the glory of ancient Rome as a bastion of selfless virtue and love of the commonweal, and it is Rome that constitutes the relevant example for Britain. Speaking of Rome, the personified Liberty says:

> HERE from the fairer, not the greater, Plan
> Of GREECE I vary'd; whose unmixing States,
> By the keen Soul of Emulation pierc'd,
> Long wage'd alone the bloodless War of Arts,
> And their *best* Empire gain'd. But to diffuse
> O'er Men an Empire was my purpose now:
> To let my martial Majesty abroad;
> Into the Vortex of one State to draw
> The whole mix'd Force, and *Liberty*, on Earth;
> To conquer Tyrants, and set Nations free.[16]

Greece may be fairer, but she is not greater than Rome. Rather, Rome perfects the initial virtues of Greece—her arts and her liberty—and, through empire ("martial Majesty") she spreads them abroad. Rome conquers tyrants and frees nations. She is not just a free state, but a liberating empire. In this way, Greece is a model for Rome, but because

---

[14] Judith Chernaik, *The Lyrics of Shelley* (Cleveland, OH: Press of Case Western Reserve University, 1972), 98.

[15] For a helpful introduction to the increasing interest in Greece during the eighteenth century with a selection of contemporary texts that develop the Grecian taste, see Timothy Webb, *English Romantic Hellenism, 1700–1824* (Manchester: Manchester University Press, 1982).

[16] Book 3, lines 78–87, in *Liberty, The Castle of Indolence and Other Poems*, ed. James Sambrook (Oxford: Clarendon Press, 1986), 75.

Rome perfectly fulfills the promise of Greece, it is the Roman example that is more important for later generations—and also more apposite for England: just as Rome imitated Greece, so England, Thomson implies, is now in a position to imitate the example of Rome as a liberating empire.

In Shelley's "Ode," liberty also arises in Greece, and it is here and not in Rome that she achieves her perfection. Athens is described as "a divine work" (69), whose "all-creative skill" produces the forms of Grecian architecture, forms of "marble immortality" (74). Shelley thus reaffirms the intimate connection between the quality of political life and the quality of art expressed previously by Thomson and more recently in his own *Philosophical View*. These Grecian forms and the idea that they represent for Shelley constitute the immortal spirit of liberty:

> Within the surface of Time's fleeting river
> Its wrinkled image lies, as then it lay
> Immovably unquiet, and for ever
> It trembles, but it cannot pass away! (76–79)

Across the river of time, religion and oppression may veil the eyes of liberty, but her spirit remains—most particularly in the idea of Athens, which stands for Shelley as what Timothy Webb calls a "thought-based monument to human potentiality."[17] After Athens, liberty next appears in Rome, where Shelley's enthusiasm is more qualified. "Like a wolf-cub from a Cadmæan Mænad," Rome "drew the milk of greatness, though thy dearest/ From that Elysian food was yet unweaned" (92–94). Despite her presence in Rome, Athens remains the "dearest" to liberty, and there is something monstrous about the simile that introduces Rome, with its reference to *The Bacchae* and wolf cubs suckling human maidens; there is even a hint of impropriety implied in the suggestion that Rome would draw the milk of liberty before Athens was weaned. The reference may also allude to Rome's founding myth of Romulus and Remus, who were purportedly suckled by wolves when abandoned as infants. This ambivalent tone continues as Shelley introduces deeds "of terrible uprightness" sanctified in Rome by liberty's "sweet love." The suggestion that Roman

---

[17] Timothy Webb, *Shelley: A Voice Not Understood* (Atlantic Highlands, NJ: Humanities Press, 1977), 203.

uprightness was somehow terrible distinguishes Shelley's more skeptical praise of Rome from the triumphant tone struck by Thomson.

Shelley does, however, single out two Roman figures, "saintly Camillus" and "firm Atilius," for particular praise. Both are figures from Livy, books 5 and 28, respectively. During Rome's war with the Falisci, the Roman general Camillus returns the Falerii schoolchildren whose corrupt master had delivered them into Roman hands. Camillus insists that the Romans have no quarrel with noncombatants, and his high principles quickly win peace from the Falerii and respect among his fellow Romans. Atilius Regulus, having been taken hostage by the Carthaginians, was sent on a peace mission to Rome, where he urged the Romans to continue the war, and then, honor-bound, returned to Carthage and his own certain death. Both figures are illustrative of action without calculation of immediate gain, and while the mention of these two legendary Romans is brief and might appear insignificant, it shows Shelley using—for the first time—legendary Romans as exemplary heroes. It is the same sort of exemplarity that Shelley so objected to in Godwin's essay "Of the Classics," and his willingness to deploy this device, especially as a counterweight to an otherwise extremely qualified homage to Rome, suggests that Shelley now sees potentially useful merit in the legendary figures of early republican Rome.

Rome itself may be a model of imperial domination, but within the Roman case, Shelley suggests, there may still be figures worthy of imitation. Yet Shelley's use of Camillus and Regulus raises the possibility that the model of exemplary heroism now has a different significance, one suggestive of a shift in the understanding of history and historical process. Throughout the eighteenth century, Montesquieu, Bolingbroke, Gibbon, Hume, and others operating on the belief that human nature is always the same repeatedly assert the direct, exemplary relevance of ancient civilization to contemporary life. For them as for Godwin, such exemplarity was *the* point, whereas for Shelley it remains a smaller aspect of the larger presentation of a historicized vision of the trajectory of liberty. Both are meant to be directly applicable to the present, but as his presentation of the history of liberty shows, Shelley's conception of the past replaces the assumption of direct, transparent relevance with a more nuanced vision in which antiquity continues to be relevant for the present, but only as mediated through an understanding of the complex historical process by which the legacy of the past is transmitted to the present.

The "Ode to Liberty," then, manifests for the first time in verse Shelley's reconsideration of the Roman legacy. Shelley's approval of Rome remains qualified, however, and Athens continues to dominate Shelley's imagination as history's foremost example of liberty and aesthetic beauty. But the "Ode to Liberty" gestures toward a rearrangement in Shelley's historical understanding, and a significant rethinking of the relationship between Greece and Rome. The first stanza of the "Ode" frames the poem with a description of the poet's inspiration, and the final stanza, with its prolonged series of similes, elaborates on the departure of the spirit of liberty and, by implication, of poetic inspiration. This departure of the spirit to its "abyss" is imagined alternately as a wild swan struck by lightning and sunk headlong, as the dissolution of summer clouds, as the fading of candlelight, and as the death of a "brief insect." Comparing this ending to "Prufrock" and the "Ancient Mariner," Webb suggests that the final stanza depicts the painful wrench of "the return to normal everyday consciousness."[18] Chernaik, in contrast, reads the ending as much more ambivalent than a simple return, and she suggests that the imagery of the final stanza seems to qualify the overt doctrine of the "Ode to Liberty" with its faith in the high will of man and its praise for secular virtues.[19] The presence of this ambivalence, the way that it reframes the poem in dualism by whispering against its dominant strain, places the "Ode" squarely alongside similar poems in the Shelley corpus, especially *Hellas* or *The Triumph of Life*. Indeed, the violent imagery in the final stanza suggests despair and hopelessness and adds a profound ambivalence to Shelley's attachment to the idea that man can triumph over adversity and want and to his impassioned call for Germany, Italy, and England to rise up in search of liberty. It also suggests the potential vulnerability of Athens in Shelley's historical framework, for Athens represents both the disembodied ideal of liberty and a specific manifestation of freedom in history. Shelley's historical vision in the "Ode," as in the *Philosophical View*, traces the trajectory of liberty from Athens through its later appearances and the logic of this vision is historical in a prescriptive way: it suggests that

---

[18] Webb, *Shelley*, 41–42.
[19] Chernaik, *Lyrics of Shelley*, 108.

the telos of history is liberty, that the triumph of liberty and of the ideal of Athens is inevitable and irresistible. Placed in the context of the final stanza, however, the logic of this vision cannot hold, and the possibility that Athens is a lapsed ideal and not the "immovably unquiet" instigator of a movement to worldwide freedom creeps into the verse. But the possible shattering of Shelley's confidence in the course of the Athenian ideal should not be read so much as the departure of that ideal as its qualification, as part of Shelley's movement into the world—a world in which the ideal of Athens does not exclude Rome and where there may even be room for a reappraisal of Rome alongside the democratic glories of Athens.

ROME AND *HELLAS*

With its placement of liberty in historical frame and its powerful expression of hope conditioned by a final blast of despair, the "Ode to Liberty" is structurally similar to Shelley's later verse drama *Hellas* (1822). Both poems respond to recent political movements and suggest that hope for the success of these movements must come from thoughtful and critical meditation on history.[20] If the "Ode" is a song of liberty animated by the spirit of Athens, then *Hellas* is a song of Athens animated by the spirit of liberty. Set in the present, *Hellas* acts as a rallying cry for the Greeks in their ongoing struggle for independence—it may even, as Carl Woodring argues, have been designed to assist the insurgents' efforts to raise money in England.[21] The immediacy of the present cause

---

[20] For an account of how *Hellas* relates to diplomatic strategies and contemporary political movements, see Mark Kipperman, "History and Ideality: The Politics of Shelley's *Hellas*," *Studies in Romanticism* 30 (1991): 147–168. Positioning himself against those who see Shelley's Hellenism as handmaiden to reactionary imperialism, Kipperman draws upon Frankfurt School theory and argues that Shelley's utopianism also functions as engaged politics. Although persuasive, his account is ultimately unconvincing, for he overlooks the alternative possibility that Shelley's Hellenism may already be in the service of his historicism. It is this connection, I am suggesting, that can be seen only when we consider the *relationship* of Athens and Rome in Shelley's thought. In this respect, it is telling that in his opening quotation of Shelley's preface to *Hellas*, Kipperman omits the sentence that links Rome to Greece.

[21] See Woodring, *Politics*, 313–319.

does not prevent Shelley from infusing the poem with a broader historical sense, and, in what reads as a redacted version of the "Ode to Liberty," the chorus of Greek captive women sing of the movement of liberty from Greece and Rome to America, France, and contemporary Europe (1. 46–93). Yet for all of its historical sense, the Greek chorus also describes Athens in richly mythological and biblical terms, as when the emergence of Athens is described thus:

> Let there be light! said Liberty
> And like sunrise from the sea,
> Athens arose! (1. 682–84)

Greece is regarded as an eternal set of values derived outside the context of political struggle and war, as something conceived "on the chrystalline sea Of thought" (1. 698–699) and not the sullied world of imperial strife and national struggle. Just as he had famously suggested in the preface that "we are all Greeks," Shelley reaffirms that Greek thought provides the foundation for contemporary Europe, for the legendary citizens of Greece "Rule the present from the past" (1. 701). But as that prefatory point was immediately followed with reference to Rome, so too the uniqueness of Athens is established comparatively:

> Through exile, persecution and despair,
> Rome was, and young Atlantis shall become
> The wonder, or the terror or the tomb
> Of all whose step wakes Power lulled in her savage lair:
> But Greece was as a hermit child,
> Whose fairest thoughts and limbs were built
> To woman's growth, by dreams so mild,
> She knew not pain or guilt
> And now—O Victory, blush! and Empire, tremble
> When ye desert the free—
> If Greece must be
> A wreck, yet shall its fragments reassemble
> And build themselves again impregnably
> In a diviner clime
> To Amphionic music on some cape sublime
> Which frowns above the idle foam of Time. (1. 992–1007)

These lines show Shelley drawing a categorical distinction between Rome and the United States ("young Atlantis") and Greece. In linking

Rome and the United States, Shelley associates Rome with freedom, but the lines also contain a warning, one that leaves open what the fate of the young Republic will be: wonder, terror, or tomb. But the lines are perhaps most revealing for the way that they associate Rome and the United States with *Power* and her "savage lair." These are states, Shelley maintains, whose values and thought are imbricated with the "pain" and "guilt" of practical politics. Greece, in contrast, is a locus of ideals, ideals built by mild dreams somehow feminine, in contrast to the masculine virtues of Rome and America. And the passage continues to suggest that the unique situation in which Greek ideals were forged enabled them to resist the corrosive effects of time. Rome may have produced a great empire, but her accomplishments and thoughts are not timeless like those of Greece, and what is more, part of Rome's greatness lies, as Shelley's preface states, in the spreading of Greek ideals.

But then, with this hopeful and demonstrative emphasis on Athenian greatness in mind, what are we to make of the final chorus of *Hellas?* It opens with such emphatic hope: "The world's great age begins anew," only to end in a cri de coeur of anguished resignation:

> O cease! must hate and death return?
>   Cease! must men kill and die?
> Cease! drain not to its dregs the urn
>   Of bitter prophecy.
> The world is weary of its past,
> O might it die or rest at last! (1. 1096–1101)

These lines sit uncomfortably with the rest of the poem and make the optimistic idealization of Greece difficult to maintain. Indeed, McGann has suggested that *Hellas* represents a turning point in Shelley's poetry in that "the complete dissociation of Shelley's mythic sensibility based upon a monolithic Promethian dream of perfection was finally reached."[22] McGann describes the tension between these lines as a phenomenon of "poetic counterstatement," which he thinks pervades all of Shelley's major poetry; it is, indeed, the same type of tension that we saw in the final lines of the "Ode to Liberty." The way Greece is handled in Shelley's verse drama again reveals Shelley's

---

[22] Jerome J. McGann, "The Secrets of an Elder Day: Shelley after *Hellas*," *Keats-Shelley Journal* 15 (1966): 26.

historical sensibility, his effort to think through contemporary changes with an eye toward history. The triumphant tone of the Greek chorus suggests optimism, but the final lines of the poem bend backwards against this and acknowledge that history does not always work the way that it should. In this way, both *Hellas* and the "Ode to Liberty" manifest, in Karl Kroeber's phrase, the "skeptical scrutiny of the idealizing [they] articulate."[23] The best place to see this tension between an idealizing, mythological impulse and a more careful and critical historicism, however, is *The Defence of Poetry*.

ROME, ATHENS, AND IMITATION IN SHELLEY'S *DEFENCE OF POETRY*

The *Defence* has traditionally been read as a key example of Shelley's idealism and as one of the central texts of British Romanticism more generally for the way that it elevates both the status of poetry and the function of the individual poet. Raymond Williams, for example, uses the *Defence* as the culminating example in his discussion of how the idea of the independent creative writer, the "Romantic artist," becomes a rule in the period. For Williams, although he is sympathetic to the claims made within, the end of the *Defence* is "painful to read" and carries the "felt helplessness of a generation," for the "bearers of a high imaginative skill become suddenly the 'legislators,' at the very moment when they were being forced into practical exile."[24] But reading the *Defence* in the context of Shelley's internally differentiated classicism, with its emergent and increasingly refined distinctions between Greece and Rome, reveals the contrapuntal melody of Shelley's historicism alongside this impassioned idealism.

Because Shelley saw a close correspondence between the state of poetry and the state of social life, his *Defence* shares many points with his *Philosophical View*, and indeed, the later essay recycles, in slightly varied form, passages from the earlier. Shelley passed over

---

[23] Kroeber, *British Romantic Art*, 165.
[24] Raymond Williams, *Culture and Society: 1780–1950* (London: Hogarth Press, 1958), 30–48; quotation from 47.

Rome in the *Philosophical View* when he considered the link between political and literary developments, and we get a fuller sense of why this is when Shelley evaluates Rome in the *Defence*. The *Defence* emphasizes Greek figures and forms, often at the expense of the Roman. When, for example, Shelley expands his definition of a poet to include prose writers and philosophers, he remarks that "Plato was essentially a poet—the truth and splendour of his imagery and the melody of his language is the most intense that it is possible to conceive."[25] In contrast, Cicero, the most legendary of Roman statesmen, "sought to imitate the cadence of his [Plato's] periods but with little success."[26] Similarly, when Shelley argues that by its association with pleasure, the best poetry inspires admiration and imitation and thereby improves mankind, his archetypes are not Roman—as they were for Godwin when he made a similar point in his essay "Of the Classics" in 1797—but Greek: "Homer embodied the ideal perfection of his age in human character; nor can we doubt that those who read his verses were awakened to an ambition of becoming like to Achilles, Hector, and Ulysses" (486). In both instances, imitation is central. Shelley faults Cicero for his failed imitation of Plato while using the standard of imitation as his measure for the best poetry. Homer's work is singled out because it inspires imitation in its readers, but its greatness seems to lie, as for Plato, in its very inimitableness.

Shelley's prolonged discussion of Rome in relation to Athens centers on imitation. Throughout the *Defence*, fifth-century Athens repeatedly stands as the quintessential example of the moral capacity of poetry, and Shelley places particular emphasis on drama as a locus in which to observe this link between poetry and social good. Indeed, his key retort to Peacock's assertion of the inefficacy of poetry is to demonstrate the effect of drama upon life and manners. Shelley asserts that "the drama at Athens, or wheresoever else it may have approached its perfection, coexisted with the moral and intellectual

---

[25] Percy Bysshe Shelley, *A Defence of Poetry*, in *SPP*, 484. Subsequent references to this edition will be provided parenthetically in the text.

[26] This stark contrast between Plato and a celebrated Roman recalls a moment in Shelley's letters when he tells Peacock, "I had rather err with Plato than be right with Horace" (PBS to TLP, 23–24 January 1819, *Letters*, 2:75).

greatness of the age" (490) and that "it is indisputable that the highest perfection of human society has ever corresponded with the highest dramatic excellence" (492). When drama thrives, political and social life must be healthy, but when drama wanes, a nation is corrupt. For Shelley, drama means tragedy, and tragedy means Athens. And yet what Shelley's claim of correlation omits is the problem of causality: Does great drama inspire the best political institutions, or do the best political institutions produce the finest drama? Shelley never asserts but rather implies the former, that drama produces political greatness. He states that "as Machiavelli says of political institutions, that life may be preserved and renewed, if men should arise capable of bringing back the drama to its principles" (492). Whereas Machiavelli argues for the power of human agency to restore a society by bringing political institutions back to first principles, Shelley suggests that the same effect can be accomplished by the restoration of drama, for poetry "is the faculty which contains within itself the seeds at once of its own and of social renovation" (493). Similarly, in considering the decline of Athens, he explains that "civil war, the spoils of Asia, and the fatal predominance first of the Macedonian, and then of the Roman arms were so many symbols of the extinction or suspension of the creative faculty in Greece" (492). All of the factors traditionally attributed for the decline of Athens are for Shelley mere "symbols" of the decline of the creative faculty.

Athens, then, represents for Shelley both the apex of democratic forms and of dramatic achievement. Athenian decline indicates what happens when poetry moves away from the "inner faculties of our nature" and becomes corrupt. Having thus explained the dominance and decline of Athens, Shelley turns to Rome and observes a similar but not identical cycle: "The same revolutions within a narrower sphere had place in antient Rome; but the actions and forms of its social life never seem to have been perfectly saturated with the poetical element" (493). Shelley makes this point seemingly as a straightforward empirical claim, but it carries profound implications, for it is both a paradigm establishing claim *and* the result of Shelley's own experience with revolutions in his time. It thus becomes a structural conceptual tool for understanding history, an anticipation of the way that Marx uses imitation in the *Eighteenth Brumaire* (1852) when he notes that unheroic as bourgeois society is, it nevertheless took heroism, sacrifice, terror, civil war and battles of peoples to bring it into being. And in the classically austere traditions of the Roman republic its gladiators found the ideals and the art forms, the self-deceptions that they needed in order to conceal from themselves the bourgeois limitations of the content of their struggles and to keep their enthusiasm on the high plane of the great historical tragedy.[27]

Both Shelley and Marx recognize the importance of Rome as the model for the later stabilization of new institutional forms, as *the* formative example for the imitative efforts of any aspiration to empire.

The concept of the same revolutions within a narrower sphere allows us retrospectively to read Rome as a model for the specter of failed revolution that haunts the final chapter of the *Philosophical View*, in which the mistimed breakthrough and attempt at practical application results in retrogression. In this way, Rome comes to epitomize the failure of innovation and constitutes the original example of imitation *as* institution building. The republic imitates the forms of Athens, but when the revolution attempts to adjust this, the result is retrogression and the outfitting of the forms of the republic within the narrower sphere of the empire. And yet what Gibbon depicts in the first five chapters of *Decline and Fall*, Shelley suggests, was in fact preceded by the same move with the adaptation of Greek forms by Rome. In each case, the institution being founded—the republic, the empire—imitates the forms of that which precedes it—Greece, the republic—for a different end, and imitation as failed innovation represents the corrupting of the spirit of innovation toward the end of ongoing stability, thus raising the possibility that institutions are always a constraint on development. Such a reading exposes how Shelley's developing historical sense enables him to think through institutionalism as such and underwrites his understanding of how the Glorious Revolution contributed to the decline in political representation, the rise of the leisure class, and the national debt—which Shelley exposes in the second chapter of the *View* as the root of contemporary problems. It also explains how Shelley thinks about the failure of the French Revolution. "Institutions," Shelley avers, "made

---

[27] Karl Marx, *The Eighteenth Brumaire of Louis Bonaparte* (New York, International Publishers, 1963), 16–17.

the French what they were" (*SPP*, 236), but there, as in Rome, the revolution failed to amend the passions which are the spirit of institutional forms.

This model of imitation, then, explains why the social life of Rome was never saturated with the poetical element. Because the Romans so admired the Greeks, their forms for expressing the poetic imagination were derivative: they avoided the expression of their own condition and aimed always for the universal and for similarity with their Greek precursors. The Greeks, as the original of all imitation, are in a unique position to be both particular and universal. Indeed, for Shelley, Greece maintains especial force because it is the only place where the particular *is* the universal. Though Shelley credits Lucretius, Virgil, and Livy as creators and poets, he observes that "Horace, Catullus, Ovid, and generally the other great writers of the Virgilian age, saw man and nature in the mirror of Greece" (494). Such intense imitation of Greek perfection means the verse of these figures produces but a shadow of the Greek substance. Indeed, though he here credits Virgil with being "in a very high sense" a creator, Shelley later excludes him from the ranks of epic poets on account of his imitation: "Virgil, with a modesty which ill became his genius, had affected the fame of an imitator even whilst he created anew all that he copied" (499). Because of this heavy reliance on the Greek example, "poetry in Rome, seemed to follow rather than accompany the perfection of political and domestic society" (494).

There was, then, in Rome no correlation between poetry and political institutions; faced with a possible counterexample, a case in which the zenith of political institutions occurs prior to the production of memorable poetry, Shelley simply turns his expansive definition of poetry onto political forms and claims:

The true Poetry of Rome lived in its institutions; for whatever of beautiful, true and majestic they contained could have sprung only from the faculty which creates the order in which they consist. The life of Camillus, the death of Regulus; the expectation of the Senators, in their godlike state, of the victorious Gauls; the refusal of the Republic to make peace with Hannibal after the battle of Cannae, were not the consequences of a refined calculation of the probable personal advantage to result from such a rhythm and order in the shews of life, to those who were at once the poets and the actors of these immortal dramas. The imagination beholding the beauty of this order, created it out of itself according to its own idea: the consequence was empire, and the reward ever living fame. These things are not the less poetry, *quia carent vate sacro*. They are the episodes of the cyclic poem written by Time upon the memories of men. The Past, like an inspired rhapsodist, fills the theatre of everlasting generations with their harmony. (494–495)

Though the political institutions of Rome were "less poetical than those of Greece," Shelley here concedes—the dismissive use of "whatever" means that it remains a qualified concession—that they nevertheless contain an element of the poetic, that they must have been produced by the same imaginative faculty that gives rise to poetry. And, as proof that this faculty was extant in Rome, he points to a series of examples from the early republic—all of which are contained in Livy—that show the selflessness of early Romans, an idea from which they built their political order. Camillus and Regulus are the same figures that Shelley singled out for admiration in the "Ode to Liberty." Curiously, however, in the same passage in which Shelley dismisses Roman poetry, he quotes a Roman poet: *quia carent vate sacro* ("because they lack the sacred bard") comes from book 4, poem 9 of the *Odes*, in which Horace insists that there are others to admire besides the exemplary figures that seem the original of heroism. Many heroes lived before Agamemnon (*vixere fortes ante Agamemnona/ multi*), as Horace said in that ode, and his sentiments are akin to Shelley's reluctant recognition that Athens is not the only ancient society useful for developing an understanding of the past conducive to greater political freedom in the present.[28]

Shelley's somewhat paradoxical quotation of Horace here calls to mind his similarly arresting use of the same poet nine years previously in his first long letter to Godwin, which Shelley also closed with a quotation from Horace. The *Defence*, however, reveals just how much

---

[28] The full sentence in context is:

> vixere fortes ante Agamemenona
> multi; sed omnes illacrimabiles
> urgentur ignotique longa
> nocte, carent quia vate sacro.

["Many a brave man lived before Agamemnon; but all lie buried unwept and unknown in the long night, because they lack a sacred bard."] Shelley likely transposes the first two words because he quotes from memory. See Horace, *Odes and Epodes*, Loeb Classical Library, trans. Niall Rudd (Cambridge: Cambridge University Press, 2004), 244–245.

Shelley's position had changed since that time. We see the same philhellenism that began to emerge from Shelley's association with Peacock, and Athens is for Shelley the *locus classicus* of the correlation between the excellence of poetry and the perfection of society. When Shelley discusses Rome and Roman poets, they appear initially to serve—as in the *Philosophical View*—as a foil, as a negative ideal to the positive legacy of Greece. But a closer inspection suggests a subtle shift in Shelley's conception of Rome. When Shelley states that "The true Poetry of Rome lived in its institutions," and then offers a series of exemplary incidents from the early republic, he implies a distinction between the republic and the empire. Previously, Shelley hinted at this distinction; in his December 1812 letter to Godwin, for example, when Shelley notes the "thirst of conquest with which even republican Rome desolated the Earth," the "even" acts as a mark of distinction, and the use of "republican" implies a form of government separate from the empire. But if Shelley gestures toward difference, he does so only to undermine it, to suggest that Rome was as eager for conquest under the republic as under the empire. In the *Defence*, however, the praise for early Rome appears genuine in that Shelley lauds the early Roman heroes for their altruism, for actions that did not arise from "refined calculation of...probable personal advantage," and he suggests that it was this instinct that created the Roman order and enabled it to have an empire, which in turn bequeathed their fame and their example to future generations: "The Past, like an inspired rhapsodist, fills the theatre of everlasting generations with their harmony." When described in these lyrical terms, Rome begins to partake in the timelessness of Athens, and the metaphorical harmony conjured here recalls the Amphionic music used to suggest the permanence of Greek civilization "above the idle foam of Time" in *Hellas*.

But how do we account for this shift in Shelley's understanding of Rome? The answer can be found in Shelley's response to such profound contemporary changes as the perceived failure of the French Revolution, the fall of Napoleon, the restoration of despotic governments throughout Europe following Waterloo, and the brutal crackdown on radical movements in England. Shelley's letters, especially those from 1819 forward, refer directly to these events as Shelley's sense of impending crisis intensifies. Even before news of Peterloo reaches him, Shelley comments that "England seems to be in a very disturbed state,"[29] and then, as he learns of Peterloo, of the trial and sentence of Richard Carlile, and of the Cato Street Conspiracy, Shelley repeatedly alludes to "awful times,"[30] which he sees as "preparing for a bloody struggle."[31] Shelley clearly regards these events as part of a pattern that has recognizable past precedents. As he writes to Peacock, "These are...the distant thunders of a terrible storm which is approaching. The tyrants here, as in the French Revolution, have first shed blood."[32] Shelley's comments on these events in the letters (with the exception of a long unpublished letter on Carlile) often lack the specificity of sustained analysis, but they do prompt the historiographical impulse that leads to the more detailed scrutiny that we have seen in the *Philosophical View* and the *Defence*. Furthermore, it is these same events that consume Shelley in the overall structure of and preface to *The Revolt of Islam*, where Shelley describes a cycle of awakening hope and energy that is crushed by

> the confederacy of the Rulers of the World, and the restoration of the expelled Dynasty by foreign arms; the massacre and extermination of the Patriots, and the victory of established power; the consequences of legitimate despotism,—civil war, famine, plague, superstition, and an utter extinction of the domestic affections; the judicial murder of the advocates of Liberty; the temporary triumph of oppression, that secure earnest of its final and inevitable fall; the transient nature of ignorance and error, and the eternity of genius and virtue.[33]

Clearly, this is a transparent presentation of Shelley's understanding of the aftermath of the French Revolution and the post-Waterloo state of Europe, where the failure of linear progress maintains the possibility of advance through a cycle of hope. This presentation of a comparative understanding of history, the attempt to think through the failure of the French Revolution with all of its aftershocks to a more hopeful future (seen also in the preface to *Prometheus Unbound*), links Shelley's sense of the present moment to

---

[29] *Letters*, 2:115.   [30] *Letters*, 2:136.   [31] *Letters*, 2:149.
[32] *Letters*, 2:119.
[33] Percy Bysshe Shelley, *Poetical Works*, ed. Thomas Hutchinson (London: Oxford University Press, 1967), 32.

his understanding of classical history and the movement of liberty from antiquity to the present. This trajectory always begins in classical times and always passes from Greece through Rome to contemporary Europe. There may not be a direct parallel between imperial Rome and post-Waterloo Europe, but the fall of revolutionary idealism in the early days of the French Revolution as well as the transition from the early promise of Napoleon to the reactionary situation after Waterloo can be thought of as analogous to the decline of Rome from republic to empire in Shelley's historical imagination. This is why Shelley's trajectory of liberty must always pass through Rome: because Rome furnishes the example of a moment when the impulse toward liberty gives way to tyranny, despotism, and institution building. It is a falling off from Greece, but it also provides the possibility that these same corrupt institutions can unwittingly act to preserve exemplary instances of virtue and hence the seeds of future renewal.

THE BUREAUCRATIZATION OF THE IMAGINATIVE

Shelley's use of his understanding of the relationship between Greece and Rome—indeed, his use of the past generally—to support the placement of poetry within his political vision is an often overlooked import of the *Defence*. Shelley's prodigious claims for the value and meaning of poetry require him to think historically, and the piece clearly expresses Shelley's acute historical awareness. Like Marx, who claimed that individuals make their own history but not in contexts of their choosing, Shelley credits poetry and poets with social agency, but that agency is not unique to the individual but is rather the mouthpiece of the "spirit of the age." It is the poet, in his role as a philosopher of history, who can grasp, in a single glance, these connections: "For he not only beholds intensely the present as it is, and discovers those laws according to which present things ought to be ordered, but he beholds the future in the present, and his thoughts are the germs of the flower and the fruit of latest time" (482–483). In this way, the poet of the *Defence* is akin to the figure of Ahasuerus in *Hellas* who, as Hassan tells Mahmud

> ...from his eye looks forth
> A life of unconsumed thought which pierces
> The present, and the past, and the to-come. (1. 146–48)

Both Ahasuerus and the poet of the *Defence* are prophet figures. They are empowered to, in Wordsworth's phrase, "see into the life of things" more deeply than others, to use an understanding of the past to comprehend not just the present but also the germ of the future that it contains. But the power of their prophecy is not simply mystical; rather, it represents the power of a proper historical sense and the promise of a historiography which suggests that a clear-sighted comprehension of the past allows one to determine the logic on which the future will unfold.

The two figures thus underline key tensions and counterstatements in Shelley's later poetry and prose. They are both idealized figures, personifying thought and its idealized abstractions, but they also present a metaphor for a refined historical consciousness that is very much of the world. The doubt, insecurity, and astonishment produced by historical thinking may frighten Mahmud, but the struggle of Shelley's later work indicates a poet more willing to descend from the lofty realm of idealized abstractions and into history. The continuous retelling of this narrative of the progress of liberty belies Shelley's historical turn and its correspondent reconsideration of classical history. To watch the shifting fortunes of Athens and Rome in Shelley's late prose and poetry both confirms the importance of Shelley's undeniable Hellenism and exposes the frequently overlooked place that Rome holds in Shelley's imagination. The contrast between the two ancient civilizations partakes in a broader tension between a supernatural ideal and a more earthbound attention to the past that runs throughout Shelley's poetry. In this sense, Shelley's attitude toward history undergoes what Kenneth Burke approvingly terms the "bureaucratization of the imaginative," a term "designed to name the vexing things that happen when men try to translate some pure aim or vision into terms of its corresponding material embodiment, thus necessarily involving elements alien to the original, 'spiritual' ('imaginative') motive."[34]

---

[34] Kenneth Burke, *Attitudes toward History*, 3rd ed. (1937; Berkeley: University of California Press, 1984), introduction, n.p.

Burke's bureaucratized imaginative provides a helpful term for surveying the transformations of Shelley's historical understanding and, more specifically, for what I have described as a shift in Shelley's analysis of Roman significance. Shelley's early letters to Godwin idealistically lump Greece and Rome together as nefarious and excessively martial societies good for little in contemporary Europe except to justify further warmongering and assorted dictatorships of taste. As the critical attention focused on Shelley's Hellenism makes abundantly clear, Shelley's position would very quickly change, and demonstrative praise of Greece and Greek examples marks nearly all of Shelley's writing. Increasingly, however, Shelley's treatment of Greece shifts from an almost supernatural enthusiasm in which Greece is an enduring example of Promethean perfection to a still reverent, but more deeply skeptical and historically grounded veneration for Greece as a society in which liberty and the arts flourished first and more prevalently than in other places. And an Athens considered as part of history and returned from otherworldly abstraction leaves room also for a historically considered Rome. Sometimes Shelley's many remarks about Rome seem peripheral, whereas in other places Rome functions as a negative foil to the positive virtues of Greece, an effective vehicle with which to criticize Regency England and post-Waterloo Europe more generally.

Shelley's use of Rome, then, presents a two-sided process of concept formation and concept application. As Rome comes to seem more apposite to the case of England—with its increasingly rigid structure of franchise, its emergent bureaucracy, its push toward imperial expansion and cultural spread, its attempt to institutionalize stability with outmoded forms, and its longstanding fascination with imitating and repeating the Roman Empire—then the case of Rome becomes a conceptual frame, a paradigm of empire generally, with its cultural spread, institutionalism, and conscious imitation. This is not simply an instance of Shelley ascribing a conceptual definition to Rome nor of his claiming that England becomes similar to Rome, but rather, the very appositeness of Rome for England provokes a conceptual enhancement of what Rome means, which in turn deepens the apposition. And as the link between England and Rome becomes ever more defined, then Greece itself emerges as an alternative because it is linked oppositionally to Rome. Shelley's Hellenism can thus be conceived as a reaction not to the cult of the Germanic, but to the eighteenth-century British fascination with Rome. It becomes relevant not as a continuation and remanifestation of an earlier neoclassicism, but rather as an historically nuanced reconsideration of the classical heritage itself, a thinking through to different ends of the relationship of antiquity to the present. This is why Wallace and Kroeber are correct to note the skepticism and ambivalence of Romantic Hellenism—a seeming tentativeness that for them serves as a caution away from a politicized reading. But as we begin to read Shelley's understanding of the relationship of Greece and Rome in the context of his historicism, we can see why Shelley's thinking about the classical past was complex and ambiguous, but also why we must recognize the aggressively political implications of Shelley's thought. Far from being a simple abandonment of Shelley's ideals, the subtle compromises inherent in his reconsideration of ancient history, the bureaucratization of Shelley's imaginative ideal, reveals a maturing poet pressing a more "usable past" to the service of his passionate belief in political freedom.

Part III

Drama

Chapter Five

Rome-antic Shakespeare

Coriolanus on Stage and Page, 1789–1820

In the past decade, a number of scholars have used the theater to refine significantly our understanding of Romantic period culture.[1] Their studies and editorial projects have shown, for example, how Romanticism, with its emphasis on imagination, solitude, and critical self-consciousness, was constituted as a willful forgetting of the physicality, sensationalism, gender relations, and spectacular violence of the theater. While many of these works use theater and theatricality as a means to discuss more traditionally Romantic texts, others have focused on the Romantic stage as important in its own right. Michael Gamer and Jeffrey Cox's *Broadview Anthology of Romantic Drama* opens with a thick description of what it would have been like to attend a theatrical performance in Romantic London. Jane Moody has demonstrated

---

[1] As late as 2000, Jane Moody lamented "the theatre's virtual absence from Romantic scholarship" (3). Those scholars returning the theater to critical attention include Julie Carlson (*In the Theatre of Romanticism: Coleridge, Nationalism, Women* [Cambridge: Cambridge University Press, 1994]), Judith Pascoe (*Romantic Theatricality: Gender, Poetry, and Spectatorship* [Ithaca: Cornell University Press, 1997]), Catherine Burroughs (*Closet Stages: Joanna Baillie and the Theatre Theory of British Romantic Women Writers* [Philadelphia: University of Pennsylvania Press, 1997]), Jane Moody (*Illegitimate Theatre in London, 1770–1840* [Cambridge: Cambridge University Press, 2000]), Michael Gamer and Jeffrey Cox (*The Broadview Anthology of Romantic Drama* [Peterborough, ON: Broadview Press, 2003]), Daniel O'Quinn (*Staging Governance: Theatrical Imperialism in London* [Baltimore: Johns Hopkins University Press, 2005]), and, most recently, David Worrall (*Theatric Revolution: Drama, Censorship, and Romantic Period Subcultures, 1773–1832* [Oxford: Oxford University Press, 2006]).

the interdependence of theatrical and literary culture, how theatrical producers and consumers shaped the cultural hierarchies and critical concepts that came to define Romanticism. Most recently, David Worrall has detailed the crucial role of the theater in London radical culture and suggested that the early-nineteenth-century theater might be understood as a laboratory of reform and revolution. Collectively, this work has shown us that the theater needs to be recognized as part of what Paul Magnuson would call "public Romanticism."[2] It has, in other words, broken down the boundaries between the public institutions and physical spaces of staged performance and a closet "mental theater," whose inwardness and anti-theatricality was traditionally understood as a rejection of those institutions and spaces.[3] The theater is an explicitly public space, and in a time of extraordinary political and social upheaval marked by the British response to the French Revolution and by increasing extra-Parliamentary pressure for the expansion of the franchise, the theater was a vital locus for the struggle over political control and the consumption of culture in a democratic age. Perhaps more important, the theater was throughout the period, and especially with the revival of the parliamentary reform movement after Waterloo, a place for debating the very nature of publicness, for contesting what should count as public speech and who should be entitled to that speech. This is so especially because the theater provided one of the few kinds of leisure that included participants from all social groups.

The following two chapters engage aspects of this new interest in Romantic period drama—in particular its thinking about the political and cultural significance of the stage and its critical account of the relationship between theatrical production and the Romantic imagination—but each chapter focuses specifically on the dramatization of the Roman republic. Rome is central in unacknowledged ways

---

[2] Paul Magnuson, *Reading Public Romanticism* (Princeton, NJ: Princeton University Press, 1998).

[3] The term comes from Byron; see *Letters and Journals*, ed. Leslie Marchand (Cambridge: Belknap, 1973–1982), 8:186–187. On Romantic mental theater, see Alan Richardson, *A Mental Theater: Poetic Drama and Consciousness in the Romantic Age* (University Park: Pennsylvania State University Press, 1988).

to the concerns addressed by scholars of Romantic theater.[4] The particular staging of a Roman republican-themed play by John Kemble produced one of the most important Romantic theorizations of imagination, Hazlitt's claim that poetry is "right royal. It puts the individual for the species, the one above the infinite many, might before right."[5] Furthermore, as a political space (and a public sphere), the theater was perhaps more representative of the nation than even Parliament in the years before the 1832 Reform Bill expanded the franchise and recast the districts of representation, but it was also subject to censorship by the Lord Chamberlain. The distancing effects provided by antiquity, however, made it possible to stage volatile political issues—including regicide, the establishment of a republic, and popular participation in the political process—by displacing these concerns into a Roman setting. Hazlitt even suggested that Shakespeare's *Coriolanus* could be a more effective vehicle for political debate than works by Burke or Paine. Finally, if Roman matters were often thought to be the province of educated elites trained in classical languages, then the representation of Rome in the theater provides an example of how knowledge of Rome and Roman figures could be spread across the social spectrum even to those social groups, most notably women and the working class, who were less likely to have a classical education. Simply put, as a public, popular form attracting an audience from all levels of British society, the theater made versions of Rome available to masses and elites alike. A focus on the staging of Rome, then, reveals republican Rome's presence outside of elite literary culture and thus helps to amplify a potentially overlooked aspect of Rome's reach and significance in this period.

This chapter evaluates alternative ways that motifs and heroic figures from the Roman republic circulated in Romantic period culture with particular focus on both the staging and the print

---

[4] Diego Saglia has situated a number of Roman plays in connection with Whig political culture. See Saglia's "'The Talking Demon': Liberty and Liberal Ideologies on the 1820s British Stage," *Nineteenth-Century Contexts* 28 (2006): 347–377. I discuss Saglia's account in chapter 6.

[5] *The Complete Works of William Hazlitt*, ed. P. P. Howe (London: J. M. Dent and Sons, 1931), 5:347.

discussion of Shakespeare's *Coriolanus*. It would be an understatement to suggest that Romantic culture was fascinated with Shakespeare. As an individual figure, he stands as one of the quintessential examples of the Romantic obsession with "artistic genius," and as a body of work, the heroes and villains of Shakespeare's plays refract seemingly everywhere. On the basis of such prevalence, Jonathan Bate argues for a shift from classical allusion in the early part of the eighteenth century to allusion to the English classics in the later part. He locates this shift not only in eighteenth-century poetry, but also in political caricature, and he suggests that it is symptomatic of the forging of a "distinctly national culture."[6] But Bate's proposition of a firm shift from the classical to the English classics overstates the case. As previous chapters have demonstrated, classical antiquity continued to be a vital presence in Romantic period culture. Furthermore, Shakespeare's plays, as much as they may have contributed to English national culture, are not concerned solely with English topics. As a result, Shakespeare's Roman plays help to reveal a more complicated process whereby a national culture is fashioned from the combination of classical culture and English classics.

Of Shakespeare's three plays on Roman subjects, *Coriolanus* was staged most often through the period.[7] *Julius Caesar* and Addison's *Cato* helped to keep the Roman republic visible to Romantic

---

[6] Jonathan Bate, *Shakespearean Constitutions: Politics, Theatre, Criticism, 1730–1830* (Oxford: Clarendon Press, 1989), 19.

[7] By my count, *Coriolanus* was performed at least eighty-eight times in licensed London theaters between Kemble's first performance on 7 February 1789 and Macready's production of 1 June 1832; it was staged ninety times in regional Theatres Royal, including Edinburgh, Manchester, Birmingham, Liverpool, Bristol, and Bath. See the "Chronological Handlist of Performances, 1609–1994" in John Ripley, *Coriolanus on Stage in England and America, 1609–1994* (Madison, NJ: Fairleigh Dickinson University Press, 1998), 343–366. In contrast, *Julius Caesar* was not performed during this period until Kemble's revival of the play on 29 February 1812. By my count, it was then staged forty-six times in London between Kemble's revival and Young's performance as Brutus at Drury Lane on 26 October 1829. Perhaps in response to the success of *Julius Caesar*, *Anthony and Cleopatra* was revived on 15 November 1813, but it was repeated only eight times. See John Genest, *Some Account of the English Stage from the Restoration in 1660–1830*, 10 vols. (Bath, 1832).

theater audiences, but the late revival of *Julius Caesar* and the relative infrequency of *Cato*'s performance meant that the dominant image of Rome on the British Romantic stage was *Coriolanus*. This is because John Philip Kemble used the role to portray the rightness of patrician rule in a time of popular unrest. *Coriolanus* is a play about the nature of political power. It depicts the Roman patrician class hoarding grain while the plebeians starve, but it also dramatizes the dependence of political leaders on the approval of the people. In the context of movements to reform parliament and expand the franchise and at a time of food shortages caused by prolonged Continental warfare, *Coriolanus* was therefore an emphatically topical play for Romantic period audiences. Looking at the staging of the play in this period suggests how the legacy of ancient Rome was contested on the Romantic stage in relation to contemporary political disputes. In making this argument, I will compare Kemble's performance as Coriolanus from 1789 to 1817 with Edmund Kean's brief tenure in the role in 1820. Kemble and Kean were the two most famous actors in Romantic period culture, and their acting styles and interpretive approaches were often contrasted by commentators on Romantic drama. The staging of *Coriolanus*, in turn, provides a concrete example of how early Roman republican heroes come before Romantic audiences in popular, nontextual ways. A comparison of Kemble and Kean in the role of Coriolanus clarifies both Romantic anxieties about Shakespearean performance and Hazlitt's famous description of the imagination as an aristocratic faculty that produces his declaration that poetry is "right royal." Hazlitt's understanding of the play, however, was based less on the text of *Coriolanus* and more on Kemble's emphatically aristocratic staging of the play, whose title character Heinrich Heine would later call "the Roman Tory."[8] The performance history of *Coriolanus*, in other words, provides the crucial subtext for understanding a key Romantic period theorization of the imagination.

---

[8] For Heine's comments, which date from 1891, see *The Romantics on Shakespeare*, ed. Jonathan Bate (London: Penguin, 1992), 291–293.

SHAKESPEARE AND THE CLASSICS

Any consideration of the intersection of Shakespeare and classical antiquity in the late eighteenth and early nineteenth centuries involves complex problems of mediation and questions about how the Romantic understanding of the classical past is shaped by the transmission of antiquity through vernacular texts like Shakespeare's Roman plays. The dynamic is further complicated by an additional dimension of mediation whereby reinterpretations of the antique past could in turn affect the staging of Shakespeare's plays, as we see in Kean's 1820 staging of *Coriolanus*, which returned the set to mud huts and thus raised questions about anachronism in Kemble's grand imperial sets. Bate and others have argued that the relationship between Shakespeare and the classics is one of perceived replacement, where, with the consolidation of a national (and nationalistic) literary history, Shakespeare emerged in the Romantic period as the English national poet, and references to Shakespeare begin to replace allusions to the classics as the cornerstone of elite and learned discourse. The issue of mediation, however, suggests that Shakespeare and the classics do not need to be seen as mutually exclusive sources of cultural capital and can rather be considered as mutually reinforcing sources for shaping aspects of English national identity.

In chapter 2, I argued that Jacobin novelists were aware of anxieties that the novel would replace the classics as a source of knowledge and that they exploited this awareness by reinscribing a Plutarchian mode of history into the novel form. Charlotte Smith's *Desmond* (1792) offers an apparent counterexample. In this novel, Shakespeare and not classical texts authorize the political discourse of learned and privileged men. *Desmond* presents an eponymous hero who leaves England for France because he has fallen in love with a married woman and hopes that political turmoil will divert his attention. The novel is an overtly politicized engagement both with the principles and events of the French Revolution and with the English response to them, as Desmond reads Burke's *Reflections* and Paine's *Rights of Man*. In one letter to Erasmus Bethel, his former estate manager and long-term confidant, Desmond casually quotes Petrarch and *Henry VI* while making reference to Burke's "swinish multitude" and reporting his reading of Paine. The bulk of the letter, however, recounts Desmond's debate with Lord Fordingbridge over the state of England. Fordingbridge takes what Hazlitt would later call "the minister's side of the question"[9] and argues that "'there is no cause for complaint in England: nobody is poor, unless it be by their own fault; and nobody is oppressed.'"[10] In response, Desmond emphasizes the draconian state of English penal law, the awkward gap between rich and poor, and the need to "'amend what is acknowledged to be defective'" (*D*, 183). In calling attention to the contrast between the ornaments and jewels of illustrious personages and the poor who die from want and exposure, Desmond quotes *King Lear*:

> Take physic pomp—
> Expose thyself to feel what wretches feel; (*D*, 181)

He also makes reference to Thomson, Pope, Cowper, and other plays by Shakespeare. Such references, however, bring only scorn from his interlocutor and Mr. Cranbourne, Fordingbridge's guardian and travel companion:

"As to your poets," cried Mr Cranbourne superciliously—"there is no bringing argument against their flowery declamation: fine sounding words about rights and liberties, are imposing to superficial understandings, but cannot convince others—fine flourishing words are not arguments." (*D*, 186)

As Fordingbridge has the support of those listening, Desmond leaves him to the "the triumph of his imagined superiority," and he slinks off to solitude, resolving that if he should mix more in society, he must, like Iago, "Disguise the thing I am/ By seeming otherwise" (*D*, 187).

What is curious about this exchange is that in a debate about government and current affairs between two upper-class English gentlemen, there are no references to classical texts or authors; instead, English texts and writers are most commonly cited. In contrast to

---

[9] See William Hazlitt, *Letter to William Gifford*, in *The Complete Works of William Hazlitt*, ed. P. P. Howe (London: J. M. Dent, 1930–1934), 9:33. Subsequent page references to this edition will be abbreviated *CWH* and provided parenthetically in the text.

[10] Charlotte Smith, *Desmond*, edited with introduction and notes by Antje Blank and Janet Todd (London: Pickering and Chatto, 1997), 180. Subsequent references to this edition will be abbreviated *D* and given parenthetically in the text.

Burke—who, as I have suggested in chapter 1, utilizes both vernacular and classical references—the debate between Desmond and Fordingbridge relies entirely on the vernacular, with Desmond repeatedly drawing on Shakespearean allusions to consolidate his sympathy for the oppressed and his support of the French Revolution. To a certain extent, such use of Shakespeare complicates my argument in chapter 2 that Jacobin novels transform the public discourse of classical citation into a more broadly accessible re-encoding of certain classical virtues. Seen from a different angle, though, Smith's use of Shakespeare and other Jacobin novelists' use of the classics are two sides of the same coin. Both underscore the centrality of classical reference in public discourse through their response to it, and both offer suggestions for replacement. Desmond's persistent quotation of Shakespeare performs the replacement of the classics by enacting the legitimation of learned discourse based on a national culture of Shakespeare and other English poets.

The use of Shakespeare in Smith's novel further indicates the increasing politicization of such allusion, an impression borne out by the flurry of debate and discussion surrounding Shakespeare in the Romantic period. When calling upon English literary texts in support of the radical cause, Desmond quotes the same passage in *King Lear* that John Thelwall, the prominent Jacobin radical who was tried for treason in 1794, would later use as the epigraph to *Tribune*, No. 1, 14 March 1795. In that piece "On the proper means of arresting National Calamities," the quote from *Lear* underscores conditions of scarcity for which Thelwall faults the government, with its war and its corruption. Thelwall, who had previously offered a series of lectures on Roman history in 1795, had himself turned to Shakespeare for a new series of lectures by early 1818. If we are to believe Thelwall's subsequent comments about these lectures in the *Champion*, they "excited very popular attention."[11] Thelwall's lectures would have had considerable competition. They were offered at the same time as a set of lectures by Hazlitt at the Surrey Institution and, on the other side of the Thames, by Samuel Taylor Coleridge at the London Philosophical

---

[11] *The Champion*, 10 January 1819, 29; quoted by Bate, *Shakespearean Constitutions*, 176.

Society.[12] In addition to the simultaneous lectures on the plays by Thelwall, Hazlitt, and Coleridge, the post-Waterloo years also saw the publication of Hazlitt's *Characters from Shakespeare's Plays* in 1817, Gifford's attack on this volume in 1818, Hazlitt's reply to Gifford in his 1819 *A Letter to William Gifford*, and various responses to the entire exchange, including a long transcription from Hazlitt's *Letter* by John Keats in a letter to his émigré brother, George, in America.

The use of Shakespeare in *Desmond* and the intensity of dispute about Shakespeare throughout the Romantic period might thus be seen to confirm Bate's claim that throughout the eighteenth century, classical allusion evolved into allusion to the English classics. But Shakespeare could be used to reflect not only on English questions, but also on the relationship between England and Roman antiquity. In a review of the recent revival of *Julius Caesar*, for example, the 29 March 1812 edition of John and Leigh Hunt's weekly newspaper, the *Examiner*, suggested:

An impression is left upon us of Roman manners and greatness,—of the appearance as well as the intellect of Romans,—which to a young mind in particular must furnish an indelible picture for the assistance of his studies, resembling perhaps the clearness of local conception which is afforded by a panorama.[13]

---

[12] Although Thelwall's lectures are lost, we can get a sense of his arguments from his comments on Shakespeare in the *Tribune*, where he asks, in reference to *Coriolanus*, "Who can behold without indignation the contemptible light in which he has exhibited those virtuous tribunes to whom Rome owed such a large portion of her liberty?" See *Shakespeare: The Critical Tradition: Coriolanus*, ed. David George (New York: Thoemmes Continuum, 2004), 89. In his 1818 lectures, Coleridge, in contrast, praised *Coriolanus* for the "wonderfully philosophic impartiality of Shakespeare's Politics" (ibid, 103). Hazlitt's reading of the play will be discussed in more detail below. On the simultaneous series of lectures, see Bate, *Shakespearian Constitutions*, 175–178.

[13] Odell, *Shakespeare from Betterton to Irving* (New York: Charles Scribner's Sons, 1920), 106. The movement from staged performance to study is echoed in the prefatory remarks to James Sheridan Knowles's *Caius Gracchus* for Cumberland's British Theatre Series. Here, as part of a defense of historical drama and the blending of history and fiction more generally, D.G. suggests that "when history borrows the aid of romance to heighten and adorn its more unimportant details," and when the integrity of principle characters are maintained, then "those who, but for the dramatist, had remained ignorant of Greek and Roman story may be led to the fountains of ancient lore, and become wise—not in the every-day sense of the term—but by study, experience, and research" (*Cumberland's British Theatre* [London: John Cumberland, 1826], Vol. 6, *Caius Gracchus*, 6). D. G. is the unidentified abbreviation used in the original.

Shakespeare is here passed over in favor of classical study. A Shakespeare play becomes, in a movement counter to what we would expect from Bate's claim, not an object in itself or a reflection on English national identity, but rather a means to enhance a schoolboy's understanding of Rome. That the play should be understood in this manner, of course, reflects how English national identity was itself constructed through its understanding of Rome, and this suggests the high stakes inherent in any attempt to interpret Roman history on the English stage. We must recognize, in other words, the various levels of mediation implied in the response to Shakespeare, the way in which Shakespeare's Roman plays, *Coriolanus* especially, can be understood as an index for how republican Rome, as transmitted through Shakespeare, was used to shape aspects of English national identity. We can get a clear sense of this from Heine's later comments on *Coriolanus*, when he observes:

> As there are many events at the present day which bear a resemblance to those sad quarrels which the privileged Patricians and the degraded Plebeians formerly waged with one another, we are better able to judge of this [Shakespeare's comprehension of the spirit of these disputes]. Shakespeare might be a poet of the present day living in London, and describing the Radicals and Tories of the present time under a Roman mask. We are borne out in this opinion by the great resemblance which exists between ancient Romans and modern Englishmen, as also between their respective statesmen.[14]

Although Heine writes at the end of the nineteenth century, his comments hold no less true for the earlier part of the century, and Heine was not alone in seeing the parallel. Gifford's attack on Hazlitt turns on Hazlitt's reading of *Coriolanus*, which also emphasized contemporary parallels and which Gifford claimed slandered Shakespeare by declaring that he leaned toward the arbitrary side of the question. In his response to Gifford, Hazlitt intensified the vindictiveness of the dispute when he labeled Gifford a "*Government Critic*, a character nicely differing from that of a government spy—the invisible link, that connects literature with the police" (*CWH*, 9:13). In the dispute between Hazlitt and Gifford, the fundamental question is the relationship between

---

[14] *Romantics on Shakespeare*, 292.

literature and power; Rome is central to this quarrel, as mediated through *Coriolanus*, but also in the way that a reading of *Coriolanus* opens more questions about the excesses of the Roman emperors.

SHAKESPEARE AND ROMANTIC PERFORMANCE: KEMBLE'S *CORIOLANUS*

The strongly political undertones and themes of Shakespearean drama—whether it be the staging of historical event in the histories, the subversion and reversal of the comedies, or the many traumas of power and succession in the tragedies—make it full of potential for contemporary allusion. In October of 1789, for example, Kemble produced *Henry V* with the subtitle, "The Conquest of France"; he repeated this role sixteen times before the end of 1792, and then revived it in 1803 after the collapse of the Peace of Amiens.[15] With the question of King George III's madness, *King Lear* was kept off the London stage from 1811 to 1820.[16] And in light of the dissolute public image of the Prince Regent, a special subtext was attached to productions of *Henry IV*. Allusions to the play entered the political discourse of the Regency, and when the play was revived in the summer of 1821—having last been played in 1804—four additional scenes presenting a "Grand Coronation" were added. The prince himself commanded that the doors of Covent Garden be opened *gratis* to the public on 19 July 1821, the day of his coronation.

Not all Shakespearean allusion was triumphant, however. Mary Jacobus has shown two problems attached to the performance of *Macbeth* in the period. She notes how Macbeth's dream of a dagger makes theatrical representation problematic and, how, as a regicide play, *Macbeth* serves as a touchstone for reflections on the French Revolution.[17] *Coriolanus* shares with *Macbeth* its representation of

---

[15] Bate, *Shakespearean Constitutions*, 63.
[16] Ibid., 85.
[17] Mary Jacobus, "'That Great Stage Where Senators Perform': *Macbeth* and the Politics of Romantic Theatre," *Studies in Romanticism* 22 (1983): 353–387.

the thing feared: in *Macbeth*, regicide, in *Coriolanus*, uprising from below. The conflict between the tribunes of the people and Coriolanus, for example, results in ruminations on the nature of participatory republican government and the threat of popular uprising. It would thus seem especially apt for contemporary parallels in a period charged with pressure to extend the franchise and reform the government. As Nathan Drake described *Coriolanus* in 1817, "It affords us a picture of what may be termed a Roman electioneering mob; and the insolence of newly acquired authority on the part of the tribunes, and the ungovernable license and malignant ribaldry of the plebeians, are forcibly, but naturally expressed."[18] What *Coriolanus* has that *Macbeth* does not is what we might describe as the neutralizing effect of antiquity—the precise effect, as we saw in chapter 1, on which Thelwall relied in 1796 when he initiated his series of Roman lectures. *Coriolanus* makes it possible to explore relationships of power and hierarchy in a structured but non-monarchic pre-Christian setting.[19] In the past, this had also made it a useful vehicle through which to highlight contemporary political issues: in 1681, Nahum Tate adapted *Coriolanus* as an anti-Whig tract titled "The Ingratitude of the Commonwealth," and John Dennis produced a version of *Coriolanus* in 1719 called "The Invader of His Country." Similarly, *Julius Caesar* presents the classic republican tale of the younger Brutus and his coconspirators uniting to protect the constitution from its usurpation by a potential tyrant. In the 1740s, quotations from *Julius Caesar* were used in a caricature likening Walpole to Caesar.[20] Even *Antony and Cleopatra*, though it would seem to be more of a love story and was dismissed harshly by Johnson for its lack of decorum, could be mined for contemporary allusion. Hazlitt complained in his review of an 1813 revival of the play that "The piece seems to have been in some measure got up for the occasion, as there are several claptraps in the speeches, which

---

[18] The passage comes from Drake's *Shakespeare and His Times* (1817), and is reprinted in *Coriolanus: The Critical Tradition*, 95.

[19] See T. J. B. Spencer, "Shakespeare and the Elizabethan Romans," *Shakespeare Survey* 10 (1957): 27–38.

[20] Bate, *Shakespearean Constitutions*, 70–71.

admit of an obvious allusion to passing characters and events, and which were eagerly seized by the audience."[21]

Although this brief sketch outlines the potential topicality of Shakespeare's Roman plays in the Romantic period, their actual staging proves more complicated. David Garrick, the preeminent eighteenth-century Shakespearean actor, produced *Antony and Cleopatra* at Drury Lane in January of 1759 and then again in May.[22] The play was not seen again in London, however, until Charles Young's revival at Covent Garden on 15 November 1813.[23] *Julius Caesar* was staged from January to April of 1780, but it was not again produced in London until John Kemble's production on 29 February 1812. As a result, the dominant version of Shakespeare's Rome presented to Romantic audiences was *Coriolanus*, which was staged repeatedly throughout the period. How might this be explained?

An initial response must consider the paucity of theatrical venues in London. There were only two royally licensed theaters, Covent Garden and Drury Lane. Although the Haymarket ran a shorter series when these two theaters were out of season, notable productions of Shakespeare were limited to Covent Garden and Drury Lane. Both Theatres Royal were enormous; at Drury Lane, for example, the auditorium rose 48 feet above the pit, and the stage itself was daunting, covering an area 60 feet deep and 33 feet wide at the proscenium. In July 1805, Covent Garden could hold 3,044 people, with nightly expenses of 160 pounds, average nightly revenues of 300 pounds, and maximum revenue of 600 pounds. Drury Lane could hold 3,611, with expenses of 200 pounds per night and maximum revenues of 770 pounds and 16 shillings. Both were rebuilt to accommodate large crowds after destruction by fire in 1808 (Covent Garden) and 1809 (Drury Lane). The sheer size of each space made it difficult to hear, and matters were not helped by the audience's tendency to converse throughout the play and to interrupt speeches with prolonged

---

[21] See the *Morning Chronicle*, 16 November 1813, reprinted in *A View of the English Stage, CWH*, 5:190.
[22] See Charles Beecher Hogan, *Shakespeare in the Theatre, 1701–1800* (Oxford: Clarendon Press, 1957).
[23] Genest, *Some Account of the English Stage*, 8:417–419.

applause.[24] Criticism of the size of London theaters was routine.[25] George Coleman the Younger, for example, the actor who would become dramatic censor in 1824, delivered a prologue in which he mocked the impossibility of hearing staged drama in the Theatres-Royal:

> When people appear
> Quite unable to hear,
> 'Tis undoubtedly needless to talk;
>
> ... 'Twere better they began
> On the new invented plan,
> And with Telegraphs transmitted the plot.[26]

As a result of these poor acoustics, theaters frequently resorted to grand spectacle, and oxen, horses, even elephants were paraded across the stage. Such antics, as Jane Moody explains, show the increasingly brittle line between legitimate, licensed theater, and the spectacular effects more commonly associated with illegitimate, unlicensed drama.[27] Such distinctions were further undermined by the fact that an evening's program regularly encompassed more than one play, so that the "high" genres, tragedy and comedy, frequently shared a program with melodramas and harlequinades.[28] Clearly, the operation of such theaters was an expensive and risky venture in which production decisions were driven by potential audience more than by the possibility of timely political allusion— although the two are not necessarily unrelated. Moreover, these were royally licensed theaters operating under a strict licensing act, and they would as such be less likely to stage politically risky or innovative productions.

Production decisions were also closely connected to which actors could pack the theater in which roles. This was likely the most

[24] On the spaces and crowd dynamics of early nineteenth-century theater, see Jeffrey N. Cox and Michael Gamer, eds., *The Broadview Anthology of Romantic Drama* (Peterborough, ON: Broadview Press, 2003), vii–xxiv, and Jane Moody, *Illegitimate Theatre in London, 1770–1840* (Cambridge: Cambridge University Press, 2000).

[25] See, for example, a series of letters from "A Lover of Justice and the Drama" to the editor of the *Theatrical Inquisitor* 4 (1814): 5–6, 42–44, and 161–162; and Joanna Baillie's "To the Reader," the preface to Vol. 3 of her "Plays on the Passions," printed as *A Series of Plays* (London: Cadell and Davies, 1812), iii–xxxi, reprinted in Cox and Gamer, *Romantic Drama*, 370–378.

[26] George Coleman the Younger, "[On the Size of the Theatres]," reprinted in Cox and Gamer, *Romantic Drama*, 343.

[27] Moody, *Illegitimate Theatre*, 6.

[28] Cox and Gamer, introduction to *Romantic Drama*, vii–xxiv, esp. xii, xxiv.

prominent reason behind what got staged and what did not. As George Odell explains, "It was—and is—a question of the actors."[29] *As You Like It*, for example, was performed more than any other Shakespearean play between 1776 and 1817 at Drury Lane, whereas it was hardly ever performed in forty-one seasons at Covent Garden. This was due to the many great Rosalinds at the former theater, including Mrs. Barry, Miss Younge, and Mrs. Jordan.[30] Similarly, between 1789 and 1806, *Coriolanus* played exclusively at Drury Lane, but it then began to appear at Covent Garden. This was because Kemble left Drury Lane in 1803 when he purchased a share in Covent Garden and became an actor manager there. Kemble's diaries, which record the nightly grosses while he was managing Covent Garden, clarify this point. When Kemble played Coriolanus, his receipts were routinely the highest of the week. On 23 December 1811, Kemble as Coriolanus brought 643 pounds and 15 shillings, by far one of the highest grosses Kemble ever recorded. Charles Young, in contrast, played Coriolanus for the first time as a benefit night on 2 June 1813 and earned the considerably lesser sum of 340 pounds, 12 shillings, and 6 pence. His third performance in the role on 21 June 1813 took in a mere 177 pounds, 3 shillings, and 6 pence—the worst gross of the week by more than 100 pounds. Similarly, when William Augustus Conway acted the part at Covent Garden on 3 December 1813, he grossed 220 pounds, 1 shilling, and 6 pence; on 15 January 1814, Kemble, in his first Covent Garden appearance in two years, brought in 537 pounds and 15 shillings, the highest earnings of the week.[31] Such figures demonstrate the degree to which star players determined a theater's revenues and allowed certain dramas to become associated with certain theaters; they also further confirm Kemble's dominance of *Coriolanus*. Not until Kean attempted to challenge Kemble's interpretation of *Coriolanus* did the play appear at both Covent Garden and Drury Lane in the same season. Furthermore, because production decisions relied on the drawing power of the leading actors, certain actors, Kean and Kemble especially, had broad editorial control over what plays were staged and how

---

[29] Odell, *Shakespeare from Betterton to Irving*, 2:20.
[30] Ibid.
[31] The figures are recorded in the John Philip Kemble Diaries, British Library Add. Ms. 31972–31975.

they were produced. Kean and Kemble were both actor managers, a position comparable to contemporary Hollywood figures who garner enough box office power and enough cash to produce their own films.

Kemble was the dominant Shakespearean actor of the period, and Coriolanus was Kemble's defining role. The text Kemble used for *Coriolanus*, however, was modified from Shakespeare's original. Streamlined to create a unified line of action and a set of characters pruned to a simple and decorous grandeur, the production was based on a version by Thomas Sheridan that borrowed from a play on the same subject by James Thomson.[32] Menenius's fable of the belly (1.1.95–162), which attempts to justify patrician rule and indicates the sharp tension between the plebeians and the aristocrats, was cut from act 1. Additional cuts in scenes representing the conflict between Coriolanus and the citizens focused animosity on personal rather than political causes. Suggestions of a wider patrician-plebeian class struggle disappeared from act 1 (1.1.15–25), and, in act 3, interventions of the citizens into the struggle (3.1) and the banishment scene (3.3) were trimmed. In act 5, the famous "Oh, mother, mother!" speech (5.3.182–193) that shows Coriolanus break down was omitted to dispel all reference to the hero's weakness. As a result of these and other amendments, the tribunes became simple villains whose personal ambitions motivated their opposition to Coriolanus. Coriolanus, in turn, was no longer a complex character, and the drama presented the continuous blaze of his aristocratic integrity and fatal arrogance with refined clarity. In this way, the play becomes not a nuanced representation of the continuous push and pull between an alienated individual and collective experience, but rather a celebration of aristocratic power. As Coriolanus suffers banishment for his principles, commits treason, and is redeemed by his mother's patriotism, it remains unclear whether the might of Aufidius or the ungratefulness of the plebeians represents the greater threat to the state. With all references to the grounds of the dispute between the patricians and the plebeians removed, plebeian protest appears ridiculous and

---

[32] For a full discussion of the emendations, see Ripley, Coriolanus *on Stage*, 117–123, and Harold Child, *The Shakespearian Productions of John Phillip Kemble* (London: Published for the Shakespeare Association by Humphrey Milford, Oxford University Press, 1935), 13–16.

possibly despicable. Kemble's *Coriolanus* thus represents a commanding statement against the desirability of popular participation in the political process.

The revised version of *Coriolanus* placed firm emphasis on the power and righteousness of its protagonist. The manner in which Kemble portrayed Coriolanus minimized any sense of a tragic flaw that would make him culpable in the play's outcome and instead broadcast a formidable image of aristocratic force and merit. The imposing majesty with which Kemble played the part earned him an enormous following. Kemble's biographer notes that neither "Kemble or Mrs. Siddons achieved the fame subsequently attached to their performance of Coriolanus and Volumnia. By a course of peculiar study, antiquity became better known to Mrs. Siddons; and Mr. Kemble also grew more completely Roman."[33]

Just how Kemble and Siddons "became Roman" can be accounted for by the attention to Roman statuary and architecture in developing the production. Kemble was a close friend of Sir Joshua Reynolds and, like him, sought to distill the abstract ideal of classical art into its essence for his stage sets. For this he could draw on the development of eighteenth-century research on antique art and the presentation of stoic morality in the grave, static handling of classical subjects in the work of Gavin Hamilton and Anton Raphael Mengs. The *Times* suggested that "the scenery, which is, we believe, altogether new, exhibits a succession of Roman architecture, which exceeds any we have witnessed."[34] Kemble's sets were so stoic and so painterly that one more recent commentator suggests that

> Kemble's revivals of *Coriolanus* are virtual stage equivalents of the paintings of David. He saw in Coriolanus the kind of severe, antique hero of ancient times who would provide, like David's classic subjects, a moral example in an era of political and social upheaval.[35]

---

[33] As quoted by Odell, *Shakespeare from Betterton to Irving*, 2:87.
[34] Ibid., 2:104.
[35] Ripley, Coriolanus *on Stage*, 116. For Kemble's interest in art, architecture, and the criticism of the fine arts more generally, see 115–117. Hazlitt too observed the relation between Roman stage sets and bas relief. In his praise for Knowles's *Virginius*, Hazlitt commented on the sets' pictorial quality: "It presents a series of pictures. We might suppose each scene to be copied from a beautiful bas relief, or to have formed a group on some antique vase." As quoted by Vance, *The Victorians and Ancient Rome* (Oxford: Blackwell, 1997), 44.

The problem, though, was that what was known about Roman architecture was mainly the imperial style. As a result, a play about an early republican hero was staged on a set that showed the height of imperial Roman grandeur. Such an imperial setting, indeed, would be entirely appropriate for either of the Theatres Royal, both of which drew upon elements of neoclassical architecture for the design of interior and exterior spaces. The neoclassical qualities of the Theatres-Royal would only have been further amplified by Kemble's actual stage sets, as we can see clearly in a painting of the set for act 2 of Kemble's 1811 production at Covent Garden. The entire set exudes the grandness of imperial building projects. We see a long colonnaded gallery with its detailed lintel leading to a formidable looking building crowned with a dome and fronted by a sculptural pediment. This building is then echoed by yet another pediment-capped and colonnaded entryway deeper in the background of the picture. Compositionally the entire image is one of studied lines and sharp angles, as we see in the foreground of the picture when the front of the setting picks up the shadows of the columns. The scene exudes an imposing order and a stark imperial might whose lack of embellishment feels stoic, though the more Corinthian decorative features in the top right of the engraving add flourish, as do the rooftop sculptures on the building in the background.

George Odell explains that Kemble's 1811 production

> embodied all his best ideas on the subject of Roman architecture, dress, habits and manners, and...it was presented on a scale of great sculpturesque beauty. The Rome of his Coriolanus was of marble—the Rome of the Caesars—but granting the anachronism, it was very fine.[36]

Granting the anachronism, indeed. Romantic period culture was increasingly fascinated with historical representation and historical periodization, as evidenced most famously in separate collections of essays by Hazlitt and John Stuart Mill on the "Spirit of the Age." It should not be surprising, then, that later productions objected precisely to this anachronistic quality. As a reviewer of Charles Macready's 1838 production suggests:

---

[36] Odell, *Shakespeare from Betterton to Irving*, 2:104.

Figure 5.1. "The Roman Forum, study for theatrical scene in Shakespeare's 'Coriolanus.'" Pen and gray ink with watercolor, drawn by Hodgkin. Used as the basis for John Kemble's 1811 Covent Garden production. ©Trustees of the British Museum.

The pictures which Kemble gave when he revived the play might be splendid, but they were utterly unreal—they clustered fine buildings together with equal disregard to the proprieties of place or time—the arch of Severus or Constantine, the Coliseum, the pillar of Trajan, all the grandeurs of imperial Rome, flaunted away within three hundred years of the first birth of the city.[37]

As enacted from 1789 to 1817, then, Kemble's Rome was a neoclassical, imperial representation from its stage scenery to its costume to its characterization. It was full of gravitas, decorum, and slow, icy majesty, and marked by control and aristocratic hauteur.

---

[37] John Forster's review of W. C. Macready as Coriolanus at the Theatre Royal, Covent Garden, from the *Examiner* of 18 March 1838, reprinted in Stanley Wells, *Shakespeare in the Theatre: An Anthology of Criticism* (Oxford: Clarendon Press, 1997), 77–78.

Romantic period critics were universally in favor of this interpretation. Walter Scott, for example, praised Kemble for his "command of muscle and limb"[38] in the death scene, and Mrs. Siddons's Volumnia earned the special praise of Julian Charles Young for her defiant pride and hauteur in the procession scene introduced by Kemble into the second scene of the second act.[39] Thomas Gilliland observed a "majesty of person in Mr. Kemble.... His frame is so formed, that his stage drapery always decorates his person with a becoming elegance." Gilliland emphasized the "form and majestic lineaments" of Mr. Kemble's face and noted that no man was ever better suited to "parts that require dignity and strong expression."[40] The language of these reviews indicates clearly the kind of figure that Kemble projected as Coriolanus: he is credited with "command," "majesty," "elegance," and "dignity." Kemble's *Coriolanus* demonstrated not just his sense of himself as an actor, but also the idealization of an entire class of patrician aristocracy. Kemble is frequently characterized as an intellectual actor. Robert Speaight describes Kemble as "an abstraction of the characteristics of tragedy," and claims that his "instinct never led him where his intellect refused to follow."[41] This intellectual quality of Kemble's performance is precisely what Thomas Campbell suggested in his "Valedictory Stanzas":

> At once enobled and correct
> His mind surveyed the classic page,
> And what the actor could effect
> The scholar could presage.[42]

Although the precise referent of "classic" is unclear, Campbell's lines suggest that Kemble used his classical scholarship to inform his productions, and it would be difficult to find an actor more frequently

---

[38] Walter Scott, review of James Boaden's *Memoirs of the Life of John Philip Kemble*, in *The Quarterly Review*, 34 (June 1826), reprinted in Wells, *Shakespeare in the Theatre*, 34.

[39] Julian Charles Young, *Memoirs of Charles Mayne Young* (London, 1840), 40–41, reprinted in Wells, *Shakespeare in the Theatre*, 37–38.

[40] Thomas Gilliland, *The Dramatic Mirror* (London, 1808), 2:806–807.

[41] Robert Speaight, *Shakespeare on the Stage: An Illustrated History of Shakespearean Performance* (London: Collins, 1973), 37.

[42] Quoted by Speaight, *Shakespeare on the Stage*, 37.

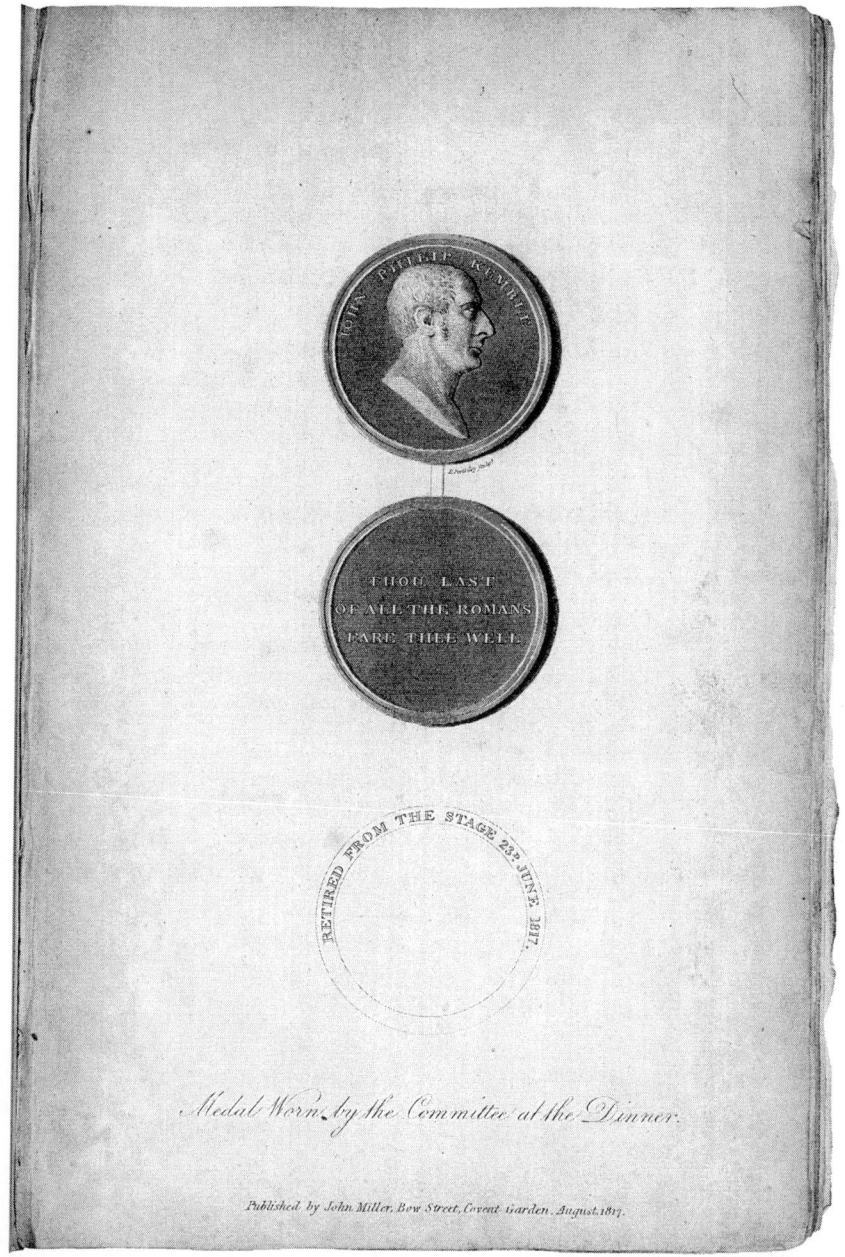

Figure 5.2. Medal worn by the committee at the farewell dinner for John Kemble, from *An Authentic Narrative of Mr. Kemble's Retirement from the Stage* (London: John Miller, 1817). By permission of the Folger Shakespeare Library.

praised in this period for his rigorous classicism. Kemble, quite simply, *was* Rome from 1789 to 1817. On the occasion of his retirement from the stage, Kemble was presented with a commemorative medallion at his farewell dinner, one worn by all the guests. This image presents a bas relief profile of Kemble in the manner of a Roman coin, while its reverse states "THOU LAST OF ALL THE ROMANS FARE THEE WELL." This phrase, a variant on *ultimus Romanorum*, was apparently first applied to Cassius and Marcus Junius Brutus in defense of their assassination of Caesar to save the Republic. It is also cited by Tacitus to lament the end of the Roman republic.[43] The irony is that the image of Rome that Kemble presented was imperial and aristocratic, a powerful projection of the rightness of patrician rule and thus a defense of the established order.

Kemble's interpretation of *Coriolanus* had a profound impact on the period, and made almost any other way of staging the text untenable, as Kean discovered in 1820. Within the context of the turbulent political situation of the 1790s and renewed calls for reform and popular political participation after Waterloo, Kemble's minimizing of tensions between the aristocrats and the plebeians had the advantage of glorifying Coriolanus's aristocratic patriotism while diminishing the citizens to mere blocks of clay. This effect was achieved not just by trimming Shakespeare's text, but also by adding to it. In act 2, when Coriolanus returns from his initial battle with the Volscians, Kemble added a procession scene. This allowed him to marshal a large crowd (reportedly 240 actors)[44] in a controlled and carefully organized manner.[45] The parade included musicians rendering "See the conquering hero comes!" from Handel's *Julius Caesar*. Kemble clearly did not care about the strangeness of celebrating the figure who ended the Roman republic in a play about an early republican hero, for the odd pairing reinforced his notions of exemplary heroism and the distilled essence of classical culture. The celebration of Caesar only further underscores the production's emphasis on absolute authority and control,

---

[43] See Norman Vance, *The Victorians and Ancient Rome* (Oxford: Blackwell, 1997), 9–10. The Tacitus reference can be found in *Annals* 4.34.

[44] Young, *Memoirs of Charles Mayne Young*, reprinted in Wells, *Shakespeare in the Theatre*, 37.

[45] In recognizing the significance of an interpolated crowd scene, I am indebted to Bate, *Shakespearean Constitutions*, 63.

though there remains a tension in invoking Caesar, a figure associated by classical scholars with the popular party, in connection with Coriolanus, who so doggedly opposes the plebeians. In the procession, Coriolanus brings up the rear of this crowd, and when they have all exited the stage, he stands beneath a triumphal arch. It was an overwhelmingly dramatic moment, as one spectator reported:

> The spoils, the captives, the soldiers, the citizens had passed over, and there, *alone*, beneath the triumphal arch, stood the hero, in his simple graceful, crimson robe, with his black head uncovered, and his attitude dictated by the very spirit of classic taste!...The exquisite beauty of the statue struck even the most uncultivated mind, and...the spectators were in an absolute ecstasy of delight.[46]

Despite this, *Coriolanus* was withdrawn from production from 1797 to 1806, for, as Mrs. Inchbald observed, "When the lower order of people are in good plight they will bear contempt with cheerfulness, and even with mirth; but poverty puts them out of humour at the slightest disrespect. Certain sentences in this play are, therefore, of dangerous tendency at certain times."[47]

Still, if anything could quell that "dangerous tendency," it was Kemble's larger-than-life representation of aristocratic force. This sense is further evident in the visual record of Kemble's representation of Coriolanus. Sir Thomas Lawrence was a much sought-after portrait painter whose subjects included the King and other royalty, nobility, and similarly elevated figures. That Kemble features among these illustrious subjects indicates his stature, and Lawrence's painting of Kemble as Coriolanus underscores the importance of that role for the actor. In Lawrence's portrait, Kemble dominates over the background, appearing to be double its scale gazing off into the distance with one foot firmly planted at the bottom of the image. He resembles nothing less than the anchored solidity of a classical column, with his sandaled foot as its base and his curly hair as its capitol, a last pillar of the old Roman order, a projection of patrician dignity and force.

---

[46] William Robeson, *The Old Play Goer* (1846), 35, as quoted by Ripley, *Coriolanus on Stage*, 129.

[47] Quoted by Ripley, *Coriolanus on Stage*, 114. One exception should be noted. In May 1804, *Coriolanus* was produced at Drury Lane with George Cooke in the title role.

Figure 5.3. John Philip Kemble as Coriolanus, oil painting by Sir Thomas Lawrence, 1798. Courtesy of the Guildhall Art Gallery, City of London.

Figure 5.4. Coriolanus, act 5, scene 3. From *A Collection of Prints...from the Dramatic Works of Shakespeare* (London, John and Josiah Boydell, 1803). By permission of the Folger Shakespeare Library.

Kemble's projection of aristocratic hauteur also influenced contemporary images of Coriolanus that make no mention of Kemble, as in the image from act 5, scene 3 from Boydell's Shakespeare Gallery. Though this is not Kemble, it suggests a portrayal of the hero similar to that in Kemble's production. Here, Coriolanus approaches the Roman matrons, and the image, with an open background, is organized around the front of Coriolanus and the back of Volumnia, each placed one third from opposite borders. The two so dominate the other figures in size that they appear to be of a superhuman race, while the broad, sinewy front of Coriolanus and the huge sword he holds in his right hand make him the emblem of aristocratic power gazing with compassion upon his suppliant wife and child who occupy the center of the picture.

Figure 5.5. George Cruikshank, *Coriolanus addressing the Plebeians*. ©Trustees of the British Museum.

George Cruikshank's caricature of Coriolanus confronting the plebeians further reveals the statuesque imperiousness with which Coriolanus was portrayed in the visual tradition. Coriolanus stands apart from the plebeians among late Roman architecture with prominent columns and arches. Even accounting for perspective, he appears double their size and girth. They slouch, tremble, and bend, and they have elongated, almost grotesque faces while he defiantly stares them down. He is distinguished by a toga worn over what appears to be a breastplate, and with his gaze rising above their heads, he more closely resembles one of the enormous columns in the background than he does a man. Cruikshank draws upon the visual tropes of Boydell's engraver and of Lawrence to represent the enormity of the confrontation. He also calls our attention to the explicit politicization of the play. One banner reads "Burdett forever," in

Figure 5.6. Peterloo massacre. Courtesy of Manchester Archives and Local Studies, Manchester Central Library.

reference to Sir Francis Burdett, a leading member of the opposition and a fervent campaigner for parliamentary reform, while the plebeians hold banners calling for "Parliamentary Reform" and "Liberty of the Press." These are precisely the slogans of the reform movement seen prominently in images of the 1819 massacre called Peterloo, which proceeded when the cavalry of the Manchester yeomanry charged a large group of peaceful demonstrators at St. Peter's Fields, killing more than ten and injuring hundreds. Ministers at the time were fiercely unapologetic for the actions of the yeomanry.[48] These visual echoes of the iconography of Peterloo underscore the topicality of *Coriolanus* in this period, the way that the play was so consistently seen by Hazlitt and others to dramatize matters of immediate contemporary parallel. Given the dominance of

---

[48] For a full description of Peterloo, see E. P. Thompson, *The Making of the English Working Class* (New York: Vintage, 1966), 669–700; for a sense of the relationship between Peterloo and the representational strategies of the period, see also James Chandler, *England in 1819* (Chicago: University of Chicago Press, 1998).

Kemble over the role of Coriolanus and the statuesque majesty that he projected in the role, Kemble's staging of the play intensified its topicality in a way that made possible Cruikshank's caricatures.

KEAN'S CHALLENGE TO KEMBLE'S *CORIOLANUS*

This marmoreal *Coriolanus* of Kemble, however, was not without its challengers. On 25 January 1820, five months after Peterloo, Kean and theater manager Robert Elliston staged a revival of *Coriolanus* at Covent Garden using the original Shakespeare text with deletions only. If Kemble's Coriolanus drew his strength and position as the representative of an aristocratic class and his pride as the trademark of aristocratic society, Kean's portrayal can be described as stereotypically Romantic, Byronic even. The staging was flushed with a dramatic and passionate individuality in which pride was the product of a unique psyche. As in Kemble's production, political and military content were deemphasized in favor of character revelation, and action and spectacle were preferred to speech. Again, the production was built around its star, who was never long absent from the stage. Though we have no visual record of the production, we do know that Ellison argued that the visual milieu should represent the early period of Coriolanus's triumph and downfall and not Kemble's imperial splendor. Authenticity was crucial, and the production staked its uniqueness on these grounds.[49] As Ellison states in the acting edition, "Not even a fragment remains to us of the Roman buildings or dresses in the time of Coriolanus."[50] He therefore drew on bas relief and vase paintings for his scenery, which attracted hardly any censure. Consistent with this reading, Kean played Coriolanus not in the manner of Kemble, as an elegant Roman of later times, but rather as a rough soldier of the early republic: a proud, impetuous, primitive creature of absolute *virtus* colliding with a temporizing society; in short, "a kind of Byronic hero."[51]

[49] Ripley, Coriolanus *on Stage*, 144.
[50] Quoted by Ripley, Coriolanus *on Stage*, 150.
[51] Ripley, Coriolanus *on Stage*, 148.

The distinction between the two productions would have been striking, and Kean's effort to overcome Kemble's anachronism must be interpreted as a direct challenge to Kemble's aristocratic version of the play and, more, as an attempt to reimagine Rome in a manner different from Kemble's emphasis on the rightness of patrician rule. When Kean staged *Coriolanus*, war with France was five years in the past, and the movement for parliamentary reform was again vigorous. Peterloo would have been fresh in the audience's memory as the conjunction of that event with Coriolanus in Cruikshank's caricature indicates. In an atmosphere of unrest, Kemble's imperial set used anachronism to dramatize control—both neoclassical, stoic self-control and, in the way that the scale of the set dominated the crowds, the embodiment of the state's control of its populace. Kean's attempt to return the play to an early republican set challenged Kemble's imperial vision, and Kean shattered the moral and political certainties of the Kemble era.

Kean himself presented an almost unrecognizable contrast to the controlled and imperious version of Kemble. If Kemble was statuesque and forbidding, Kean was energetic and full of passion. In a review for the *Champion*, Keats writes of Kean's "sensual grandeur," and of "an indescribable gusto in his voice, by which we feel that the utterer is thinking of the past and the future, while speaking of the instant," a quality to which he subsequently refers as "this intense power of anatomizing the passion of every syllable."[52] Byron, after seeing Kean as Richard, exclaimed, "By Jove, he is a soul!," while Mrs. Trench thought "constantly of Bonaparte—that restless quickness, that Catiline inquietude, that fearful somewhat *[sic]* resembling the impatience of a lion in its cage."[53] Despite such force, indeed perhaps because of it, most critics (including Hazlitt) agreed that Kean was ill suited to play Coriolanus. Reviews were almost universally unfavorable, and the production was staged only four times. Kean's small stature was seen as a distraction, and nearly all reviewers commented on Kean's energy, on the way that his style relied on flamboyant, discreet

---

[52] Keats, review in the *Champion*, 21 December 1817, reprinted in Wells, *Shakespeare in the Theatre*, 51.
[53] Both citations from William Clark Russell, *Representative Actors* (London: F. Warne, 1888), as quoted by Speaight, *Shakespeare on the Stage*, 43.

moments and not the steady accretion of detail. Crowds and critics alike insisted on Kemble's icy imperiousness. Trench's analogy between Kean and Napoleon suggests a political polarity in the portrayal of Coriolanus, a struggle over the proper legacy of Rome in which Kemble stands for the decorum, majesty, and autocratic authority of Rome under the empire—ironic, perhaps, for he is after all portraying a republican hero—and Kean as Bonaparte presents a wildly energetic, uncontrolled upstart threat to Kemble's legacy, much like that of Napoleon and the French Revolution to dynastic, aristocratic Europe. The reference to Kean's "Catiline inquietude" further aligns Kean with another upstart whose plot against Rome drew the eloquent invective of both Cicero and Sallust.[54] In the terms of this analogy, Kemble would be the established, legitimate republic, with Kean as the feisty malcontent who hopes to overthrow the Kemble legacy by backhanded, insidious manipulation and conspiracy.

Such associations were not lost on contemporaries. In a review of Kean's opening performance, the critic for the *European Magazine* commented that "Mr. Kean was a Plebeian, not a Patrician Coriolanus; and he appeared much more like a mob-orator, than a noble Roman."[55] The association with a mob orator links Kean to one of the more prominent anxieties surrounding the parliamentary reform movement, the concern that it was not a popular movement at all, but an effort by demagogues to play for power outside of parliamentary channels. This seems to be precisely the point: what the same critic described as Kemble's "grand and imposing dignity" was what both audiences and critics wanted Coriolanus to be such that any other version was seen as a threat to the state. The struggle over *Coriolanus*, in other words, can be understood as a struggle over the proper legacy of Rome in the Romantic period. Mediated through Shakespeare, this contest turns around a representation of Rome as a fundamental legitimation of aristocratic authority (one that essentially transposes the Rome of the republic into that of the empire) and a challenge to that understanding that questions precisely its aristocratic authority. This is why

[54] I discuss the changing Romantic significance of Catiline in the next chapter.
[55] *European Magazine*, 25 January 1820; reprinted in Gamini Salgado, *Eyewitness of Shakespeare: First Hand Accounts of Performances 1590–1890* (New York: Barnes and Noble, 1975), 327.

the distinction between Kean and Kemble, as it becomes a distinction between different interpretations of the Roman legacy, takes on such distinctly polarizing overtones. We may not agree with the critic from *European Magazine* that Kean was a "Plebeian Coriolanus"—one recent critic even suggests that Kean's *Coriolanus* was "a celebration of bourgeois individualism"[56]—but we should nonetheless recognize the affront that Kean's staging would have presented to those complacent about the stability of rank and patrician rule, hence the invocation of Bonaparte, of Catiline, and of the mob orator.

HAZLITT, *CORIOLANUS*, AND THE ARISTOCRATIC IMAGINATION

Hazlitt's comments on *Coriolanus* clarify the struggle over the play's interpretation and the representation of Rome more broadly. Hazlitt's is certainly the period's most dramatic and startling reading of the play, for it is here that Hazlitt articulates his understanding of poetry as "right royal" and of the imagination as an aristocratic faculty. A close reading of Hazlitt's remarks demonstrates the centrality of Kemble's performance of *Coriolanus* to Hazlitt's theory of the imagination. We often associate Romantic theories of imagination with the solitary encounter between an elevated subjectivity and the external world, where imagination is the mediator between man and nature, mind and world. Whether it is Blake on lambs and tigers, Coleridge in his lime tree bower, Wordsworth in a field of daffodils, Shelley meditating on Mont Blanc, or Keats addressing a nightingale, the focus is not on external nature itself, but rather on how the mind relates to it. As Coleridge describes it in a much-quoted passage from book 13 of the *Biographia*, the "primary" imagination is "the living power and prime agent of all human perception, and...a repetition in the finite mind of the eternal act of creation in the infinite I AM."[57] As for

---

[56] Ripley, Coriolanus *on Stage*, 144.
[57] Coleridge, *Biographia Litteraria*, ed. James Engell and W. Jackson Bate, in *The Collected Works of Samuel Taylor Coleridge* (Princeton, NJ: Princeton University Press, 1983), 7:304.

Coleridge, for many other poets of the Romantic period, the imagination is a sympathetic, perhaps even redemptive faculty that, in linking mind and world, can also link humans to each other. For Hazlitt, in contrast, imagination is "an exaggerating and exclusive faculty" (5:347). Poetry is not democratic and participatory, but rather "right royal" (5:348). These comments appear in Hazlitt's interpretation of *Coriolanus*, and the source of his distinctions is the stage and not the page. Hazlitt's justifiably famous and contentious comments about *Coriolanus* are underwritten not by the isolated encounter of his private imagination with the text, but rather by the indelible impression left upon him by Kemble's version of the role.

Critics of the Romantic period have long noted a distinction within the period between the staging of Shakespeare's work and an interpretation of it as written text. Not coincidentally, the Romantic period manifests the increasing importance of the concept of "character" in Shakespearean interpretation and the denigration of stage performance. Charles Lamb's essay "On the Tragedies of Shakespeare Considered with Reference to Their Fitness for Stage Representation" (1811) forms the most famous and the most explicit argument that Shakespeare is not suited for performance on stage. Lamb's characterization of the hierarchical function of imagination resembles Hazlitt's later description of imagination as exaggerating and exclusive, and a comparison between the two underscores the complicated politics of Hazlitt's claim.

In asserting that Shakespeare is unfit for performance, Lamb argues that it is impossible to do justice in production to the complexity and sublimity of Shakespeare's text. The problem is one of speed and depth. A problem of speed, because when the text is staged in real time, it is presented too quickly for the viewer to engage the subtlety of the text. Instead, the viewer is left only with the interpretation of the actor. As Lamb notes, "Such is the instantaneous nature of the impressions which we take in at the eye and ear at a play-house that we are apt not only to sink the play-writer in the consideration which we pay to the actor, but even to identify in our minds, in a perverse manner, the actor with the character which he represents."[58] There is,

---

[58] *The Complete Works and Letters of Charles Lamb* (New York: Modern Library, 1935), 291. Subsequent references to page numbers in this edition will be given parenthetically in the text.

in addition, a problem of depth because for Lamb the plays are grounded so deep in nature that "the depth of them lies out of the reach of most of us" (294). Depth is a significant factor of Lamb's analysis in other ways as well, for he is continuously drawing hierarchical distinctions between the literate and the "meanly lettered" (291) and between the active, intrepid, withdrawn imagination and the "common auditor" (294). Indeed, according to Lamb, it is this common auditor who does not read the works of Shakespeare in isolation and who is thus most likely to mistake the actor for the character, the production of the play for the thing itself.

As quick as Lamb is to draw such distinctions among those viewing Shakespeare's plays, he does not blame the viewer for his failure to distinguish the character from the actor. Rather, he concludes that "there is something in the nature of acting which levels all distinctions" (296). And this, it immediately becomes clear, is the problem. Lamb refers repeatedly to the leveling effects of stage production. When he wrote this essay, Lamb had turned from his earlier radical leanings to the cultivation of a genteel inwardness. The leveling that Lamb resents, it is worth noting, was a loaded term in the Romantic period, and Lamb's use of "levels" resonates with the proliferation in the 1790s of conservative loyalist groups known as the "Reevite Associations Against Levellers and Republicans" and the infamous Levellers of the Putney debates of the seventeenth-century interregnum. Lamb's use of the term allows us to extrapolate a political significance from his seemingly innocuous comments. Shakespeare, for Lamb, is all about the preservation of distinctions. Only from the slow "vantage ground of abstraction" (298) can the *reader* of Shakespeare properly grasp "the inner structure and workings of mind in a character" (292), for "the sublime images, the poetry alone, is that which is present to our minds in the reading" (298). In sharp contrast, "upon the stage, *when the imagination is no longer the ruling faculty*...we are left to our poor unassisted senses" (299, emphasis mine). In isolated reading, then, the imagination rules over the senses. Although Lamb's comments seem to preserve Shakespeare for the isolated reader, the way that Lamb figures the imagination as a faculty that preserves distinctions and prevents their leveling—as a faculty that should *rule*—suggests the deeply hierarchical significance that he attaches to the concept of imagination.

Lamb's reservations about the stage indicate a desire to redeem Shakespeare for the self and thus remove him from political appropriation. Perhaps more important, they also represent the fear of an explosive audience, a fear that Alan Richardson notes was "intensified if not directly inspired by the living theater of the French Revolution, when (as Nodier wrote in 1841) 'le peuple entier venait de jouer dans le plus grand drame de l'histoire.'"[59] But if Lamb's emphasis on the written text is consistent with his attempt to describe the hierarchical function of imagination and to prevent a radical Shakespeare, what, given Hazlitt's sympathies for the reform movement, are we to make of the ambivalent politics of Hazlitt's similar concession that the imagination is an aristocratic faculty?

Hazlitt's original comments on *Coriolanus* come directly from his evaluation of Kemble in the role, printed in a review for the *Examiner*. The review, however, makes only limited, belated mention of the specific performance. Instead, in a brilliant piece of paratactic rhetoric, Hazlitt picks up on the resonance of the issues at stake in the play for contemporary English political discourse. The review begins: "*Coriolanus* is a storehouse of political common-places. Any one who studies it may save himself the trouble of reading Burke's *Reflections*, or Paine's *Rights of Man*, or the Debates in both Houses of Parliament since the French Revolution or our own" (*CWH*, 5:347). The piece continues in a barrage of pert, declarative statements as Hazlitt quickly and famously concludes that "Shakespeare himself seems to have had a leaning to the arbitrary side of the question" (*CWH*, 5:347), and he then extends this point to poetry in general and declares that "poetry naturally falls in with the language of power" (*CWH*, 5:347). From this follows Hazlitt's often cited distinction between the imagination and the understanding:

> The imagination is an exaggerating and exclusive faculty: it takes from one thing to add to another: it accumulates circumstances together to give the greatest possible effect to a favourite object. The understanding is a dividing and measuring faculty: it judges of things not according to their immediate impression on the mind, but according to their relations to one another. The one is a monopolizing faculty, which seeks the greatest quantity of present

---

[59] Richardson, *A Mental Theater*, 3; see also Bate, *Shakespearean Constitutions*, 134.

excitement by inequality and disproportion; the other is a distributive faculty, which seeks the greatest quantity of ultimate good by justice and proportion. The one is an aristocratical, the other a republican faculty. The principal of poetry is a very anti-levelling principle. It aims at effect, it exists by contrast. It admits of no medium. It is everything by excess.... Poetry is right royal. It puts the individual for the species, the one above the infinite many, might before right. (*CWH*, 5:347–348)

Hazlitt's distinction here between imagination and understanding recalls Shelley's later opening paragraph of the *Defence of Poetry* with its emphasis on the difference between reason and imagination. Shelley subordinates reason to imagination "as the instrument to the agent" (*SPP*, 2nd, 510–511). Hazlitt, in contrast, explicitly politicizes the difference when he claims reason for the republican cause and leaves poetry to the minister's side of the question (which may explain why Hazlitt concludes his *Letter to Gifford* with an explication of his earlier philosophical work). Only once he has established this absolute premise does Hazlitt move into an explanation of *Coriolanus*, the moral of which, he states, "is that those who have little shall have less, and that those who have much shall take all that others have left" *(CWH,* 5:349), and this, he concludes, "is the logic of the imagination and the passions" (*CWH*, 5:349).[60] Poetry, by this inflexible conclusion, can only be tyrannical.

This, however, presents a problem for Hazlitt. Lamb's emphasis on Shakespeare as a written text is consistent with an attempt to prevent a radical Shakespeare, but why is it that Hazlitt, who sympathizes with the cause of Reform, is so willing to concede the moral of *Coriolanus* and indeed, Shakespeare himself, to the forces of reaction? Why does he leave poetry to power in his essays on *Coriolanus* while he elsewhere claims a more humanizing role for it? Part of the explanation lies in Hazlitt's acknowledged willingness to sustain and even court contradiction throughout his writing—and especially

---

[60] The reference here is of course biblical, and refers to the sayings of Jesus. Matthew 25:29, for example, reads in the King James Version, "For unto every one that hath shall be given, and he shall have abundance: but from him that hath not shall be taken away even that which he hath." Similar sentiments can be found in Mark 4:25; Luke 8:18, 19:26. The same sentiments are also invoked by Shelley in the *Defence*, where he associates them with political economy.

in relation to radical opposition and Edmund Burke.[61] In the particular instance of *Coriolanus*, however, tensions within Hazlitt's position arise less from his reveling in ambivalence per se than from the distinctions between Kemble's and Kean's stagings of the play. Kevin Gilmartin acknowledges Hazlitt's tendency "to play out in the sphere of mind or art a set of issues (independence, opposition, contradiction, egotism, hatred, self-interest) that popular radicalism wanted to treat as resolutely social and political."[62] Hazlitt's handling of *Coriolanus* stands as a case in point, but it is especially distinctive for the way that Hazlitt's very reading of the play creates this relationship between politics and the sphere of art; here, however, it is a relationship influenced not by Hazlitt's usual felicity with a move to the realm of abstraction but rather with the concrete particularity of Hazlitt's encounter with the Romantic period staging of the play.

Hazlitt felt that *Coriolanus* was Shakespeare's most political play, and he wrote about it on a number of occasions, including reviews reprinted in *The Characters of Shakespeare's Plays* (1817) and *A View of the English Stage* (1818). The two volumes differ markedly—the first is an attempt to assess the characters of Shakespeare's plays as a reader, whereas the second is a collection of Hazlitt's theatrical reviews. Telling here is that Hazlitt's description of *Coriolanus* is virtually unchanged in his essay on Kemble's specific performance reprinted in *A View of the English Stage*, and his more general essay on Coriolanus as a Shakespearean character in *The Characters of Shakespeare's Plays*. This suggests that Hazlitt has so conflated his reading of *Coriolanus* with Kemble's staging of the play that such distinctions between text and performance have become irrelevant.

---

[61] David Bromwich, for example, notes Hazlitt's "faculty of holding two opposed ideas in his mind at the same time" (*Hazlitt: The Mind of a Critic* [New York: Oxford University Press, 1983], 59–60). Gilmartin observes that Hazlitt not only tested fellow radicals as to whether they could acknowledge the greatness of Burke, but that he also divided his sympathies toward Burke himself. See Gilmartin, *Print Politics: The Press and Radical Opposition in Early Nineteenth-Century England* (Cambridge: Cambridge University Press, 1996), 227–233, esp. 230–33; and John Whale, "Hazlitt on Burke: The Ambivalent Position of a Radical Essayist," *Studies in Romanticism* 25 (1986): 465–481. On broader questions of contradiction as a function of post-Waterloo radical politics, see Gilmartin, *Print Politics*, 31–33, 39–42.

[62] Gilmartin, *Print Politics*, 230.

Hazlitt's admiration for Kemble, as he explicitly acknowledges, is imbued with a religious, almost idolatrous enthusiasm. In his review of Kemble's *King John*, reprinted in *A View of the English Stage*, Hazlitt writes:

> We wish we had never seen Mr. Kean. He has destroyed the Kemble religion; and it is this religion in which we were brought up. Never again shall we behold Mr. Kemble with the same pleasure that we did, nor see Mr. Kean with the same pleasure that we have seen Mr. Kemble formerly. We used to admire Mr. Kemble's figure and manner, and had no idea that there was any want of art or nature. We feel the force and nature of Mr. Kean's acting, but then we feel the want of Mr. Kemble's person. Thus an old and delightful prejudice is destroyed, and no new enthusiasm, no second idolatry comes to take its place. (*CWH*, 5:345)

Even if Kean has shattered the Kemble religion, he here serves as a testament to the depth of Hazlitt's admiration for Kemble. Coriolanus is the role in which Kemble takes his leave of the stage, and it is one of the first in which Hazlitt remembers seeing him, "and it was one in which we were not sorry to part with him," Hazlitt writes in "Mr. Kemble's Retirement," "for we wished to see him appear like himself to the last" (*CWH*, 5:375). Just as, for Lamb, while we read Lear, "we see not Lear, but we are Lear" (296), and, for Byron, "Kean is Richard,"[63] for Hazlitt, Kemble is Coriolanus. Indeed, the impression made by Kemble's Coriolanus is one that cannot be changed by time or distance:

> It is near twenty years ago since we first saw Mr. Kemble in the same character—yet how short the interval seems! The impression appears as distinct as if it were yesterday. In fact, intellectual objects, in proportion as they are lasting, may be said to shorten life. Time has no effect upon them. (*CWH*, 5:374)

What, then, did Kemble's Coriolanus represent for Hazlitt?

As Coriolanus, Kemble "exhibited the ruling passion with the same unshaken firmness, he preserved the same haughty dignity of demeanour, the same energy of will, and the same unbending sternness of temper throughout. He was swayed by a single impulse" (5:376). We see this in Hazlitt's claim that Kemble cannot play

---

[63] Quoted by Speaight, *Shakespeare on the Stage*, 43.

Brutus despite the suggestion that "Mr. Kemble chiefly excelled in his Roman characters" (*CWH*, 5:379). This is because Kemble can only impersonate those characters who "imply a certain stoicism of feeling and energy of will" (*CWH*, 5:379). Brutus, in contrast, "is not a stoic, but a humane enthusiast. There is a tenderness of nature under the garb of assumed severity; an inward current of generous feelings, which, burst out, in spite of circumstances, with bleeding freshness" (*CWH*, 5:379). Kemble, therefore, can certainly play Cato, and in his review of Kemble in this role, Hazlitt praises him as "the most classical of actors.... His person, manner, and dress, seemed cast in the very mould of Roman elegance and dignity" (*CWH*, 5:342). For Hazlitt, clearly, Kemble's Coriolanus is reserved and lofty, single-minded in his purpose, rigorously unbending; he partakes entirely of a kind of Roman *dignitas*. This is what Peter Manning implies when he characterizes Kemble as an actor of "neoclassic decorum" with a "dignified oratorical manner."[64] Contrary to Lamb's general point, Kemble's Coriolanus does not level all distinctions, but he rather promotes and enforces them. Further, he produces in Hazlitt an indelible conception of *Coriolanus* which cannot help but color his reading of the play. To quote Lamb, Hazlitt may even be guilty of identifying "in a perverse manner, the actor with the character which he represents."[65]

In contrast to his attachment to Kemble as Coriolanus, Hazlitt thought little of Kean in the role. While he elsewhere approved of Kean's playing, as Coriolanus, "Mr. Kean's acting is not of the patrician order; he is one of the people, and what might be termed a *radical performer*" (*CWH*, 18:290). Hazlitt insistently wants to read *Coriolanus* in the terms of

---

[64] Peter J. Manning, "Edmund Kean and Byron's Plays," *Keats-Shelley Journal* 21–22 (1972–1973), 190, 191.

[65] In conflating Kemble with his characters, Hazlitt was certainly not alone. Indeed, there must have been something in Kemble's acting style that encouraged precisely this conflation. In her remarks on *The Mountaineers*, for example, Mrs. Inchbald suggested that without Kemble, the play would hardly be capable of representation: "Those persons who have never seen Mr. Kemble in *Octavian*, will yet receive delight in reading this well-written play; but those who *have* seen him, will weep as they read, and tremble as they weep, for it is most certain they have not forgotten him. Those, again, who have seen any other actor in the character will peruse the play, possessed of all its claims to attention, with indifference." See *The British Theatre*, ed. Mrs. Inchbald (London, n.d.), Vol. 21. I thank Joe Bray for pointing out this reference.

contemporary political dispute. He so associates Kemble's interpretation of the play as the last word that any other interpretation is untenable. This recalls the critic for *European Magazine* who described Kean as "a Plebeian, not a Patrician Coriolanus" and likened him to "a mob-orator." Both read the class-based divisions of the play onto the actors staging it. Hazlitt further complains of Kean's performance that "the intolerable airs and aristocratical pretensions of which he is the slave, and to which he falls victim, did not seem *legitimate* in him" (*CWH*, 18:290). "Legitimate" and "legitimacy," as Stuart Semmel suggests, were politically charged terms with novel implications in this period: "'Legitimacy' was at once an actual vision of monarchy advanced by advocates of hereditary rule—and a monolithic rhetorical adversary constructed by the dynasts' enemies."[66] Hazlitt was skeptical of the term. In "What Is the People?" he associates it with divine right doctrine, and the preface to his 1819 *Political Essays* celebrates Napoleon as illegitimate, as the manifestation of a principle opposite to legitimacy.[67] The italics used in connection with Kean are Hazlitt's own, and in their suggestion that Kean fails to be legitimate they imply a connection between Kemble's staging of the play and legitimacy, which Hazlitt associates with the Establishment and with claims for hereditary, absolute rule. In contrast, Kean's acting is characterized by what Hazlitt calls "energy," a term which would have suggested Franklin and Priestley's experiments with electricity, and which likely also would have suggested enthusiasm, another concept associated with the radical movement.[68] Elsewhere, in his first review of Kean as Richard, Hazlitt faults him for having too much exuberance. For Hazlitt, a perfect performance is a matter of sustained intensity: "It should have a little more solidity, depth, sustained, and impassioned feeling, with somewhat less brilliancy, with fewer glancing lights, pointed transitions, and pantomimic evolutions" (*CWH*, 5:181). Kean, however, lacks precisely this solidity. Hazlitt concludes in his second review of Kean as Richard by noting that Kean "presents a perpetual succession of striking pictures. He bids fair to supply us with the best Shakespear Gallery we have had!"(*CWH*, 5:184).

---

[66] Stuart Semmel, "British Radicals and 'Legitimacy': Napoleon in the Mirror of History," *Past and Present* 167 (2000): 153.
[67] Ibid., 149, 161.
[68] Bate, *Shakespearian Constitutions*, 139–140.

Such movement and energy were qualities associated with revolution, and this suggests that the Kemble-Kean opposition can be mapped onto the earlier opposition between Burke and Paine. Bate suggests that there is a quality not in the particularity, but in the structure of Hazlitt's prose that aligns the Kean-Kemble contrast with that of Burke and Paine.[69] Here, Kemble's intensity matches Burke's, and when Hazlitt describes Burke's style, he quotes from *Coriolanus*,[70] whereas the electricity and enthusiasm so prominent in Hazlitt's and others' descriptions of Kean were terms used frequently in attacks on radicals. The contrast further suggests the possible source of Hazlitt's comments on the distinction between imagination and understanding. It is no accident that Hazlitt sought to separate performance from text, for Kemble was so persuasive in the role of Coriolanus that as much as Hazlitt sympathized with the cause of the plebeians and drew the obvious parallel to the reform movement, any other way of staging the play became inconceivable. And Hazlitt's dilemma, in turn, suggests that despite the movement to avoid anachronism on stage, the image of Rome that survived in the popular imagination was an imperial, and not a republican, vision.

This becomes clearer in the vituperative exchange between Hazlitt and William Gifford over Hazlitt's comments on *Coriolanus*. In his attack on Hazlitt's claim that poetry falls in with arbitrary power, Gifford introduces a counterexample: "If we look to the history of mankind, we shall learn from this new theory of the 'pleasures of the imagination,' that it is not natural for us to sympathize with the distresses of suffering virtue, but that whatever we may pretend, we are, in truth, gratified by the cruelties of Domitian and Nero."[71] Faced with an attack on his belief that poetry should help to preserve what he earlier calls "degree" and good order, Gifford reaches for the most extreme examples of wanton cruelty that he can find, the emperors Domitian and Nero. He then immediately links the excesses of these two to revolutionary France: "The crimes of revolutionary France were of a still blacker dye." Gifford attempts to

---

[69] Ibid., 138–139.
[70] See Hazlitt, *The Plain Speaker* in *The Complete Works of William Hazlitt*, ed. P. P. Howe (London: J. M. Dent and Sons, 1931), 12:228.
[71] *Quarterly Review* 18 (1818): 465.

move the Roman parallel in the direction of France by aligning the cruelties of the emperors with the cruelties of Robespierre and Carnot. Hazlitt, in his *Letter to William Gifford*, pushes the analogy in a different direction, however:

> You ask "are we gratified by the cruelties of Domitian or Nero?" No, not we—they were too petty and cowardly to strike the imagination at a distance; but the Roman Senate tolerated them, addressed their perpetrators, exalted them into Gods, the Fathers of their people; they had pimps and scribblers of all sorts in their pay, their Senecas, etc. till a turbulent rabble thinking that there were no injuries to society greater than the endurance of unlimited and wanton oppression, put an end to the farce, and abated the nuisance as well as they could. Had you and I lived in those times, we should have been what we are now, I a "sour mal-content," and you "a sweet courtier." (*CWH*, 9:38)

Hazlitt counters the link between Rome and France in order to imply a parallel between Rome and Britain. There as here, he suggests, a corrupt Senate not only tolerates but exalts a corrupt ruler, and they are aided in this by a corrupt press ("pimps and scribblers of all sorts"). Charles Mahoney argues that Hazlitt's comments on *Coriolanus* need to be read "as a crucial pivot in Hazlitt's always overdetermined appraisal of the collusion of poetry and power in the English sublimation of the French Revolution."[72] I agree but would add that as the exchange between Hazlitt and Gifford suggests, we cannot overlook the role that the Roman setting of *Coriolanus* plays in mitigating the terms of that relationship between poetry and power. In this way the dispute between Hazlitt and Gifford also becomes a dispute over the proper reading of a parallel between Roman precedent and the British present. It is curious that the dispute over a play set in republican Rome should lend itself to a quarrel over imperial precedent, but this, like Hazlitt's theory of the aristocratic imagination, can be explained by Kemble's staging of the play, which transposed the republican episode into an imperial context.

When Hazlitt talks about poetry's sympathy with power, David Bromwich has argued, he is in fact expressing his admiration for energy of mind, which allows a love of power to be natural but not necessarily

---

[72] Charles Mahoney, "Upstaging the Fall: *Coriolanus* and the Spectacle of Romantic Apostasy," *Studies in Romanticism* 38 (1999): 43.

prevalent. But poetry's interest in the individual over the species does, for Bromwich, represent a turn against revolutionary politics because only by abstraction and the understanding can the imaginative self-worshiper hold to radical beliefs.[73] This is precisely what Hazlitt decries. Bate reasons that Hazlitt is likely responding to the politicization of Shakespeare's legacy by deliberately exaggerating his comments to provoke a response—which is exactly what he gets from Gifford. But Hazlitt's position can best be explained when we consider the prominent place that Kemble's interpretation of *Coriolanus* held for Hazlitt. The explicit relation between the staging of *Coriolanus* and Hazlitt's theory of imagination is an overlooked chapter in the history of the Romantic imagination. It is also a paradoxical one. If, as in a standard reading of Romanticism, Coleridge, Wordsworth, Shelley, and others forge a theory of imagination in the isolated encounter of mind and world, it is an encounter that conceives of the imagination as a sympathetic faculty and implicitly holds open the possibility of sociability. Hazlitt's theory of the imagination, however, is not formed in isolation, but rather in a context of explicit sociability—in the theater. And yet for Hazlitt, the imagination becomes an exaggerating, monopolizing faculty that places "the one above the infinite many, might before right."

---

[73] Bromwich, *Hazlitt*, 314–320.

Chapter Six

What Is the People?

Rome on the Romantic Stage after Kemble

On 12 October 1817, William Hazlitt began publishing a series of essays in the *Champion* on the question "What is the people?" So impatient was Hazlitt to address the issue, that the title of the essay served as its opening line and the actual body of the piece—beginning with the anticipated response of "And who are you to ask the question?"—provided a reply to the title, thus starting an imagined dialogue on the topic in which Hazlitt berated the perceived corruptions of the monarchy and advanced the claims of the people as the best foundation for stable and consistent government. Hazlitt's essay is an attack on what he perceives as a parasitical court and Crown and an attempt to define the populace as a necessary check on the powers of those institutions. For Hazlitt, "The people is the hand, heart, and head of the whole community acting to one purpose and with a mutual and thorough consent." The will of this people, according to Hazlitt, "necessarily tends to the general good as its end" so long as it is guided by popular feeling and by public opinion, "as arising out of the impartial reason and enlightened intellect of the community."[1] He continues:

What is it that determines the opinion of any number of persons in things they actually feel in their practical and home results? Their common interest.

---

[1] *The Complete Works of William Hazlitt*, ed. P. P. Howe (London: J. M. Dent, 1930–1934), 7:267. Subsequent page references to this edition will be abbreviated *CWH* and provided parenthetically in the text.

What is it that determines their opinion in things of general inquiry, beyond their immediate experience or interest? Abstract reason. In matters of feeling and common sense, of which each individual is the best judge, the majority are in the right; in things requiring a greater strength of mind to comprehend them, the greatest power of understanding will prevail, if it has but fair play. (*CWH*, 7:267–268)

Hazlitt's concept of the people is inclusive. Nobody is explicitly barred from it based on standards of property ownership or occupation, though we might wonder whether he includes women. At bottom, "What is the People?" is an essay about the balance of powers, whereby an all-inclusive people exercising its will through what Hazlitt calls public opinion serves as a check on the powers of the Crown and court. "The power of an arbitrary King or an aspiring Minister," Hazlitt asserts, "does not increase with the liberty of the subject, but must be circumscribed by it" (*CWH*, 7:265).

Furthermore, in Hazlitt's conception this inclusive populace will, if given free rein, develop through the guide of independent feeling and abstract reason into the articulation of a public opinion that must necessarily lead to truth. Lack of interference is crucial, for as Hazlitt adds, "The vox populi is the vox Dei only when it springs from the individual, unbiased feelings, and unfettered, independent opinion of the people" (*CWH* 7:272). Free and open communication, unrestricted discourse, allows public opinion to develop into truth. But if everyone can be considered part of the people, how can this enormous mass be disciplined to the extent that it can express and articulate a coherent popular voice or public will? The answer, for Hazlitt, lies in the press. The press serves as the court of public opinion, the area in which ideas can be disputed until a consensus about public opinion can be achieved, and "it is the press that has done every thing for the people, and even for Governments" (*CWH* 7:269). For Hazlitt, then, there is a close connection between the idea of the populace, the popular press, and what he calls public opinion.

The question that Hazlitt poses so directly and insistently—What is the people?—and the related issue of what the role of this people should be in political decision making was the central question in post-Waterloo British popular politics. On what grounds was an individual entitled to participate in the political process? How could that individual guarantee his independence? Was it on the basis of property in land (the contemporary status quo), or should it be immovable property like a household (the eventual solution of the 1832 Reform Bill)?[2] Or, moving in a more radical direction, did the capacity to labor or the use of reason (as Hazlitt would have it) provide sufficient guarantee of independence and thus entitle one to political participation?[3] Arising from these questions were a further set of related issues: if the present system failed to conform to one's understanding of political enfranchisement, on what grounds could authority be resisted?[4] The corollary to an expanded understanding of the people was, of course, fear of the mob, on the assumption that an expansion of the franchise would represent mob rule and pose a grave threat to the rights of property. How could an expanded role for common people in the political process be balanced against the fear that such inclusiveness would encourage mob violence and pose a threat to property? As extra-parliamentary agitation for an expansion of the franchise and more regular Parliaments intensified, public debate turned on disputes over which elements of the populace should count as "the people" in a reformed political process.

Given these questions, it is unsurprising that Hazlitt's essay, which poses the problem so directly, was repeatedly reprinted, first in two parts in a radical newspaper, the *Yellow Dwarf* on 1818

---

[2] On the link between property and political independence, personal autonomy, and a stable identity, see J. G. A. Pocock, *The Machiavellian Moment* (Princeton, NJ: Princeton University Press, 1975), 464–466; and Pocock, *Virtue, Commerce, and History* (Cambridge: Cambridge University Press, 1985), 103–104, 108–112.

[3] For a clear and eloquent articulation of the relationship between a theory of politics grounded in labor and one based on property, see Kevin Gilmartin, *Print Politics: The Press and Radical Opposition in Early Nineteenth-Century England* (Cambridge: Cambridge University Press, 1996), 33–35. As Gilmartin explains, the radical movement, like the classical republican tradition, sought to ground independence in the material world, "yet the new material foundation was a process ("labor") or an experience ("poverty and distress") rather than a product ("property")" (35).

[4] The question of popular resistance to authority is a profound one in British political culture, especially from Locke forward. For a much debated account of Locke's *Second Treatise* as a revolutionary tract and a prescription for revolt, see Richard Ashcraft, *Revolutionary Politics and Locke's Two Treatises of Government* (Princeton, NJ: Princeton University Press, 1986). For evidence of armed resistance in the popular press, see Gilmartin, *Print Politics*, 21–22.

March 7 and 14, and then the following year by the radical publisher William Hone in Hazlitt's *Political Essays, with Sketches of Public Characters*. Such reprinting underscores Hazlitt's point about the importance of the popular press in establishing debate over matters of public concern and its role in forming and shaping public opinion. The press, however, was not the only force active in shaping the populace's understanding of itself and its role in the political process.[5] The recent increase of scholarly attention to Romantic period theater has demonstrated convincingly the prominent place of the theater in Romantic period culture and the close relationship between a pervasive theatricality and the period's political culture.

This chapter extends the claims of recent scholarship on the political importance of the stage to a reading of early-nineteenth-century plays on Roman themes. A close look at the history of the Theatres Royal in the second and third decades of the nineteenth century reveals a significant resurgence of interest in events from Roman republican history. John Howard Payne's *Brutus* (1818) was the first of these plays to appear on stage, and was quickly followed by James Sheridan Knowles's *Virginius: A Tragedy* at Drury Lane (1820), by an anonymous *Virginius* at Covent Garden (1820),[6] and by Knowles's *Caius Gracchus* (1823). The regular staging of both *Coriolanus* and *Julius Caesar*, and the less frequent performance of Addison's *Cato* complemented this proliferation of republican-themed drama; in addition, numerous plays set in Rome were published but not staged, including George Croly's *Catiline: A Tragedy* (1822); Joseph Lunn's *Amor Patriae; A Dramatic Poem* (1823); *Camillus: An Historical Play* (1827); and the English translation of M. Jouy's *Sylla: A Tragedy* (1824). Even when they were not staged, many of these dramas were intended for the stage and attracted comment in the public journals of the period after their publication.

---

[5] As Gilmartin claims, "No account of the radical movement, even one that focuses on print, can overlook the meetings and debates that provided a key forum for public deliberation" (*Print Politics*, 20). To this we can add the theater.

[6] This play was not printed, and to the best of my knowledge exists only in the licensing copy, Huntington Manuscript LA2152. It was the version acted by Kean at Drury Lane in 1820 at roughly the same time that Macready was starring in Knowles's *Virginius* at Covent Garden.

Collectively, the appearance of these works points to what we might call a "Roman Revival" in the theater that followed the defeat of Napoleon in 1815 and Kemble's retirement from the stage in 1817. With Kemble—who had dominated the popular imagination of ancient Rome for so long with his performance of an imperial, and imperious, Coriolanus—gone, Rome was again up for grabs, and it was, moreover, suddenly available at a time when the French experiment with Roman precedent had come to an ignominious ending and when travel to Italy was again possible.[7] As the *Edinburgh Review* remarked in an 1814 review of Joseph Forsythe's Italian travels that appeared just one year after its review of John Eustace's similar tour: "Perhaps the reader may now take a livelier interest in guides to Italy, than could reasonably be felt on the former occasion [the review of Eustace from 1813]. We then had about as much connexion with that fair country, as if it lay on another planet, and not much greater chance of seeing it."[8] Whether one chose to take that travel opportunity or not, the Roman Revival made versions of republican Rome available to those who remained in London from 1814 through the 1820s and beyond.

This chapter demonstrates the importance of the Roman Revival for our understanding of Romantic period theater and Romantic period culture more broadly. For much of this period, the staging of *Coriolanus* provided a means of asserting a position on the nature of participatory republican government, the threat of popular uprising, the role of the people in political decision making, and—especially— on the potential of the stage to shape contemporary debate on these issues. Although the performance of *Coriolanus* was less frequent after Kemble's retirement from the stage in 1817, the issues that Kemble addressed in his staging of the play did not disappear. They were, rather, rearticulated in a series of plays on Roman themes, all of which

---

[7] On the French use of Roman examples, see, most famously, Karl Marx, *The Eighteenth Brumaire of Louis Bonaparte* (New York: International Publishers, 1963). See also Harold T. Parker, *The Cult of Antiquity and the French Revolutionaries* (Chicago: University of Chicago Press, 1937); Robert L. Herbert, *David, Voltaire,* Brutus *and the French Revolution: An Essay in Art and Politics* (New York: Viking Press, 1972); and Mona Ozouf, *Festivals and the French Revolution* (Cambridge: Harvard University Press, 1988), 271–278.

[8] *Edinburgh Review* 22.44 (January 1814): 379–380. The earlier review of Eustace appears in *Edinburgh Review* 21.42 (July 1813): 378–424.

attempted to transform the topical relevance of *Coriolanus* into vibrant new historical tragedies.

David Worrall argues that "the London theatres of the 1800s were a kind of laboratory for both revolution and reform."[9] This is especially true in the staging of republican Rome. All of the plays on Roman themes present significant crises in the Roman state—issues that would have been emphatically topical in the second and third decades of the nineteenth century, including problems of rulers who fail to respect the laws, foreign wars, shortages of grain, corruptions in the political system itself, and conspiracies or revolts, which attempt to remedy those corruptions or which serve as further proof of their existence, alongside more general questions about the use of violence for political ends—and in addressing these issues, all of these plays question the role of the people during crises of state. Although Kemble's staging of *Coriolanus* implies that the people constituted an undisciplined threat to property rights and the effective functioning of the state, other Roman plays rarely present the position this starkly, and what makes the plays of the Roman revival so engaging is their framing of contemporary questions about the people through the invocation of legendary episodes of republican history. Similar to the antirevolutionary dramas discussed by Jeffrey Cox,[10] Roman-themed plays do not enact contemporary events; but in their handling of figures from Rome's republican past, including the elder Brutus, Caius Gracchus, Virginius, and Catiline, they all utilize what Diego Saglia succinctly describes as "the vocabulary of reform, despotism, rebellion, repression, and liberty that haunted British governments from the revolutionary decade of the 1790s to the Great Reform Bill and beyond."[11] The effect of this displacement is complex. Frequently, the

---

[9] David Worrall, *Theatric Revolution: Drama, Censorship, and Romantic Period Subcultures, 1773–1832* (Oxford: Oxford University Press, 2006), 230. On links between the theater and popular politics, see also Marc Baer, *Theatre and Disorder in Late Georgian London* (Oxford: Clarendon Press, 1992) and Julia Swindells, *Glorious Causes: The Grand Theatre of Political Change, 1789–1833* (Oxford: Oxford University Press, 2001).

[10] Jeffrey N. Cox, "Ideology and Genre in the British Antirevolutionary Drama of the 1790s," *ELH* 58 (1991): 579–610.

[11] Saglia, "'The Illegitimate Assistance of Political Allusion': Politics and the Hybridization of Romantic Tragedy in the Drama of Richard Lalor Sheil," *Theatre Journal* 58 (2006): 266.

evocation of precedent in Roman dramas works, like Kemble's production of *Coriolanus*, to contain the possibilities of changing social and political conditions by implying that such changes are simply a variant of the timeless struggle between elites and the masses and that any similar struggle can best be clarified through reference to Rome. Sometimes, however, as with Croly's *Catiline*, Roman dramas reimagine the Roman republican past in an effort to understand the present in bold new ways. My interpretation of the Roman Revival begins with Payne's *Brutus*, the first and most successful of these plays. It then turns to Knowles's *Caius Gracchus*, which also became a fixture in the repertoire, before concluding with George Croly's *Catiline*. Each of these plays raises questions about the role of the populace in political crisis; collectively, they show in concrete detail how the history of the Roman republic was used to shape debate over such contemporary concerns as popular politics, agricultural unrest, the resistance to authority, the relationship between popular democracy and empire, and, indeed, the very organization of the British political system.

One final comment before I turn to the plays. Hazlitt's notion of a court of public opinion worked out in the absence of external restriction through the operation of abstract reason in the pages of the popular press sounds, of course, very much like Jürgen Habermas's much-discussed concept of the public sphere.[12] The public sphere functions between the private sphere and the state where, in Habermas's description, the middle class organized itself into a public through the eighteenth century by means of reasoned debate in such social spaces as coffee shops and the newspaper press. Habermas asserts that such a public is formed through a type of social intercourse that disregards status and allows for the discussion of matters of common concern among an unrestricted public, one with the freedom to assemble and express their opinions: "The issues discussed become 'general' not merely in their significance, but also in their

---

[12] One crucial distinction that I will not address here is that in contrast to Habermas, for whom the constitution of a public is an affair of abstract reason, for Hazlitt it is a matter of abstract reason but also of affect. Note, for example, the frequent conjunction of feeling and abstract reason in the passages of Hazlitt's "What is the People" cited at the opening of this chapter.

accessibility: everyone had to *be able* to participate."[13] For Habermas, the medium of engagement in the public sphere is reason, "the authority of the better argument."[14] There has been a longstanding academic debate about the timing of the public sphere's emergence[15] and about the normative basis for Habermas's sphere of communicative rationality, one turning around which groups have access to the public sphere and whether such a place of unrestricted conversation ever did or could exist.[16] In response, revisionist scholars like Bruce Robbins multiply the concept of the public sphere and speak of "alternative public spheres" and "counterpublics." Such emphasis on the competitive and conflictual nature of the public sphere is especially important for early-nineteenth-century radical culture.[17] The recognition of competition among a variety of publics, however important, should not, as Kevin Gilmartin points out, cause us to overlook "that such contests were never entirely contained within [a structured setting] but came to be waged over structure and setting as well."[18] Similarly, John Plotz has suggested that the more important problem for thinking about the public sphere in the early nineteenth century concerns contests over what counted or failed to count as public speech. Plotz argues that "the public sphere in early nineteenth-century Britain was not a site where rational-critical conversation either took place or failed to take place, but the arena wherein the disputes between

---

[13] Jürgen Habermas, *The Structural Transformation of the Public Sphere: An Inquiry into a Category of Bourgeois Society* (Cambridge: MIT Press, 1989), 37.

[14] Habermas, *Structural Transformation*, 36. As Habermas declares explicitly elsewhere, "Public opinion can only come into existence when a reasoning public is presupposed." See "The Public Sphere: An Encyclopedia Article (1964)," *New German Critique* 3 (1974): 50.

[15] See most recently *The Politics of the Public Sphere in Early Modern England*, ed. Peter Lake and Steven Pincus (Manchester: Manchester University Press, 2007).

[16] See *Habermas and the Public Sphere*, ed. Craig Calhoun (Cambridge: MIT Press, 1992); Oskar Negt and Alexander Kluge, *Public Sphere and Experience: Towards an Analysis of the Bourgeois and Proletarian Public Sphere*, trans. Peter Labanyi (Minneapolis: University of Minnesota Press, 1993); *The Phantom Public Sphere*, ed. Bruce Robbins (Minneapolis: University of Minnesota Press, 1993). See also Gilmartin, *Print Politics*, 3–10.

[17] See Geoff Eley, "Nations, Publics, and Political Cultures: Placing Habermas in the Nineteenth Century," in *Habermas and the Public Sphere*, ed. Craig Calhoun (Cambridge: MIT Press, 1992), 289–339.

[18] Gilmartin, *Print Politics*, 8.

various discursive logics were staged: the space, one might say, in which it was decided what would come to count as public conversation at all."[19] Both Gilmartin and Plotz, then, extend an understanding of the public sphere beyond print culture to include other social phenomena that move into public awareness like meetings and debates or even crowd activity, all of which shift the debate over what constituted public speech and action as part of a "contest to determine what sorts of discourses would count as central to public speech and performance."[20] Such an expanded account of the locus, activities, and concerns that constitute a public sphere or spheres should also include the theater. The theater was, after all, a public space that included members of all social groups, one that negotiates as much as print journalism or crowd actions the central questions about what constitutes the populace and on what basis a populace so constituted can articulate public opinion and ground its claim to participation in the public sphere and the process of political representation.[21]

At first glance the insistence that theatrical performance constitutes public discourse and thus participates in the sort of critical debate that Habermas associates with the public sphere would seem so obvious as hardly to need stating. Still, the theater of the early nineteenth century was subject to state censorship under the 1737 Licensing Act and was thus a far cry from the unrestricted rational-critical conversation idealized by Habermas. Nonetheless, this does not mean that the censor handled all plays alike. Although such dramas as Richard

---

[19] John Plotz, *The Crowd: British Literature and Public Politics* (Berkeley: University of California Press, 2000), 10.

[20] Ibid.

[21] For a recent reevaluation of the theater's influence over public opinion and its place in the kind of public debate associated by Habermas with the public sphere, see Diego Saglia, " 'The Talking Demon': Liberty and Liberal Ideologies on the 1820s British Stage," *Nineteenth-Century Contexts* 28.4 (December 2006): 347–377. Saglia provides a rich contextualization of relations between patrons, authors, and actors to show "how a whole set of theatrical practices collaborated with and were implicit in the emergence of liberal ideologies and the sociopolitical transformations in post-Waterloo Britain" (351–352). In Saglia's reading, the drama of the 1820s elides ideological complications by smoothing public sphere tensions into private plots, but these acts of reduction also serve to bring into focus obstacles and flaws in the "extrication of liberal values from traditional forms of monarchic and dynastic allegiance" (369). I engage Saglia's interpretation in my discussion of Knowles's *Caius Gracchus* below.

Cumberland's *Richard the Second*, Edmund Eyre's *The Maid of Normandy*, and Eglantine Wallace's *The Whim*, as Worrall shows, were subjected to heavy censorship and even banned outright by the censor John Larpent (with the assistance of his wife, Anna), the Roman plays under discussion in this chapter were censored hardly at all. The reason was likely generic: tragedy was a high genre, featuring exceptional heroes and thus possibly on its face more respectable and less threatening than other sorts of entertainment submitted for licensing. The Roman setting, furthermore, may also have played a part, with the distancing effect of antiquity working to conceal potentially inflammatory situations behind the veil of classical respectability.[22] There may also have been an element of self-censorship, whereby playwrights wary of a refusal of licensing were careful to omit any language or circumstance that they thought might provoke the suspicion of the censor.

Whatever the explanation, the licensing submissions of plays on Roman themes contain remarkably few objections from the censor, although there are in some cases significant discrepancies between the copy submitted for licensing and those actually printed. Such absence of markings is curious. In the most recent and thorough account of theatrical censorship in England, Worrall describes the censorship principles of the Larpents as "totally unaccountable."[23] He also notes that the Larpents were especially sensitive to faults of their own class and that "the day-to-day reactions and perceptions by the Larpents of the movement of politics became the chaotic cues for their repression of drama."[24] This makes it all the more surprising that dramas that depict the overthrow of legitimate kings (*Brutus*), a similar resistance to the authority of the zealous decimvir Appius that results in his murder (*Virginius*), or the cruelty of the Roman aristocracy toward the starving plebeians (*Caius Gracchus*) should reach the stage largely in the form in which they were submitted. How can such tolerance be explained?

---

[22] On the treatment of historical distance in the period more generally, see Mark Salber Phillips, "Relocating Inwardness: Historical Distance and the Transition from Enlightenment to Romantic Historiography," *PMLA: Publications of the Modern Language Association of America* 118 (2003): 436–449.

[23] Worrall, *Theatric Revolution*, 126.   [24] Ibid., 131.

Any explanation must recognize the distancing effect of antiquity. Setting immediate contemporary issues, like the role of common people in political decision making or the manner and justification for resisting corrupt and ineffective leaders, in the antique past provided a safety net for censors concerned with the effects of staged drama on popular audiences. Plays depicting the overthrow of the Roman monarchy were palatable in a way that *The Maid of Normandy*, with its depiction of the more recent death of Marie Antoinette, was not. Still, such distancing effects may not tell the whole story. A consideration of how plays set in the Roman republic handle Hazlitt's question "What is the people?" reveals that their ambivalence about the role of the masses in political activity worked to combat certain potentially insurrectionary aspects of their plot and likely made them acceptable to the censor. This is not to suggest that these are fundamentally conservative plays, although some of them, like Croly's *Catiline* no doubt are; rather, these are plays that, in their depiction of popular political activity, question and undermine the claims of the people to participate in the political process and, by extension, the very possibility of articulating a rational-critical public opinion based on abstract reason.

JOHN HOWARD PAYNE'S *BRUTUS*: STAGING REGICIDE AFTER THE REVOLUTION

The first of the dramas from the Roman Revival to reach the London stage, John Howard Payne's *Brutus* enacts, for the first time after the French Revolution and the Napoleonic Wars, this story of rebellion, regicide, and the transition from a monarchy to a republic. The play opened in London at Drury Lane on 3 December 1818, with Kean in the title role of Lucius Junius Brutus, and the performance was a resounding popular success. It became a signature role for Kean and was performed fifty-two times, becoming a stable part of the dramatic repertoire at the Theatres Royal through 1830 and beyond. In 1826, it was anthologized alongside Shakespeare, Massinger, Farquhar, Addison, Goldsmith, Otway, and Jonson in John Cumberland's multivolume anthology *Cumberland's British Theatre*. The play's appeal also extended abroad, and shortly after its London debut, it opened in New York on 15 March 1819.[25]

The play must have generated controversy given the lingering memory of the establishment of the French republic and the beheading of Louis XVI, as well as the more immediate domestic disturbances seen in the Spa Fields riots, the alleged attack on the prince regent in December 1817, and the subsequent crackdown on the reform movement, which included the repeal of Habeas Corpus and the Gagging Acts.[26] Such resonances were further overlaid by associations of the Brutus story with the widespread cult of Brutus in the early years of the French Revolution.[27]

Given the widespread calls for reform and the anxiety over extraparliamentary politics and popular disturbances, how does *Brutus* figure the establishment of Roman republican liberty, and how does that liberty relate to the demands of the Roman populace? What is "the people" in *Brutus*, and does the drama itself treat this as an important question? Is liberty presented as something historically inevitable, or as the contingent result of particular individual actions? Do the people clamor for liberty? Are they seen to ally themselves with demagogues who exploit this desire for liberty? Or, alternatively, is liberty presented as something beyond their asking? The following section addresses these concerns through an analysis of the play's content, staging, and reception. *Brutus* was clearly understood as a response to the aristocratic version of Rome presented in Kemble's *Coriolanus*, and, while it sometimes appears sympathetic to popular politics and the cause of political reform, it is in fact deeply ambivalent about the role and relevance of common people in establishing the Roman republic.

---

[25] As a curious side note, when the play toured the United States, it was with an actor appropriately named Lucius Junius Booth. One of Booth's sons, John Wilkes Booth, later shot President Abraham Lincoln in a Washington, D.C., theater in 1865. See Herbert, *David, Voltaire,* Brutus, 148.

[26] For more on these events, see the classic account in E. P. Thompson, *The Making of the English Working Class* (New York: Vintage, 1966), 603–710.

[27] On the use of the Brutus legend in France read in conjunction with David's "Lictors Returning to Brutus to Bodies of His Sons," see Herbert, *David, Voltaire,* Brutus, esp. 50–51. Also note that in choosing Brutus for his subject, David rejected an earlier plan to paint Coriolanus. Herbert points out that the heroic stories of Coriolanus, Brutus, and Regulus all share the theme of "heroic self-abnegation in which the pleas of women and children feature prominently" (54).

The plot of *Brutus* derives from two episodes in the life of Rome's first consul, Brutus. Both originate in Livy's history of Rome, *Ab Urbe Condita*. The first episode tells the story of the rape of Lucretia by Sextus Tarquinius, the son of Rome's king, and her subsequent suicide out of shame, after which Brutus cast off his ruse of incompetence and led a revolt against the Crown that resulted in the establishment of the Roman republic and its institution of consular leadership.[28] The drama then concludes with a second episode in which Brutus, having assumed the role of consul and facing a conspiracy to restore the Tarquins to power, sentenced his sons to death for their participation in the conspiracy. This would have been a familiar story to many early-nineteenth-century theatergoers. As one reviewer noted, "All the events of Roman history are as familiar to persons with any tincture of learning as those of our own; and the story of Lucretia, and the consequential overthrow of the Tarquins, is known to every schoolboy."[29] In both of these episodes, Payne sticks closely to the structure of the Brutus story as narrated by Livy, though he departs from his ancient source in giving Brutus one son, rather than two; in furnishing Tarquin with both a faithful army and a strong camp at Ardea; and in shifting the conspiracy plot of his sons away from a political motivation and toward a romantic one. Brutus's son, Titus, participates in the conspiracy not out of political principles, but rather because he is in love with Tarquin's daughter Tarquinia. The play thus blends the high dramatic conflicts of tragic action with a forcible appeal to sentiment and feeling, one that is able to tell the story of a stern patriot while still including elements of the more popular romantic melodrama. Furthermore, the staging combined an appeal to high Roman heroism with the sort of spectacle that audiences loved but that many critics had begun to condemn. *Brutus* was faulted, for example, for its "melo-dramatic *tableau*."[30]

Brutus dramatizes the transition from a monarchy to a republic. One way to read the play would underscore the danger of replacing a seemingly corrupt monarch with a new republic. In such a reading,

---

[28] For this episode, see Livy, I.57–60, in Livy, *Livy: Books I and II*, Loeb Classical Library, trans. B. O. Foster (Cambridge: Harvard University Press, 1919), 196–209.
[29] *Theatrical Inquisitor* 13 (1818): 450.   [30] Ibid., 452.

which echoes strongly a common understanding of the French Revolution, the overthrow of the Tarquins results merely in their replacement by another absolute ruler. Tullia, Tarquin's wife and the queen of Rome, for example, dismisses Brutus as "the king of Rome."[31] Act 5, in which Brutus sentences his own son to death, can then be read as proof of his autocracy. The play itself, in this reading, becomes a warning that although the establishment of a republic appears to effect a change in government, it merely leads to a different form of monarchy. Republicanism itself thus becomes a chimerical impossibility.[32] This certainly provides an explanation for why a play about the establishment of a republic met with the approval of the censor, but it obscures significant complexities in the play. Brutus's sentencing of his son, for example, could be read as evidence not of a restrictive autocracy, but rather as an explicit recognition that under a republic, all citizens, regardless of their rank and family connection, are subject equally to the laws. This in itself is a compelling definition of liberty, and it provides a more optimistic take on the establishment of the republic in *Brutus*. The manner in which *Brutus* deploys the rhetoric of liberty and freedom further demonstrates its complexity and points away from a reading of *Brutus* as merely condemning republicanism. Liberty and freedom were, of course, charged terms in the early nineteenth century, and the frequency with which they are invoked in *Brutus* suggests the drama's participation in a broader attempt to define these terms. Liberty can imply the freedom of the subject from the arbitrary power wielded by an absolute ruler (in this case, Sextus Tarquin). Similarly, it can represent a value protected by the rule of law that guarantees the equal position of all beneath the law. Finally, the idea of liberty also invokes the more dubious possibility of license and a lack of constraint. *Brutus* invokes all of these possibilities and the manner in which it does so highlights its efforts to shape the way that its audience understood liberty and freedom.

---

[31] John Howard Payne, *Brutus; or, the Fall of Tarquin* (London, 1819), act 4, scene 3.

[32] This is the reading offered by the play's only modern editor. See *Shakespeare Imitations, Parodies, and Forgeries, 1710–1820*, ed. Jeffrey Kahan (London: Routledge, 2004), Vol. 3.

In act 3, for example, when Brutus first sees Lucretia's dead body and withdraws her bloody dagger, he bids "Rome be free."[33] Since the tyranny of the Tarquins represents the central problem of the first four acts, Brutus's declaration implies that "freedom" can be achieved by the removal of tyranny. It does not, however, make any suggestions for what will replace this tyranny. Furthermore, the conjunction of Lucretia's body with the dagger and freedom pairs freedom and liberty with vengeance and violence, and the play is marked by repeated calls for revenge. Brutus asks his allies to swear on the dagger to "revenge her fall." In act 3, scene 4, he repeatedly tells the people that the acts of the Tarquins cry for revenge and later, he confronts Tullia with the cry "Justice! Vengeance!"[34] Elsewhere, Tullia reports the Roman people "in arms and thundering at our gates/ For just revenge."[35] Similar language recurs throughout the text, but the linking of freedom and liberty with revenge represents a problem for the play, for how can those seeking revenge prevent their deeds from instigating a violent cycle of vengeance that prevents the establishment of their very goal of freedom, liberty, and justice? This has, of course, been a consistent problem for violent revolutionaries, and it recalls Paine's effort to explain the bloodthirstiness of the Paris peasantry in the early days of the revolution. Paine notes that the attack on the Bastille was largely peaceful and that the few who were killed died at the hands of the mob and not the people. Such "vulgar" and "ignorant" people arise "as an unavoidable consequence, out of the ill construction of all old governments in Europe," Paine claims. "They learn from the governments they live under, and retaliate the punishments they have been accustomed to behold."[36]

Brutus, too, implicitly weighs this dilemma, as suggested by his frequent use of organic metaphors of gestation to describe the emergence of liberty. In the first act, for example, when Brutus announces his

---

[33] Payne, *Brutus* (London, 1819), act 3, scene 2, p. 27. Subsequent references to page numbers in this edition will be given parenthetically in the text along with act and scene numbers.

[34] The lines appear in the handwritten version of the play submitted for licensing, which can be found in the Larpent Collection of the Huntington Library, manuscript number LA2059.

[35] Act 4, scene 1, LA2059.

[36] Thomas Paine, *The Rights of Man* (Oxford: Oxford University Press, 1995), 108–109.

sense of liberty's imminent approach, he declares that liberty "presses to the birth—I see it in the forming womb of time—The embryo liberty" (1.3, p. 8). Toward the end of act four, scene 1 when Brutus asserts to his son that he is wholly in his right mind—"I am not mad but as the lion is/ When he breaks down the toils that tyrant craft/ Hath spread to catch him" (4.1, p. 35)—and that the Tarquins must be punished, Titus asks pointedly whether the punishment represents justice. Brutus's reply repeats the figure of liberty as an embryo:

> At the birth of Freedom
> Frantic and wild are the first struggling throes
> That cast the mighty embrio on the world
> Cradled in blood the Herculean infant lies
> Till grown into nature strength he casts
> The film of imperfection. Peace and Justice
> And comely order welcome his approach
> And loves and graces triumph his train.[37]

Passages like this, with their strong linking of freedom and violence, recognize that the transition from tyranny to republican liberty will be painful. The use of organic figures of growth, however, implies that maturing to perfection is an inevitable result of the establishment of a republic, and this allows even the violent pangs of vengeance to seem a necessary and natural step in the establishment of what the villainous Horatius calls "the Roman Rights."[38] A similarly sanguine belief that the overthrow of tyranny will create the possibility of freedom can be found when Valerius explains that he joys not in the falling of palaces, but rather in the hopes that follow:

> It is the day-spring of revising freedom,
> The dawn of brighter hopes, that cheers my bosom,
> And makes these terrors pass away like clouds
> Before the uprising Sun.[39]

---

[37] The lines appear in LA2059. They come straight from Cumberland's earlier dramatization of the Brutus story and are one of a number of instances where long-winded speeches from Cumberland are cut to make a more streamlined drama. See Richard Cumberland, *The Sybil; or The Elder Brutus. A Tragedy; from The Posthumous Dramatick Works of the Late Richard Cumberland* (London: G. and W. Nichol, 1813).

[38] Again, these lines appear only in LA2059, and are cut from the printed text.

[39] Act 4, scene i, LA2059.

Valerius's optimism about the transition to a free republic is expressed not through an organic metaphor of growth but in the classic Enlightenment image of the dawning day, with all of the implications that we might expect such language to carry.

The play itself seems to support Valerius's optimism, as demonstrated by its depiction of the force of law under the new Roman republic after the ousting of the Tarquins. Repeatedly, the law is shown to apply equally to all citizens and to guarantee freedom from the arbitrary abuse of power. Indeed, once the play has solved the problem of tyranny, it increasingly defines liberty and freedom through the principle of the rule of law. The contrast between the rule of law under the Roman republic and license under the rule of the Tarquins reveals the problem of non-republican forms of government in which rulers are set above the law and authorities are able to ignore the law with impunity. When, for example, the Tarquins have been deposed and Lucretius and Valerius encounter Horatius and Celius, two allies of the Tarquins, Lucretius immediately wants to arrest them. But Valerius stops him and says:

> Let them be watch'd. We must not venture farther.
> To arrest a Roman upon bare surmise
> Would be at once to imitate the tyrant
> Whom we renounce and from his throne have driven! (4.1, p. 40)

This strong defense of habeas corpus comes directly from William Duncombe's *Junius Brutus: A Tragedy* (1735), where it is preceded by the acknowledgment that "the Laws and Rights, of which we are the Guardians,/ Restrain our hands from Arbitrary Sway."[40] The episode shows the respect for due process in the new republic. As used here by Payne, the lines provide a concrete instance of a moment where republicans have an opportunity to repeat the practices of a tyrant— indeed, are inclined to such practices, as Lucretius's instinct shows— but deliberately choose not to. Such sentiments repeat themselves in the organic terms associated with liberty's inevitability when Brutus declares that once the republic has been established, he will resign consular power: "once freedom shall be firmly rooted/ Then...will

---

[40] William Duncombe, *Junius Brutus: A Tragedy* (London, 1735), 76.

your Consul/ Exchange the splendid miseries of power, / For the calm comforts of a happy home" (5.1, p. 43). Moments like this suggest a political system governed not by particular men, but by laws more generally. This is why act 5, which some contemporary reviewers considered superfluous to the main action, is so important. When Brutus is called out of retirement to pass judgment on his son, who, out of love for Tarquinia, has participated in the conspiracy to return the Tarquins to power, Brutus's sentence of death seems stern and unsentimental. But it establishes definitively the rule of law. Moreover, when Brutus embraces his son and declares "the sovereign magistrate of injured Rome condemns/ A crime thy father's bleeding heart forgives" (5.3), he effects a clear separation between the domestic role of father and the impartial and anonymous offices of state.

The fifth act of *Brutus*, then, establishes liberty to mean rule by law applied equally to all citizens. This becomes even more apparent in the contrast between the rule of law under the republic and the understanding of liberty articulated by the Tarquins, where liberty is repeatedly figured negatively as mere license, especially sexual license. Throughout the first four acts of *Brutus*, the central problem is the license of the monarchy, which manifests itself as an extension of political license, of rule without accountability, into sexual license, specifically rape. In the second act, for example, when Tarquin and his generals lay bets on whose wife is the most faithful, liberty figures as feminine depravity, and the problematic relationship between righteous liberty and decadent license becomes clear. Tarquin speculates that the generals will find each wife "Making the most of this, their liberty./ Why 'tis the sex: enjoying to the full/ The swing of licence which their husband's absence/ Affords" (2.1, p. 15). Tarquin can see liberty only as carnal license, which, with the emergent discourse of liberty, was a common counterrevolutionary tactic from the 1790s onward; such reactionaries saw the call for increased liberty as a threat both to the nation's political life and to female chastity.[41] By associating Tarquin, the villain of the play, with these positions, the drama implies that these fears represent the paranoia of the authoritarian

---

[41] See Nicola Watson, *Revolution and the Form of the British Novel 1790–1825* (Oxford: Clarendon Press, 1994); and Cox, "Ideology and Genre."

elite. The irony, of course, is that the Roman wives, as exemplified by Lucretia, are not at all licentious. Liberty as license is, rather, reserved for the Tarquins themselves, who, ruling from a position above the law, can act with legal impunity. The threat to female chastity and the moral health of the nation comes not from below, from the increased license of the people, but rather from above, from the willingness of those in power to exploit their position and to act as if beyond the reach of the law. Burke resorted to sentimental politics to depict the actions of the Paris mob against the royal family in the famous passage culminating in his praise for Marie Antoinette,[42] but the *Brutus* plot reverses the poles of that argument. The threat in each case is sexualized, but in the Brutus story, it comes not from the crowd below, but rather from the monarch above. In the previous chapter, I argued that Hazlitt's dismissal of poetry as "right royal," as inevitably aligned with monarchy and "the minister's side of the question," was rooted in Kemble's performance of *Coriolanus*. Payne's drama can be read as a response to this very position, as an attempt to enlist poetry and drama for the progressive cause. The prologue refers obliquely to "our cause," and the play itself, as it presents the replacement of tyranny by a republic, figures liberty as the accountability of all, even leaders, to the rule of law.

But if *Brutus* locates the threat to national stability in the extralegal license of those in power and not in the perceived fickleness of the masses, this does not mean that it endorses the possibility that positive change comes from popular action. Rather, *Brutus* grapples with the problem of collective agency and the role of popular actions in the establishment of the republic. The text of the play does not initially seem to take a strong position for or against mass action, although certain aspects of the play suggest a sanguine view toward popular political activity. For a start, the only figures in the drama that demean and dismiss the Roman populace are its villains. Tullia, for example, when told that the palace is in flames, refuses to meet death at the hands of the people: "to perish/ By the vile scum of Rome, hunted by dogs,/ Baited to death by brawling, base mechanics—/

---

[42] See Edmund Burke, *Reflections on the Revolution in France*, ed. J. G. A. Pocock (Indianapolis, IN: Hackett, 1987), 60–67.

Shame insupportable" (4.1; LA2059). Such sentiments, which repeatedly deny the potential of common people to hold viable political positions, are later echoed by Horatius, who describes the populace as a "giddy throng" (4.2; LA2059). Both of these passages appear in the submission for licensing but not in the print copy. The omissions may be an attempt to tone down perceived support for popular actions, but they more likely result from an effort to achieve dramatic economy.[43] In addition to generating sympathy for the masses by placing scorn for the people in the mouths of the play's villains, there is evidence that when the play was staged, it included scenes showing coordinated popular action. One reviewer described the opening of the fourth act as including "the outer gate of Tarquin's palace...beat down by the populace; the stage is covered with the ruins, and the glare of burning buildings is thrown upon the scene."[44] Moments like this attribute great power to the people and show their active participation in political change. On the other hand, a stage covered with ruins and the glare of burning buildings raises the possibility that collective agency, the actions of a mob with no property of their own and hence no vested interest in the state, will always pose a dangerous threat to property. The moment asks pointedly whether the old must be entirely destroyed before the new can be established. Moreover, because collective action of this sort does not involve spoken lines, it would not need to be described in the play's submission for licensing, thus promoting the censor's approval.

Such attributions of collective agency in *Brutus* can be read as a response to the crowd scenes of Kemble's *Coriolanus*, where the aristocratic hero of the play is shown dominating a group of more than two hundred actors on stage. The difference in each play's attitude toward rank is evidenced further even at the level of the cast of characters. In Kemble's *Coriolanus*, the cast is listed not by appearance or importance, but strictly by rank. Payne's *Brutus* lists the cast by importance, with Lucius Junius first and Sextus Tarquin, who by order of rank as the king's son would be listed first by Kemble, listed third. The contrast between the two plays might then underscore the degree to which

---

[43] The canceled lines come straight from Cumberland's *Sybil*.
[44] *Theatrical Inquisitor* 13 (1818): 452.

What Is the People?

Brutus aligns itself with the approval of popular participation in the political process, a position that might even be associated with post-Waterloo agitation for reform and with the key claims of early-nineteenth-century popular politics more broadly. Despite such possibilities, *Brutus*'s representation of common people remains far from triumphant. To begin with, at the end of act 3, scene 3, Flavius Corunna, one of Tullia's servants, describes Brutus addressing the Roman people from behind the exposed body of Lucretia. Brutus "harangues assembled Rome" (line19), Corunna reports. The choice of verb calls to mind a demagogue, one who uses the people to his own end rather than one who seeks the cooperation of the people for coordinated action. Corunna confirms this impression when he adds that

> all the people hear him
> With wildest admiration and applause;
> He speaks as if he held the souls of men
> In his own hand, and moulded them at pleasure.
> They look on him as they would view a god,
> Who from a darkness which invested him,
> Springs forth, and knitting his stern brow in frowns,
> Proclaims the vengeful will of angry Jove. (lines 21–28)

The description comes from one aligned with the Tarquins and so might be another example of the tendency of the play's villains to dismiss the populace; nonetheless, it raises the haunting specter that an impassioned leader could stir common people into acts of violence and produce not an ordered state but mob rule and mere anarchy.

Against this prospect, the play suggests, we can rely only on the exceptional virtue of leaders who win the trust of the masses. Such emphasis on individual virtue reveals a generic tension in the attempt to use tragedy to advance a populist or democratic position, which again recalls Hazlitt's reading of *Coriolanus* and his assertion that poetry is "right royal." Payne's *Brutus* represents itself as "an historical tragedy." The choice of genre is important because tragedy most commonly emphasizes the dominant, singular individual over other forces and agents. In this sense it might be related to exemplarity, which is, as I suggested in chapter 2, a Plutarchian mode. If exemplarity works by paralleling historical events, it most commonly parallels historical personages and invites those who think through example to idealize not the impersonal values of a state or a culture but rather the very personal situations of individuals seen to represent and uphold those values. Exemplarity most frequently turns history into biography, and, as a consequence, its response to crisis locates its solution only in the strong leader or exemplary hero. In this way, exemplarity as a way of understanding the past through precedent has much in common with tragedy, which similarly locates its action and sense of crisis in powerful (but flawed) individuals.

The choice of the Brutus plot initially minimizes the problem of the people to focus instead on the problem of monarchy. While the play may retain the possibility of popular political agency, the solution to its central crisis—the license of the monarchy—becomes not mass action, but individual virtue. There is thus a tension in the play between its emphasis on the great individual, Brutus, and its heralding of the emergence of a democratic republic. In this way, Payne's play faces a problem opposite to that of the antirevolutionary drama of the 1790s as described by Jeffrey Cox. Those dramas were defined by their "double assault upon popular rebellion and sexual liberation," and they used traditional tragedy as "a formal means for discounting the importance of the mass actions portrayed in revolutionary historical spectaculars."[45] The crux, however, was that the conservative form (tragedy) could not contain its radical content (images of revolution). "The antirevolutionary drama had to incorporate the imagery of the pro-revolutionary drama in order to combat it," Cox claims, "but in doing so it recreated for the audience the powerful icons of revolt whose significance had already been established for them by radical literary culture."[46] In contrast, Payne's play uses a conservative form to deliver potentially progressive content. Rebellion and a complete change of political system are preferable to a tyrant who sits so far above the law as to threaten female chastity. Such a transition might be violent, but if led by an individual with exemplary virtue and respect for the law, it is possible to establish a republic where liberty and freedom—in the sense of the equal application of the law to all citizens—reign supreme. Read this way, the story of Brutus and the founding of the Roman republic stands as a

---

[45] Cox, "Ideology and Genre," 586, 596.
[46] Ibid., 605.

counterexample to the disasters of the French Revolution. But such potentially insurrectionary implications are held in check by the form of the work itself, which emphasizes the heroic individual alone as the motor of change and implies that only the virtuous leader can save the state from tyranny. The play thus stops far short of advocating any kind of popular revolution, and it ultimately questions the possibility of popular politics more generally. This, combined with the distancing effect of its classical setting, provides an explanation for why *Brutus* was hardly touched by the censor.

If Larpent, the censor, was kind to the play, the critics were not. *Brutus* received at best lukewarm reviews, and more often highly negative ones. The *Theatrical Inquisitor*, for example, praised the fifth act in which Brutus must condemn his son as producing that "solemn gloom, almost approaching to awe, which is the noblest attribute of genuine tragedy,"[47] but it objected to the play's marked anachronism, its violation of the unities, its handling of character, and the low quality of its poetry. The *British Critic* applauded the constant movement of *Brutus*, its "*hurry-skurry*," but it saw little else to admire in the play: "The language of it is very indifferent; the action is managed without any skill or the slightest regard to any canon of dramatic criticism; the sentiments are for the most part common place, and the characters partake, as might be expected, of the same nature."[48]

---

[47] *Theatrical Inquisitor* 13 (1818): 452.

[48] *British Critic*, n.s. 11 (January–June 1819): 75. Such shortcomings, however, might also be explained by the fact that Payne plagiarized his drama nearly in its entirety from two source texts, Hugh Downman's *Lucius Junius Brutus; or, the Expulsion of the Tarquins: An Historical Play* (1779) and Richard Cumberland, *The Sybil; or The Elder Brutus: A Tragedy* (published posthumously in 1813). Payne credits these sources in his preface, where he notes that "he has had no hesitation in adopting the conceptions and language of his predecessors, wherever they seemed likely to strengthen the plan which he had prescribed to himself" (n.p.). Nonetheless, Payne continues to claim that "no assistance can be available without an effort almost if not altogether as laborious as original composition" (n.p.). Comparisons of Payne's source texts with the copy submitted for licensing and the published version allows speculations about how certain aspects of Downman and Cumberland might have come to seem objectionable and threatening in the politically charged climate of London after Waterloo. The Brutus story, moreover, has a long history of political interpretation and had been used in the eighteenth century as a transparent justification of the Glorious Revolution and subsequent Whig rule. Another of Payne's sources, William Duncombe's *Junius Brutus: A Tragedy* (1735), for example, suggests the rich potential for

The harshest review of the play, however, came from the *Quarterly Review*. Although the reviewer complains initially that the facts of the story were "too strictly political to suffice for the interest of a regular tragedy,"[49] the objections that follow are aesthetic rather than political. Brutus's son Titus is poorly handled: "Mr. Payne had no way of making us feel for him but by so diminishing his guilt, that we become dissatisfied with what seems a more strained and severe punctilio in Brutus" (*QR*, 405). Brutus himself was overly simple and single-minded: "He has no conflicting passions in his heart, or double purposes in his conduct, and he is exhibited not under a variety of trials, but exposed to one only, and under circumstances, which...leave no room for uncertainty, or wavering conduct" (*QR*, 405–406). Ultimately, both Payne and the play were damningly dismissed in a burst of critical vitriol:

> We declare, then, that he appears to us to have no one quality which we should require in a tragic poet; he has neither comprehended nor arranged his subject properly, he has not surmounted its difficulties, nor profited by its advantages:—we will not dwell upon his faults, the foolish and presumptuous imitation of one of the most beautiful speeches in Shakespeare, the absurd mummeries, and pantomimic tricks, too long tolerated with patience by an audience, which might have commanded for their delight and instruction, the noblest productions of human nature,—it is enough to say conscientiously, that we cannot find in the whole play, a single character finely conceived, or rightly sustained, a single incident well managed, a single speech, nay, a single sentence of good poetry. (*QR*, 407)

analogies between the Brutus story and contemporary events. The play is dedicated to the Right Honourable the Lord Hardwicke, lord chief justice of His Majesty's Court of King's Bench, with the claim that "my design in the following scenes being to excite a zeal for public good, a reverence for the law, and a just veneration for that heroic [page break] prince, whom providence raised up in the day of distress, to rescue these nations from civil and ecclesiastical tyranny, and fix our liberties on a firm and lasting foundation" (*Junius Brutus* [London, 1735], n.p.]). This statement presents the play as a justification of 1688 and a paean to William as the Brutus-like father of his country. The play is a sustained plea for rule of law over arbitrary monarchical government, but since it does not claim that rule of law is possible only under a republic, it partakes of the eighteenth-century idea of a mixed government and does not seem republican so much as thoroughly Whig.

[49] *Quarterly Review* 22 (1820): 404. Subsequent page references to this volume will be provided parenthetically in the text with the abbreviation *QR*.

Brutus may question the viability of collective agency and reject popular politics, but it nonetheless represents the possibility of revolt in a manner that would have been objectionable to Tory audiences. This suggests that the *Quarterly*'s aesthetic objections to the play might be seen as motivated by a political objection to Payne's subject matter, a position asserted by Vindex in a letter to the *Theatrical Inquisitor*. Vindex claimed, "The chief merit of Shakespeare, in his English historical plays, proceeds, according to the Quarterly Reviewers, from his not having dwelled upon 'PUBLIC REVOLUTIONS, A DISCONTENTED PEOPLE, OR RIVAL FACTIONS;' this is the grand test to which dramatic power is subjected; and as the pages of 'Brutus' are replete with these disinterested exceptions, hence the virulent animosity with which its author is assailed."[50] The *Quarterly*'s position, Vindex claims, is marked by an opposition to the representation of popular movements, and its "hireling hatred of human liberty," but *Brutus*

abounds in excitements to democratic virtue; its details, as the reviewers observe, are chiefly of a political nature; and when this fact is combined with an assurance that the drama not only agitates, but forms and directs the public mind, a probable conjecture may be hazarded of the dark and desperate venality I have attempted to detect. The Quarterly Reviewers have rolled the black current of their critical opinions across the pages of Mr. Payne, but like the inundations of the Nile, their encroachments will be followed by renovated verdure, and redoubled fertility.[51]

Vindex rightly notes that *Brutus* "forms and directs the public mind," and, as he suggests, *Brutus* can be read as a sustained plea for liberty. But he overlooks the tension, discussed above, between this plea and the drama's location of liberty not in popular action, but in the heightened virtue of a particular individual. Still, if Vindex overstates the democratic implications of *Brutus*, he does at least emphasize its progressive tendencies, which are further underscored by the play's casting of Edmund Kean in the title role. A number of critics who did not respond well to the drama raved about the quality of the acting, with special plaudits for Kean. When Keats saw the play, for example, his response in a letter to his brother George succinctly reflected the

[50] *Theatrical Inquisitor* 16 (1820): 128–129.
[51] Ibid., 134.

critical consensus, "Kean was excellent—the play was very bad."[52] Kean's presence encouraged critics to compare his version of Rome with Kemble's, and this comparison was explicitly politicized.

Comments from the *Theatrical Inquisitor*, for example, suggest a closed economy of comparison between Kean and Kemble whereby to defend Kean was to diminish Kemble, but to prefer Kean to Kemble in Roman roles went even further and stood as a comparison and a judgment of the version of Rome presented by each actor. "What now becomes of that assertion," the reviewer asked in his praise for Kean, "that he is a quack, that the success of his performance depends on one or two tricks, that he has but one manner of acting, that he is without dignity, and above all, that he cannot personate the Roman character?" Moreover, the reviewer continued that Kean's representation of Brutus as father in act 5 "is the true sublime; never has the Roman dignity been more adequately sustained; Mr. Kemble's was dignity of person, Mr. Kean's seems true dignity of soul. Mr. Kemble's *Coriolanus* will not, for the future, rank above Mr. Kean's *Brutus*."[53] Comments of this sort demonstrate clearly that Kean was being explicitly compared to Kemble—which is no surprise given that the two were both enormously popular figures who acted with completely different styles.[54] The highly aesthetic qualities for which Kean is praised, moreover, suggest a situation similar to the review from *The Quarterly*, where aesthetic preferences speak for political positions.

Kemble's *Coriolanus*, with its imperious, aristocratic hero marshaling large crowds on stage and then haughtily banishing the people as he towered over them, was the dominant representation of Rome on the English stage until Kemble's retirement in 1817, and it was a decidedly antipopular enactment, one that came down, as Hazlitt suggested, "on

---

[52] JK to the George Keatses, 16 December 1818–4 January 1819, *The Letters of John Keats*, ed. Robert Gittings (Oxford: Oxford University Press, 1970), 178.

[53] *Theatrical Inquisitor* 13 (1818): 457.

[54] Hazlitt constantly compared the two. In his comments on Kean from the preface to *A View of the English Stage*, Hazlitt noted detractors that complained of Kean: "He was not tall. He had not a fine voice. He did not play at Covent Garden. He was not John Kemble" (quoted in William Hazlitt, *Selected Writings*, ed. Jon Cook [Oxford: Oxford University Press, 1991], 244). Hazlitt, in contrast, in his first review of Kean's Shylock published in the *Morning Chronicle* of 27 January 1814, compared Kemble and Kean to Kean's favor: "It is not saying too much of Mr. Kean, though it is saying a great deal, that he has all that Mr. Kemble *wants* of perfection" (Hazlitt, *Selected Writings*, 249).

the minister's side of the question." Kean's *Brutus*, in contrast, resists this aristocratic hauteur for a different understanding of the Roman republican past and its contemporary application. This version of Rome was progressive in its condemnation of tyranny, its examination of the grounds for rebellion, and its attempt to clarify an understanding of liberty and freedom grounded in the equal subjection of all citizens to the law. *Brutus*, however, stops far short of ascribing a coherent political agency to the Roman populace, and, in its firm focus on the exceptional virtue of Brutus, it undermines the claims of a fully enfranchised democracy and the possibility of popular politics more generally. Faced with Hazlitt's question, "What is the people," *Brutus* returns an ambivalent response. For certain characters, like Collonus and Tullia, "the people" are a mob that Brutus can easily work into a frenzy with his harangue, and they are capable, perhaps desirous, of acts of destructive violence. But if the play as a whole rejects this position and suggests that the people are a necessary support for Brutus's cries of revenge and his institution of a new form of government, it certainly does not show them as capable of exerting their own coherent political will, let alone anything approaching Hazlitt's conception of "public opinion" operating "beyond immediate experience or interest" grounded in "abstract reason."

J. S. KNOWLES'S *CAIUS GRACCHUS*: AGRARIAN REVOLT AND THE POLITICS OF CORN

John Howard Payne was not the only playwright challenging Kemble's version of ancient Rome. Payne too spawned imitators, most prominently James Sheridan Knowles, whose *Virginius* premiered at Covent Garden on 17 May 1820 and became the defining role for Charles Macready. The tragedy brought Knowles his first theatrical success, which he then followed with the less successful *Caius Gracchus* (Covent Garden, 18 November 1823).[55] Like Payne's *Brutus*, Knowles's

---

[55] It should be noted, however, that *Caius Gracchus* debuted earlier, on 13 February 1815, in Belfast. The version that was staged at Covent Garden was somewhat different from this one. On the initial history of the play in 1815 and the negotiations with the censor in 1823, see Saglia, "Talking Demon," 355; and L. W. Conolly, *The Censorship of English Drama* (San Marino, CA: Huntington Library, 1976), 110–111.

Virginius tells the story of a powerful aristocratic figure who seeks absolute dominion over Rome and whose sense of being above the law is exposed by an act of injustice against a woman. But unlike *Brutus*, *Virginius* takes place after the founding of the republic, and the telos of its action is not the establishment of a republic based on the rule of law but the restoration of that republic. The people are consistently shown to be ungrateful and unwilling to assert their interests boldly, and instead such action is reserved for singular heroic figures like Virginius. *Brutus* takes a dim view of popular collective action; *Virginius* is even more extreme in its dismissal of the general populace's political participation.[56] With its emphasis on Virginius's feelings over the killing of his daughter to save her from the lust of Appius, *Virginius* is more sentimental than *Brutus*, and its potentially volatile politics are contained by the emphasis on a private plot involving the love of Virginius for his daughter. It therefore makes better sense to compare *Brutus* with *Caius Gracchus*, in which Knowles more clearly shapes his understanding of the populace in connection with issues such as tyranny, the right to resistance, the need for reform, the uses of political violence, and the relationship between leaders and the people in the face of a corrupt government.

Caius Gracchus tells the story from Livy and Plutarch of the younger Gracchus brother who as tribune in 123 and 122 BCE pushed for an ambitious series of agrarian reforms that earned him the enmity of the Senate and resulted in his death in 121 after a crackdown on his supporters by the aristocrat Opimius.[57] The drama attends little to the

---

[56] For a recent reading of *Virginius* that links the play to *Coriolanus* and recognizes its "dangerously reformist politics," see Saglia, "Talking Demon," 356–359. Saglia argues that while the play was pruned of passages that would have been sensitive to the new monarch, it might still be read as an indictment of monarchy in general and of George IV in particular and thus "remained a vehicle for subversive contents" (358). See also Norman Vance, *The Victorians and Ancient Rome* (Oxford: Blackwell, 1997), 43–44. For the apocryphal story that George IV himself censored Knowles's play, see Conolly, *Censorship*, 109–110.

[57] The main source here is "Caius Gracchus" in *Plutarch's Lives*, Vol. 10, Loeb Classical Library, trans. Bernadotte Perrin (Cambridge: Harvard University Press, 1921), 196–241. On Caius's legal reforms, see v.1–vi.4 (206–213); on the Senate's use of Livius Drusus, see viii.3–x.2 (214–219). Plutarch says little of Caius's mother, Cornelia; see iv.3–4 (206–207) and xix.1–3 (238–241). Caius Gracchus's reforms are also described in the summary of Livy's lost book lx. See Livy, *Livy: Summaries*, Loeb

details of Caius's reforms, but it does stage the rivalry between Caius and Opimius and presents Caius as torn between the love of domesticity encouraged by his wife, Licinia, and the political ambitions of his mother, Cornelia. As the rivalry between Opimius and Caius deepens, a plot by Opimius to use his ally, the tribune Drusus, to draw popular support away from Caius by promising the people an ever greater and more demagogic program of rewards succeeds. To win their favor, Caius must go before the people and beg for it. He refuses to do this, and his ruin follows shortly after an exchange between Caius and his mother, who initially begs him to stay away from politics because the people are fickle and do not deserve his help, but then urges him to take action: "Go! You are Cornelia's son."[58] A narrative of populist, some would say demagogic, land reform becomes instead a tale of popular ingratitude and aristocratic vindictiveness played out in the context of a son's close relationship with his ambitious mother.[59] In this way, the themes, language, and dramatic emphasis of the play all obviously mimic the plot of *Coriolanus*, so much so that one commentator complained that Knowles too frequently draws on Shakespeare's play: "We have the lofty spirit of Caius Marcius, the heroic grandeur of Volumnia, the quaint jests of Menenius, and the deafening shouts of the Roman multitude, all brought to our remembrance in regular succession."[60]

Classical Library, trans. Alfred C. Schlessinger (Cambridge: Harvard University Press, 1959), 70–71.

[58] James Sheridan Knowles, *Caius Gracchus*, in *The Dramatic Works of James Sheridan Knowles* (London: G. Routledge, 1856), act 4, scene 2, p. 42. Subsequent references to act, scene, and page number in this edition will be provided parenthetically in the text.

[59] Norman Vance argues that the play's domestic theme, the tension between Gracchus and his wife, who wants him to stay home, and his mother, who wants him actively to confront tyranny, "helped to soften the alarming politics which revolutionary France had reinfused into the republic" (*Victorians and Ancient Rome*, 43). I differ from Vance in emphasizing the play's political resonance. Although I agree that the play softens the potentially alarming politics of the Gracchi story, I locate this softening not in the domestic plot but rather in the dismissive attitude that the play projects onto the Roman populace.

[60] D.G., "Remarks" preceding *Caius Gracchus* in *Cumberland's British Theatre*, Vol. 6 (London: John Cumberland, 1826), 5. D. G. is the anonymous abbreviation used in the original. One contemporary viewer also saw the citizens in *Caius Gracchus* as reminiscent of the populace in *Julius Caesar* and *Coriolanus*. See "Literary Review: Caius Gracchus," *The Mirror of the Stage* 3 (1 December 1823): 133–134.

Like *Brutus*, the prologue of *Caius Gracchus* draws upon the logic of exemplarity to offer Rome as a model for contemporary Britain. It further underscores the exemplary value of Roman history more generally for such progressive causes as the Spanish and Greek revolutions. "Tonight our vent'rous Poet," the prologue begins:

> dares presume
> To touch the story of immortal Rome;
> Oh! That his Muse could with the theme aspire
> And animate the scene with Roman fire;
> Then might he catch the Patriot's noble zeal
> And ev'ry Briton kindred ardour feel
> Then might his Heroes Latian spirit shew
> Reflect like Brutus or like Caius glow,
> To proudest heights of ancient virtue soar
> And Britain hence become like Rome of yore.[61]

The explicit link drawn between Caius Gracchus and Brutus invites a comparison with Payne's *Brutus*. In each case, the hero of the play, and Rome more generally, functions in an exemplary manner, where the example is meant to inspire a particular kind of behavior: virtue—obviously—but virtue directed at the "noble zeal" of a patriot. Rome is here seen as the original example of virtuous patriotism. Its status as original might imply that it is therefore unsurpassable; such deference to Rome, however, does not continue throughout the prologue, and the logic of exemplarity by which Britain imitates Rome quickly turns to a logic of substitution that celebrates British accomplishments over and against the Romans: "Yet let us not while Roman worth we trace/ Forget the merits that our annals grace." In a series of equivalencies, Virgil is replaced by Shakespeare, the Roman actor Roscius by David Garrick (the eighteenth-century's most renowned Shakespearean actor), and seventeenth-century Whig martyrs Algernon Sydney and Lord William Russell come to stand in for the earlier mention of Brutus and Caius Gracchus as Britain's contribution to the annals of self-denying patriotism. Again we see the biographical

---

[61] Knowles, *Caius Gracchus*, Larpent copy: Huntington Manuscript LA 2384, 1st and 4th page of the m.s. Subsequent references to the prologue are all to this manuscript.

emphasis of exemplarity whereby the replacement of Rome by England is emphasized through a series of explicit individual figures. Praise for Sydney and Russell, furthermore, suggests a kind of Whig resistance, perhaps a republicanism, but a resistance to the Establishment in any case that is made even clearer when the prologue concludes with a link between the patriot zeal of its eponymous hero and more contemporary nationalist struggles:

> Nor let us while to native worth we bow
> Forget the Patriot zeal that struggles now.
> Lo! Greece to break her galling chains essays,
> And pants to realize Homeric lays,
> Deems life in Freedom's cause a glorious loss,
> If o'er the crescent, tow'rs the hallowed cross.
> Spain too, tho' bent by foreign force today,
> Tomorrow may throw off th' opprobrious sway;
> Spread the pure flame of Liberty around,
> And Tyranny on Earth no more be found.

These lines, with their explicit support for nationalist revolutionary movements in Greece and Spain, clearly align the drama that follows with the liberal cause and with reform politics.[62] They thus expand the exemplary relevance of republican Rome beyond a litany of great figures and into a more general republican model of liberty as a powerful force perpetually in opposition to tyranny, and they suggest that the legacy of republican Rome is one that can inspire contemporary republican movements abroad and, possibly, at home. The prologue's support for nationalist revolutionary movements and the rhetoric of freedom, liberty, and tyranny, when combined with an episode of grain shortages and agrarian reform, suggest that *Caius Gracchus* will align itself with the progressive politics of the reform movement.

The play that follows, however, is more ambiguous. It demonizes the aristocrats who resist the reformist measures of the younger Gracchus, but the threat of such figures is complemented, and perhaps

---

[62] For a discussion of liberalism as "a network of ideologies" linked especially by "the notion that the state sanctions individual freedom even as it refrains from intruding upon the private sphere," see Saglia, "Talking Demon," 350–351.

even exceeded, by a ruthless attack on the undependability and fickle loyalty of common people, the very group that Caius is shown wanting to help. From the start, tensions between the people and the aristocrats frame the play, and these tensions are shown to be so deep as to corrupt the entire legal system. *Brutus* made clear that liberty and freedom were fundamentally linked to the ideal of equal protection under the law. In *Caius Gracchus*, such values are in jeopardy; the law has become a tool for aristocratic power. In the opening scene, Vettius, a friend of Caius Gracchus's, is accused of treason. A chorus of plebeians make clear that Vettius is a friend of the people, and therefore sure to be condemned. Licinius, Caius Gracchus's brother-in-law, challenges this claim, and the following exchange occurs with Marcus, a plebeian:

LICINIUS: Are not the Patricians just?
MARCUS: Not to the people.
LICINIUS: Why not?
MARCUS: Because they have the power to be otherwise. They have as great dominion over the people, as over their oxen and so they treat them like their oxen. (Act 1, scene 1, p. 4)

The passage highlights the aristocratic dominance over the legal system and it further emphasizes that the legal system is a function not of justice but of power. Isaiah Berlin's well-known concepts of positive and negative liberty may be helpful here. For Berlin, negative liberty refers to the freedom from the arbitrary exercise of tyranny and coercion, whereas positive liberty implies the freedom to exercise the civil rights indicative of participatory government, such as voting and holding office.[63] In *Caius Gracchus*, it is negative liberty that the citizens clamor for. Specifically, they do not want to be accused of treason without cause, but, more generally, they resent being subject to the arbitrary exercise of power by the patricians. But however much the people bristle at the injustice of the Senate's charges, they do not have any sense of how to amend the system. Positive liberty does not figure at all in their protest.

The situation for the common people of Rome is clearly dire, and when Caius Gracchus returns to public life after a long absence to

---

[63] See Isaiah Berlin, *Two Concepts of Liberty* (Oxford: Clarendon Press, 1958).

defend Vettius, he aligns himself with their cause. Gracchus's defense of Vettius further underscores the depth of Rome's corruption; he argues that a punishment worse than death or banishment would be to allow Vettius to remain in Rome, given how badly the city suffers from political corruption, usury, and starvation. The patrician dominance of Rome's legal and political system has become so extreme that the people can hardly be considered citizens. Indeed, they are repeatedly compared to animals—oxen in the passage above and herd animals later, as when Gracchus tells the people that the consul Opimius would rate them "as we rate our herds" and use them "as we use our herds" (3.1, p. 27). Gracchus emerges as the people's champion, but their response to his support of their cause is revealed to be lukewarm at best. As Gracchus's star rises, the patricians control him by simply outdoing each of the favors that he promises the people. The supposed corruptions of the aristocracy are thus enabled by the fickleness and greed of the Roman populace. The people are shown to be unaware of their true interest and unable to exert a coherent political will. They are, rather, a mob to be purchased by the highest bidder.

They are also violent. When Opimius insults Gracchus, the people vow revenge, and in a fit of rage they kill a lictor. The moment recalls the violent cycle of vengeance in Payne's play, especially when Lucretius wants to arrest two allies of the Tarquins without cause and is stopped by Horatius, who explains that to do so would repeat the mistakes of a tyrant. Here, however, the impulse remains unchecked, and it is even more extreme because it involves not just an arrest but a killing. A comparison of the two scenes underscores the extreme mistrust of the populace manifest in *Caius Gracchus*. The evident corruption of the Roman aristocracy is matched only by that of the people, and in the end Gracchus damns them for their lack of support: "May they crawl/ Ever in bondage and in misery,/ And never know the blessed rights of freemen!" (5.3, p. 57). Gracchus here pointedly refers to the "rights of freemen."[64]

---

[64] It is curious to note that here and in *Brutus*, where Horatius refers to the "Roman Rights," republican Rome is used to invoke not a language of duty, which we might be led to expect from Pocock's theory of civic humanism, but a more Lockean discourse of natural rights.

Gracchus, like Coriolanus before him, expects the support of the masses by right and merit, and the tragedy centers on the pride of Gracchus, his refusal to seek actively the support of the people. One could argue that the drama condemns not the people but Gracchus himself, insofar as Gracchus's prideful refusal to plead for popular support provokes their disloyalty. But this overstates the case, for although Gracchus's pride is shown to be his fatal flaw, there is no attempt to rescue the populace from charges of craven self-interest and fickle disloyalty. Part of the problem is that they fail to recognize their own interest and are all too willing to abandon Gracchus for immediate short-term gain. The reforms proposed by Caius Gracchus do not deliver immediate rewards; rather, they address the structural problems that corrupt the legal system. Specifically, Gracchus promises the people not money, but *land*, and his program highlights the relationship between the "rights of freemen" to which he refers, and the ownership of real property in land. Land reform as a solution to corruption implies that it is inequalities in wealth that produce injustice in law. To redistribute land to give all a more equal share in the commonwealth underscores a fundamental connection between property and the rhetoric of liberty and freedom, whereby only the redress of wide disparities in property distribution can guarantee liberty in the sense of equality before the law. In this sense, there is a close connection between liberty and property; but there is also a tension between the ideal of economic equality and the protection of property rights, for on what grounds can the seizure of the property to be redistributed be justified?

The prologue of *Caius Gracchus* invites us to read the play in connection with contemporary Britain through the lessons of patriotism and its hero's exemplary virtue. Although omitted by the prologue, there is a further parallel between post-Waterloo England and Rome at the time of the Gracchi: grain shortage. In England, the passage of the Corn Laws in 1815, which protected English farmers from Continental imports and kept the price of grain artificially high, was one cause of national unrest and of frequent radical complaints that targeted government corruption as the source of national ills.[65] Although

---

[65] For a recent evaluation of the Corn Laws, see Boyd Hilton, *A Mad, Bad, and Dangerous People: England 1783–1846* (Oxford: Oxford University Press, 2006), 264–268.

the Gracchi appear infrequently in the political discourse of the 1790s and beyond, they do play a central role in the eighteenth-century interpretation of ancient Roman history, as Frank Turner has shown. Because the central feature of the Gracchi were their proposals for land reform, they were used by Nathaniel Hooke and others for classical republican arguments that deny the equation of political liberty with parliamentary supremacy and propose instead a connection between political liberty and wider land ownership.[66] In Turner's account, the chief critique of this position came from Adam Ferguson, who argued that political reform through economic equality was impossible because the size and scale of Rome made democracy and equality incompatible. "The distinction of poor and rich, in States of any considerable extent," Ferguson claimed:

> are as necessary as labour and good government itself. The poor being destined to labour, the rich, by the advantages of education, independence and leisure, are qualified for public affairs.... The project [of the Gracchi] seemed to be as ruinous to government as it was to the security of property, and tended to place members of the commonwealth, by one rash and precipitate step, in situations in which they were not qualified to act.[67]

In Ferguson's conception, democratic equality is an issue of scale, and political equality can be a feature only of small agrarian republics. The trouble with the Gracchi, in other words, is that by pointing to the alleged corruption of the aristocrats in power, they set a precedent for the direct appeal to the people and the recognition of popular leaders—one of the very issues in the struggle over political reform in early-nineteenth-century Britain.

To produce a tragedy on the subject of the Gracchi was thus necessarily controversial, and, as Turner shows, the controversy has its roots in the eighteenth-century interpretation of Roman history. A look at the drama's application for license supports this sense of volatility. Roman Revival dramas show little evidence of the censor's hand. This can be explained by self-censorship, the

---

[66] For a discussion of this issue, see Frank M. Turner, "British Politics and the Roman Republic," *Historical Journal* 29 (1986): 584.

[67] Adam Ferguson, *The History of the Progress and Termination of the Roman Republic* (Edinburgh, 1799), 1:390; quoted by Turner, "British Politics and the Roman Republic," 585.

censor's respect for high genres like tragedy, and the distancing effect of antiquity. *Caius Gracchus*, however, was initially rejected for license and only after complicated negotiation and significant cuts was the play approved. Even so, the final manuscript of *Caius Gracchus* reveals the presence of the censor at a number of points, and the lines that draw attention are those that invoke the language of liberty and the law and connect it to the class warfare between patricians and plebeians.[68] In act 2, for example, when Caius seeks to be the people's tribune, the censor intervenes in the populist rhetoric of his speeches. In one, Caius denies the patriotism of the patricians:

> Your great men boast no more the love of country.
> They enlarge their palaces—dress forth their banquets & with their floods
> Of ripe Falernian, drown the little left
> Of virtue! Romans, I ask the office
> of your Tribune![69]

Here, the lines calling attention to the size of patrician palaces (~~They enlarge their palaces—dress forth their banquets~~) are cancelled and a more innocuous suggestion: "They count their talents—measure their domains," is substituted instead. By the time the text was printed, the original lines were restored, and the censor's amendment integrated:

> Your great men boast no more the love of country.
> They count their talents—measure their domains—
> Number their slaves—make lists of knights and clients—
> Enlarge their palaces—dress forth their banquets,
> Awake their lyres and timbrels—and with their floods
> Of ripe Falernian, drown the little left
> Of virtue! (2.3, p. 22)

Although this change is relatively minor, later lines on the laws reveal more heavy-handed censorship. In the printed text, Caius asks with regard to the laws:

---

[68] For an account of the history of *Caius Gracchus* and Knowles's negotiations with the censor, see the sources given in note 55 above.

[69] James Sheridan Knowles, *Caius Gracchus*, application copy for licensing, Huntington Manuscript LA2384.

What Is the People?

> Why do they guard the rich man's cloak from a rent,
> And tear the poor man's garment from his back?
> Why are they, in the proud man's grasp a sword,
> And, in the hand of the humble man, a reed?
> The laws! The laws! I ask you for the laws!
> Demand them in my country's sacred name!
> Still silent? Reckless still of my appeal? (2.3, p. 23)

When the same lines appear in the application copy nearly four lines are struck through:

> Why do they guard the rich man's cloak from a rent,
> And tear the poor man's garment ~~from his back?~~
> ~~Why are they, in the proud man's grasp a sword,~~
> ~~And, in the hand of the humble man, a reed?~~
> ~~The laws! The laws! I ask you for the laws!~~
> ~~Still silent?~~ Reckless still of my appeal? (2.3, LA 2384)

Clearly, the censor is alarmed by lines that call attention to class-based inequalities and that use the presence of such inequalities to call the entire legal system into question. Still later, when Caius tells the people not to fear the Senate:

PRINT:
C. Grac: Some coldness there has been between us; but
We know the cause, and so are friends again.
Our enemies may once prevail by cunning,
But not a second time. Now, show yourselves
The men you should be.—If your liberties
And rights are dear to you, be faithful to them.—
Be freemen! none will dare to make you slaves

Fear not the Senate.—Call upon the tribes.—
Be freemen—none will dare to make you slaves!
(4.3, p. 44)

APPLICATION:
C. Grac: Now, show yourselves,
The men you should be.—~~if your liberties~~
~~And rights are dear to you, be faithful to them.—~~
~~Fear not the Senate.—~~Call upon the tribes.—
(4.3, LA2384)

Caius Gracchus's reference to the tribes and his admonition not to fear the Senate might be read as an appeal to the kind of extra-parliamentary agitation that was increasingly common after Waterloo and that drew the repressive crackdown by the government in the face of the Peterloo massacre. Indeed, the speeches of Caius Gracchus are potentially insurrectionary. They consistently draw attention to marked disparities between great men and the plebeians, disparities cast as distinctions between rich and poor. Moreover, such economic disparities reveal the corruption in the Roman legal system whereby all are not equal under the law. Caius repeatedly calls for the redress of these wrongs in the rights-based language of liberty and freedom, and this language is precisely that to which the censor objects. He bristles at the deliberate attention called to luxuries ("palaces and Falernian wine") and income disparity, but his most prominent deletions are those directed at the connections that Caius makes between such disparities and the corruption of the legal system and at Caius's suggestion that such matters be settled by an appeal outside the Senate. That the censor's deletions fall almost exclusively on the speeches of Caius Gracchus highlights the danger that the censor would have recognized in the use of a figure like Gracchus. Gracchus's direct appeal to the people raises the prospect of the demagogue and recalls Horatius's description of Brutus in Payne's play. The difference here, however, is that the populace fail to listen to Caius, and for this failure they are dismissed as fickle cowards unwilling or unable to recognize their common interest.[70]

Even with the deletions of the censor, *Caius Gracchus* still presents a charismatic leader rousing the people to claim their rights and freedoms through exceptional means, and it can be read as a subversive and potentially insurrectionary drama. Why was it allowed on stage when appeals of this sort were feared by the government to a degree that led to the Six Acts, which so severely constrained exactly this kind of extra-parliamentary appeal?[71] As with *Brutus*, the generic issue of tragedy and its focus on exceptional individuals provides an initial explanation. *Caius Gracchus* does not dwell on the details of Gracchus's land reforms or on the debate surrounding them; it does

---

[70] One review noted both the "noisy and fickle populace" and the play's depiction of "one of those accomplished demagogues who used to spring up in the tempestuous times of the Roman republic with the most alarming frequency" (quoted by Saglia, "Talking Demon," 356).

[71] The so-called Six Acts comprised the Training Prevention Act (60 Geo III cap. 1), the Seizure of Arms Act (60 Geo III cap. 2), the Seditious Meetings Act (60 Geo III,

not attend to the problems of balancing a need for greater equality with the inviolability of property rights. Rather, it focuses more closely on Caius Gracchus himself. Gracchus is, like most tragic heroes, a flawed hero. In response to his flaws, however, the drama refuses to align itself with either the aristocracy or the people. Gracchus is proud, but he sympathizes with the sufferings of the people and is committed to alleviating their misfortunes. In this sense, he is the opposite of Coriolanus, who shows nothing but contempt for the Roman populace. But like *Coriolanus*, *Caius Gracchus* becomes a tragedy about a popular hero unappreciated by the people he hopes to serve. It suggests that the way to fix the corruption of the Roman system, with its perversion of justice and its massive inequality between rich and poor, the aristocrats and the people, is through the force of a single strong leader.

Furthermore, while Gracchus raises the prospect of a demagogue through the manner in which he makes a direct appeal to the people about the corruptions of the Roman system, the drama does not dwell on his proposed solutions. The implications and justifications for his land reform are notably muted. In this way, *Caius Gracchus* provides a language for articulating perceived corruptions—specifically a rhetoric of liberty and freedom that would have been echoed by the reform movement—but it does not produce any kind of similarly resonant call for specific action. In this sense, it might be seen to underscore not the relevance of Roman examples, but their untranslatability, whereby it shows the impossibility of converting the rhetoric of liberty and freedom into any kind of coherent program. Finally, and most important, even if *Caius Gracchus* had dealt more specifically with the details and implications of Caius's land reform, the people most certainly would not have listened. They are presented as so vile as to be undeserving of any political rights. Indeed, *Caius Gracchus* condemns conjointly the aristocrats and the plebeians and suggests that *both* contribute equally to the corruptions of Rome. As the remarks preceding the reprinting of *Caius Gracchus* in *Cumberland's British Theatre* assert:

---

cap. 6), the Blasphemous and Seditious Libels Act (60 Geo III, cap. 4), the Misdemeanours Act (60 Geo III, cap. 8), and the Newspaper Stamp Duties Act (60 Geo III, cap. 9). Collectively, the acts curtailed radical reform meetings, raised the taxes on printed materials, and made it easier to prosecute for libel.

The Fall of the Gracchi is one of the many evidences of the glory and degeneracy of the Roman nation. Of its glory, in producing such illustrious examples of true greatness—of its degeneracy, in abandoning and leading them forth to sacrifice and death. The annals of the republic exhibit little else but continual struggles between the *nobles* and the *people*; and it is difficult to say which party, in the pursuit of their several ends, adopted the most unjustifiable means. If the patricians were haughty, ambitious, and tyrannical, the plebeians were fickle, treacherous and cruel. The former made their common cause against liberty; the latter sought *license* rather than *liberty*—the indulgence of private and party animosity, not the good order and just government of the state. The cowardice of the people was as flagrant as their ingratitude.[72]

This portrayal of the populace significantly diminishes the insurrectionary potential of Caius Gracchus's speeches. The people in *Caius Gracchus* are nothing—they are irrational, fickle, greedy, and fundamentally incapable of articulating any kind of will or interest that could form the basis for participation in political life. The nation, *Caius Gracchus* implies, can only be restored by the singular virtue of the leader—and even then, the fate of Caius makes explicit, there is no guarantee of success.

Although after the prologue the play never makes explicit its sense of parallel between past and present, the sense of connection between contemporary Britain and republican Rome works as a vehicle for a series of displaced concerns. If the history of the Roman republic is understood not as a succession of heroic self-sacrificing patriots, but as a prolonged struggle to accommodate within its republican forms the divergent and clashing interests of different classes of its citizens (as a struggle, in other words, between the aristocracy and the people) then the Roman example might help to clarify aspects of the contemporary situation—especially the complex relationship between the rulers and the ruled, masses and individuals, the people and the aristocracy—at a time when Parliament faced intense pressure for universal male suffrage and to change the districts of representation to eliminate "rotten" boroughs and include representatives from the rapidly expanding industrial districts of the north and west. Along these lines, Diego Saglia reads a strongly reformist, protoliberal agenda into Knowles's dramas. Saglia argues that Knowles's short-lived Glasgow newspaper (*Free Press*,

---

[72] *Cumberland's British Theatre* (London: John Cumberland, 1826), Vol. 6, *Caius Gracchus*, 5.

1823–1824), a firmly antiestablishment venture that promoted a strongly reformist agenda, provides an "ideological key to his plays' customary displacements of current political issues towards other geocultural and historical dimensions." Similarly, Saglia underscores how Macready's attraction to these plays was because "his personal political convictions were firmly on the side of social and institutional reform."[73] The negotiations with the censor and the kind of material marked for deletion further underscore the subversive potential of *Caius Gracchus*. While *Caius Gracchus* thus has an obviously reformist appeal, certain tensions nonetheless persist. The choice of a story from the Roman republic both empowers and limits the contentious ideological message of the play—empowers because it allows for a displaced exploration of contemporary concerns, but limits because given the historic outcomes of the Gracchi's land reform and their ultimate betrayal by the Roman populace, the subject matter encourages a negative depiction of the Roman populace, an attitude of scorn and dismissal that coheres uneasily with the play's more progressive sympathies. In this way, if the play encourages a displaced critique of the failings of contemporary Britain, it also emphasizes the difficulties and contradictions in consolidating public opinion, in increasing the possibilities for engagement within the public sphere, and in expanding the participation in political decision making by a populace that it implies can only function as a mob and is therefore incapable of becoming a people.

CATILINE: DEMOCRACY, EMPIRE, AND THE REACTION TO THE ROMAN REVIVAL

Both Payne's *Brutus* and Knowles's *Caius Gracchus* attempt to rewrite the patrician *Coriolanus* staged by Kemble. In the face of evident legal corruption—rulers who place themselves above the law in the case of *Brutus* and a legal system corrupted by patrician wealth in the case of *Caius Gracchus*—both plays use the rhetoric of liberty and freedom to explore possible remedies. While *Brutus* considers the possibility of

---

[73] See Saglia, "Talking Demon," 355, 358.

rebellion and a change of political system, *Caius Gracchus* introduces land reform and economic redistribution as the cure for legal corruption and food shortages. Both plays echoed contemporary issues in post-Waterloo Britain, and they can in many ways be considered progressive, including their willingness to recognize fundamental flaws in the government and their conception of these flaws as related to competing interests between the government, on one hand, and the people and their leaders, on the other. Nonetheless, such potential is balanced by their handling of the Roman populace—toward whom *Brutus* remains ambivalent and *Caius Gracchus* is outright dismissive. Both plays thus raise serious questions about the very possibility of popular politics and suggest that only a virtuous leader can help the Roman state. The way in which these plays use republican Rome to frame issues of contemporary concern did not go unchallenged, and one result of the cultural struggle over the meaning of the Roman legacy was George Croly's *Catiline*, which attempts to recapture Rome in favor of empire and in opposition to reform and the rights-based rhetoric of liberty and freedom. Unlike *Brutus* and *Caius Gracchus*, *Catiline* was not staged, though a rewriting of it by H.M. Milner was produced in 1827. Nonetheless, the play merits attention for the striking way that it handles its title figure. In *Catiline*, the source of corruption is not the Roman legal system and the excessive influence of the patricians (as in *Caius Gracchus*) or a tyrannical monarchy (as in *Brutus*), but rather a democratic political system that forces leaders to take lucrative imperial appointments to pillage the maximum possible amount of wealth, which can then be used to buy votes from the people. *Catiline*, in other words, presents the populace as the sole problem facing republican Rome. Catiline himself is an important figure for this argument because throughout the eighteenth century he serves as an index for anxieties about revolution, revolt, and conspiracy.

Catiline was a Roman aristocrat who, after his defeat for the consulship by Cicero in 63 BCE, plotted to take the office by force. The exposure of his conspiracy made him the subject of four speeches by Cicero and a biography by Sallust. Both sources treat Catiline negatively, as an ambitious, greedy plotter willing to use any means necessary to gain the consulship that he had lost in the popular vote. Most modern scholarly editions gloss references to him in precisely this way. J. C. D. Clark does so in his critical edition of Burke's *Reflections*, where he says of Catiline, "Repeatedly disappointed in elections for the consulate, he organized a conspiracy to seize power which was frustrated by Cicero."[74] Indeed, Cicero used his prosecution of Catiline to secure his consular authority, and he benefited from the prosecution to such a degree that classical scholars have consistently speculated that the conspiracy may have been less an actual plot by Catiline than one imagined and fabricated by Cicero. Frank Turner, for example, in his notes to the Yale University Press edition of Burke, is more diplomatic in his gloss of Catiline, whom he describes as "leader of a rebellion against the late Roman Republic whom Cicero defeated and *portrayed* as a traitor."[75] George Croly picks up on exactly this ambivalence when he notes in his preface that "the story of a public man, after his fall, must be received with caution," and he continues to speculate: "Had Catiline triumphed, history would probably have described him as not more culpable than the other successive masters of the state. It might have spoken with contempt of the private charges which even rivals and enemies ventured to give only upon rumour; and found room for panegyric in the talents, by which an individual, without opulence, remarkable family connexion, or military means was able to collect upon himself the eyes of Rome, and of the world. It would represent the other sovereigns of Rome as seizing the throne, by the coarse and simple agencies of armies: but Catiline, as the only man who mastered it by the nobler superiority of the mind."[76] Croly's remarks revise the significance of Catiline, whose portrayal in British letters had been consistently negative.

Ben Jonson followed both Sallust and Cicero in his 1611 tragedy, *Catiline*, which presents Catiline as an evil plotter confronting desperate choices who turns to Rome a face metaphorically likened to

---

[74] Edmund Burke, *Reflections on the Revolution in France*, ed. J. C. D. Clark (Stanford, CA: Stanford University Press, 2001), 228.
[75] Edmund Burke, *Reflections on the Revolution in France*, ed. Frank M. Turner (New Haven, CT: Yale University Press, 2003), 296. Emphasis mine.
[76] George Croly, *Catiline: A Tragedy with Other Poems* (London: Hurst, Robinson, 1822), xi–xii. Subsequent page references to this edition will be provided parenthetically in the text.

"public ruin"[77] and seeks to grasp the state with his "rebellious parts" (act 5, line 688). Indeed, Petreius says of Catiline, "His count'nance was a civil war itself" (act 5, line 644). Subsequently, Catiline was a figure often invoked throughout the seventeenth and eighteenth centuries. As J. G. A. Pocock explains, "Eighteenth-century fears of revolution regularly took a Catilinarian form,"[78] one based on the apprehension that a member of the ruling inner circle might betray his class. Pocock focuses especially on the conservative Josiah Tucker, for whom figures such as Locke, Algernon Sidney, and Lord William Russell were desperate aristocratic radicals; in Pocock's words, "the Catilines of their age,"[79] men who initiate a tradition of déclassé patricians, extending through Richard Price and Joseph Priestley, and who employ individualist rhetoric to stir up underemployed Londoners for their various causes.

Catiline is also a particularly forceful figure for Burke. Burke refers to Catiline as part of his critique of the National Assembly, early in the *Reflections* as he builds toward his sentimental description of Marie Antoinette. In describing the illegitimacy and consequent impotence of the Assembly, Burke notes:

It is notorious that all their measures are decided before they are debated. It is beyond doubt, that under the terror of the bayonet and the lamp post, and the torch to their houses, they are obligated to adopt all the crude and desperate measures suggested by clubs composed of a monstrous medley of all conditions, tongues, and nations. Among these are found persons, in comparison of whom Catiline would be thought scrupulous.[80]

The association between Catiline, the French National Assembly, and their English supporters in the *Reflections* works to demean aristocratic politicians on both sides of the channel who enlist themselves in radical causes to advance their pursuit of elected office. Burke, of

---

[77] *Catiline*, in *The Complete Plays of Ben Jonson*, ed. G. A. Wilkes (Oxford: Clarendon Press, 1982), 3:477. The quotation is from act 5, line 643. Subsequent act and line references to this edition will be given parenthetically in the text.

[78] J. G. A. Pocock, *Virtue, Commerce, History* (Cambridge: Cambridge University Press, 1985), 263.

[79] Ibid., 178.

[80] Edmund Burke, *Reflections on the Revolution in France*, ed. J. G. A. Pocock (Indianapolis, IN: Hackett, 1987), 59–60.

course, famously describes all of the early events of the French Revolution as a conspiracy of the monied interests—all those provincial lawyers—against the legitimacy of the aristocracy and the church, and his reference to Catiline here associates events in France with a notorious conspiracy from ancient history. There is, however, an important difference. In Burke's hands, Catiline is less a figure of conspiracy from above, as Pocock describes him through the eighteenth century, and more a symbol of revolutionary depravity: a threat not because of a sophisticated conspiracy, but because of a degraded and deranged nature. Described this way, Catiline's derangement becomes a broad symbol for both the revolutionaries and their English supporters.

This is also how Catiline is deployed in other conservative tracts of the revolution controversy. Among the early responses to Paine, for example, was "A Protest against T. Paine's 'Rights of Man:' Addressed to the Members of a Book Society" (1792), by the government-paid propagandist John Bowles. Bowles argues that "under the mask of discussion" Paine's writings "really point to action," and he claims that Paine's words will work on "the restlessness inherent in man" to overthrow the constitution and "stimulate the people to sedition and rebellion."[81] As if, Bowles says, the absurdity of Paine's ideas is not enough, they also appeal to dangerous malcontents:

The doctrines I allude to are particularly intended to unite and call into action the unprincipled and turbulent part of mankind, the common pests of Society, who are ever ready to second any attempts which lead to tumult and disorder. Desperate, ambitious, and malignant, their views are promoted, or their feelings gratified by riot and confusion; and they depend for their harvest upon the convulsion of kingdoms and empires.... Such persons, who from the nature of their dispositions and pursuits are abundantly more watchful and active than the friends of Order, are obliged to anybody who will furnish them with a shadow of a pretext for raising a clamour against imaginary defects in any part of the existing Government; they flock to a declaration of absurd, fictitious, and impracticable Rights, as to a Manifesto

---

[81] "A Protest against T. Paine's 'Rights of Man:' Addressed to the Members of a Book Society," in *The Political Writings of the 1790s*, ed. Gregory Claeys (London: Pickering and Chatto, 1995), 6:43–44. Subsequent references to this edition, referred to as "Claeys," will be provided parenthetically in the text.

of Rebellion or a Standard of Revolt—happy in an occasion to blow the flame which may catch all that is combustible in a State—thrice happy to find a head whether a TYLER, a CADE, or a CATILINE, who may lead them to the attack, or give consistence and effect to their conspiracies. (Claeys, 6:45–46).

Catiline is here linked with two famous home-grown rebels, Wat Tyler and Jack Cade, both of whom led peasant rebellions, and the threat posed by Catiline's example has shifted neatly from above to below. Similarly, an earlier anonymous pamphlet published in Dublin in response to Burke suggests that "some societies, composed of the extravagant, the impoverished, the seditious, and the unprincipled, have gone to unwarrantable excesses in all their fictitious plans of patriotism, and have bound themselves (as Catiline handed the bloody goblet round the circle of his partizans) by mutual attestation, to perform and carry through their measures" (Claeys, 7:44). A note from the author adds that "Catiline's conspiracy is the first instance we meet with in history of a real Round Robin—the object was the same with one of our days, the subversion of the established government. Pity they do not assimilate in the conclusion" (Claeys, 7:44). By the 1790s, of course, if there remained any fear of a conspiracy to overthrow the government from above and within, it had long been subverted by the overwhelming fear of popular revolt, of revolution from below, and the figure of Catiline adapted handily to the more prevalent anxiety. Catiline becomes a symbol of depraved nature, of one who takes active pleasure in sowing discord and confusion. Note that both Bowles and his anonymous precursor used the same descriptive adjective: "unprincipled." The figure of Catiline thus shifts from its eighteenth-century association with aristocratic conspiracy to an association with the more current and far greater fear of revolution from below, and the move is accomplished by linking Catiline to depravity—the kind of excess or unhinging that most conservatives thought necessary to any kind of popular revolt.

Catiline, then, might be thought of as an especially powerful figure because he picks up on all of the eighteenth-century fears of conspiracy, treachery, and treason, but then adapts them, through his association with depravity, to more contemporary anxieties. In this way, he could be used to great rhetorical effect in denouncing the French Revolution and its English sympathizers. By the end of the period, however, with the culmination of the counterrevolutionary wars, in the face of agrarian misery and rebellion, industrial change, an expanding empire, and renewed agitation for the franchise, Catiline began to assume different connotations. For some, he became a figure in need of revision, as the clamor for voting reform and the spread of the empire put Britons in a position to reinterpret his actions. In this context, Croly's *Catiline* counters the traditional reading of Catiline as a deranged, morally bankrupt plotter seen prominently in the revolution controversy. It presents him instead as one forced into his actions by flaws in the Roman state, and it shows how his conspiracy was produced not by the corruptions inherent in the aristocratic character but as a response to the lunacy and inherent sleaze of popular participation in the electoral process.

The play begins with Cicero's defeat of Catiline for the consulship. Cicero is portrayed as an upstart, a "master of the crowd" whose oratorical skills pander to the people, whereas Catiline, in contrast, is seen as an aristocrat, indeed as the representative of nobility and one doomed by the fickleness of the people. Catiline's response to this loss, however, is not a conspiracy against the state. Instead, it is the Carthaginian leader Hamilcar who establishes the conspiracy to attack Rome. Hamilcar seeks to have revenge on Rome and thinks Catiline will be vulnerable to his overtures. Catiline is initially reluctant, and it is not until his wife, Aurelia, encourages him to stand up and stave off his ruin with revolt that he even begins to consider the possibility. Meanwhile, there is a slave revolt, and, through no fault of his own, crowds run through Rome with banners for Catiline, who is soon summoned to face the Senate. In this way, Catiline's plot against Rome is shown not as a knee-jerk response of frustrated ambition, but rather as something thrust upon him to which he consents only when the corruption of the Senate forces him into revolt to avoid the fallout of their corrupt maneuvers. Having settled upon rebellion, Catiline seeks the support of the Allobroges, a Gallic tribe who greet him as "the great patrician" (*C*, 69). Catiline presents himself as the most wronged man in Rome, and he acknowledges that he is now "Rome's eternal foe." Up to this point, we can recognize how Croly's play combines both *Macbeth*, the protagonist of which is a frustrated aristocrat edged into revolt by his ambitious wife, and *Coriolanus*, the story of a great Roman hero who turns against Rome and seeks the support of a hostile tribe.

Even though it means declaring open enmity for the powers in Rome, the Allobroges join Catiline. Their reasons are manifest in a long discussion of freedom, in which it becomes clear just how much the Gauls have done for Rome, although they have been robbed of their freedom and turned into tribute payers while Roman proconsuls pillage their lands. The result of the rebellion, however, is predictable. It fails when Hamilcar's lover, the Roman maiden Aspasia, betrays the conspiracy to Cicero in hopes that her betrayal will save Hamilcar from the fate of the other conspirators. With Hamilcar seized, Cicero coaxes details of the plot from him, and Catiline is foiled. The people hail Cicero as their savior, and Catiline's rebel army is hunted down and destroyed. Catiline himself dies while announcing his desire to be "King! Dictator!" (*C*, 157). Ordinarily, this might seem to be a revelation of his warped ambitions, but within the politics of the play, it stands for something quite different, for in Croly's drama, it is not Catiline but Rome that is corrupt and degenerate.

Croly's *Catiline* is significant for two reasons. First, for its critique of Roman democracy. The revision of Catiline's character shows that all of his noble qualities could not succeed against the combination of a skilled orator and a willing populace; indeed, it is further implied that the entire electoral system is corrupt and that one needs vast amounts of money to win election to any position of authority in Rome. The only way to generate such sums is through the pillaging of conquered territories through proconsular appointments. This, in turn, provides the second critical significance of Croly's play: its link between democracy and empire or, more specifically, between democracy and bad imperial governance. The first of Croly's footnotes, on the order and dignity of Roman elections, clarifies the logic of this connection. The note suggests that such elections must have their origins in northern tribes rather than in "Italian barbarism." The entire note is a diatribe against popular elections, and Croly claims that the decorum of the Roman system "puts to shame the extravagance of our modern hustings. But human nature has been, probably, always the same; and the popular suffrage was solicited, in every mode that inflames the passions, or seduces the cupidity of the multitude" (*C*, 160). The logic here is that the more the best men are forced to pander to the awful masses for their favor, the more money they lavish on silly entertainment for the populace, and thus the more they need to plunder the colonies for their wealth. An expanded franchise would not only destabilize government by turning elections into a commodity to be bought by the highest bidder—a common critique—but would ruin the growing imperial project by providing both incentive and means to see colonies as no more than easy spoil.

As if the refiguration of Catiline's legacy were not enough to make its politics plain, the play's preface carefully considers the context in which Catiline's conspiracy transpired. It reads throughout as an argument in favor of the political stability conveyed best by hereditary monarchy and as a warning of the dangers imposed by popular sovereignty and democratic government. The preface reconsiders the military conflicts that led to the fall of the republic, and claims that "a hereditary throne might have forced the violence of these mighty competitors into the channel of public utility" (C, iv), but, even so, the battles between the Roman generals can be best described as military revolution, a type of revolution that may have shattered the foundations of Rome without totally ruining them. As such, military revolution is far preferable to democratic revolution. "Military revolution may be sanguinary," Croly writes, "but it is democratic revolution, with its boundless meanness and perfidies, its sleepless suspicions, and its merciless scaffolds, that extinguishes a national mind.... Military domination may turn an empire into a camp; but democracy, with its low, personal malice, and searching, insatiable cupidity, and bloody fears, turns it into a dungeon and a grave" (C, v–vi).

As comments like these show, Croly is no less reactionary than Burke,[82] but for him, Catiline becomes an honorable but frustrated patrician forced to plot against the state because the spread of popular democracy has made election as consul too expensive. Other, less honorable aspirants, however, raise this money through exploitative, plundering governance in pro-consular appointments elsewhere in the empire. In this way, Catiline's plot is seen as returning the republic to virtue, and the play becomes a far-reaching critique of popular democracy, one that blames the expansion of suffrage for political corruption at home and for the mismanagement of the empire

---

[82] In this context, it is interesting to note that Croly later published *A Memoir of the Political Life of the Right Honourable Edmund Burke* (Edinburgh: Blackwood and Sons, 1840).

abroad. With the clamor for voting reform that resumed after Waterloo, Croly's position functions as an especially powerful critique of the expansion of the franchise. It suggests that democracy is not only inimical to the British government and the domestic health of the state, but also that it contributes to the exploitation of colonial resources and bad provincial government and thus undermines the basis of a stable and well-governed empire.

None of Croly's sources, to the best of my knowledge, present a similarly favorable reading of Catiline's conspiracy. From Ben Jonson through the eighteenth century and into the revolution controversy, Catiline has uniformly negative associations. Croly's *Catiline* represents an attempt to reconsider the received historical record, to rethink sources, and to imagine an understanding of the past different from the way it had been presented. It should therefore be understood as part of a new confidence about the writing of ancient history, one that started with Gibbon's willingness to write a history in the classical style but that, in Croly's work, considers the events of antiquity through a more critical lens.

Finally, Croly's *Catiline* might be understood as part of a cultural struggle over the English stage. In its review of *Brutus*, the *Quarterly Review* claimed that "the national character is impressed strongly on the drama, while our drama is not the least potent of many agents to form and to cherish the peculiarities of our national character" (*QR*, 402). Therefore, as the reviewer makes clear, the presentation of popular revolts, regicide, and demagoguery were seen as threatening. Even if *Brutus* and *Caius Gracchus* ultimately reject the possibility that the populace could articulate a coherent political will and thus undermine the relevance of popular politics more generally, they do present a critique of the status quo that explores alternative possibilities and might thus be seen as progressive. Croly enters the dispute from the other side, to dramatize and reinterpret an event from Roman republican history in a manner that firmly rejects all of the proposed benefits of reform and that throws the fault for any political problems entirely on the populace and on democratic participation in the political process. That he should be compelled to do so suggests that other representations of Rome were not firm enough in their rejection of democratic politics. Still, none of these plays is sanguine about the role of the populace in the political process, and this, in the end, might be their most enduring legacy. In response to the question from Hazlitt with which this chapter began, the plays discussed above, even taking into account their considerable differences, return a much less enthusiastic answer than did Hazlitt himself, one that might sidestep the original question and reply that however we define the people, they have no claim to political participation because it is impossible for the populace to articulate a coherent political will. In this sense, their Roman setting is significant because it allows these plays to frame the problem of popular politics in a distant past when conditions were fundamentally different. The choice of a Roman republican setting, in other words, acts to restrict and simplify present conditions and to limit future possibilities. Most prominently, the Roman setting allows these plays to overlook what Kevin Gilmartin calls "print politics," and the use of the press to shape popular political movements.[83] This is precisely Hazlitt's claim, that public opinion can be articulated through print, and the turn backward to dramatizing issues of contemporary importance in their Roman setting thus has the effect not only of creating safety through distance, but also of eliminating the need to consider factors that might distinguish the present from the antique past, most notably the rise of print culture and the flourishing of a plebeian public sphere.

[83] Kevin Gilmartin, *Print Politics: The Press and Radical Opposition in Early Nineteenth-Century England* (Cambridge: Cambridge University Press, 1996).

Conclusion

In October of 1832, the year that earlier saw the passage of the First Reform Bill with its modest expansion of the franchise,[1] Thomas De Quincey published the first of his essays on the Caesars in *Blackwood's Edinburgh Magazine*. The piece begins with a lengthy general introduction on the importance of Rome and then turns to a biography of Julius Caesar. De Quincey produces a spirited defense of the greatness of the Roman Empire. "It is false to say that with Caesar came the destruction of Roman greatness," De Quincey declares, and he continues to assert that Rome lost no liberties under Julius Caesar.[2] Rather, the unitary power consolidated under Caesar helped Rome achieve perfection. De Quincey is fascinated by this concentration of power, and he claims that "after the Roman Caesars all modern kings, kesars, or emperors, are mere phantoms of royalty. The Caesar of Western Rome—He only of all earthly potentates, past or to come, could be said to reign as a *monarch*, that is, as a solitary king" (9:7). He is equally captivated by the breadth and power of the Roman Empire: "Vast, therefore, unexampled, immeasurable, was the basis of natural power upon which the Roman throne reposed" (9:10). Such power, furthermore, "involved every mode of strength, with absolute immunity from all kinds and degrees of weakness" (9:11). This rousing

---

[1] The bill's most significant provisions redistributed districts of representation to accommodate growing industrial towns and lowered electoral qualifications to permit voting by smaller property holders. Although the bill was fiercely resisted by the Tories, it did not extend the vote to the working classes and many of the lower-middle class and was thus a far cry from the universal male suffrage called for by the more radical reformers.

[2] Thomas De Quincey, *The Works of Thomas De Quincey*, ed. Grevel Lindop (London: Pickering and Chatto, 2001), 9:6. Subsequent page references to this edition will be provided parenthetically in the text.

acclamation of the greatness and power of Rome's empire and emperors then justifies the biographies of Roman rulers that follow in the series.[3]

It might seem strange to conclude a study of the Roman republic with a defense of the Roman Empire. But De Quincey's defense of imperial power must account for the transition from the republic to the empire and must defend the empire against those with republican sympathies who mark the transition as "the destruction of Roman greatness" (9:6). De Quincey's introduction to the essays can therefore be read as an assessment of the Roman republic. Furthermore, De Quincey's essays amplify a number of important themes from this study. For a start, De Quincey's interpretation of Rome aligns with a particular position in contemporary British politics. During his extended panegyric to the Roman Empire, De Quincey makes a telling analogy. The Roman Caesar

was not the greatest of princes, simply because there was no other but himself. There were doubtless a few outlying rulers, of unknown names and titles upon the margins of his empire, there were tributary lieutenants and barbarous *reguli*, the obscure vassals of his scepter, whose homage was offered on the lowest step of his throne, and scarcely known to him but as objects of disdain. But these feudatories could no more break the unity of his empire...than at this day the British empire on the sea can be brought into question or made conditional, because some chief of Owhyhee or Tongataboo should proclaim a momentary independence of the British trident or should even offer a transient outrage to her sovereign flag. (9:7)

The link between the Roman and British empires allows us to read De Quincey's fantasy of Roman power as a fantasy also of British power (one especially contemptuous and dismissive of those natives that come under its sway), and De Quincey's praise for the strength of the Caesars as a particular vision for the British monarchy and the British polity more generally. This is certainly how Thomas Carlyle read it when he wrote to John Stuart Mill about De Quincey's essays and noted that De Quincey "is one of the most irreclaimable Tories now

---

[3] The essays continued sporadically until August 1834, ultimately totaling six parts and continuing through the reign of Diocletian (ruled 284–305 CE).

extant."[4] Accordingly, De Quincey's essays on the Caesars perform moves similar to all of the figures that I have discussed thus far in their attempt to engage in the cultural struggle over the meaning and relevance of the Roman example for contemporary Britain. All invoke the timelessness of the classical past to make authoritative sense of the present, what Christopher Stray calls "classicizing." De Quincey constructs a reading of the Roman imperial past and the "everlasting" (9:7) city to authorize a particular idea of the British present, in this case his vision of a strong empire governed by a strong monarch with absolute power. In this sense, we can also link De Quincey to an internally differentiated classicism. De Quincey clearly does not worship antiquity as such; rather, he sees it as reaching its apotheosis in the empire established by Julius Caesar. In praising that empire, De Quincey makes a distinction between the Roman republic and the Roman Empire to suggest that the more relevant model for contemporary Britain is not the republic but rather the empire, with its strong leader and its territorial sway.

In addition to using an interpretation of the Roman past to sanction an understanding of the British present, De Quincey's essays show the persistence of exemplary thinking. He uses the Caesars emblematically, as figures of absolute power who, regardless of their vices, still have something sacred about them that commands obedience and even reverence. But alongside this mode of thinking, De Quincey remains aware of changes in historiographical thinking and the new emphasis on critical interrogation of the sources of ancient history. Of Julius Caesar he says, "It is certain that many parts of his life require investigation much keener than has ever been applied to them, and that many might easily be placed in a new light. Indeed the whole of this most momentous section of ancient history ought to be recomposed with the critical skepticism of a Niebuhr, and upon the same comprehensive collation of authorities" (9:26). In the context of De Quincey's essay, however, this skepticism about sources translates into an opportunity to discredit any sources that offer evidence of flaws in Caesar's character. Finally, De Quincey's defense of the Roman Empire invokes the possibility of another position, the claim that the coming

---

[4] As quoted in the editor's introduction to the essays. See De Quincey, *Works*, 9:4.

of Caesar and the end of the republic destroyed the greatness of Rome. The vehemence with which De Quincey attempts to tout the virtues of the empire over the republic therefore implies the strong presence of this contrary position in public debate. Indeed, those figures that De Quincey dismisses as "rhetoricians, false threnodists of false liberty! Hollow chanters over the ashes of a hollow republic!" (9:7), we might read as defenders of republican liberties like Godwin, Thelwall, Hays, Byron, Shelley, Hazlitt, Payne, and Knowles.

As the preceding chapters have suggested, the Roman republic retains a prominent place in the symbolic landscape of Britain in the Romantic period. Though he writes much later, Henry James, in the opening to *The Golden Bowl* (1904), provides us with an image of Roman continuity:

The Prince had always liked his London, when it had come to him; he was one of the Modern Romans who find by the Thames a more convincing image of the truth of the ancient state than any they have left by the Tiber. Brought up on the legend of the City to which the world paid tribute, he recognized in the present London much more than in contemporary Rome the real dimensions of such a case. If it was a question of an *Imperium*, he said to himself, and if one wished, as a Roman, to recover a little sense of that, the place to do so was on London Bridge, or even, on a fine afternoon in May, at Hyde Park Corner.[5]

Admittedly, James seems to have the Roman Empire in mind, but we should not forget that Roman *Imperium* begins under the republic. In the way that this passage suggests how a particular historic locale can sometimes be more authentically experienced elsewhere, it underlines both the permanence and the discontinuity of the Roman legacy and provides a fitting moment for a study of the receptions of republican Rome in British Romanticism and beyond. The passage recalls the complex temporality of Mary Wollstonecraft's vision of London in ruins, of Byron's memory of Servius Sulpicius in *Childe Harold*, canto IV, and of Macaulay's fantasy of a future visitor from New Zealand standing on the ruins of London. Rome exists on at least two levels here: as Rome, a historical city and empire subject to inevitable decline

---

[5] Henry James, *The Golden Bowl*, ed. Gore Vidal (Harmondsworth: Penguin, 1985), 43.

and decay, and as "Rome," the permanent marker of lasting empire and world-historical significance. The incidents, figures, and texts discussed in this book all implicitly engage this doubleness. They do not present a continuous, teleological narrative, but they do show the persistence of thinking about Rome, and especially republican Rome, throughout the period. Moreover—while always recognizing that Rome's long and diverse history gives it an unprecedented capacity for oversignification that often makes the meaning of its use elusive—this book suggests a change in the meaning of Rome during the Romantic period.

The deployment of Roman examples is not simply the continuity or resurgence of a persistent neoclassicism. Even in those moments where Roman references appear most neoclassical in mode—Burke's Latin citation, Godwin's emphasis on the exemplarity of Roman heroes, or in the Jacobin novel's attempt to reencode the exemplary logic of republicanism—such references are used to forge a distinctly modern and future-directed sensibility. Burke's claim that the past defines the parameters of the present and future—that society is a contract between the living, the dead, and the not-yet-born—undermines the transparent relevance of Roman examples to contemporary issues in favor of a more organic conception of the nation. The past may be prologue, but it is not analogue. In contrast, the Jacobin novelists' recasting of Roman exemplarity attempts to bring the pedagogical functions and moral seriousness of ancient history into the novel form and thereby to enlist the Roman example in the service of progressive causes like expanded popular participation in the political process.

This Janus-faced quality of Rome, its usability for diverse ends, is even more evident in the work of Byron and Shelley. In *Childe Harold*, canto IV, Byron uses Roman ruins to amplify his expression of self but also to develop a particular post-Waterloo reengagement with history. A focus on Rome allows us to see that, if Byron's Romanticism is self-absorbed, it ultimately moves beyond solipsism because he comes to see the self in which he is absorbed as historically conditioned. In later writings, and especially in his participation in the so-called Pope controversy, Byron wields this historical sensibility (here an awareness of Roman literary history) to condone the imitation of Roman examples and to condemn his poetic peers for what he sees as

Conclusion 277

the derivative imitation of each other. Shelley, meanwhile, often dismisses Rome as a lesser copy of Greece. Yet close inspection shows that Shelley's conception of Greece as a land of imagination and freedom depends on his construction of "Rome" as rigid imitation. Although Shelley's relationship to Rome is thus mediated by his philhellenism, he does reconsider the Roman legacy as he struggles to use his understanding of the ancient past to comprehend the logic of the present and anticipate the future rule of liberty. Byron, then, uses imitation to promote Rome, and Shelley uses the same concept to denounce Rome. The contrast shows not just Rome's potential for contradictory signification, but also how Romanticism's conception of imitation and its relation to imagination is mediated by its sense of the meaning and modes of Roman antiquity.

Clearly, the Roman example has a powerful presence in the prose and poetry of the Romantic period. Its influence, however, was not simply textual. Representations of republican Rome persisted in the Theatres Royal from the start of the period to the end. In an age marked by foreign wars, food shortages, and domestic unrest, the distancing effect of classical antiquity allowed Roman episodes to serve as an analogy for contemporary experience, and the meaning of the Roman legacy was fiercely contested on the Romantic stage. John Kemble's staging of *Coriolanus* presented audiences with a vision of republican Rome transposed into imperial Rome as it dramatized the rightness of patrician rule. In response to Kemble's aristocratic staging, Edmund Kean reinterpreted Coriolanus as a rough hero of the early republic in a portrayal that was even described as "plebeian." While Kean's production was ultimately a failure, he had already achieved great success in recasting Kemble's Roman legacy as the title character in John Howard Payne's *Brutus*. This now-forgotten drama was part of a prolonged struggle over the relevance of the Roman republic for the early nineteenth century that sparked the production and publication of numerous further episodes from the republican past.

Together, these incidents force a reevaluation of the common assumption that Rome, from the late eighteenth century onward, was displaced from a position of dominant cultural authority. They further suggest that what has been thought of as a shift from republicanism to historicism is neither a smooth nor an abrupt transition, but rather a set of mutually reinforcing modes for the reencoding and redescription of Roman antiquity that together help to create a distinctly modern sensibility. As the brief passage from James would suggest, this is a process that continues through the nineteenth and into the twentieth century. The continuity underscores Rome's capacity for multiple and conflicting signification, but it also suggests that despite our obsession with modernity as a break from the ancient past, we cannot overlook the enduring presence of Rome. We might even modify T. S. Eliot's claim[6] and say, "We are all still citizens of the Roman republic."

---

[6] "Virgil and the Christian World," in *On Poetry and Poets* (London: Faber and Faber, 1957), 130. The original declares, "We are all, so far as we inherit the civilizations of Europe, still citizens of the Roman empire."

Bibliography

Abrams, M. H. *The Mirror and the Lamp: Romantic Theory and the Critical Tradition.* New York: Oxford University Press, 1953.

———. *Natural Supernaturalism: Tradition and Revolution in Romantic Literature.* New York: Norton, 1971.

Ashcraft, Richard. *Revolutionary Politics and Locke's Two Treatises of Government.* Princeton, NJ: Princeton University Press, 1986.

Ayres, Philip. *Classical Culture and the Idea of Rome in Eighteenth-Century England.* Cambridge: Cambridge University Press, 1997.

Baer, Marc. *Theatre and Disorder in Late Georgian London.* Oxford: Clarendon Press, 1992.

Bakhtin, Mikhail M. *The Dialogic Imagination: Four Essays.* Translated by Caryl Emerson and Michael Holquist. Austin: University of Texas Press, 1981.

Bann, Stephen. *Romanticism and the Rise of History.* New York: Twayne, 1995.

Barnett, George L., ed. *Eighteenth-Century British Novelists on the Novel.* New York: Appleton-Century-Crofts, 1968.

Baron, Hans. *The Crisis of the Early Italian Renaissance: Civic Humanism and Republican Liberty in an Age of Classicism and Tyranny.* Princeton, NJ: Princeton University Press, 1966.

Bate, Jonathan. *Shakespearean Constitutions: Politics, Theatre, Criticism, 1730–1830.* Oxford: Clarendon Press, 1989.

———, ed. *The Romantics on Shakespeare.* London: Penguin, 1992.

Bate, Walter Jackson. *From Classic to Romantic.* Cambridge: Harvard University Press, 1946.

———. *John Keats.* Cambridge: Harvard University Press, 1963.

Benjamin, Walter. *Illuminations.* Edited by Hannah Arendt. New York: Schocken Books, 1969.

Berlin, Isaiah. *Two Concepts of Liberty.* Oxford: Clarendon Press, 1958.

Blake, William. *The Complete Poetry and Prose of William Blake.* Edited by David Erdman. Berkeley: University of California Press, 1982.

Bohm, Arnd. "Just Beauty: Ovid and the Argument of Keats's 'Ode on a Grecian Urn,'" *Modern Language Quarterly* 68.1 (March 2007): 1–26.

Bolton, Betsy. *Women, Nationalism, and the Romantic Stage: Theatre and Politics in Britain, 1780–1800.* Cambridge: Cambridge University Press, 2001.

Boulton, James T. *The Language of Politics in the Age of Wilkes and Burke*. London: Routledge and Kegan Paul, 1963.
Brand, C. P. *Italy and the English Romantics: The Italianate Fashion in Early Nineteenth-Century England*. Cambridge: Cambridge University Press, 1957.
Brewer, John. "English Radicalism in the Age of George III." In *Three British Revolutions: 1641, 1688, 1776*, ed. J. G. A. Pocock, 323–367. Princeton, NJ: Princeton University Press, 1980.
Bromwich, David. *Hazlitt: The Mind of a Critic*. New York: Oxford University Press, 1983.
Burroughs, Catherine. *Closet Stages: Joanna Baillie and the Theatre Theory of British Romantic Women Writers*. Philadelphia: University of Pennsylvania Press, 1997.
Burke, Edmund. *Reflections on the Revolution in France*. Edited by Frank M. Turner. New Haven, CT: Yale University Press, 2003.
———. *Reflections on the Revolution in France*. Edited by and with an introduction by J. G. A. Pocock. Indianapolis, IN: Hackett, 1987.
———. *Reflections on the Revolution in France*. Edited by J. C. D. Clark. Stanford, CA: Stanford University Press, 2001.
Burke, Kenneth. *Attitudes toward History*. 3rd ed. Berkeley: University of California Press, 1984.
Butler, Marilyn. *Jane Austen and the War of Ideas*. Oxford: Clarendon Press, 1975.
———. "Romanticism in England." In *Romanticism in National Context*, ed. Roy Porter and Mikulas Teich, 37–67. Cambridge: Cambridge University Press, 1988.
———. *Romantics, Rebels, and Reactionaries: English Literature and Its Background 1760–1830*. Oxford: Oxford University Press, 1981.
Buxton, John. *The Grecian Taste: Literature in the Age of Neo-Classicism, 1740–1820*. New York: Barnes and Noble, 1978.
Byron, George Gordon Lord. *Byron's Letters and Journals*. Edited by Leslie Marchand. 12 vols. Cambridge: Harvard University Press, Belknap Press, 1973–1982.
———. *The Complete Miscellaneous Prose*. Edited by Andrew Nicholson. Oxford: Clarendon Press, 1991.
Calhoun, Craig, ed. *Habermas and the Public Sphere*. Cambridge: MIT Press, 1992.
Carlson, Julie. *In the Theatre of Romanticism: Coleridge, Nationalism, Women*. Cambridge: Cambridge University Press, 1994.
Carter, Paul. "Shelley & the Greek Spirit." *Art and Artists* 11 (1977): 511–519.
Cavaliero, Roderick. *Italia Romantica: English Romantics and Italian Freedom*. London: Palgrave, 2005.

Cestre, Charles. *John Thelwall*. Paris: L. Liard, 1906.
Chandler, James K. *England in 1819: The Politics of Literary Culture and the Case of Romantic Historicism*. Chicago: University of Chicago Press, 1998.
———. "The Pope Controversy: Romantic Poetics and the English Canon." *Critical Inquiry* 10 (1984): 481–509.
Chapman, Allison, and Jane Stabler, eds. *Unfolding the South: Nineteenth-Century British Women Writers and Artists in Italy*. Manchester: Manchester University Press, 2003.
Chapman, Gerard Wester, ed. *Literary Criticism in England, 1660–1800*. New York: Alfred A. Knopf, 1966.
Cheeke, Stephen. "The Sword 'Which eats into itself': Romanticism, Napoleon and the Roman Parallel." *Romanticism* 10.2 (2004): 209–227.
———. "'What So Many Have Told, Who Would Tell Again': Romanticism and the Commonplaces of Rome." *European Romantic Review* 17 (2006): 521–541.
Chernaik, Judith. *The Lyrics of Shelley*. Cleveland, OH: Press of Case Western Reserve University, 1972.
Child, Harold. *The Shakespearian Productions of John Phillip Kemble*. London: Published for the Shakespeare Association by Humphrey Milford, Oxford University Press, 1935.
Christensen, Jerome. *Lord Byron's Strength: Romantic Writing and Commercial Society*. Baltimore: Johns Hopkins University Press, 1993.
Churchill, Kenneth. *Italy and English Literature, 1764–1930*. Totowa, NJ: Barnes and Noble Books, 1980.
Cicero, Marcus Tullius. *De Officiis*. Loeb Classical Library. Trans. Walter Miller. Cambridge: Harvard University Press, 1913.
———. *De Re Publica De Legibus*. Loeb Classical Library. Trans. Clinton Walker Keyes. Cambridge: Harvard University Press, 1943.
———. *The Speeches: Pro Sestio and In Vatinium*. Loeb Classical Library. Trans. R. Gardner. Cambridge: Harvard University Press, 1958.
Claeys, Gregory. "The Origins of the Rights of Labor: Republicanism, Commerce, and the Construction of Modern Social Theory in Britain, 1796–1805." *Journal of Modern History* 66 (June 1994): 249–290.
———. "Republicanism versus Commercial Society: Paine, Burke, and the French Revolution Debate." *History of European Ideas* 11 (1989): 313–324.
———. "The *Reflections* Refracted: The Critical Reception of Burke's *Reflections on the Revolution in France* during the Early 1790s." In *Edmund Burke's Reflections on the Revolution in France: New Interdisciplinary Essays*, ed. John Whale, 44–59. Manchester: Manchester University Press, 2000.
———, ed. *The Political Writings of the 1790s*. 8 vols. London: Pickering and Chatto, 1995.

Clark, J. C. D. *English Society, 1688–1832: Ideology, Social Structure, and Political Practice during the Ancien Regime.* Cambridge: Cambridge University Press, 1985.
Clarke, M. L. *Classical Education in Britain, 1500–1900.* Cambridge: Cambridge University Press, 1959.
Clemit, Pamela. *The Godwinian Novel: The Rational Fictions of Godwin, Brockden Brown, Mary Shelley.* Oxford: Clarendon Press, 1993.
Coleridge, Samuel Taylor. *The Collected Works of Samuel Taylor Coleridge,* 16 vols. General editor, Kathleen Coburn. Princeton, NJ: Princeton University Press, 1969–.
Coltman, Viccy. *Fabricating the Antique: Neoclassicism in Britain, 1760–1800.* Chicago: University of Chicago Press, 2006.
———. "Representation, Replication, and Collecting in Charles Townley's Late Eighteenth-Century Library." *Art History* 29 (2006): 304–324.
Conolly, L. W. *The Censorship of English Drama.* San Marino, CA: Huntington Library, 1976.
Connery, Brian A., and Kirk Combe, eds. *Theorizing Satire: Essays in Literary Criticism.* New York: St. Martin's Press, 1995.
Cox, Jeffrey N. "Ideology and Genre in the British Antirevolutionary Drama of the 1790s." *ELH* 58.3 (1991): 579–610.
———. *Poetry and Politics in the Cockney School: Keats, Shelley, Hunt, and Their Circle.* Cambridge: Cambridge University Press, 1998.
Cox, Jeffrey N., and Michael Gamer, eds. *The Broadview Anthology of Romantic Period Drama.* Peterborough, ON: Broadview, 2003.
Croly, George. *A Memoir of the Political Life of the Right Honourable Edmund Burke.* 2 vols. Edinburgh: Blackwood and Sons, 1840.
———. *Catiline: A Tragedy with Other Poems.* London: Hurst, Robinson, 1822.
Cumberland, Richard. *The Posthumous Dramatick Works of the Late Richard Cumberland.* London: G. and W. Nichol, 1813.
Curran, Stuart, ed. *The Cambridge Companion to British Romanticism.* Cambridge: Cambridge University Press, 1993.
———. *Shelley's Annus Mirabilis: The Maturing of an Epic Vision.* San Marino, CA: Huntington Library, 1975.
De Bruyn, Frans. "William Shakespeare and Edmund Burke: Literary Allusion in Eighteenth-Century British Political Rhetoric." In *Shakespeare and the Eighteenth Century,* ed. Peter Sabor and Paul Yachnin, 85–102. Aldershot, UK: Ashgate Press, 2008.
De Quincey, Thomas. *The Works of Thomas De Quincey.* 21 vols. Edited by Grevel Lindop. London: Pickering and Chatto, 2001.
Dickinson, H. T., ed. *Britain and the French Revolution, 1789–1815.* Basingstoke, UK: Macmillan, 1989.

Dowling, Linda. *Hellenism and Homosexuality in Victorian Oxford*. Ithaca, NY: Cornell University Press, 1994.
Downman, Hugh. *Lucius Junius Brutus; or, the Expulsion of the Tarquins: An Historical Play*. London, 1779.
Duncombe, William. *Junius Brutus: A Tragedy*. London, 1735.
Dyer, Gary. *British Satire and the Politics of Style, 1789–1832*. Cambridge: Cambridge University Press, 1997.
Edwards, Catherine, ed. *Roman Presences: Receptions of Rome in European Culture, 1789–1945*. Cambridge: Cambridge University Press, 1999.
Eliot, T. S. *On Poetry and Poets*. London: Faber and Faber, 1957.
Eley, Geoff. "Nations, Publics, and Political Cultures: Placing Habermas in the Nineteenth Century." In *Habermas and the Public Sphere*, ed. Craig Calhoun, 289–339. Cambridge: MIT Press, 1992.
Epstein, James. *Radical Expression: Political Language, Ritual, and Symbol in England, 1790–1850*. New York: Oxford University Press, 1994.
Erdman, David. *Blake: Prophet against Empire*. Princeton, NJ: Princeton University Press, 1954.
Erskine-Hill, Howard. *The Augustan Idea in English Literature*. London: Edward Arnold, 1983.
Ferguson, Adam. *History of the Progress and Termination of the Roman Republic*. 2nd ed. 5 vols. Edinburgh: Bell and Bradfute, 1799.
Fielding, Henry. *Joseph Andrews*. Edited by Martin C. Battestin. London: Methuen, 1961.
Franta, Andrew. *Romanticism and the Rise of the Mass Public*. Cambridge: Cambridge University Press, 2007.
Fry, Paul H. "Classical Standards in the Period." In *The Cambridge History of Literary Criticism*, Vol. 5: *Romanticism*, ed. Marshall Brown, 7–28. Cambridge: Cambridge University Press, 2000.
Furniss, Tom. *Edmund Burke's Aesthetic Ideology: Language, Gender, and Political Economy in Revolution*. Cambridge: Cambridge University Press, 1993.
Gallagher, Catherine. *Nobody's Story: The Vanishing Acts of Women Writers in the Marketplace, 1670–1820*. Berkeley: University of California Press, 1994.
Gaull, Marilyn. "Romans and Romanticism." *Wordsworth Circle* 36.1 (2005): 15–20.
Genest, John. *Some Account of the English Stage from the Restoration in 1660–1830*. 10 vols. Bath, 1832.
George, David, ed. *Shakespeare: The Critical Tradition: Coriolanus*. New York: Thoemmes Continuum, 2004.
Gibbon, Edward. *The History of the Decline and Fall of the Roman Empire*. 3 vols. Edited by David Womersley. London: Allen Lane, 1994.

Gilmartin, Kevin. *Print Politics: The Press and Radical Opposition in Early Nineteenth-Century England*. Cambridge: Cambridge University Press, 1996.

———. *Writing against Revolution: Literary Conservatism in Britain, 1790–1832*. Cambridge: Cambridge University Press, 2007.

Godwin, William. *Caleb Williams*. Edited by Maurice Hindle. Harmondsworth: Penguin, 1988.

———. *The Enquirer: Reflections on Education, Manners, and Literature*. London: G. G. and J. Robinson, 1797.

———. *Enquiry Concerning Political Justice*. Edited by Isaac Kramnick. Harmondsworth: Penguin, 1976.

———. *The Political and Philosophical Writings of William Godwin*. Edited by Mark Philp. 7 vols. London: William Pickering, 1993.

Goldhill, Simon. *Who Needs Greek: Contests in the Cultural History of Hellenism*. Cambridge: Cambridge University Press, 2002.

Goodman, Kevis. *Georgic Modernity and British Romanticism: Poetry and the Mediation of History*. Cambridge: Cambridge University Press, 2004.

Graver, Bruce. "Romanticism." In *A Companion to the Classical Tradition*, ed. Craig Kallendorf, 72–85. Oxford: Blackwell, 2007.

Griffin, Robert J. *Wordsworth's Pope: A Study in Literary Historiography*. Cambridge: Cambridge University Press, 1995.

Habermas, Jürgen. "The Public Sphere: An Encyclopedia Article (1964)." *New German Critique* 3 (1974): 49–55.

———. *The Structural Transformation of the Public Sphere: An Inquiry into a Category of Bourgeois Society*. Cambridge: MIT Press, 1989.

Hampsher-Monk, Iain. "John Thelwall and the Eighteenth-Century Radical Response to Political Economy." *Historical Journal* 34 (1991): 1–20.

Handwerk, Gary. "History, Trauma, and the Limits of the Liberal Imagination: William Godwin's Historical Fiction." In *Romanticism, History and the Possibilities of Genre: Re-forming Literature 1789–1837*, ed. Tilottama Rajan and Julia M. Wright, 64–85. Cambridge: Cambridge University Press, 1998.

Haskell, Francis, and Nicholas Penny. *Taste and the Antique: The Lure of Classical Sculpture, 1500–1900*. New Haven, CT: Yale University Press, 1981.

Hays, Mary. *Memoirs of Emma Courtney*. Edited by Eleanor Ty. Oxford: Oxford University Press, 1996.

Hazlitt, William. *The Complete Works of William Hazlitt*. 21 vols. Edited by P. P. Howe. London: J. M. Dent and Sons, 1930–1934.

———. *Selected Writings*. Ed. Jon Cook. Oxford: Oxford University Press, 1991.

Heitland, William. *The Roman Republic*. London, 1902.

Herbert, Robert L. *David, Voltaire,* Brutus, *and the French Revolution: An Essay in Art and Politics*. New York: Viking Press, 1972.

Hilton, Boyd. *A Mad, Bad, and Dangerous People: England 1783–1846*. Oxford: Oxford University Press, 2006.

Hitchens, Christopher. *The Elgin Marbles: Should They Be Returned to Greece?* London: Chatto and Windus, 1987.

Hogan, Charles Beecher. *Shakespeare in the Theatre, 1701–1800*. Oxford: Clarendon Press, 1957.

Holcroft, Thomas. *Anna St. Ives*. Edited by Peter Faulkner. Oxford English Novels. London: Oxford University Press, 1970.

———. *Hugh Trevor*. Edited by Seamus Deane. Oxford English Novels. London: Oxford University Press, 1973.

Hole, Robert. *From Jacobite to Conservative: Reaction and Orthodoxy in Britain, c. 1760–1832*. Cambridge: Cambridge University Press, 1993.

Holmes, Richard. *Coleridge: Early Visions*. London: Hodder and Stoughton, 1989.

Horace [Quintus Horatius Flaccus]. *Odes and Epodes*. Loeb Classical Library. Trans. Niall Rudd. Cambridge, MA: Harvard University Press, 2004.

———. *Satires, Epistles, and Ars Poetica*. Loeb Classical Library. Trans. H. Rushton Fairclough. Cambridge: Harvard University Press, 1929.

Hume, David. *Essays: Moral, Political, and Literary*. Edited by Eugene F. Miller. Indianapolis, IN: Liberty Classics, 1987.

Inchbald, Elizabeth. *Nature and Art*. Edited by Shawn L. Maurer. London: Pickering and Chatto, 1997.

Jacobus, Mary. "'That Great Stage Where Senators Perform': *Macbeth* and the Politics of Romantic Theatre." *Studies in Romanticism* 22 (1983): 353–387.

———. *Tradition and Experiment in Wordsworth's "Lyrical Ballads" (1798)*. Oxford: Clarendon Press, 1976.

James, Henry. *The Golden Bowl*. Edited by Gore Vidal. Harmondsworth: Penguin, 1985.

Jenkyns, Richard. *The Victorians and Ancient Greece*. Oxford: Basil Blackwell, 1980.

Johnson, J. W. *The Formation of English Neo-Classical Thought*. Princeton, NJ: Princeton University Press, 1967.

Johnson, Nancy E. *The English Jacobin Novel on Rights, Property and the Law: Critiquing the Contract*. Basingstoke, UK: Palgrave Macmillan, 2004.

Jones, Steven E. *Satire and Romanticism*. New York: St. Martin's, 2000.

Jonson, Ben. *The Complete Plays of Ben Jonson*. 4 vols. Edited by G. A. Wilkes. Oxford: Clarendon Press, 1982.

Juvenal [Decimus Iunius Iuvenalis]. *Juvenal and Persius.* Loeb Classical Library. Ed and trans. G. G. Ramsay. Cambridge: Harvard University Press, 1940.

Kahan, Jeffrey, ed. *Shakespeare Imitations, Parodies, and Forgeries, 1710–1820.* 3 vols. London: Routledge, 2004.

Kallendorf, Craig, ed. *A Companion to the Classical Tradition.* Oxford: Blackwell, 2007.

Kaminski, Thomas. "Rehabilitating 'Augustanism': On the Roots of 'Polite Letters' in England." *Eighteenth-Century Life* 20.3 (1996): 49–65.

Keats, John. *The Letters of John Keats.* Edited by Robert Gittings. Oxford: Oxford University Press, 1970.

Keen, Paul. *The Crisis of Literature in the 1790s: Print Culture and the Public Sphere.* Cambridge: Cambridge University Press, 1999.

Kelly, Gary. *The English Jacobin Novel 1780–1805.* Oxford: Clarendon Press, 1976.

Kipperman, Mark. "History and Ideality: The Politics of Shelley's *Hellas*." *Studies in Romanticism* 30 (1991): 147–168.

Klancher, John. "Godwin and the Republican Romance: Genre, Politics, and Contingency in Cultural History." *Modern Language Quarterly* 56 (1995): 145–165.

———. "Godwin and the Genre Reformers: On Necessity and Contingency in Romantic Narrative Theory." In *Romanticism, History and the Possibilities of Genre: Re-forming Literature, 1789–1837*, ed. Tilottama Rajan and Julia M. Wright, 21–38. Cambridge: Cambridge University Press, 1998.

Knowles, James Sheridan. *Caius Gracchus: A Tragedy in Five Acts.* London: T. Dolby, [1823].

———. *The Dramatic Works of James Sheridan Knowles.* London: G. Routledge, 1856.

Koselleck, Reinhart. *Futures Past: On the Semantics of Historical Time.* Translated by Keith Tribe. Cambridge: MIT Press, 1985.

Kramnick, Isaac. *The Rage of Edmund Burke: Portrait of an Ambivalent Conservative.* New York: Basic Books, 1977.

Kroeber, Karl. *The Artifice of Reality: Poetic Style in Wordsworth, Foscolo, Keats, and Leopardi.* Madison: University of Wisconsin Press, 1964.

———. *British Romantic Art.* Berkeley: University of California Press, 1986.

Kucich, Greg. "Eternity and the Ruins of Time: Shelley and the Construction of Cultural History." In *Shelley: Poet and Legislator of the World*, ed. Betty T. Bennett and Stuart Curran, 14–29. Baltimore: Johns Hopkins University Press, 1996.

Lamb, Charles. *The Complete Works and Letters of Charles Lamb.* New York: Modern Library, 1935.

Lang-Peralta, Linda, ed. *Women, Revolution, and the Novels of the 1790s*. Lansing: Michigan State University Press, 1999.

Lake, Peter, and Steven Pincus, eds. *The Politics of the Public Sphere in Early Modern England*. Manchester: Manchester University Press, 2007.

Levinson, Marjorie. *Wordsworth's Great Period Poems*. Cambridge: Cambridge University Press, 1986.

Levinson, Marjorie et al., editors. *Rethinking Historicism: Critical Readings in Romantic History*. New York: Blackwell, 1989.

Lipking, Lawrence. *The Ordering of the Arts in Eighteenth-Century England*. Princeton, NJ: Princeton University Press, 1970.

Liu, Alan. *Wordsworth: The Sense of History*. Stanford, CA: Stanford University Press, 1989.

Livy [Titus Livius]. *Livy*. Loeb Classical Library, 14 vols. Cambridge: Harvard University Press, 1925.

Lukács, Georg. *The Historical Novel*. Translated by Hannah Mitchell and Stanley Mitchell. Lincoln: University of Nebraska Press, 1983.

———. *The Theory of the Novel*. Translated by Anna Bostock. Cambridge: Harvard University Press, 1971.

Macpherson, C. B. *Burke*. Oxford: Oxford University Press, 1980.

Magnuson, Paul. *Reading Public Romanticism*. Princeton, NJ: Princeton University Press, 1998.

Mahoney, Charles. "Upstaging the Fall: Coriolanus and the Spectacle of Romantic Apostasy." *Studies in Romanticism* 38 (1999): 29–50.

Manning, Peter. "Cleansing the Images: Wordsworth, Rome, and the Rise of Historicism." *Texas Studies in Literature and Language* 33 (1991): 271–326.

———. "Edmund Kean and Byron's Plays." *Keats-Shelley Journal* 21–22 (1972–1973): 188–206.

———. *Reading Romantics: Texts and Contexts*. New York: Oxford University Press, 1994.

Marshall, Peter. *William Godwin*. New Haven, CT: Yale University Press, 1984.

Marx, Karl. *The Eighteenth Brumaire of Louis Bonaparte*. New York: International Publishers, 1963.

McCalman, Iain. *Radical Underworld: Prophets, Revolutionaries, and Pornographers in London, 1795–1840*. Cambridge: Cambridge University Press, 1988.

———, ed. *The Oxford Companion to the Romantic Age: British Culture 1776–1832*. Oxford: Oxford University Press, 1999.

McGann, Jerome J. *The Beauty of Inflections: Literary Investigations in Historical Method and Theory*. New York: Oxford University Press, 1985.

———. *The Romantic Ideology: A Critical Investigation.* Chicago: University of Chicago Press, 1983.

———. "The Secrets of an Elder Day: Shelley after *Hellas.*" *Keats-Shelley Journal* 15 (1966): 25–41.

McKeon, Michael. *The Origins of the English Novel: 1600–1740.* Baltimore: Johns Hopkins University Press, 1987.

———. "Prose Fiction: Great Britain." In *The Cambridge History of Literary Criticism: The Eighteenth Century*, ed. H. B. Nisbet and Claude Rawson, 238–263. Cambridge: Cambridge University Press, 1997.

[Mill, John Stuart.] "The Spirit of the Age." *The Examiner.* 9 January 1831: 20–21.

Moody, Jane. *Illegitimate Theatre in London, 1770–1840.* Cambridge: Cambridge University Press, 2000.

Most, Glenn W. "On the Use and Abuse of Ancient Greece for Life." *Cultura Tedesca* 20 (2002): 31–53.

Myrone, Martin. *Bodybuilding: Reforming Masculinities in British Art, 1750–1810.* New Haven, CT: Yale University Press, 2005.

Negt, Oskar, and Alexander Kluge. *Public Sphere and Experience: Towards an Analysis of the Bourgeois and Proletarian Public Sphere.* Translated by Peter Labanyi. Minneapolis: University of Minnesota Press, 1993.

O'Brien, Conor Cruise. *The Great Melody.* Chicago: University of Chicago Press, 1992.

Odell, George. *Shakespeare from Betterton to Irving.* New York: Charles Scribner's Sons, 1920.

Ortega y Gassat, José. *Meditations on Quixote.* Translated by Evelyn Rugg and Diego Marín. New York: Norton, 1961.

O'Quinn, Daniel. *Staging Governance: Theatrical Imperialism in London, 1770–1800.* Baltimore: Johns Hopkins University Press, 2005.

Ozouf, Mona. *Festivals and the French Revolution.* Cambridge: Harvard University Press, 1988.

Paine, Thomas. *Rights of Man, Common Sense, and Other Political Writings.* Edited by Mark Philp. Oxford: Oxford University Press, 1995.

Parker, Harold T. *The Cult of Antiquity and the French Revolutionaries.* Chicago: University of Chicago Press, 1937.

Pascoe, Judith. *Romantic Theatricality: Gender, Poetry, and Spectatorship.* Ithaca, NY: Cornell University Press, 1997.

Paulson, Ronald. *Representations of Revolution (1789–1820).* New Haven, CT: Yale University Press, 1983.

Payne, John Howard. *Brutus or the Fall of Tarquin.* London: Richard White, 1819.

Phillips, Mark Salber. "Relocating Inwardness: Historical Distance and the Transition from Enlightenment to Romantic Historiography." *PMLA:*

Publications of the Modern Language Association of America 118 (2003): 436–449.

———. *Society and Sentiment: Genres of Historical Writing in Britain, 1740–1820.* Princeton, NJ: Princeton University Press, 2000.

Philp, Mark. *Godwin's Political Justice.* Ithaca, NY: Cornell University Press, 1986.

Pincus, Steven C. A. "Whigs, Political Economy, and the Revolution of 1688–89." In *Cultures of Whiggism: New Essays on English Literature and Culture in the Long Eighteenth Century,* ed. David Womersley, Paddy Bullard, and Abigail Williams, 62–85. Newark: University of Delaware Press, 2005.

Plotz, John. *The Crowd: British Literature and Public Politics.* Berkeley: University of California Press, 2000.

Plutarch [Lucius Mestrius Plutarchus]. *Plutarch's Lives.* Loeb Classical Library. 11vols. Cambridge: Harvard University Press. 1914–1926.

Pocock, J. G. A. *The Machiavellian Moment: Florentine Political Thought and the Atlantic Republican Tradition.* Princeton, NJ: Princeton University Press, 1975.

———. *Virtue, Commerce, and History.* Cambridge: Cambridge University Press, 1985.

Porter, James I. "What Is 'Classical' about Classical Antiquity? Eight Propositions." *Arion* 13.1 (2005): 111–145.

Price, Richard. *Political Writings.* Edited by D. O. Thomas. Cambridge: Cambridge University Press, 1991.

Richardson, Alan. *A Mental Theater: Poetic Drama and Consciousness in the Romantic Age.* University Park: Pennsylvania State University Press, 1988.

Ripley, John. *Coriolanus on Stage in England and America, 1609–1994.* London: Associated University Presses, 1998.

Robbins, Bruce, ed. *The Phantom Public Sphere.* Minneapolis: University of Minnesota Press, 1993.

Rosenblum, Robert. *Transformations in Late Eighteenth-Century Art.* Princeton, NJ: Princeton University Press, 1967.

Rousseau, Jean-Jacques. *Confessions.* Edited by P. N. Furbank. New York: Everyman, 1992.

Saglia, Diego. "'The Illegitimate Assistance of Political Allusion': Politics and the Hybridization of Romantic Tragedy in the Drama of Richard Lalor Sheil." *Theatre Journal* 58 (2006): 249–267.

———. "'The Talking Demon': Liberty and Liberal Ideologies on the 1820s British Stage." *Nineteenth-Century Contexts* 28 (2006): 347–377.

Salgado, Gamini. *Eyewitness of Shakespeare: First Hand Accounts of Performances 1590–1890* New York: Barnes and Noble, 1975.

Sallust [Gaius Sallustius Crispus]. *Sallust*. Loeb Classical Library. Trans. J. C. Rolfe. Cambridge: Harvard University Press, 1921.
Scriptores Historiae Augustae. Loeb Classical Library. Trans. David Magie. 3 vols. Cambridge: Harvard University Press, 1921–1932.
Semmel, Stuart. "British Radicals and 'Legitimacy': Napoleon in the Mirror of History." *Past and Present* 167 (2000): 140–175.
Shelley, Mary Wollstonecraft. *The Letters of Mary Wollstonecraft Shelley*. Edited by Betty T. Bennett. 3 vols. Baltimore: Johns Hopkins University Press, 1980.
Shelley, Percy Bysshe. *Letters of Percy Bysshe Shelley*. Edited by Frederick L. Jones. Oxford: Clarendon Press, 1964.
———. *Poetical Works*. Edited by Thomas Hutchinson. London: Oxford University Press, 1967.
———. *Shelley's Poetry and Prose*. Edited by Donald H. Reiman and Sharon B. Powers. New York: W. W. Norton, 1977.
———. *Shelley's Prose, or the Trumpet of a Prophecy*. Edited by David Lee Clark. Albuquerque: University of New Mexico Press, 1954.
Simpson, David. *Wordsworth's Historical Imagination: The Poetry of Displacement*. New York: Methuen, 1987.
Smith, Charlotte. *Desmond*. Edited with introduction and notes by Antje Blank and Janet Todd. London: Pickering and Chatto, 1997.
Sonensher, Michael. *Before the Deluge: Public Debt, Inequality, and the Intellectual Origins of the French Revolution*. Princeton, NJ: Princeton University Press, 2007.
Speaight, Robert. *Shakespeare on the Stage: An Illustrated History of Shakespearean Performance*. London: Collins, 1973.
Spencer, T. J. B. "Shakespeare and the Elizabethan Romans." *Shakespeare Survey* 10 (1957): 27–38.
St. Clair, William. *Lord Elgin and the Marbles*. Oxford: Oxford University Press, 1967.
———. *The Reading Nation in the Romantic Period*. Cambridge: Cambridge University Press, 2004.
Stabler, Jane. *Byron, Poetics, and History*. Cambridge: Cambridge University Press, 2002.
Stauffer, Andrew. *Anger, Revolution, and Romanticism*. Cambridge: Cambridge University Press, 2005.
Stray, Christopher. *Classics Transformed: Schools, Universities, and Society in England, 1830–1960*. Oxford: Clarendon Press, 1998.
Sullivan, Jr., Garret A. "'A Story to Be Hastily Gobbled Up': *Caleb Williams* and Print Culture." *Studies in Romanticism* 32 (1993): 323–337.

Swindells, Julia. *Glorious Causes: The Grand Theatre of Political Change, 1789–1833*. Oxford: Oxford University Press, 2001.
Tacitus, Cornelius. *The Complete Works of Tacitus: The Annals. The History. The Life of Cnaeus Julius Agricola. Germany and Its Tribes. A Dialogue on Oratory*. Trans. Alfred John Church and William Jackson Brodribb. Edited with an introduction by Moses Hadas. New York: Modern Library, 1942.
Thelwall, John. *An Appeal to Popular Opinion against Kidnapping and Murder*. London, 1796.
———. *Ode to Science; John Gilpin's Ghost; Poems; The Trident of Albion*. Edited by Donald Reiman. New York: Garland Publishing, 1978.
———. *The Politics of English Jacobinism: Writings of John Thelwall*. Edited with an introduction by Gregory Claeys. University Park: Pennsylvania State University Press, 1995.
———. *Prospectus of a Course of Lectures...in Strict Conformity with the Restrictions of Mr Pitt's Convention Act*. London, 1796.
Thomas, Sophie. "Assembling History: Fragments and Ruins." *European Romantic Review* 14 (2003): 177–186.
Thompson, E. P. *The Making of the English Working Class*. New York: Vintage, 1966.
Thomson, James. *Liberty, The Castle of Indolence and Other Poems*. Edited by James Sambrook. Oxford: Clarendon Press, 1986.
Turner, Frank. "British Politics and the Demise of the Roman Republic: 1700–1939." *Historical Journal* 29.3 (1986): 577–599.
———. *The Greek Heritage in Victorian Britain*. New Haven, CT: Yale University Press, 1981.
———. "Why the Greeks and Not the Romans in Victorian Britain?" In *Rediscovering Hellenism*, ed. G. W. Clarke, 61–81. Cambridge: Cambridge University Press, 1989.
Ty, Eleanor. *Unsexed Revolutionaries: Five Women Novelists of the 1790s*. Toronto: University of Toronto Press, 1993.
Vance, Norman. *The Victorians and Ancient Rome*. Oxford: Blackwell, 1997.
Wallace, Jennifer. *Shelley and Greece: Rethinking Romantic Hellenism*. New York: St. Martin's Press, 1997.
Watson, Nicola. *Revolution and the Form of the British Novel, 1790–1825*. Oxford: Clarendon Press, 1994.
Watt, Ian. *The Augustan Age*. Greenwich, CT: Fawcett Publications, 1968.
———. *The Rise of the Novel: Studies in Defoe, Richardson, Fielding*. Berkeley: University of California Press, 1957.

Webb, Timothy, ed. *English Romantic Hellenism, 1700–1824*. Manchester: Manchester University Press, 1982.
———. "Romantic Hellensim." In *The Cambridge Companion to British Romanticism*, ed. Stuart Curran, 148–176. Cambridge: Cambridge University Press, 1993.
———. *Shelley: A Voice Not Understood*. Atlantic Highlands, NJ: Humanities Press, 1977.
———. *The Violet in the Crucible: Shelley in Translation*. Oxford: Clarendon Press, 1976.
Weinbrot, Howard D. *Augustus Caesar in Augustan England: The Decline of a Classical Norm*. Princeton, NJ: Princeton University Press, 1978
———. "The Emperor's Old Toga: Augustanism and the Scholarship of Nostalgia." *Modern Philology* 83 (1986): 286–297.
———. *Brittania's Issue: The Rise of British Literature from Dryden to Ossian*. Cambridge: Cambridge University Press, 1993.
Wells, Stanley. *Shakespeare in the Theatre: An Anthology of Criticism*. Oxford: Clarendon Press, 1997.
Whale, John, ed. *Edmund Burke's Reflections on the Revolution in France: New Interdisciplinary Essays*. Manchester: Manchester University Press, 2000.
———. "Hazlitt on Burke: The Ambivalent Position of a Radical Essayist." *Studies in Romanticism* 25 (1986): 465–481.
White, Daniel E. *Early Romanticism and Religious Dissent*. Cambridge: Cambridge University Press, 2006.
Wilkins, B. T. *The Problem of Burke's Political Philosophy*. Oxford: Clarendon Press, 1967.
Williams, Ioan M., ed. *Novel and Romance, 1700–1800: A Documentary History*. New York: Barnes and Noble, 1970.
Williams, Raymond. *Culture and Society, 1780–1950*. London: Hogarth Press, 1958.
Wollstonecraft, Mary. *Mary and The Wrongs of Women*, ed. Gary Kelly. Oxford: Oxford University Press, 1976.
———. *A Vindication of the Rights of Men and A Vindication of the Rights of Woman*. Edited by Sylvana Tomaselli. Cambridge: Cambridge University Press, 1995.
Wood, Marcus. *Radical Satire and Print Culture, 1790–1822*. Oxford: Clarendon Press, 1994.
Woodring, Carl M. *Politics in English Romantic Poetry*. Cambridge: Harvard University Press, 1970.
Wooton, David. *Republicanism, Liberty, and Commercial Society*. Stanford, CA: Stanford University Press, 1995.

Womersley, David, ed. *Cultures of Whiggism: New Essays on English Literature and Culture in the Long Eighteenth Century*. Newark: University of Delaware Press, 2005.

Worrall, David. *Radical Culture: Discourse, Resistance, and Surveillance, 1790–1820*. Detroit: Wayne State University Press, 1992.

———. *Theatric Revolution: Drama, Censorship, and Romantic Period Subcultures, 1773–1832*. Oxford: Oxford University Press, 2006.

Index

Addison, Joseph 231
  Cato 182–183, 216, 224
Alexander III of Macedon (Alexander the Great) 100
Analytical Review 92
Antoinette, Marie 54, 231, 239, 264
Aristotle 105, 130
Athens
  in Byron's writing 133
  climate of 13
  in Shelley's writing 44, 148, 149, 151, 155, 158, 160–166
  See also Greece
Augustan age 1, 31–32
Augustus, Gaius Julius Caesar (Octavian) 10, 31–34, 50, 88, 138
Ayres, Philip 33–34, 50

Bage, Robert
  Hermsprong 79
Bankes, Henry
  Civil and Constitutional History of Rome 17
Bann, Stephen 5, 75
Bate, Jonathan 182, 184, 188, 218, 220
Bate, Walter Jackson
  on Keats and history 38–39
Benjamin, Walter 15–16
Berlin, Isaiah 252
Blackwood's Edinburgh Magazine 6, 272
Blake, William 17 n. 28, 209
Boccaccio, Giovanni 137
Bolingbroke, Henry St. John, 1st Viscount 159
Bowles, John 265
Bowles, William Lisle 123, 131
Boydell, John 203
  Shakespeare Gallery 203, 217
British Critic 243
Bromwich, David 219
Brougham, Henry 131
Brutus, Lucius Junius 28, 137, 216, 233
  Godwin and the punishment of his sons 72
Brutus, Marcus Junius 200

Burdett, Sir Francis 205
Burgoyne, John (General) 67
Burke, Edmund 22, 57, 98, 181, 214, 218, 276
  on Catiline 62–63, 264–265
  Philosophical Inquiry into the ... Sublime and Beautiful 61
  Reflections on the Revolution in France 22, 26, 212, 239
  on British government 53–56
  compared to Godwin 51–52
  read by Desmond 184
  response to Richard Price 52–53
  Roman references in 40–41, 51–65, 276
  Speech on Fox's East India Bill 61
  use of Cicero 22, 51, 60–63
  use of Horace 57–59
  use of Juvenal 59–60
Burke, Kenneth 116, 145, 173–174
"Burke Problem" 56–57
Butler, Marilyn 27, 101
  on changes in Romantic reading audiences 41–42
  on the Jacobin novel, 76, 79, 93, 98, 100
  on Romantic Hellenism 35, 149 n. 7
Byron, George Gordon, sixth baron 6, 20
  Childe Harold's Pilgrimage 43, 115, 118, 133–145, 275–277
  Romanticism of 134–135
  Roman ruins in 136–137, 140–145, 276
  comparison of ancient and British literary history 117, 125, 129–130, 276
  on the decline of literature 115–131
  on didactic poetry 128
  Don Juan 119–121, 130
  "English Bards and Scotch Reviewers" 131–133, 144
  Hours of Idleness 132
  and Italian culture 27
  on Kean 207, 215

Byron (*continued*)
　Letter to **** ******
　　[John Murray] 115–131
　and Marlow circle 35
　and Pope controversy 42–43,
　　122–131, 276–277
　rejection of Romantic poetics 6,
　　42–43, 115–131
　and Romanticism 140–145
　Sardanapalus 124
　self-construction of 118, 140–145,
　　276–277

Cade, Jack 266
Caesar, Julius 33, 201
　assassination of 200
　compared to Napoleon 138–139
　De Quincey on 272–275
Caligula 100
Cameron, Kenneth 152
Camillus, Marcus Furius 159, 168, 169
Camillus: An Historical Play 224
Campbell, Thomas 117, 119, 122
　on John Kemble 198
　response to Bowles in Pope
　　Controversy 123
Canning, George 91
canons, literary 123–124, 126, 127, 129
　English in relation to Roman 42–43,
　　130
Carlile, Richard 171
Carlyle, Thomas 273
Carnot, Lazare 219
Carthage
　and Britain 16, 133
Cary, Lucius, 2nd Viscount Falkland 98
Cassius (Gaius Cassius Longinus) 200
Castlereagh, Robert Stuart,
　　Viscount 121
Catiline (Lucius Sergius Catilina) 65,
　　101, 207–209, 262–267
　Burke on 62–63
　Cicero's prosecution of 62, 262–263
　representation in British letters
　　263–267
Cato Street Conspiracy 171
Cato the Younger (Marcus Porcius Cato
　　Uticensis) 28, 58–59, 70, 216
　and *Anna St. Ives* 102–104
　Godwin on suicide of 72

Catullus, Gaius Valerius 168
　and British Romanticism 27,
　　27 n. 49
censorship 181
Champion 207, 221
Chandler, James
　on *Don Juan* 121
　on Romantic historicity 5, 25
　on the Pope Controversy 123–124,
　　125, 132
　on Shelley 150
Cheeke, Stephen 20, 37–38
Chernaik, Judith 156–157, 160
Christensen, Jerome 118, 135 n. 23
Christian religion 10
Christie, Thomas 53
Cicero 10, 28, 58, 105, 107
　and Burke 51, 56, 60–63
　in *Childe Harold's Pilgrimage*
　　136–137, 143
　De Legibus 60–61
　De Officiis 62
　Godwin's praise for 67–68, 69
　and Plato 165
　prosecution of Catiline 62, 208,
　　262–263
　prosecution of Verres 67–68
　Pro Sestio 61
Cincinnatus, Lucius Quinctius 28
civic humanism. *See* republicanism
Clark, J. C. D. 32, 263
Claudian 117, 119
classical history 80–82, 85–86, 97,
　　173, 274
　and present state of Europe 117, 150,
　　156, 172
　mediation of 13–16, 159–160,
　　184–189, 208–209
classical learning 7–9, 19, 103
　and bellicosity 105, 107
　contrasted to novel reading 77–78,
　　84–85
　Jacobin novel's critique of 101–108
　and masculine virtue 85–86, 105
　and political conservatism 9, 17–18
　and political reform 10, 17
　and public discourse 56, 105
classical languages 9
　learning of 10, 69, 104–105, 108
classical tradition 122, 125–126, 131

classicism
    and historical mediation 13–16
    internal differentiations within 11–12,
        12 n. 15, 87, 103, 122, 126, 131,
        148–150, 274
    in nineteenth-century Germany 11
        n. 14
    and Romantic culture wars 21
Clemit, Pamela 80 n. 8, 98
Coleman, George (the Younger) 192
Coleridge, Samuel Taylor 20, 37, 119,
    121, 122
    Biographia Litteraria 209–210
    on imagination 209–210, 220
    lectures on Shakespeare 186–187
commercial society 4, 76, 118, 135 n. 23,
    142 n. 27
Condorcet, Marquis de 116
conspiracy 63, 262–271
Corneille, Pierre 127
Corn Laws (1815) 254–255
Cornwall, Barry (Brian Waller
    Proctor) 119, 121
Conway, William Augustus 193
Covent Garden 25, 189, 191, 193, 206,
    224, 247
Cowper, William 185
Cox, Jeffrey 21, 27, 179, 226, 242
Crabbe, George 117
Crebillon, Claude-Prosper Jolyot
    de 127
Croly, George 119, 121
    Catiline 45, 224, 227, 231, 262–271
        analysis of 268–270
        critique of democracy in
            268–270
        plot of 267–268
Cromwell, Oliver 138
Cruikshank, George 204, 207
Cumberland, John
    Cumberland's British Theatre 231,
        259
Cumberland, Richard
    Richard the Second 230

Dante (Dante Alighieri) 127, 137, 155
David, Jacques-Louis 195
decline of literature 42–43, 116–131
Demosthenes 105
Dennis, John 190

De Quincey, Thomas 38
    essays on the Caesars 6, 272–275
D'Israeli, Isaac 123
Domitian 218–219
Drake, Nathan 190
Drury Lane 25, 191, 193, 224, 231
Dryden, John 132
    and Augustanism 31
    and English canon 43, 125, 127
Duncombe, William
    Junius Brutus 237
Dundas, Henry 67
Dyer, Gary 60

Edinburgh Review 35, 225
Edgeworth, Maria 81
Eliot, T. S. 278
Elliston, Robert 206
enthusiasm 217
Epictetus 95
Epstein, James 50–51
Erskine-Hill, Howard 31–32
European Magazine 208, 209, 217
Eustace, John 225
Examiner 187–188, 212
exemplarity 8, 29
    and the British republican
        tradition 28
    and *Caius Gracchus* 250–251
    and De Quincey's essays on the
        Caesars 274
    Godwin's use of 23, 66–68, 72–74,
        100–101
    and historicism 39–41, 274
    and the Jacobin novel 24, 41, 80–82,
        97, 100–101, 108, 110–111
    related to Burkean prejudice 73
    and Rome 8
    Shelley's use of 159
    and tragedy 241–242
Eyre, Edmund
    The Maid of Normandy 230, 231

Fabricius 7, 8 n. 10, 28
    as Godwinian model of virtue 7, 74
Farquhar, George 231
Ferguson, Adam 16
    *History of the Progress and
        Termination of the Roman
        Republic* 16, 255

Fielding, Henry 90
Forsythe, Joseph 225
Fox, Charles James 56, 66
Franklin, Benjamin 217
Free Press (Glasgow) 260–261
French Revolution 4, 6
  appropriation of antiquity 14–16
  British response to 6, 21, 34, 39–40, 80, 219 (*see also* Revolution Controversy)
  and Brutus 15, 232
  compared to Catiline's conspiracy by Burke 62–63
  Constituent Assembly 15
  in *Defence of Poetry* 167, 170–171
  and historical parallels 39, 218–219
  National Convention 15
  and Payne's *Brutus* 231–232
  as theater 212
  use of Roman republic in 4, 14–16, 34, 37
Fry, Paul 36

Gallagher, Catherine 81–82, 110
Gamer, Michael 179
Garrick, David 191, 250
George III, King 189
George IV, Prince of Wales, Prince Regent and later King 189
Gibbon, Edward 116, 154, 155, 159, 270
  History of the Decline and Fall of the Roman Empire 16, 63, 140, 167
  on Claudian 119
Gifford, William
  attack of Hazlitt 187–188, 218–220
Gilchrist, Oliver 123
Gilliland, Thomas 198
Gilmartin, Kevin 214, 228–229, 271
Glorious Revolution 21, 53–54, 167
  Burke's interpretation of 53–54, 57
Godwin, William 7, 23, 86, 275–276
  "An Account of the Seminary" 68–69
  Caleb Williams 79, 92, 94, 98–101, 106
  and *Emma Courtney* 98–99
  representation of reading in 99–100
  Enquirer 7–8, 23, 41, 95
  "Of the Study of the Classics" 7–8, 11–12, 36, 147, 159, 165
  exchange with Shelley on classics 8–12, 21, 147, 169–170, 174
  "Of History and Romance" 75–76, 95–98
  History of Rome (as Edward Baldwin) 17
  and the Jacobin novel 41
  Political Herald and Review "Mucius" letters 66–68, 106
  Political Justice 7, 8, 23, 41
  print technology in 94
  selfless benevolence and Roman heroism in 66, 72–74
  use of Rome in 69–74
  on the Renaissance 14, 155
  on Roman aristocracy 71–72
  use of Roman precedents 7–12, 23, 40–41, 51–52, 65–76, 276
Goethe, Johann Wolfgang von 20, 141
Goldsmith, Oliver 16, 231
  Roman History 16–17
Gracchi, mother of (Cornelia Scipionis Africana) 69
Gracchus, Caius 33, 69
Gracchus, Tiberius 33, 69
Greece, ancient 4
  Byron on 117, 121–122, 133, 136, 138
  in *Emma Courtney* 86–87
  and Rome 7–13, 20, 34–35, 147–175, 277
  Shelley on 43–44, 147–175, 277
  Thomson on 157
Griffin, Robert 43, 124, 141

Habermas, Jürgen 227–228
Hamilton, Gavin 195
Handel, George Frideric
  Julius Caesar 200
Hannibal 136, 168
Hardy, Thomas 49
Hare, Julius 17
Harrington, James 49
Hastings, Warren
  prosecution of 67–68
Hays, Mary 23, 41, 275
  Memoirs of Emma Courtney 82–90, 93, 106
  and *Caleb Williams* 98–99
  representation of reading 82–90

Hazlitt, William 6, 20, 44, 185, 275
  A View of the English Stage 214, 215
  on *Antony and Cleopatra* 190
  and Burke 56–57
  and contradiction 213–214
  on *Coriolanus* 6, 26, 45, 181, 183,
    209–220
  and Payne's *Brutus* 239, 241
  Characters of Shakespeare's Plays 187,
    214
  comparison of Kean and Kemble
    215–218
  distinction between imagination and
    understanding 212–213
  lectures on Shakespeare 186
  Letter to William Gifford 187,
    188–189, 213, 218–220
  and Marlow circle 35
  Political Essays 217, 224
  Spirit of the Age 196
  "What is the People?" 217, 221–224,
    227, 231, 247, 171
Hegel, Georg Wilhelm Friedrich 116
Heine, Heinrich 183, 188
Hellenism. *See also* Romantic
    Hellenism
  and Homer 13
  rise of 4, 12–13
  and Shelley 6, 12, 147–175
  Victorian 4
Hesiod 128
historicity 5, 25
  and satire 130–131
historicism 6
  rise of 28–29, 38–39
  Romantic 6, 24–25, 29, 36
  and Shelley 159, 164–175
Hobhouse, John Cam 119
Hogg, Thomas Jefferson 10
Holcroft, Thomas 23, 41, 101
  Anna St. Ives 102–104
  Hugh Trevor 88, 102, 104–107
  and *Caleb Williams* 106
  and *Emma Courtney* 106
  representation of reading 104–105
  representation of writing 105–107
Homer 18, 78, 84, 103, 127
  and Virgil 133
  Shelley on 165
Hone, William 224

Hooke, Nathaniel 255
Horace 10, 31, 91, 117, 120, 168
  Ars Poetica 57–58
  Burke's citation of 56, 57–59
  and Byron 131, 136, 138
  Epistles 10, 58–59
  Godwin's praise for 69, 97
  Odes 169
  read by Caleb Williams 100
Hume, David 75, 116, 159
  "Of Civil Liberty" 29
Hunt, John 187
Hunt, Leigh 187
  and Marlow circle 35
  Examiner 187–188
Hurd, Richard 90, 93

Inchbald, Elizabeth (Mrs.) 41, 101, 216n
  on *Coriolanus* 201
  Nature and Art 107–108
  A Simple Story 84
Italy
  in *Childe Harold's Pilgrimage*
    134–135, 137
  in *A Philosophical View of Reform* 155
  travel to 225

Jacobin novel 6, 23–24, 75–76, 77–111,
    184
  and classical history 80–82
  critique of classical learning
    in 101–108
  and exemplarity 24, 41–42, 80–81,
    96–98, 100–101, 108, 110–111
  and historical novel 97
  as Plutarchian mode 81–82, 96–98,
    100–101, 108, 110–111
  recasting of classical virtues in 89–90,
    93, 97, 101–102, 104, 110–111,
    186, 276
  and relationship between historical
    change and literary form 79–80
  representation of discursive practices
    in 81–90, 94–95, 99–100,
    104–111
Jacobus, Mary 189
James, Henry 278
  The Golden Bowl 275–276
Johnson, Richard
  New Roman History 17

Johnson, Samuel 91, 93
Jonson, Ben 231
 Catiline 263–264
Juvenal
 and British Romanticism 27, 27n
 Burke's citation of 56, 59–60
 and Byron 132, 138, 144
 Satire IV 59–60

Kant, Immanuel 116
Kean, Edmund 25, 193–194
 as Brutus 231, 245–247, 277
 compared to Kemble 206–209,
  215–218, 246–247, 277
 production of *Coriolanus* 45, 183,
  184, 206–209, 277
 reviews of 207–209
 sets of 206
 as Richard 207, 215
Keats, John 119, 187, 209
 and Italian culture 27
 on Kean 207, 245
 and Marlow circle 35
 Shelley on 152
Kelly, Gary 79, 93, 98, 109
Kemble, John 181
 compared to Kean 206–209, 215–218,
  246–247, 277
 as King John 215
 portrait of by Thomas Lawrence
  201–202
 production of *Coriolanus* 6, 16, 25,
  26, 44–45, 183, 189–206, 277
 compared to Brutus 240–241
 nightly grosses for 193
 reviews of 198–200
 and Romantic period politics
  200–201, 205
 sets of 195–197, 207
 text of 194–195
 use of statuary 195
 retirement of 225, 246
Kipperman, Mark 161 n. 20
Knight, Richard Payne 13
Knowles, James Sheridan 25, 275
 Virginius 25, 224, 230, 247–248
 Caius Gracchus 45, 224, 227, 230,
  247–261, 270–271
 analysis of 251–255
 censorship of 255–258
 compared to *Brutus* 250, 253, 261–262

compared to *Coriolanus* 249
 plot of 248–249
Knox, Vicesimus 77–78, 84, 88, 90
Koselleck, Reinhart 41, 65, 66, 68, 139
 on exemplarity and historicism 38
Kramnick, Isaac 57
Kroeber, Karl 149 n. 7, 164, 175
Kucich, Greg 116, 153

Lamb, Charles 210–212, 216
Landor, Walter Savage 119
Larpent, Anna 230
Larpent, John 230, 243
Latin language 7, 10, 108
Lawrence, Sir Thomas
 portrait of Kemble 201–202
legitimacy 217
Levellers 211
Licensing Act (1737) 229
Livy 14, 36, 78, 169, 248
 on Brutus 233
 in *Childe Harold's Pilgrimage* 136,
  137, 138, 143
 Godwin's praise for 7
 on Gaius Mucius Scaevola 67
 on Romulus 70
Locke, John 49, 264
Louis XIV, King 33
Louis XVI, King 232
Lucretius 9, 128, 130, 168
Lukàcs 97
 on the novel and epic 78
Lunn, Joseph
 Amor Patriae 224

Macaulay, Catherine 53
Macaulay, Thomas 275
Machiavelli, Niccolò 29, 166
Mackintosh, James 53
Macready, Charles 25, 196, 247, 261
Magnuson, Paul 180
Mahoney, Charles 219
Mandeville, Bernard 55
Manning, Peter 118, 128 n. 20, 216
Marius, Gaius 33
Marx, Karl 15, 39, 172
 Eighteenth Brumaire 15, 37, 151,
  166–167
Massinger, Philip 231
McGann, Jerome 19–20, 131, 141, 163
 on Romanticism and Roman ruins 20

Index

McKeon, Michael 79, 92, 93, 110–111
Mengs, Anton Raphael 195
Michelangelo (Michelangelo
    Buonarroti) 155
Michelet, Jules
    Histoire romaine 17
Mill, John Stuart 29, 196, 273
Milner, H.M. 262
Milton, John 95, 132
    and English canon 43, 125, 127, 129
Montesquieu 14, 159
Moody, Jane 179–180, 192
Moore, John 91, 92, 93
Moore, Thomas 115, 117, 119, 122
Most, Glenn W. 11
Mucius (Gaius Mucius Scaevola) 66–68,
    72, 74
Murray, John 42, 115

Napoleon (Bonaparte) 20, 170,
    207–209, 217, 225
    Byron's invocation of 119, 136, 138
    and Caesar 138–9
neoclassicism 30, 30n, 35, 175, 276
    and Theatres Royal 196
Nero 100, 151, 218–219
Nicholson, Andrew 124, 125
Niebuhr, Barthold Georg 20, 274
    Römische Geschichte 17
novel
    and appetite 84
    and classical learning 77–78,
        84–85, 91
    and historical narrative 95–98
    moral effects of 77–78, 90–93, 96–97
    and romance 91–92
    and social change 93–101

Odell, George 193, 196
Otway, Thomas 231
Ovid 10, 168
Ozouf, Mona 37

Paine, Thomas 41, 49, 181, 218
    and revolutionary violence 235
    and Revolution Controversy 50–51
    Rights of Man 26, 44, 51, 55, 212
        read by Desmond 184
Parnassus 122
Parthenon (or Elgin) Marbles 13, 43
Payne, John Howard 275

Brutus 45, 224, 227, 230, 231–247,
    248, 270–271, 277
    analysis of 233–243
    and *Caius Gracchus* 250, 253,
        261–262
    difference from Livy 233
    and Hazlitt's reading of
        Coriolanus 239
    plot of 233
    and relationship between political
        and sexual license 238–239
    as response to Kemble's
        Coriolanus 240–241, 277
    reviews of 243–246
    sources 243 n. 48
Peace of Amiens 189
Peacock, Thomas Love 146, 153, 165,
    170, 171
    and Marlow circle 35
Peterloo Massacre 148, 170–171, 205,
    206, 258
Petrarch (Francesco Petrarcha) 137, 184
Philp, Mark 66
Phlipon, Manon (Mme. Roland) 14
Pitt, William (the Elder) 18
Plato 165
Plotz, John 228–229
Plutarch 14, 69, 76, 97, 109
    and the Jacobin novel 80–82, 96–98,
        110–111, 108
    Parallel Lives 84, 97
        read by Emma Courtney 85, 87, 109
        read by Rousseau 85
    as source for *Caius Gracchus* 248–249
Pocock, J.G.A. 264, 265
Political Herald and Review 66–68,
    69, 70
Pope, Alexander 117, 125, 132, 185
    and Augustanism 31
    translation of Homer 84
Pope Controversy 42–43, 122–131, 132,
    276
Porter, James 21
Portland, 3rd Duke of 66
Price, Richard 52–53, 60, 264
Priestley, Joseph 217, 264
print culture 19, 72, 94, 229, 271
public opinion 45, 221–224, 247, 261, 271
public sphere 227–229, 261, 271
Punic Wars 136
Putney Debates 211

Index

Quarterly Review 35, 244–246, 270

Racine, Jean 127
Raphael 155
Reeve, Clara 92
Reevite Associations Against Levellers
  and Republicans 211
Reform Bill of 1832 (First Reform
  Bill) 6, 26, 32, 46, 181, 223, 272
Reform movement (parliamentary)
  17, 22–23, 41, 45, 148, 180,
  207, 251
  and *Coriolanus* 190, 200, 205, 208
  and Hazlitt 212, 213, 218
  and literary taste 8–12, 119, 132
  suppression of 232, 258
Regulus, Marcus Atilius 104, 159, 168,
  169
Renaissance 14, 155
republicanism
  and British classical republican
    tradition 14, 28, 40, 40
    n. 74, 251
Revolution Controversy 49–76,
  264–267
  Burke and Paine in 50–51
Reynolds, Sir Joshua 195
Richardson, Alan 212
Richardson, Samuel 102, 105
Robbins, Bruce 228
Robertson, William 75
Robespierre, Maximilien 219
Rogers, Samuel 117, 122
Roman Empire
  De Quincey on 272–275
  Shelley on 148, 154–155, 170, 174
Romantic Hellenism 18–19, 24, 35
  Shelley and 43–44, 147–175
Romantic theater 25–27, 179–181, 277
  censorship of 181, 229–231
  production conditions 191–194
  as public space 26, 45, 180–181,
    229–231
  representation of the populace 45–46,
    226–227, 232–261
  and "Roman Revival" 224–227
  and Romantic imagination 26, 183
  and Romantic period culture 224–231
Romanticism
  and Byron 115–131, 141–145

  in *Childe Harold's Pilgrimage*
    134–135
  and classical models 18, 18 n. 30, 36
  and classicism of 30
  and historical understanding 5–6,
    38–39, 46, 75–76
  and historiography 28
  and imagination 209–220, 277
  and Kean's *Coriolanus* 206
  and neoclassicism 30
  and Pope 124
  and theater 179
  and Rome 4–5, 277
  use of Roman models in 1, 6
Roman republic
  aristocracy of 71–72, 194
  in *Caius Gracchus* 252–255
  bellicosity of 70–71, 170
  British dispute over the legacy of
    17, 23, 27, 40, 49, 183,
    208–209, 225–227, 231–271,
    275–277
  and French Revolution 4, 14–16, 34,
    37, 39–40, 62–63
  Godwin's reverence for heroes of
    66–68, 72–74
  and historical mediation 14
  imperialism of 9, 71
  as model for eighteenth-century
    Britain 1, 33
  as model of masculine virtue
    7–8, 163
  in Parliamentary debate 16, 16n, 18
  and popular democracy 22, 49–50, 51
  representation on British stage 25–26,
    44–46, 180–183, 187–220,
    224–271, 277
  of populace 45–46, 194–195,
    226–227, 232–261, 262, 270–271
  and Romantic aesthetics 27
  and Romanticism 1, 4–5
  and Romantic period Britain 1, 9, 11,
    12, 34–35, 49–50, 150–151,
    174–175, 200–201, 225–227,
    230–271, 273–277
Rome
  archaeological excavation of 13
  Burke's use of 56–65, 276
  and Byron's concept of decline
    115–131

decline of as related to Britain 60, 275–276
and eighteenth-century Britain 32, 157
in "English Bards and Scotch Reviewers" 133, 138–145
and European politics 138–139, 150, 156, 250–251
and exemplarity 30, 138–139, 274
and Godwin 71–72
and Greece 133, 147–175, 277
and historical parallels 20, 37–38, 64–65, 66–68, 118–119, 138–139, 150–151, 156, 166–172, 174–175, 191, 200–201, 218–219, 225–226, 250–251, 254–255, 273–275.
See also exemplarity
historiography of 16–17, 36, 274
literary history of 42–43, 276
and national identity 6, 32–33, 118, 188
ruins of 136–137, 140–145, 152, 276
and Shelley's Hellenism 43–44, 146–175
violence of 88
virtues of 7–9, 25, 28, 71–72, 87
Roscius 250
Rous, George 53
Rousseau, Jean Jacques 14, 109, 116
Confessions 85, 88
La Nouvelle Héloïse 86, 87
Russell, Lord William 250, 264

Saglia, Diego 226, 260
Sallust 7, 36, 78
Bellum Catilinae 101, 208, 262–263
Godwin's praise for 7, 101
satire 60, 130–132
Schiller, Friedrich 116
Schlegel, Friedrich 127
Scott, Walter 111, 117, 119, 121–122, 127
on Kemble's production of *Coriolanus* 198
Scottish Enlightenment 127
Senmel, Stuart 217
Seneca 95, 104
sensibility 82–83
Shakespeare 95, 127, 129, 231, 245
Antony and Cleopatra 190–191
As You Like It 193
and classical antiquity 184–189

Coriolanus 6, 14, 44, 181, 182, 183, 188–220, 224, 267, 277
and *Caius Gracchus* 249, 259
Kemble's production of 6, 16, 25, 44–45, 183, 189–206, 277
Kean's production of 206–209, 277
Henry IV 120, 189
Henry V 189
Henry VI 184
Julius Caesar 182–183, 187–188, 190–191, 224
King John 215
King Lear 185–186, 215
Macbeth 121, 189–190, 267
Othello 185
Richard III 207, 215
and Romantic period culture 182, 184–189
and stage performance 210–212
and Virgil 250
Shelley, Harriet Westbrook 10
Shelley, Percy Bysshe 6, 8, 41
Adonais 148, 152
Defence of Poetry 44, 133, 148, 164–173, 213
exchange with Godwin on classics 8–12, 21, 147, 169–170, 174
Hellas 43–44, 147, 148, 149, 160, 161–164, 170, 172–173
Hellenism of 6, 12, 43–44
and Italian culture 27
and Marlow circle 35
"Ode to Liberty" 44, 148, 156–161, 162, 163
"Ode to the West Wind" 152–153
Philosophical View of Reform 44, 148, 154–156, 158, 164, 167, 171
Prometheus Unbound 148, 152, 171
Queen Mab 151–152
The Revolt of Islam 171
and the Romantic imagination 209, 220
The Triumph of Life 160
use of Rome 43–44, 133, 146–175, 277
Sheridan, Richard Brinsley 56
Siddons, Sarah (Mrs.) 25, 195, 198
Six Acts (1819) 258
Smith, Adam 55

Smith, Charlotte
  Desmond 184–186
Smollett, Tobias 102
Socrates 10
Sonensher, Michael 142 n. 27
Southey, Robert 117, 119, 120, 121, 122
Spa Fields riots 232
Speaight, Robert 198
Stabler, Jane 27, 119
Staël, Germaine de 127, 141
Stendahl (Marie-Henri Bayle) 20
Stray, Christopher 5, 20–21, 274
Sulla, Lucius Cornelius 138–139
Sylla (M. Jouy) 224
Sullivan, Garrett 94
Sulpicius (Servius Sulpicius Rufus) 136–137, 275
Swift, Jonathan 31
Sydney, Algernon 49, 250, 264

Tacitus 7, 36, 200
Tate, Nahum 190
Terence (Publius Terentius Afer) 56
Theatres Royal 25, 191–194, 196, 224, 231, 277
Theatrical Inquisitor 243, 245–246
Thelwall, John 22–23, 40, 44, 56, 275
  Champion 186
  lectures on Roman history 22–23, 49–51, 68, 71, 190
  lectures on Shakespeare 186
  Tribune 186
Thirlwall, Connop 17
Thirty Tyrants (of Rome) 120
Thomson, James 185
  Liberty 156–158
  Seasons 84
Times (London) 195
Tooke, Horne 49
Tory Party 33, 183, 188, 245, 273
Treason Trials (1794) 49
Trench, Mrs. 207–208
Tucker, Josiah 264
Turner, Frank 5, 6, 64, 255, 263
Two Acts (1795) 22, 22 n. 39, 49, 68
Ty, Eleanor 81 n. 9, 89 n. 19
Tyler, Wat 266

United States 162–163

Vance, Norman 249 n. 59
Virgil 18, 31, 78, 127, 130, 168
  Aeneid 153
  and British Romanticism 27
  Burke's citation of 56
  in *Childe Harold's Pilgrimage* 136, 137, 138, 143
  Georgics 10, 128
  and Godwin 69, 97
  and Homer 133
  and Shakespeare 250
Volney, Constantin François de Chassebœuf, comte de 116
  Les Ruines 63
Voltaire (François-Marie Arouet) 127

Wallace, Eglantine
  The Whim 230
Wallace, Jennifer 149 n. 7, 175
Waterloo 170
Watson, Nicola 80
Watt, Ian 78, 92
Webb, Timothy 12, 147, 149 n. 7, 158, 160
Weinbrot, Howard 31–32
Wharton, Joseph and Thomas
  An Essay on the Genius and Writings of Pope 124
Whig Party 56, 66, 67, 250–251
Wilkins, B.T. 55
Williams, Ioan 77
Williams, Raymond 164
Winckelmann, Johann Joachim 13
Wollstonecraft, Mary 55, 275
  Vindication of the Rights of Men 63–64
Woodring, Carl 149, 161
Wordsworth, William 20, 117, 121, 122, 173
  and *Child Harold's Pilgrimage* 134
  and the Romantic imagination 209, 220
Worrall, David 180, 226, 230

Yadav, Alok, 33n
Yellow Dwarf 223
Young, Charles 191, 193
Young, Julian Charles 198